Sir Arthur Bryant was born in 1899 at the twilight of the Victorian age, in a house on the royal Sandringham Estate. He served in the Royal Flying Corps in the First World War and taught and wrote history for the rest of his life. His reputation was established by his biography of Charles II in 1931; his biography of Pepys, his history of the Napoleonic Wars and his analysis of the Second World War through the war diaries of Field Marshal Alanbrooke, among his many other classic books, became recognized as the standard works on the subject. Through them he pioneered a neglected art – the writing of history as literature. Indeed Professor John Foster, reviewing Arthur Bryant's last work of medieval history, wrote, 'One cannot put it down. Some men are great writers. Some are great historians. Just a few, like Gibbon, are both. And one of the few is Sir Arthur'. He wrote the Diary in the *Illustrated London News* since inheriting the column from G. K. Chesterton in 1936. He was knighted in 1954 and created Companion of Honour in 1967. Sir Arthur Bryant died in January 1985.

By the same author

Macaulay
The National Character
The Letters and Speeches of Charles II (editor)
The England of Charles II
The American Ideal

The Story of England
Makers of the Realm B.C.–1272
The Age of Chivalry 1272–1381
The Elizabethan Deliverance
King Charles II 1630–1685
Restoration England 1660–1703
English Saga 1840–1940

Samuel Pepys
The Man in the Making 1633–1669
The Years of Peril 1669–1683
Pepys and the Revolution

The Napoleonic Wars
The Years of Endurance 1793–1802
Years of Victory 1802–1812
The Age of Elegance 1812–1822
Nelson
The Great Duke

The Alanbrooke Diaries
The Turn of the Tide 1939–1943
Triumph in the West 1943–1946

English Social History
The Medieval Foundation
Protestant Island

The Fire and the Rose
The Lion and the Unicorn
Jimmy
Jackets of Green
A Thousand Years of British Monarchy
Spirit of England

A History of Britain and the British People
Set in a Silver Sea

ARTHUR BRYANT

Samuel Pepys

The Saviour of the Navy

PANTHER
Granada Publishing

Panther Books
Granada Publishing Ltd
8 Grafton Street, London W1X 3LA

Published by Panther Books 1985

First published in Great Britain by
Collins 1938
New edition 1949

Copyright in this edition © Sir Arthur Bryant 1949

ISBN 0-586-06472-9

Printed and bound in Great Britain by
Collins, Glasgow

Set in Baskerville

Contents

LONDON

UNDER CHARLES II

The dotted line encloses the
district destroyed by the
Great Fire

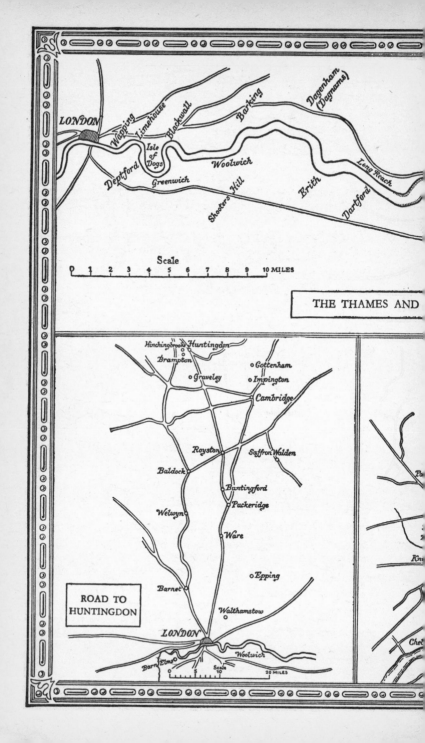

LONDON

Wapping
Limehouse
Blackwall
Isle of Dogs
Barking
Dagenham (Dagnams)
Deptford
Woolwich
Greenwich
Shooters Hill
Erith
Long Reach
Dartford

Scale

0 1 2 3 4 5 6 7 8 9 10 MILES

THE THAMES AND

Hinchingbrook Huntingdon
Brampton
Graveley
Cottenham
Impington
Cambridge

Royston
Saffron Walden
Baldock
Buntingford
Puckeridge
Welwyn
Ware

Epping

Barnet

Walthamstow

ROAD TO
HUNTINGDON

LONDON
Woolwich
Barn Elms

Scale
5 10 20 MILES

Chel

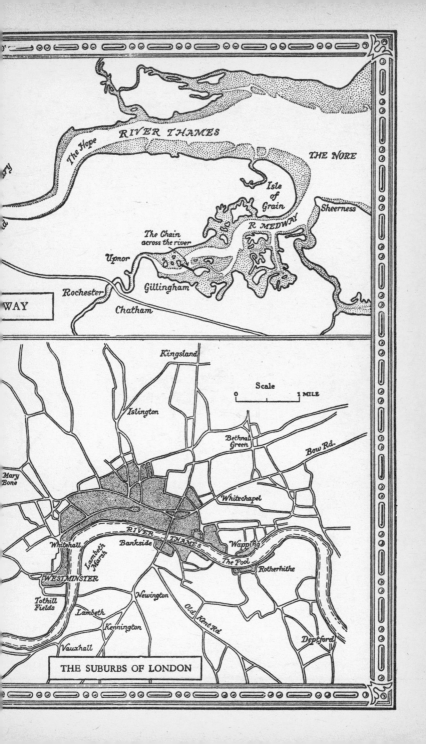

RIVER THAMES

The Hope

THE NORE

Isle of Grain

Sheerness

R. MEDWAY

The Chain across the river

Upnor

Gillingham

Rochester

WAY

Chatham

Kingsland

Scale

0   1 MILE

Islington

Bethnal Green

Bow Rd.

Mary Bone

Whitechapel

Whitehall

RIVER THAMES

Bankside

Wapping

The Pool

Lambeth Marsh

Rotherhithe

WESTMINSTER

Newington

Tothill Fields

Lambeth

Old Kent Rd.

Kennington

Vauxhall

Deptford

THE SUBURBS OF LONDON

Preface

Eleven years have passed since I published this book: years that probably few of us would wish to live again. So, I dare say, in the Indian summer of his last decade, in the little paradise he had made overlooking the river above Inigo Jones's Watergate, Samuel Pepys looked back in old age on the years recorded in this volume. They witnessed, with much else that he could recall with pride, the nemesis and ruin of his world. The Court of the Stuarts, the political ideals that prevailed there, and Pepys's own hard-won and honourable place in it, vanished as though they had never been. The men he had hated, who had plotted against his life, who had broken – as he thought, though wrongly – the work to which he had given so much, inherited the power and the glory of the new world. And Pepys, lucky to escape in peace, retired into the shades.

Yet, as so often in England, the twilight proved the pleasantest part of the day, and in Pepys's case it was long and summery. The story of it belongs to a later and final book still to be written: of our hero, ambition laid aside, all passion spent, learning to accept defeat, growing old gracefully and forming, amid the society of his learned friends, the exquisite little library that bears his name. The present, and third, volume of Pepys's biography, carries the story of his life from his fifty-first to his fifty-seventh year. These five and a half years, between the autumn of 1683 and the spring of 1689, were the most important of his career. They cover the voyage to Tangier and Spain, during which he learnt the full extent of the decay into which the Navy had sunk in his absence, the second and greatest of his two periods of rule at the Admiralty, and his fall from power during and after the Revolution of 1688. His highest achievement – that by virtue of which his country so long ruled the sea – belongs to these middle years of endeavour.

The story of that achievement, here recorded, is taken largely from the many thousands of Pepys's official letters entered in his last six Admiralty Letter Books. These vast folios, unlike the earlier volumes of his first Secretaryship, have never been calendared, though Dr J. R. Tanner made an important use of them in his later writings, particularly in the introductory volume of the Catalogue of Naval Manuscripts in the Pepysian Library. But he was prevented by death from completing his task, and the final Letter Books contain much still unpublished. So do the invaluable volumes of unsorted Pepysian letters and papers among the Rawlinson MSS. in the Bodleian Library. On the other hand the tale of the voyage to Tangier, told by Pepys in his last shorthand journal, has already been printed more than once, most recently by the late Edwin Chappell in his admirable edition of the *Tangier Papers* published by the Navy Records Society before the War. His transcription I have been able to collate with an earlier and unpublished transcription made for me in 1932 by Dr W. Matthews. To the latter I also owe my transcription of Pepys's shorthand parliamentary notes.

I should like once more to record my debt to Sir Owen Morshead, to Commander John Owen, R.N., to the late Francis McMurtrie and to Sir Charles Petrie. Most of all I am indebted to Francis Turner, Pepys Librarian, and to the Master and Fellows of Magdalene College, Cambridge, from whom I have received, in the course of writing this volume and its two predecessors, kindnesses and hospitality beyond acknowledgement.

As in the earlier volumes, I have modernized the spelling and punctuation of the letters quoted, and used the old or English calendar and notation of years.

ARTHUR BRYANT

Smedmore
March 1949

1

Voyage to Tangier

'Captain Hume is bound to sea
    Hey boys, ho! boys!
Captain Hume is bound to sea
    Ho!
Captain Hume is bound to sea
And his brave company
    Hey, the brave Grenadiers
Ho!

When we come to Tangier shore
    Hey boys, ho! boys!
When we come to Tangier shore
    Ho!
When we land on Tangier shore
We'll make our grenades to roar
    Hey, the brave Grenadiers
Ho!'
           'The Grenadiers' Rant.' *Roxburghe Ballads*, ii, 582.

As the fleet rounded Rame Head and the friendly slopes and roofs of Plymouth fell away into the August haze, Samuel Pepys, outward bound on the deck of Lord Dartmouth's flagship, passed from one life into another. Behind him were the tangled nightmares of four years of persecution and proscription – the angry Parliament men who had shouted him down, the Tower jailors with their chains clanging down stony corridors, the accusers who had perjured themselves under the rafters of Westminster Hall while the mob outside shouted for his blood. John Scott, who had risen like some satanic spirit from the underworld to lie away his office, his honour and his life, was again a penniless fugitive in a far country humbly soliciting forgiveness; James the butler, who had betrayed him with false evidence, had died in anguished repentance; Shaftesbury, 'the great little lord', was dead and defeated. Only the fine gentleman Harbord remained, clinging precariously to the fringes of a Court whose enigmatic King was either too good-humoured to harry a dishonoured traitor or too polite to remind a well-bred scoundrel of his villainy: no one could say which.

Ahead, far to the southward, was Tangier – the beleaguered city Pepys had never seen, which his country had held for a generation against barbarous Moors and pirates, and out of which his own mushroom fortunes had grown. During his fifteen years as its Treasurer nearly a million and a quarter had passed through his hands to pay its officers and garrison, and his closest friend and former clerk, Will Hewer, who had succeeded him, had fingered a quarter of a million more on the same account. And in the seventeenth century public money had a way of sticking to private fingers, even to those that were accounted honest.

Once, twenty-one years before, when England had taken over the place from the Portuguese as part of Queen Catherine's marriage portion, Tangier had seemed to Englishmen the gateway to the dominion of the Mediterranean and a Christian Empire in Africa. In pursuit of that mirage many thousands of British lives and vast sums of treasure had been lost between the ocean and the Moor-ridden mountains, and the rulers of England, from the King who paid for it to the back-benchers who refused to vote supplies for its defence, had grown weary of the very name of Tangier. Pepys, who had been one of its first Commissioners, could remember the whole story. Now his friend, Lord Dartmouth, was sailing with secret orders to evacuate the garrison and inhabitants and destroy town, fortifications and harbour, while he, recalled after four years of unmerited disgrace to the service of the Crown, was accompanying him as his confidential adviser at the King's request.[1]

Whatever the political outcome might be, it was not an unpleasing prospect. Since his enforced resignation from the Secretaryship of the Admiralty Commission in 1679, Pepys had suffered enough to teach him to be a philosopher. For four years he had known dishonour, imprisonment, fear of death and almost constant anxiety. Yet he was still alive and thriving, with his zest for enjoyment and work unimpaired. At the age of 50 – say 60 as years were then reckoned – he was in better health than he had been for a decade. He was even keeping a journal in shorthand, a thing his eyes had not permitted him to do since he closed his first diary fourteen years before.

In the first new ship that carried him at the head of the fleet – and

it added to his satisfaction that it had been of his own laying down –
were many who shared his interests and two of his dearest friends.
These were Will Hewer and Henry Shere, the great engineer who
had completed the Mole at Tangier and who once long ago had read
poetry to poor Elizabeth. With them were Dartmouth – the hot-
tempered, lovable George Legge whom Pepys had quarrelled with
four years before* but whom he had since learnt to love for his
loyalty to their common patron, the Duke of York – Dr Trumbull,
the brilliant young civilian learned in law and history, Dr Lawrence,
the physician, and the sweet-voiced divine, Thomas Ken, known to
our age as the author of the Evening Hymn. In less than two
months, if all went as Pepys intended, he would be back with his
books and his friends in York Buildings. In the meantime he would
see Africa, and perhaps Spain and Portugal. Nor, though he was a
man of substance and long used to doing without the King's wages,
did it lessen his enjoyment to reflect that he was earning £4 for every
day spent in such pleasant service.†

The rough fishermen and shepherds of south Cornwall gazing out
to sea must have speculated curiously as to the destination and
purpose of the flock of sails that clustered past their shores and
slowly vanished into the August night. More sophisticated persons,
standing before stone manor-houses, or riding, cloaked and top-
booted, down the narrow highways, spoke knowingly of Tangier and
mysteries of State.‡[2]

There were twenty-one sail in all spread across the sea, nine of
them King's ships, gilded and bright with pennants in all the
pageantry of power with which the State was wont to interpret its
mystery and majesty to the common man. Of the three ships of the
line, the *Grafton* was several hundred tons larger than her consorts,
Henrietta and *Montagu* – a two-decked 3rd rate of the latest design of

* See *The Years of Peril*, 192.

† That Pepys should have been paid the equivalent of £20 a day in modern money
for this not very exacting employment shows how highly Charles II and his brother
had come to value his services, though they had long been prevented by the state of
English political opinion from using them.

‡ 'Lord Dartmouth's design is still a secret, but 'tis said his *rendezvous* will be at
Tangier, where he will have 25 sail of ships in his fleet. Mr Pepys is gone as his
Lordship's secretary, Dr Ken as his chaplain, and Dr Turnbull (*sic*) the civilian is also
gone with him.' John Verney to Edmund Verney, Aug. 27th, 1683. *H.M.C. 7th Rep.*
(*Verney*, 481).

1174 tons* carrying 380 men and 62 guns. The five 4th rates that accompanied them – the frigates *Oxford*, *St David*, *Woolwich*, *Bonaventure* and *Mary Rose* – averaged 600 tons and carried 46 guns each. A 6th rate of 184 tons, the *Greyhound*, completed the squadron. The rest were merchantmen.

Though of minute burden, the expanses of white sail above the ships gave them an impression of size greater than their tonnage warranted. Joined with the ten or twelve frigates already operating in the Straits against the Sallee pirates of western Morocco, they constituted, after five years of Admiralty rule by inept and ignorant politicians, almost the entire peacetime effective of Britain.[3]

With the lazy, quivering, sleep-inducing motion of sailing ships they gave themselves to the swell. Tired after the early rise he had made to get off his letters before the fleet sailed, Pepys celebrated his first day at sea by going early to bed. Nor did he rise next morning until the ship's tailor had finished altering the sleeves of his doublet according to the sea fashion. For, though that was long ago, he had not been called Dapper Dicky for nothing. And when aboard the fleet he liked to do as the fleet did.

That Friday, August 24th, 1683, the fleet, plunging off the Lizard, came up with ten sail of merchantmen southward bound. The time-honoured ceremony so dear to the Navy was performed, two of the strangers coming up under the *Grafton*'s stern to strike their topsails. Next day another merchantman encountered off Land's End, omitting the ceremony, had a gun fired across his bows to remind him of his duty. Here the *Anne* yacht hove into sight returning from Tangier; her captain, amazed to see the fleet, was ordered to turn and follow. But Pepys, sitting alone in his cabin, copying out Dartmouth's instructions and swaying with the ever increasing swell, for the moment took little zest in these naval occasions. Shortly before sailing he had speculated curiously whether all peoples were equally subject to sea-sickness. He was no longer in any doubt. 'At night to bed a little sickish,' he wrote in his shorthand journal of the voyage, 'the weather being bad, and very bad indeed it was all night.' For the first time in his life the former Admiralty Secretary was on the broad Atlantic.

* The figures are taken from Pepys' own Register of Ships (*C.P.* MSS. 1, 268). A volume in the Admiralty Library gives the burden of the *Grafton* as 1096 tons and another list printed in *The Mariner's Mirror* from Sergison's MSS. as 1053 tons only.

He slept little, for the flagship rolled ever more steeply, and the tramping of the helmsman's feet sounded all night above his head. At one moment one of the attendant merchantmen was reported in distress: at another the *St David* loomed out of the darkness, all but falling foul of the *Grafton*. But though Pepys kept his cabin on Sunday morning, he did not surrender easily. All afternoon the little man sat making notes on his Tangier commission. That evening he attended prayers, supped with Lord Dartmouth and walked the quarter-deck, talking of matters maritime and watching the moon rising above the restless seas.

Monday was a day of storm. Pepys battled against it sturdily. 'The wind still fresh,' he wrote, 'but against us so as we made very little way. I up and to my Lord by agreement for him to take my notes from me in his own hand, but the motion of the ship was such that I could do nothing there. So upon the quarter-deck and there walking all the morning, the sea running very high. My stomach so ill I could not go down to dinner, but in my cabin talking with Dr Trumbull all the afternoon.' Even the *Grafton*'s log-book admitted the foulness of the weather. The little *Anne* yacht shipped so much water that her captain reported that she could not safely keep the seas and had to ask leave to run for Plymouth. Yet that night when the seamen danced to the harp and sang, Pepys still stood on the quarter-deck, watching and listening till midnight.[4]

For though his head might turn dizzily and his stomach rebel and the long Atlantic rollers lap hungrily at the ship's sides, Pepys did not forget his self-dedication to the sea nor cease to honour the rough virtues of the men who lived by her. 'Towards showing the hardship of the seaman's trade', he noted in his memorandum book, 'it is mighty observable the strange difficulties they suffer in the dark nights in storms, when men must go up to hand their sails etc. in the night.' Of their needs he spoke earnestly with the ship's lieutenant as he paced the deck with him: of how much they rejoiced at a good commander who saw that all bore their share equally, and how much they could suffer from ignorant, careless and corrupt captains who bestowed favour on worthless servants and left the real work of their ships to be borne unrewarded by a few. Their diet was harsh and unpalatable, with putrid water and meat that caused diseases which could only be cured ashore. All the days of their perilous lives, they were learners in a world of mysterious tides and shoals. Neither in peace nor war were they ever free from danger. It was good to see them dance and hear them sing.[5]

On Tuesday, the 28th, the fifth day out, Pepys being pretty well and the sea a little smoother, he and Dartmouth locked themselves after dinner in the latter's cabin to prepare their papers for the important business which they had left England to transact. They were still the only people in the expedition who knew what it was. While Pepys dictated Dartmouth took down the heads of the Commission which he was to give him and Trumbull for valuing the properties of Tangier and compensating their owners. Afterwards on deck Pepys examined the proposals of Major Beckmann, the Swedish engineer, for demolishing the Mole and fortifications.

But Dr Trumbull, that rising young civilian, who was accustomed to see his learning given universal consideration, was not pleased. He did not like locked doors between himself and the great lord at whose request he had left his thriving practice and comfortable home. There was no friendly chat of laws and antiquities for Pepys next day: instead he had to content himself by reading *Hudibras* and going early to bed. Even Will Hewer, prostrate in his cabin with sea-sickness, failed him that night.

For the Atlantic was rougher than ever. Next day, which, though only Thursday, Pepys hazily took for Sunday, the Admiral himself stayed below. The fleet, driven far out of its course to the north, ran through driving spray and rain towards the coast of Ireland. Pepys was forced to spend the afternoon sitting in one of the little deck cabins to keep himself dry and not sick. At supper time he gave up the unequal struggle and went to bed.

Then, as so often happens at sea, a bad day was followed by one of calm. In the night the gale dropped. On August 31st the sun restored everyone's good humour, even Dr Trumbull's. During the afternoon in Pepys' cabin there was a great deal of dancing and good humour, followed by a pleasant walk on deck with Lord Dartmouth. 'And in the evening Dr Trumbull and I alone in our cabin reading of Dr Zouch his book of the Admiralty,' the diarist recorded, 'with great pleasure in our mutual discoursing thereon, and so after supper to bed.'[6]

Yet it was not till Wednesday, September 5th, that the headwinds finally dropped and the fleet with a favouring gale turned due south towards Tangier. Next day at noon Pepys walking the quarter-deck heard that they had made a run of 126 miles in twenty-four hours. Before night he had seen his first shoal of porpoises, swimming several thousand strong beside the ship, and on Friday morning woke to feel an unwonted warmth and see the sailors putting up the awning. The fleet was in the latitude of Finisterre, the 'north cape' as the sailors called it, though still far out at sea.[7]

That day, 'the sea being very smooth and pleasant', Sir William Booth, the captain of the *Grafton*, Henry Shere, Will Hewer and Pepys dined in the *Henrietta* as the guests of her commander, Sir John Berry. When dinner was done, Berry, who was a fat, jolly, little man, played on the violin until, the company growing serious, talk turned to the state of the Navy.

Both captains declared that the discipline of the Service had never been kept up as in Pepys' time and was now quite lost. Of this they gave examples, every one of which showed the wisdom of all that he had contended for in the past. The ignorant politicians and country gentlemen who had taken his place at the Admiralty – the 'land Admirals' as the seamen called them – recognized no other qualification for promotion but a good estate and ancient lineage. The ships were commanded by men who knew little or nothing of the sea but relied solely on their spirit as gentlemen and men of honour to do the King's business.

Pepys asked for a brief definition of the difference between a tarpaulin and a gentleman commander. Booth, who himself came of good family, replied that it was hard to give, but that a captain who did not understand the particular use of every rope, line and block could never give the King the proper benefit of his ship's service. However brave he might be, he could easily be kept out of action through some pretended disaster to mast or rope, which his inferiors, more anxious to save their skins than to win him honour which they could not share, would be sure to exaggerate. Booth cited his own case, recalling how in the midst of a fight with a Turkish corsair his officers had urged him to fly, on the ground that the ship was disabled; yet, when he had sent the fellows about their business, the Turk had quickly been made a prize. No mere 'land captain' knew what course to steer upon sight of an enemy, nor how to make the best of the wind to lay himself alongside. 'I never go on the deck', he said, 'but I see something or other out of order, either a strap or rope galled or something else that gives me occasion of giving order for remedying the same. All which a land captain overlooks and never thinks of and so is surprised by an enemy, whereas I always observe that he that seeks his enemy to surprise him, keeps himself always ready and is never surprised but has many advantages above him that is attacked first.'

What was true of commanders was equally true of inferior officers. Booth, Berry and Shere were unanimous in their praise of Pepys' Establishment for examining Reformados and Volunteers before granting them Lieutenants' commissions. Yet under the present Admiralty Board, Pepys' rule was universally ignored. Herbert, till lately Commander-in-Chief in the Straits, had given commands to two worthless confidants of his vices, neither of whom had served his time as Lieutenant and one of whom had been his *valet-de-chambre*. Booth knew of four or five other instances where senior officers' footmen had been promoted without any sea knowledge and who now reckoned themselves among the fine fellows and gentlemen commanders of the fleet. On which Pepys observed that apparently by 'gentleman-captain' was meant anyone who was not a bred and experienced seaman. Under such discouragements the true race of 'tarpaulins', from whose ranks such men as Myngs, Lawson and Berry himself had sprung, would soon be no more.[8]

All this Pepys, justly or unjustly, set down next morning in his shorthand notes. And that night, on his return to the *Grafton*, he remained looking long upon the stars trying to learn them, for another of the ills of the Navy had begun to vex him. During the voyage he had several times examined the flagship's chart and followed as best he could the course she was taking. After a conversation with one of the engineers, a young man named Phillips interested in the still primitive science of navigation, he had persuaded the Admiral to order an account of the ship's course to be kept by all who could make a reckoning. On the day of Pepys' visit to the *Henrietta*, Dartmouth at his request called for these reckonings, and found every one of them different. Such discrepancy gave an Elder Brother of Trinity House some cause to think.

Worse followed. On the 10th the fleet sighted the Burlings. Yet at that moment not one of the twelve reckonings made the *Grafton* within twenty-five leagues of them. For some time the navigators even contended that the Portuguese coast beyond was a fog bank. As

Pepys stared at the rugged islands, he thought how lucky it was they had not encountered them in the night or the whole fleet might have foundered like the *Gloucester* a year before.

All this led to much examining of charts, which were found to contain a host of inaccuracies. In some the Burlings were shown just south of the North Cape, in others to the east of it. Rather than admit their mistakes, masters preferred to conceal such discrepancies which were thus left permanently uncorrected. It was natural, of course, but symptomatic of the slovenly, haphazard way in which everything in the Service was now done. 'In short,' Pepys wrote, 'it is most plain from the confusion all these people are to be in how to make good their accounts (even each man's with itself) and the nonsensical arguments they would make use of to do it, and disorder they are in about it, that the skill of the whole lies in very little room. And yet is very little obtained among them, so as that it is by God Almighty's providence and great chance and the wideness of the sea that there are not a great many more misfortunes and ill chances in navigation than there are.'[9]

For the moment there was some relief from these disturbing reflections in the excitement of beholding a new world. There were the dry, green hills of Portugal dotted with white houses, and all next day the expectation of sighting Cape St Vincent. That evening passed cheerfully enough in Dartmouth's cabin, where the virtuosos of the expedition supped and listened to a warm dispute about ghosts between Dr Ken who believed in them and Pepys who did not. Later they adjourned to the captain's cabin to drink a glass of wine and water and partake of 'mighty pretty music upon the flutes in the night, and so to bed'.

After a further evening's debate about the existence of spirits and a hot restless night, Pepys was woken early in the morning of September 13th, with news that Cape Spartel was in sight. As soon as he had finished feasting his eyes on Africa he went back, like the good man of business he was, to the memorandum he was preparing in his cabin to help Dartmouth convince the garrison and inhabitants of Tangier of the necessity for its destruction. That done he hurried back to the quarter-deck to see the fleet sailing 'now fair in sight of the entrance into the Straits between the two shores'. It was a pleasant sight, described a few years before in verse by a naval chaplain who like Pepys was also a secret diarist:

No sooner from our top-mast head we see
The Turkish hills, the coast of Barbary,
But Spain salutes us and her shores discloses,
And lofty hills against the Turk opposes.
We sail 'twixt both, playing at handy dandy
With noble bowls of punch and quarts of brandy.[10]

At daybreak on Friday the 14th, after a night spent sheltering under Cape Spartel from a Levanter – the damp, searching, easterly wind of the Mediterranean – the *Grafton* weighed anchor and ran into the mouth of the Straits.

Standing on the quarter-deck Pepys could see at once the coasts of Europe and Africa, to his great pleasure. From these green, rolling shores was borne to the fleet a variety of pleasant scents – 'a most odoriferous smell like to the fume of cedar or juniper'. Pepys had been three weeks away from his mother earth, the longest period of absence from it he had ever known. 'Nothing', he noted, was 'so welcome to a seaman as after being at sea a little time to set his foot on shore, though it be the most barren place in the world.'

About ten o'clock the fleet rounded the long stone Mole and came into Tangier Bay. By the water's edge was a little town of flat roofs huddled together behind battlemented walls that climbed up a steep hill to meet in a fortress not unreminiscent of the Tower of London, with the Union Flag blowing straight above it in the easterly breeze. Nearer at hand was a smaller castle standing on a mound above the quay-side. This last, like the Mole which jutted out from it for a quarter of a mile into the Straits, was crowded with warehouses and cannon. Yet to Pepys' searching eyes the whole scene was somehow intensely pathetic, and even a little contemptible. Here was this vaunted imperial outpost, this African stronghold at the Mediterranean gateway, into which England had poured so much treasure (not without some honest profit to himself) and which anyone could see at a glance was useless and untenable. 'But Lord!' he wrote that night in his diary, 'how could ever anybody think this place fit to be kept at this charge, that by its being overlooked by so many hills can never be secured against an enemy?' For there on those very hills he could see the army of the Alcaïd, the cruel, spear-encircling Moors who ever watched and waited the hour when the infidels should be driven back into the sea, and all Barbary be theirs again.

As the English fleet came into the bay the Castle guns thundered in salute. A straggler left behind at Plymouth with orders to follow had escaped the long south-westerly gale which had delayed the Admiral, and so brought news of his coming before him. Presently Colonel Kirke, the Governor, came on board. Before they dined Dartmouth, in the privacy of his cabin, confided to him the reason of the expedition. Not that there seemed much need. From the excited conversation of the officers who crowded on to the *Grafton*'s quarter-deck and into the great cabin, it was plain that the closely-guarded secret was already common gossip. 'And all say', Pepys noted with some satisfaction, 'that my and Mr Hewer's coming makes more talk than my Lord's.'

After dinner there was a consultation between the Governor, Trumbull, Pepys and Dartmouth in the latter's cabin. Kirke, with whom Pepys had occasionally corresponded* and whose wife he had admired of old in England, appeared unexpectedly forward in the affair and was full of suggestions. Afterwards on the crowded quarter-deck, Pepys encountered his brother-in-law, Balty St Michel – mightily altered in his looks and full of the hard usage he had suffered. For under the persecution of Admiral Herbert, the Agent-General-for-the-Affairs-of-his-Majesty's-Navy-at-Tangier, as Balty liked to call himself, had suffered something of a martyrdom. The poor, whining creature had got something to complain of at last.[11]

The east wind still continued. 'To bed and the scuttle being open it blew very hard into my cabin upon my bed all night, and being at anchor we lay much more still than hitherto and so I slept well.' Saturday morning found Pepys gazing through his perspective glass at the Moors' camp upon the hills. The rest of the day was taken up with business: dictating to Dartmouth an abstract of his instructions to help his memory, talking with the officers of the garrison at dinner and conferring afterwards with Dartmouth, Trumbull and Shere – 'our first Council of Four' – on the forthcoming Commission of Enquiry into the proprieties of the town, the victualling of the garrison and fleet and the troubled relationships between the Governor and the Alcaïd. These last seemed

* Earlier in the year Kirke had written begging Pepys to 'preserve me some place in your remembrance as a person that has all imaginable esteem for you, and would be glad of any occasion to express the great vigour I have for your friendship'. *Rawl. MSS. A.* 190, f. 23.

likely to prove embarrassing, for the presence of a hostile army was a liability on which the evacuators had not counted.

Though Hewer went ashore in the afternoon, Pepys did not accompany him but remained on board with Dartmouth. It was a pleasant evening and he noted with customary zest how much lower the Pole Star appeared in the sky.[12]

On the morning of September the 17th, amid a pleasing rattle of artillery from ships and shore, the Admiral landed with the King's Commission Extraordinary as Captain-General and Governor of Tangier. Pepys, bewigged and laced, landed by his side. From the crowded quay-side, along roadways lined with red-coats and slashed with green, bathed in unfamiliar sunshine and assailed by the scent of southern gardens and the still stronger odours of Africa, they marched in solemn state up the steep hill to the Castle. Here in the Governor's house, with its beautiful view over the Bay and Straits, they sat down to dine and afterwards saw the Governor's famed wife, the Lady Mary. Pepys thought her mightily changed. And though he approved the grapes and Spanish pomegranates they set before him, he did not revise his view of the town. 'An ordinary place,' he thought it, 'but overseen by the Moors, so as to be amazed to think how that the King has laid out all this money upon it.' That night he was infinitely bitten by chinches.[13]

2

African Adventure

'A little camp trading in drink and subject to the usual disorders.' Sir Hugh Cholmley. (Routh, *Tangier*.)

Many who visited Tangier during its twenty-one years of British occupation found it a charming place. After the grey skies of England it was delightful to find a clear blue heaven and a sun that suggested perpetual warmth and fruitfulness. The town was rich in trees and gardens, filling the narrow, dirty streets in spring with aromatic scents and blossom. Hardly a house, wrote a traveller, 'without a little garden full of sweet herbs and pleasant trees, especially vines which run up upon pillars made of stone and espaliers made of great reeds, all their walks and backsides and spare-places covered and shaded with vines, mightily loaden with excellent grapes of divers sorts, sizes and shapes'. Small wonder that Evelyn, pioneering with horticulture in the cloudy Thames valley, wrote to his friend Pepys to 'remember the *poor gardener*' and secure him some kernels and seeds.

Others who were not gardeners were charmed with the lazy and plentiful life of the place and the princely hospitality of its officials and traders. 'After this,' wrote Chaplain Teonge of one of them, 'he took us into his cellar, where he feasted us with roast beef cold, Westfalia polony-pudding, parmesan; gave us cucumbers, musk-mellons, salads and a reeve of Spanish onion as thick as my thigh; stowed us with good wine; and then, loth to let us go, he sent one of his corporals with us to see us safe to our pinnace. Such a hearty entertainment I never saw before from a mere stranger.' Nearly £100,000 of the King's money flowed every year into this little station of some six or seven hundred civilians and a thousand or so soldiers. There was therefore plenty of money in circulation.

Nature was equally abundant, providing chickens, capons, geese, turkeys, pigeons and ducks of rare fatness with a generous choice of vegetables and fruit – peas, beans, artichokes and wild asparagus from the surrounding fields, 'melons so plentiful, so various in shape

and kind that it cannot be described to understanding and belief',
apricots, peaches and calabashes. And outside the town was 'a land
very rich and pleasant, abundantly luxurious in the production of
fine flowers and sweet-smelling plants, so that the hay made there by
the garrison is only a withered nosegay of rosemary, thyme,
marjoram, pennyroyal and other sweet-smelling herbs'. Here, san-
guine newcomers reflected, forgetting dry, dusty winds, long weeks
of monotonous confinement and the peering Moors who bided their
cruel purpose in the hills beyond the gates, was England's place in
the sun.[1]

But Pepys, curiously walking the streets of the town on the day
after his arrival, was under no delusions. He was a very different
person now to the excited young clerk who so joyously described the
sights of Holland in the spring of 1660. Close on a quarter of a
century's experience – of long, close, unremitting labour, vast
responsibilities and unjust persecution – had left its impress. Those
still curious eyes saw a world that was no longer rose-tinted. He felt
hot, out of order with the change and unwonted climate, and
woefully bitten. When after dinner Dartmouth and Kirke made him
ride out to view the fields around the town, he did so without
pleasure, 'but with great danger, I thought, and so did W. Hewer,
and wondered all the way at the folly of the King's being at all this
charge upon this town'. A mere saunter into the country involved
the risk of death and slavery; the very water supply was dependent
on the Moors. As they rode back he could see their cavalry
exercising upon the shore. It was a disturbing spectacle. And the
chinches were even worse. Before he retired to sleep he tried to
defeat them with lime and the use of candles and by moving his bed.
But he was still bitten.

Next morning he visited the Bagnio, where the jade in charge
told him that the women of Tangier were such whores that mothers
and daughters called each other so publicly. As a change he
inspected the Moor with five fingers and toes on one foot – a
delegate from the Alcaïd – and spent an enjoyable evening in
Henry Shere's garden, 'listening and dancing to the harp and
guitar with mighty pleasure'. But that night his wonted supper of a
quart of milk cost him the shameful price of 8*d*., and, though he
made his bed upon chairs and covered his hands and face against
the chinches, he was again mercilessly bitten. 'A hell of brimstone

and fire and Egypt's plagues . . . in a hellish torrid zone', poor Balty in one of his numerous laments had called the place.* Pepys had already come to agree with him.[2]

He was not sorry therefore to start work on his commission for valuing the town. It was, after all, what he had come for, and the sooner begun, the sooner ended. On September 19th the proprietors were summoned by proclamation to attend at the Town House with evidence of their tenures. Next morning, attended by his fellow-Commissioners, Trumbull and Frederick Bacher, the Admiralty Judge of Tangier, Pepys opened proceedings in the presence of the Mayor, resplendently but unsuitably clad in scarlet robes and ermine.

With his usual method Pepys had drawn up elaborate instructions for the guidance of himself and his fellow-Commissioners and had got Lord Dartmouth (who, poor man, had been made to copy them out in tabulated form in his own hand) to present them formally. They were to enquire of every claimant by what right he held his tenement, what covenants had been entered into with the Crown and whether they had been duly kept, what rents had been reserved and whether paid, what encroachments had been made and at whose charge repairs had been effected and whether out of the King's stores and materials. They were also to ascertain what sums the proprietors owed to the Crown or foreign merchants and, before certifying their claims, to make the necessary adjustments. In doing so they were to deal first with the Portuguese, whose rights had been guaranteed by the Queen's marriage treaty, next with other foreign proprietors, then with the English civilians, and last of all with the garrison, it having been privately determined to evacuate them in this order.[3]

It was a task in equity to test any man's industry and patience. But Pepys was used to titanic tasks and faced it with equanimity. He reckoned however without the proverbial indolence and carelessness of the Tangerines. For the proprietors could not yet be told the reason of the enquiry. When the Commission opened, in spite of the previous day's Proclamation, scarcely any of them appeared, though they had been informed that the value set upon their holdings would depend on their doing so. Only the black-robed Fathers of the

* B. St Michel to S. P., June 27th, 1683. *Rawl. MSS. A.* 190, f. 42.

Portuguese Church, fretful after the manner of their kind for Holy Church's property, were there vigorously asserting their rights. Afterwards the good men bore Pepys away to view their buildings and library. But he seems to have been more impressed by the admirable grapes and pomegranates, roast fowl and sweetmeats which Shere brought home that night after a friendly visit to the Alcaïd.

Next morning – happily the chinches had been less successful in their night attack – the Portuguese Fathers were again the only proprietors to appear. But as their titles were in Spanish and had to be sent away to be translated, the Commissioners, having nothing to do, were forced to adjourn. In the afternoon a few other claims dribbled in, but all so imperfectly drawn that what remained of the day was spent instructing the claimants how to remedy them.

When all this tiresome business was over Pepys walked the Parade with Trumbull and little Ken to see fashionable Tangier taking the evening air. Afterwards they supped off Spanish onions, which Pepys thought 'mighty good', and drank wine deliciously cooled in salt-petre. But their pleasure was spoiled by Lord Dartmouth, who, softened by the gift of a wild boar from the Alcaïd, began to speak of entrusting that wily Moor with his plans for demolishing the town. From this they did their best, though in vain, to dissuade him. Shere was particularly gloomy about the time the work of destruction must take: he did not see how it could be done in less than three months.[4]

The continued indifference of the proprietors deepened Pepys' depression. His hopes of an early return to England and of eating his Christmas dinner of brawn with the Headmaster of St Paul's and his pretty cousin, Barbara Gale, were fast vanishing. He did his best, however, getting Dartmouth to supply him with twelve clerks to prepare elaborate forms for the guidance of the proprietors. With such this good civil servant in Wonderland hoped that something might be done. He also drafted another Proclamation calling a general meeting of claimants on the Monday.[5]

During these labours he and Trumbull, according to the official practice of the age, were forced to take their midday dinner at a separate table at the Castle – an honour which, accustomed to a more informal way of life, they regarded as useless foolery. Pepys occasionally broke his rule against supping* by taking a little fruit and vegetables with his customary milk at Dartmouth's table. There one evening he was much interested to find a young Moor, who had run away from the Alcaïd's army and professed a desire to enter the English service and become a Christian. 'He seems', he wrote, 'a very sober, good, well-looked youth, and says to my asking him that it was God only that put it into his heart to be a Christian and he has laboured several days to get to us and could not till last night. I bid him show the manner of his saying his prayers, and he did it with so much reverence in his manner, speech, the motion of his hands and eyes and sound of his voice and most of all in his prostrations, that I never was more taken with any appearance of devotion in my life.' It was an agreeable deception. For the English had not yet grasped their destiny and had still to apprehend the imperial and commercial advantages of disbelieving natives.[6]

On his first Sunday in Tangier Pepys returned to his old habit, discontinued since leaving England, of shaving himself. Then he accompanied Lord Dartmouth, the Mayor and Aldermen and the officers of the garrison to church. Dr Ken preached an excellent sermon, full, he noted, of the skill of a preacher but empty of all natural philosophy – nothing, in short, but forced meat. For in his religion, as in his discourse and reading, Pepys was now a thorough-paced virtuoso. 'I saw', he added, 'very few women that appeared gentlewomen.' When he returned to renew his devotions after a post-prandial hour over a book, he was more fortunate, for there in the same pew was the Governor's wife – 'a lady I have long admired for her beauty, but she is mightily altered. And they do tell stories of her on her part, while her husband minds pleasure of the same kind on his.' After service he led her to her chair – for Tangier, like London, had its fashionable sedans – and asked her how the place agreed with her. Nor was Lady Mary Kirke the only object that interested him in church. 'Here I first observed crawling upon the side of the church windows some lizards and sticking in the windows to bask themselves in the sun', his journal records. 'And at noon we had a great locust leapt of a sudden on the table, and this morning in my chamber the most extraordinary spider that ever I saw, at least

* See *The Years of Peril*, 309–10.

ten times as big as an ordinary spider. Such things this country do mightily abound with.'[7]

On Monday, September 24th, the Commissioners, Dartmouth himself attending to give them countenance, took their places early with their hundred and twenty beautifully copied questionnaires before them. But so few of the proprietors appeared that a further Proclamation had to be drafted, giving them till ten o'clock on the following Thursday. And such answers as we received were so full of faults that it looked as though the task of settling them must take a great deal longer than that of blowing up Tangier. It was therefore resolved to divide the work between the Commissioners. Bacher, who had been long acquainted with the town, took the freeholds, Trumbull the older leaseholds and Pepys the more recent ones.[8]

The day ended with a melancholy conversation. As Pepys was getting into bed and disposing himself under the mosquito net which Dartmouth had lent him, his Lordship himself came into the room. He seemed despondent, and Pepys, by repeating to him all the stories he had heard of the time it must take to demolish the Mole, began by making him still gloomier. But when, abandoning conjectures and excuses, Dartmouth frankly admitted the true state of affairs, Pepys would speak no more of fears.

The position was grave enough. Instead of the supplies from England which the Lord Treasurer had promised, not a single victualling ship had arrived. Of the provisions brought with the fleet, 16,000 rotting pieces of pork had had to be condemned as unfit to eat. In a few days the seamen would have to go on short allowance. Nor was there anything with which to feed the civilian population on the voyage home. Dartmouth, too easy a despairer by nature, was now convinced that the expedition was meant to fail by the great men who had had him sent on it. He believed himself fated to be such another sacrifice as Lord Sandwich.

But Pepys, though he admitted the gravity of things, refused to despair. He urged the younger man not to yield to the temptation of revealing his plight to the apparently friendly Alcaïd, but rather to submit himself to God and do the best he could. After which Dartmouth, a little comforted, went away, while Pepys, from behind the frail defences of his net, resumed his unequal war against the mosquitoes and chinches.[9]

Yet he felt gloomy himself in the morning, for his enemies had had many successes. As he walked at dawn by the water's edge and listened to Major Beckmann telling him how ill-provided the engineers were with everything needed for their work, his depression deepened. And though he sat close at his business, from eight till one and from two-thirty till eight, it seemed to little purpose, 'without anything more observable than the slowness of the proprietors coming in with their titles and the infinite unreadiness in those that did to make them good'.* At this rate the work would never be done.

It seemed worse than ever on Thursday morning, for when ten o'clock came, despite the Proclamation there were not ten people in Court. A final and very stern Proclamation was therefore issued giving the neglectful proprietors till that evening only. After that they poured in, and Pepys was kept hard at it till past nine at night. 'But in one word', he wrote, 'so silly and supine from all of them, even the people of most understanding among them, that it is plain there was a habit of disorder and forgetfulness of all method and discipline in all they did, even in their own private concernments, taking such evidence for their security as would not be worth sixpence in Westminster Hall.' To make matters worse, Trumbull, who like Pepys had been hearing gloomy stories, was in a terrible state, complaining peevishly of Dartmouth for having beguiled him from his thriving practice on so uncomfortable and hazardous an enterprise. Pepys knew it was such but could not forgive the young lawyer for saying so.[10]

Friday, September 28th, was a holiday. No one went to the office, everyone making for the hills outside the town where the formal meeting was to take place between Dartmouth and the Alcaïd. Pepys, who still retained his old love for a spectacle, was up early to watch the seamen land, every man in a blue and white striped linen jacket with musket, pike or poleaxe. He was proud to see them turn out so well and to give as good a volley, or better, with their small shot as the soldiers themselves.

About eleven o'clock Dartmouth, accompanied by Pepys and the officers of his staff, rode out of the town to review the two armies drawn up among the hills and beside the sea. At the water's-edge, under the guns of the smaller vessels of the fleet, Dartmouth received the Alcaïd, who with fitting oriental gravity made several long

* *Rawl. MSS. A.* 196, f. 24.

speeches, graver and better, Pepys thought, than Dartmouth's, 'though he did also extremely well'. After a truce had been propounded and an agreement reached for Commissioners to meet next day, the rival forces exercised. Pepys was fascinated by the Moorish manoeuvres, especially by the Alcaïd's son – 'a pretty youth who exercised very neatly and sometimes attacked his very father himself, and now and then the father (who is no old man, not fifty, though his habit makes him appear otherwise) would hit him with his lance'. The Alcaïd was no doubt also impressed and therefore more polite than usual, for the red-coats now numbered over 4000. For once in the troubled history of British Tangier the Moors were confronted with a display of force greater than their own.

But Pepys knew that such ceremonies, however pretty, could not solve the expedition's difficulties. After dinner Dartmouth, who wanted him to be one of the Commissioners, held a council about the proposed truce. Pepys contended that it would not give the engineers time to complete their work, since they needed at least four, and perhaps six, months to destroy the Mole. At this there was a scene. Dartmouth angrily replied that those who said so did not understand their business; he had a secret way that would do it in a fortnight. 'To which Kirke', recorded Pepys, who was beginning to loathe the Governor, 'immediately added, God damn him, he would do it all in a fortnight or he would be contented to be hanged.' Pepys said no more.[11]

Next day he went back to the office, and worked regardless of the heat from eight in the morning till nine at night with only an hour's break for dinner. Surveying the titles the straggling townsmen brought him, his contempt for the ways of Tangier increased: 'never surely was ever any town governed in all matters both public and private as this place has been.' Nor was he pleased at being consulted again about the negotiations with the Alcaïd, which he now regarded as useless. He left Dartmouth as soon as he could and returned to work. And so after a frugal supper 'to bed and slept mighty well, and the better that the business of my being employed in a foolish treaty is over'.[12]

Having come to the conclusion that the only way to straighten out the townsmen's claims was by a survey, Pepys spent his Sunday drafting a report for Dartmouth on its necessity. He managed, however, to attend church twice and take his fill of gazing at Lady Mary Kirke, even better dressed than a week before, though still not so fine as he had sometimes seen her. During the sermon, which was about the vices of the town, he blushed severely for her husband and his officers, though it struck him as a fruitless essay in oratory, for they took not the least notice.

Ken's sermon was deserved: 'nothing', Pepys noted among his memoranda, 'but vice in the whole place of all sorts, for swearing, cursing, drinking and whoring.' One could not pass an open door without hearing people blaspheming, the women as much as the men. The Governor himself, at Dartmouth's table, boasted publicly how one wench – 'her name, Joyce, as I remember', Pepys recorded, 'a mighty pretty creature' – had at sixteen given her disease to no less than four hundred of his soldiers, and seemed much amused because his own secretary 'was one that got it most pockly'.* Horrified and indignant Pepys carefully wrote it down: how Kirke had got his wife's sister with child so that she had had to hurry to Spain to be brought to bed, how he had taught a captured Moor with his first lisping phrase of English to drink healths to an unmentionable word and how, whenever he was 'with his whores at his little bathing house which was furnished with a jade a-purpose', his wife whom he kept in awe would send for her gallants and 'play the jade by herself at home'.[13]

All next week Pepys struggled with the dreary business of putting the claims of the feckless townsmen in order. Only the Portuguese Fathers showed any energy in the matter: from them the Commissioners received almost ceaseless communications. Dartmouth, agreeing at last to ignore the Moors whose bark seemed likely to be worse than their bite, resolved to make his mission public. Already the discourse of the town was of little else. On the evening of October 2nd he read over to Pepys and Trumbull the draft of his speech for the occasion, 'wholly taken', Pepys observed, 'out of my notes that I gave him, but with many good improvements that were really very good and wise and shows him to me to be a man of very good understanding and consideration'.

That was perhaps the lowest day in the fortunes of the expedition. In the afternoon the Moorish envoys parted with high words and in

* *Rawl. MSS. C.* 859, f. 249v.

the evening Dartmouth spoke openly of his fear that the King would be persuaded by those about him to disown the whole affair. At the back of everyone's mind was dread of Lord Sunderland, the Secretary of State and the most shifty politician in the three kingdoms. Pepys, who was in his grimmest mood, remarked that he was sorry for Dartmouth, but that he would not be the first to be so used while obeying the King's commands. This roused Dartmouth sufficiently to declare that he would go through with the thing and see it well done, though it should cost him his life. Pepys replied that 'the well doing of the thing did not lie in flinging away himself, but preserving himself to see it done . . . Upon which he answered that he did not intend to fling away himself, for he too well remembered the case of my lord of Sandwich and Sir William Berkeley and others and what they got by it when they were dead and out of the way, . . . but would labour to do the work so as that his life should not be spared if that were necessary for the accomplishing of it. This said, we took leave and the Doctor and I after a turn or two in my chamber, discoursing of what had now passed between us, to bed.'[14]

That was the worst. Afterwards things cheered up. Already there was news from England that three victualling ships were on their way, and that night the long drought ended in a sudden downpour which, however damaging to the engineering prospects, had a reviving effect on jaded spirits. In any case, Pepys reflected, as he listened to the sound of the rain, it would be worse for the Moors in the fields outside. On Thursday the 4th, Dartmouth, in the Town House, publicly revealed the great secret to the joy of all.[15]

Pepys passed it on next day to James Houblon in England, assuring him that, however much it might be censured by ignorant politicians at home, the evacuation was an act of necessity and wisdom. According to his practice in correspondence he praised his chief and colleagues – an approval which we know from his journal he was far from feeling towards one of them: he even described Dr Trumbull as a 'worthy sober gentleman'. The greater part of his letter dealt with his employments – 'an office wherein I have it equally in hand to serve the King against impostures from them whose demands are so apt to fly too high, as the poor proprietors against others whose want of tenderness might betray them to making offers of satisfaction too low . . . Under a pressure of business equal, at least, to all that ever you knew us in at Derby House . . . both my duty and charity meet with a good degree of content.'

'But to tell you the truth,' he concluded, 'I am at this very moment upon winding up a great many poor people's pretences, who have very little time to turn themselves in . . . I am in most perfect health, full of just remembrances of all my friends and their friendships in England, and yours in the front of all; greedy to make an end here in hopes of making a step over to Spain while our sulphur-mongers are preparing a Doomsday for this unfortunate place . . . And now I end with prayers for you and your dear tribe, to every of whom ten thousand blessings. And so God send us a good meeting!'*[16]

The work of winding up the townsmen's claims was finished by October the 18th. Three days before, a solemn debate was held before Lord Dartmouth in which the proprietors argued their objections to the assessments and Pepys replied for the Commissioners. The gist of his answer was that the present level of rents in Tangier was fictitious, being greatly enhanced by the reinforcements which had been poured into the town since 1680, and that it was unjust to expect the King to pay for his own kindness. If the present swollen garrison were reduced to the normal establishment, rents would soon fall to their proper level. As it was, not four houses had been sold in Tangier during the past twelve months. 'Nay,' Pepys asked, 'what would not people have taken for their houses had this been known six months ago, for who that had heard that would ever have imagined that the King would have done that which is now offered?'

In the end it was settled that the Commissioners' rates of compensation should stand, leaving the King the option of increasing them if he chose. The Portuguese received £600 and the English £11,000. The main work in all this had been Pepys'. When on October 18th, he and Trumbull presented their formal report on the completion of their commission, he could not refrain from noting with scorn 'how weakly and yet impudently would this Doctor pretend to interpose in discourse with my Lord upon it when he

* S. P. to J. Houblon. *Howarth*, 158–60. It is there dated October 14th, so Pepys obviously used the *new style*, for according to his journal it was posted on October 5th, *old style*.

knows and owns to me, and so do my Lord too, that he has done nothing in the world in the thing'.[17]

But by October 18th Pepys' contempt for Trumbull had become almost boundless. A little while before Dartmouth had told him how, on the first day of term, the sheepish Doctor, who had a young wife waiting for him in England, had come to him moaning about all the guineas he might have been earning at that moment in Westminster Hall. Every day his gloom and sickness became more intolerable. Pepys at last suggested that he should be given a passage to England by the next ship. This pleased everybody, even the Doctor, who immediately became quite brisk, telling everyone that he was being sent home with despatches. 'A man of the meanest mind as to courage that ever was born', was the diarist's verdict. On October 20th he departed with the mails, Pepys prudently giving him a farewell bottle of wine and a good send-off, 'that he might be useful in England.* And so the fool went away, every creature of the house laughing at him.'[18]

Pepys did not share poor Trumbull's fears. Though a Moorish attack was expected, he wrote to Dr Gale that they were in no pain concerning it, believing that the fleet could keep them secure against all Barbary. He himself became increasingly daring. At his arrival the merest sally beyond the town gates had seemed dangerous; after October 10th, when he first walked in the fields by Fountain Fort, he made one almost daily.

At first Pepys' comments on these expeditions were chiefly of their peril – of the folly of the place in being overlooked everywhere, of his own obvious value as a prize and how the Moorish sentries had seemed mighty close and intent upon him. Yet after a day or two his inherent curiosity overcame these fears. He watched the Moors mending a boat, chatted 'in a kind of Frank' with the Armenian traders who brought their wares to the shore, and even talked with the sentries so as to be rebuked on his return for his rashness: 'but this I am glad I have once done to know the most of the place and some of the history of it against the Moors'. During these solitary rambles the long dead poet in him awoke again; after dining with

---

* Lord Dartmouth saw fit a week later to write Trumbull a very civil letter, thanking him for his attendance and hoping that it would turn to his good. 'I am sure it was so intended by his Majesty and his Royal Highness and all your real friends.' *H.M.C. Downshire* II, i. 20–1.

Captain Killigrew aboard the *Mountagu*, he described how he rowed himself round the Bay to see the ruins of old Tangier and 'coming back upon the water first saw how blue the remote hills will look in the evening about the sun's going down, as I have sometimes seen them painted but never believed it natural'.[19]

Meanwhile the work of the engineers on the Mole went on but slowly. In his more optimistic moments Dartmouth announced that all would be done in three weeks. But Pepys, who was a daily and interested spectator of the operations which he frequently talked over with Shere, Phillips and Major Beckmann, never believed it. On October 19th he watched Captain Leake, the Master Gunner of England, make an unsuccessful trial of two bombs under the Mole arches, while Colonel Kirke kept up a ceaseless accompaniment of bawdy talk, asking the young Controller whether he had yet got himself a mistress and offering to help him to a little one of his own size before all were got aboard the ships.

Towards the end of the month, Dartmouth, taking advantage of the moonlight nights, brought all hands from the easier work on the fortifications to the Mole. After that, under Shere's direction, things went better, and Pepys, who frequently spent his evenings with his old friend in the mines, witnessed 'some very good execution, even to wonder with so little quantity of powder'. One day he was brought hurrying up from his dinner to the house top by a message to see Shere's great mine crack the Mole from side to side and shower stones over ships and harbour: on another he watched from the dining-room window by Dartmouth's side while fragments of masonry fell all round them as the Mole's end shot up into the night.

But to demolish every trace of a Mole 1500 feet long and 110 wide and weighing over 167,000 tons, was no easy task by seventeenth-century standards. Sir Hugh Cholmley and Shere – its joint creators – had done their work well, for all their quarrels. The half-million or so which the King had sunk on it had taken a more permanent form than usually attended his expenditure. And when the rains set in again in mid-November, the work of destruction was still far from complete.[20]

Pepys' own task was sooner done: he had his own way of getting through things and he wished to visit Spain. In spite of a cold in his throat that made it difficult to speak or swallow, he drew up a long report on every petition against the Commissioners' findings. This he finished at eleven o'clock on the night of October 25th, not stirring till it was over. Dartmouth, to whom he presented it next day, was 'mightily pleased' with it, observing that 'it was surely the first time ever such a general report was ever done upon petitions. And I believe so too', Pepys added.[21]

His official task was not his only one. His passionate sense of justice had impelled him to another. While he, Dartmouth and the Governor were walking one late October morning up and down the Mole, the town apothecary approached them with a complaint that the departing shopkeepers were selling off their sour wine cheap to the soldiers. Kirke at once demanded that it should all be staved and, receiving Dartmouth's consent, went off to see it done. Presently he returned with a bottle of white wine in his hand, crying out, *God damn him*, that it was vinegar. He was followed by its owner, a modest-looking creature, who assured Dartmouth, with tears in his eyes, that the wine was good and was only sold cheaply because he had no other means of disposing of it. But Kirke only ranted the more, calling the poor man dog and swearing all the merchants in the town were rogues who would poison his men.

Pepys, who tasted the wine for himself, set down the rest of the story in his note book. 'My lord calmly bade the man dispose of what he had otherwise, and not sell it to the soldiers. "Nay, God damn him," says Kirke, "he must gather it up then from the ground, for I have staved it." However the man (whether he had any more that was not staved or not, I know not) withdrew himself weeping and without complaint, to the making my heart ache. And when the man was gone, I whispered to my lord that I did not find the wine so sour as Kirke represented it, and my lord concurred with me. And, the man being gone, did say openly to Kirke in the hearing of the company, "Now we are by ourselves, I must needs say the wine is not so bad as you make it, and I believe it is better than you give your soldiers at other times", to which he answered, God damn him, but it was not. I said, and I said truly, that I had drunk worse a hundred times in some of the best inland market towns in England. And Mr Session, my lord's servant, among others being by and saying the same thing or to the same purpose, Kirke swore God damn him, he wished he might never drink better wine as long as he lived, and other words very sharp. Upon which Session answered (and so did I) that he had often drank worse. However the thing went off without any more, my lord having in his good nature told the owner that there should be no more of his wine staved, but bid him to sell no more to the soldiers of it, and yielded to a motion of Kirke's for a proclamation to be made by beat of drum (telling my lord it was not necessary, nor usual here, to have some things done in writing) to forbid the selling of any more white wine.'

The sequel occurred in an hour or two, when just after Dartmouth had sat down to dinner, one of the aldermen appeared in a panic to beg protection from soldiers who had got into his wine cellar and were staving, not only his stock-in-trade, but the very Canary and Muscatella which he drank at his own table. This was quickly followed by further alarms, the military breaking into private houses, robbing and beating their owners, snatching hats off the heads of passers by and even assaulting government clerks and officials. Pepys promptly warned Dartmouth to punish such excesses for which he would otherwise be blamed in England. As a result a proclamation was issued imposing the death penalty for any further disorders.[22]

This affair caused Pepys to compile a private record of Kirke's misdemeanours. He had not far to seek for material. Shere told him how the Governor owed £1500 to the townsmen, who could get no other response to their entreaties for payment but a 'God damn me, why did you trust me?' Dr Ken described how Kirke had forced the brother of his own mistress upon the parish as Reader – a fellow that swore, drank and talked bawdy. From others Pepys learnt how he had done two of his men to death for threatening to complain of his injustices, how he had tied a serjeant to a post and thrashed him with his own hands, and how he had sent a poor refugee Jew and his wife back to Spain to be burned by the Inquisition. Those who served under such a commander behaved as might have been expected: everywhere at night officers and men could be seen lying drunk in the streets. 'And to show how little he makes of drunkenness (though he will beat a fellow for having a dirty face or band) I have seen a soldier reel upon him as he has been walking with me in the street as drunk as a dog, and at this busy time too, when everybody that is not upon the guard is at work. And he has only laughed at him and cried, "God damn me, the fellow has got a good morning's draught already", and so let him go without one word of reprehension.'[23]

The more Pepys saw of Kirke the more he loathed him. The bold, brutal, slap-dash fellow with his go-as-you-please, devil-may-care manner, was utterly repugnant to his own careful temperament. That Kirke was one of the most successful of Tangier's military Governors, adored by his rough men and the founder of a regimental tradition that, in a moderated and more decorous form, was to flourish for generations in the British Army, was beyond the compass of Pepys' vision. All he could see was an overbearing red-coat, who, speaking with the impudent assurance of a gentleman, outraged every decency and mocked every prudent, diligent rule that his own experience had taught him to honour. The dislike between the two men was spontaneous and natural.

The middle-aged moralist who carefully noted in his neat short-hand the Colonel's bestialities presumably found a certain satisfaction in doing so. There is a gusto in these passages of prurient gossip that recalls Pepys' chronicle of his own earlier transgressions. In minute detail he recorded how Kirke and his myrmidons defamed every woman who would not yield to their invitations, how he had employed the town bawd 'to get the maidenhood of a young pretty girl, a kinswoman of this whore's newly come over', and how he boasted publicly at table of his shameful conquests. Words that in his earlier diary he had disguised in a queer jargon of half a dozen foreign languages, he now made no attempt to disguise at all. Much of that record of other men's vices is unprintable.[24]

It was not only the dormant and probably dying passion of sex that stirred Pepys to record the hated Governor's misdoings, but that sense of justice which lay at the core of his intellectual being. Here was tyranny, and in its most hated form – unlicensed power. To Pepys himself power was something sacrosanct, to be pursued earnestly for good ends and to be linked rigidly with law. Kirke used power as though it was a personal toy, mocked at rules and precedents and flung drunken oaths at those set to administer them. 'The Recorder tells me of Kirke's saying to him in public Court, *God damn the Law*, and to the jury, *God damn their consciences*, he would make them stretch their consciences. And would say that the Recorder was his dog.'

No man living could make Pepys stretch his conscience. With Ken at his side, he openly charged the Governor with his looseness of speech and the morals of Tangier. It was knowledge of this that caused the peace-loving Dartmouth to entrust Pepys with the examination of an extraordinary petition from one of the departing townsmen. It appeared that this wretched man had been unlawfully beaten and carried off to the guard-house, where his wife on coming to visit him was ravished by three soldiers while his house was broken into and robbed. Pepys pursued the matter with his usual thoroughness, examined an officer of the guard and secured without much difficulty his admission that the woman had been lain with by three of his men. Later the officer, feeling his honour impeached, denied it, and when Kirke pressed him, sulkily replied he had no need to lie with any woman, for he had a wife of his own at home. 'Yes, and a handsome one,' thundered the Governor, 'but that is no argument, for I have a wife too, and yet I lie with other women.' 'To which', Pepys recorded, 'my lord very worthily answered but that was not necessary for him to publish to everybody as if it were a thing to be boasted of.' 'Why, my lord,' says Kirke, 'I don't pretend to be a saint!'[25]

In this military Bedlam, Pepys felt he could come to no certain conclusion on the matter, for the petitioner and his wife had already left Tangier with the Portuguese. 'But though I believe some part of their report', he wrote in his summary, 'that the woman might be a light woman and her husband an idle fellow, yet there was too much confessed to show the bestiality of this place.' It was not surprising that in his chamber that day, he and Ken, dining together, agreed that it was time for God Almighty to destroy the town.

Pepys expressed the same sentiments in his letters to James Houblon, contrasting the peace and innocence of his friend's home with the scene of debauchery in which he was placed. 'I would not wish my sweet W. or little Jemmy here; for with sorrow and indignation I speak, it is a place of the world I would last send a young man to, but to Hell. Therefore, on God's account as well as the King's, I think it high time it were dissolved.' And in his memoranda he noted how a former Recorder of the town had left his estate to a servant on condition that he never married a woman of Tangier. He even secured a copy of the will to preserve among his papers.[26]

Of the impossibility of holding Tangier Pepys had now no doubt. The elaborate reasons for its evacuation which he had prepared on the voyage out had been confirmed by experience. 'Overseen quite

round the town'; 'no water but Fountain Fort at this time, which the
Moors, if they knew and would, might prevent us of'; 'the Mole not
to be stood upon for the great seas.' . . . When some of Herbert's
young commanders made difficulties about signing a memorandum
of Dartmouth's on the uselessness of the place as a naval base, Pepys
could see nothing but downright dishonesty in their attitude.
Everything about Tangier was rotten in his eyes, even its timber and
the stone pillars by the waterside eaten away by the searching winds
and spray: the very knife and steel in his pocket were rusting.[27]

Its days were now numbered. On the evening of October 27th,
Pepys, lying in his bed, heard the Mayor and chief citizens take their
leave of Lord Dartmouth. At dawn next day they sailed for England.
By November 5th all the townsmen had departed, and only the
soldiers, the engineers and the fleet were left.[28]

The greater part of that melancholy month Pepys spent confined
to his chamber with an appalling cold. He occupied himself by
writing exhaustive reports, reading his favourite Hakluyt and
pursuing his 'navo-historical' researches. When he was well enough
he accompanied Dartmouth to dine aboard one or other of the ships
in the Bay, and once, while fishing in Alcazar Bay, was fired at by
Moorish sentries. His chief concern now was to get away on his
promised holiday to Spain with Will Hewer. Among Dartmouth's
entourage there was a good deal of humorous speculation as to
whether Mr Pepys and 'his pupil' would ever take their much talked
of pilgrimage. Pepys had no doubts: he meant to go, and he was
going. And when Dartmouth, anxious to retain him, expressed the
hope that he would be back in a fortnight, he privately made a note
in his journal that he would take the full three weeks promised him.
For the opportunity once lost might never come again.[29]

Before he went, he had a last bout with Kirke who had procured
from Dartmouth the option to purchase a prize brought in by a
Tunisian pirate. On her master declining his cruelly inadequate
offer, the Governor forbade him either to leave the port or to sell to
anyone else. After a week the poor man, penniless and half-starving,
contrived to communicate his case to Pepys, who persuaded Dartmouth to allow him to take his ship away.

But there was no end to the ways in which the Governor abused
his authority. Having begged a grant of all coals and chopped straw
left over from the King's service, he placed sentries wherever these

commodities were stored, so depriving the horses working on the Mole of their fodder and the government forges of their fuel. Yet when Pepys spoke of the way in which the Governor turned everything to his private profit, Dartmouth only shrugged his shoulders and asked what he could do. 'I came not here to stay,' he said, 'and for me to oppose and cross him for so little a time is to little purpose to the King or the subjects but a great deal to me, to the drawing of enemies about my ears at home.'[30]

It was the same with the captains of the fleet. All the while the good-natured Admiral kept yielding to their importunities to be sent off to Cadiz or to some Mediterranean port on pretence of taking in water or mending a leak or spar, but in reality to make money by private trading. He seemed to regard their right to do so as part of their employment – a reward to one man for his labour, and compensation to another for an unprofitable voyage.

Some of the captains solicited Pepys himself to plead for them with the Admiral. It made him mad. Even his friend, Sir John Wyborne, told him that unless he could get sent to Cadiz before returning to England, his service at Tangier would prove a loss. 'Perhaps after the rate they live here', Pepys admitted, 'it is true too. So that it is impossible for this thing to be in the order it should be till the business of Good Voyages be at an end, and their lives made comfortable to them by their plain salary, and severe discipline to make them perform their duty for self-preservation sake.'[31]

And the chief contributory cause of it all was Tangier – that accursed town far out of reach of every decent influence and check. Used only as a pretext to employ ships for their own profit, it had debauched every commander. Even Samuel Atkins, the faithful clerk whose Puritan conscience had once stood between Pepys and death, had fallen into the prevailing laxity. And here the diarist recalled how Herbert and his fellow officers were said to have been 'drunk and merry' a whole month together off the Portuguese coast, and one day to have caused the fleet surgeon to be stripped stark naked with one leg tied by the toe to the cabin roof and exposed in this posture to the mockery of loose women. 'This is but one instance of a whole life that they all spend here in roguery.' Perhaps Herbert and his gay young sea dogs would have replied that it was the only recreation that life on a foreign station afforded.[32]

Pepys' own last days in the place passed in a perpetual downpour of rain 'such weather for wind, thunder, lightning, rain and hail all together for eight or ten days, I never saw in my life'. Everyone was ill, and the shortness of provisions made things worse. Pepys was attacked by the old swimming sensation in his head and Hewer prostrated with a fearful headache – 'and I twice at his ill lodging to see him, and mightily troubled I was to see him lie in a room great and wide and cold, rain coming in all over the house, and no glass windows but shutters'.[33]

On the night of November 28th a great storm swept the bay. Several of the ships were driven from their moorings, one of them, the *Mountagu*, colliding with another frigate and subsequently requiring repair. The accident provided Pepys with the means of transport to Cadiz. The time for departure seemed auspicious, for the storms, while delaying operations on the Mole, temporarily removed the danger of a Moorish attack. On the last night of November, Pepys wrote his letters to England, including a 'merry, roguish but yet mysterious one' to Sarah Houblon.* Then he washed his feet and thighs with brandy and went to bed.

Next morning he rose early to collect his belongings, thinking to set sail in the damaged ship. But it was still raining and 'by and by it become so stormy . . .' After that, though he continued to fill his memorandum book with shorthand notes, he ceased any more to record his daily doings. Not till the evening of December 6th did the storm abate and Pepys with Hewer beside him sail in the *Mountagu* for Spain.[34]

---

* The initials S. H. here employed by Pepys were used by him on other occasions to denote Sarah Houblon. There seems therefore little reason to doubt that it was her that he meant, especially as she wrote him three days later from England exactly such another 'roguish but yet mysterious' letter (see *Howarth*, 163).

3
Spanish Holiday

'Spitting out of a wax taper is an Inquisition business in Spain.' Pepys'
Notes on Spain, *Tangier Papers*.

Mr Pepys took with him on his Spanish holiday his books and music
for the flute, a pot in which to boil his morning chocolate, his
bedding and sheets, sponges and wash-balls, razors and spectacles
and a sheaf of recommendatory letters. He also carried, like the
perfect tourist he was, a list of the principal places he ought to see.
He was to study Spanish laws, libraries and manufactures, buy old
plates, new books and ballads, investigate the *mal de ojo* or evil eye
and the powers, if any, of the Saludadors, and inspect a furnished
house, a christening and the Exchange of Seville.*

He carried many commissions. He was to buy horses for Dartmouth, books for Trumbull and Ken, mouchettes and stockings (one
suspects for Sarah Houblon) and a chameleon. And he was to call on
a great many people, British merchants and exiles and learned
Spaniards – Mr Pitts, Señor la Cruz at Seville, Father Ambrose,
Father Lynch and the English Catholic scholars. It was characteristic of the man that he provided himself with elaborate notes as to
how to address them:

> Al Reverendo Padre Maistro Ambrosio de St Tomás.
> Al Señor Don Alonzo de Vaues.
> Al Reverendo Padre Piedro North.[1]

At Cadiz Pepys was made welcome by his bankers, Messrs
Hodges and Reresby, James Houblon's agents in southern Spain.
Their house, presided over by Mr Hodges' young wife, became his
home† while he explored the delights of Cadiz. Part, at least, of his

---

* *Rawl. MSS. C.* 859, ff. 164, 167. Mr Chappell does not include Pepys' pencil
longhand notes in his edition of the diarist's shorthand Tangier Papers.

† They had written to him on the 14/24 Sept. 1683, begging him to 'honour us with
your good company before you return to England and accept (though of a poor) yet a
hearty welcome at our house during your stay in this place'. *Rawl. MSS. A.* 190, f. 208.

customary eye-witness' luck held. During his stay the outbreak of
war with France was proclaimed in the streets, and the Flota, the
great Spanish treasure fleet from the Indies, sailed in stately
procession into the Bay and anchored under the guns of Puntales
Castle.

Yet in other ways Pepys' luck was out. Hardly had he landed
when the westerly gales which had detained him at Tangier began
again. A week later, he was still waiting in Mr Hodges' hospitable
house for the rains to cease so that he could set out for Seville. "Tis
with impatience (on his Majesty's behalf and your lordship's as my
own)', he wrote to Dartmouth on Christmas Day,* 'I have waited a
change of weather, we having not had till yesterday one hour fair to
be able, for wind and rain, to look abroad since we came hither; and
the floods are so high in the country that, should it continue fair, as
it hath two days, my friends here tell me there will be no passing the
roads these five days more. However, such is my resolution of saving
every minute in my return towards your lordship that, sink or swim,
I will set out hence on Tuesday next, the first day the devotion of
this place will suffer either man or mule to work on.'[2]

But after two more fine days, during which Pepys had his first
chance of seeing Spain idling timelessly in its habitual sunshine – it
struck his practical English mind as strange that in a land with so
much sun there should be so few sun-dials – the gales began again.
On New Year's Day, after more than two weeks at Cadiz, he was
still flood-bound and on the verge, so he told Dartmouth, of
returning to Tangier in despair. Yet next day he wrote in a different
vein: 'The weather coming about very fair yesterday and so
continuing, I am encouraged afresh to try a few days more, being
unwilling to lose the benefit of the favour your lordship intended me
in this journey.'[3]

And though the gales and rain began again almost immediately,
he went. Malaga, which he had once set his heart on seeing, was out
of the question now. But on Monday, January 3rd, accompanied by
Hewer and Mr Fowler, a learned gentleman well acquainted with
the country, he took a boat across the bay to Puerto de Santa Maria,
or Port as the English community called it. Thence mounted on

---

* New style. The new continental time, which Pepys naturally used in Spain, was
ten days ahead of the old or English notation.

mules, with their portmanteaux and baggage borne before them, they travelled along flooded roads across the flat plain to Sanlúcar de Barrameda. As they did so, Samuel was rewarded, for through the pelting rain he saw Spain. Ever since his youth when he had taken charge of the captured son of the Viceroy of Peru for his cousin Mountagu, and learnt to read Spanish, he had longed to know more of this romantic land and people. Now, able to at last, he jotted down in rough and all too brief shorthand his notes of what he saw – the devout country people who greeted the travellers with a *Go with God* instead of the familiar English *God go with you,* the beggars who approached with the courtesies of Hidalgos and expected to be saluted as such in return, the bare-footed ploughmen who wore slashed sleeves and laced bands pinned to their ragged shirts. So proud were these people that a barber would not demean himself by washing his client's face nor a shoemaker pull off his customer's shoe, not if it were that of the Governor of Andalusia himself. Yet the houses were almost always unfinished, were without chimneys, and swarmed with fleas – 'a mighty plague', Pepys found them. And for all the formal hospitality of the people, it was uncommonly difficult to get a drink. Nor was there so much as a seat in a tavern to sit down in: one just stood and took one's quartel of wine and, it might be, a plate of olives and then hurried away. Drinking was out of fashion, and, as if to emphasize the fact, there did not appear to be a single chamber-pot in the whole country.[4]

They reached Sanlúcar on the 5th. In this pleasant little merchant town of baroque white houses, cellars of sherry and rich, vinous smells they lingered for a day or two. Pepys wrote to Dartmouth, who must have despaired as his obstinate adviser receded further and further into the north, to tell him that he was hurrying as fast as the weather would let him to the Andalusian capital. Here he promised he would endeavour with all despatch to run through whatever that place might afford of entertainment. And for Seville he now embarked with his fellow travellers, sailing between desolate floods up the broad Guadalquivir.[5]

So Pepys came to the most beautiful city on earth. He did not see it as others have seen it, with the blossom filling its streets and the sun kissing its shuttered windows. But he breathed Andalusia's intoxicating air, and, though the pitiless rain from the Atlantic fell steadily almost throughout his entire stay, could see the cathedral, the discreet, beckoning balconies and the lovely women who sometimes look down from them. There is no record to tell whether these things struck chords in a heart that had once been so sensitive to all beauty: only silence. Perhaps the rain drowned all.

Yet it did not drown Pepys' passion for improving and curious knowledge. 'I wish', his politely astonished host of Cadiz had written to him at Sanlúcar, 'the curiosities of Seville may in some respect answer your desire of a journey at so unseasonable a time of the year.' They did. For six feverish days until the ever rising floods made further sightseeing impossible, Pepys saw all that there was to be seen that could contribute to his knowledge – the courts of law, the bookshops which were served by the blind, the Saludadors, whose sanative and prophetic faculties he put to a severe test and pronounced a fraud. Each of these pious men, so it was claimed, carried a black cross in the roof of his mouth and was enabled by divine protection to sit comfortably in a red-hot oven. Pepys sought one of them out, placed him before an oven and, inviting him to display his art, received a frank and unembarrassed confession that it was all an imposition on the public. Nor was there anything, he decided after further investigation, in the *mal de ojo*. It was not for nothing that he had been a member of the Royal Society for nineteen years. Other researches revealed such humble sociological data as that for their more intimate sanitary purposes the people of Spain used cloth instead of paper, and modestly preferred doorways to the open street. These also he noted. For he was still, as he had always been, a very curious and universal observer.[6]

But the knowledge which the Pepys of middle-age prized above all else concerned the sea. While he enjoyed the hospitality of Roger Slingar and the English merchants of Seville, this ex-Master of Trinity House called at the Casa de Contratación, the learned office that superintended the golden trade to the Indies, and there sought out Don Miguel Zuero, the Cosmógrafa Fabricador or master-mapmaker of Spain. With him he discussed the traditions and mysteries of his craft, and heard the story of its decay; how by the old Spanish law, pilots had been forbidden to carry any maps or instruments but of their House's making, yet now did so, and how the Dutch mapmakers undersold them, marketing for two shillings what they could not make for four, so that the Fabricador of instruments, though the only one in Spain, could scarcely earn

enough to feed himself. Don Miguel, who had learnt his trade from
his uncle, the last Cosmógrafa Fabricador, showed him as a great
favour a new map which he was making. But Pepys was not in the
least impressed and set it down privately as 'an ordinary thing'.[7]

While at the Casa de Contratación he studied the methods of
training and examining the pilots who brought home to Spain the
wealth of the New World. It seemed that at their examinations the
Piloto Mayor never said a word lest by engaging in controversy he
might lessen the respect paid to his rank. The presiding Judge sat
under a canopy, with the Piloto Mayor and a *disputado* of the
Universidad de Mercantes on his right, the Cosmógrafa and the
Fabricador of instruments on his left, and six other master pilots
sitting bare-headed beside them, while the examinees were publicly
questioned in the science of navigation. Before becoming qualified
for examination, the students had to attend mathematical lectures
by the Piloto Mayor and the Cosmógrafa for sixty mornings.[8]

In all this there were signs of the stately paralysis which for a
century past had been sapping the giant strength of Spain. That
bright genius that had flowered so swiftly and wonderfully was
being atrophied by the innate Moorish passion for outward forms
and symbols. Slow-moving pride and dead precedent now reigned
in every department of government. It was part of the inevitable
process of decay through which all empires pass – the hour when
honour is paid alone to the holder of office and not to the doer of
work, when the fire and rhythm of speech is neglected for grammar
and spelling, when men base their actions not on their instinct
and conviction but on the precedents established for them by
others.

Pepys was not deceived by the splendid formalism of Spain,
though he compared it, as was natural in a pioneer of bureaucracy in
a young empire, a little enviously with the vigorous, rough-and-
ready mode of his own untrammelled countrymen. He saw straight
through the pompous pretences of Spanish public life to the
inefficient reality behind them. 'And though', he noted, 'here is the
most exemplary method of having justice done by there being upon
the expiration of every office ... a *Juez* to *tomar cuenta de
Residencia,* to enquire into and invite all persons to bring in their
complaints of any injustice done by this office during his time ... yet
this is all nothing, it being turned only to a thing of form, thereby to

gratify some man or other that lacks a courtesy at Court by making him a judge in this occasion only to squeeze something out of the officer whom he is to enquire after.' The same spirit of solemn humbug ran through the whole nation. Men put on spectacles to pretend that they were readers, citizens were compelled to buy a dispensation for the upkeep of a fleet against the Moors and Turks which did not exist, and everyone from peasant to beggar made out that he was of gentle birth and behaved accordingly. From this universal habit of pretence no one was free; 'the severest women all the year will hear and talk and almost do anything for three days before Lent, and their husbands bear it'.

The tyranny of legal and social fictions is not the only curse that attends the death of empires. When the living spirit leaves the body of a nation's institutions, these are administered not by the quick but by the dead. A Spaniard told Pepys how his country was under an evil fatality, its offices being filled by men untrained for them either by experience or knowledge. The kingdom was overrun with proud and worthless spongers, so that, as Pepys noticed, the foreign merchants at Seville who were his hosts found it advisable to avoid the Exchange and do their business unobtrusively on the Lonja or in their own houses lest, by being thought rich men, they should be surrounded by importunate officials and beggarly gentlemen in search of loans. Pepys saw it all and coldly deplored. 'Men of the Toga who have never been in the world do govern all in Spain, and men of the Spada are put into most employments at sea without knowing anything of their business, and so the state is governed and all will be lost. In a word, never were a people so overrun with fools in all states as they are.'[9]

Yet Pepys found something to learn from the still rich and once powerful imperial people of Spain. He particularly admired the strict law that forbade the carrying of merchandise in the King's galleons. In the intervals of sightseeing, he talked much with the English merchants of Seville about the ills that arose from failure to enforce a similar rule in the English Navy.

At that time the British community in Spain was raging at what they held to have been a needless injury to their credit and the national honour, caused by Captains Clowdisley Shovell and Matthew Aylmer hanging about Spanish harbours for freights until forced at the cannon's mouth to salute the King of Spain's

flag.* Shovell had actually been warned very civilly by the Spanish
Admiral of what must follow if he persisted in flying his flag in the
presence of a Spanish fleet in its own harbour. Pepys, furious at the
greed and indiscipline that had caused these officers to place
themselves and their country's honour in so humiliating a dilemma,
more than shared the indignation of his hosts. He even spoke of the
young captains as poltroons, comparing them unfavourably with a
French commander who, in like circumstances, had refused to salute
and had gone to the bottom with all hands. But in this he was less
than just, for both the young Irishman, Aylmer, and Shovell, who as
a Lieutenant had thrilled all England by his gallantry in the boats at
Tripoli, were famed for their courage.†

The English merchants at Seville were divided as to the wisdom of
allowing men-of-war to carry plate. All admitted the gravity of the
abuses that arose from it and agreed that the King paid dear for it.
But some argued that he ought to bear it for the good of commerce.
'It is plain that interest governs them', was Pepys' uncompromising
comment. Where the Navy was concerned he was as single-hearted
and intolerant as a Spanish Inquisitor. From them he obtained
further light on the state of discipline in the Straits fleet under its late
Commander-in-Chief. 'Ballocks', they told him was the name by
which Herbert always called his chaplain, till the poor man could
bear his bawdy talk no more and left the Service.‡ It was no longer a
place for any decent and honourable man.[10]

Pepys lingered at Seville for nearly six weeks – from Monday,
January 10th, new style, until the 19th or 20th of February. All the
while the rain, 'notwithstanding many public processions for its
amendment', came down in torrents, making it impossible to move
and very difficult to enjoy staying. He had seldom experienced such
a disappointment. Hewer was in despair, writing to Sam Atkins at
Tangier that, not for the best sight Spain could show, would he

* 'And it is plain that here was want of manners and good judgment in breeding
that led him to it in another nation's port, and may be a good argument of the use of
having gentlemen employed who can better judge of what is fitting in that kind, he
being in everything else spoken of as a man of valour and knowledge in his trade as a
seaman and a good man.' *Tangier Papers*, 167. In after years both Shovell and Aylmer,
who were to learn much from Pepys' schooling, served their country as Admirals.

† Lord Peterborough, writing of Sir Clowdisley Shovell in 1705, described him as
'brave, if I may say it, to a fault'. J. H. Owen, *War at Sea under Queen Anne*, 8

‡ 'I think his name is Haslewood, a very ingenious man.' *Tangier Papers*, 168.

endure such an affliction again. At last, after their boat – the only possible mode of travel – had waited for them for more than three weeks, the two friends were able to return to Sanlúcar. They were speeded by an anxious letter from Dartmouth, who having almost completed his operations at Tangier was in urgent need of their help in the complicated financial business of redeeming English slaves from the Moors.[11]

On the way down the Guadalquivir, the travellers passed a boat carrying fifty-six boys, who had accompanied the Flota on its voyage to America and were now returning to the Seminary of San Telmo. Pepys was much interested in this Spanish counterpart to his own Mathematical School at Christ's Hospital – now temporarily abandoned by him in despair. Subsequently, at an inn on the road from Sanlúcar to Puerto he fell into conversation with some Spaniards who, having been on the voyage, were able to tell him all about the boys. It seemed that as soon as they were old enough, they were sent to sea as cabin boys and, under the supervision of the boatswain, put to such tasks as cleaning and sweeping. During this first voyage their academic studies were confined to reading, writing and casting accounts. Having gained an insight into the practical working of a ship, they returned to school to study the theory of navigation until old enough for a further voyage, when the boatswain took them in hand again and made them working masters of their craft. It struck Pepys as an admirable scheme.[12]

At Sanlúcar, where Mr Canham, the merchant, made much of the returning travellers and promised to procure them a cask of old sherry, Pepys found his English mail. There was a long letter from James Houblon of December 3rd, giving the news of the town and of the great world and its impending wars: 'next summer you will see, in all appearance such a tragedy as Europe never saw since Julius Caesar's time.' What touched Pepys' heart more closely was what the good merchant told him of his own family, still lingering after summer had passed in the shades of Epping Forest. All was well. 'Not a friend of yours that I know of,' the dear fellow wrote, 'but is in the same state you left them in, our neighbour, sister Dolly, excepted, who is abroad again out of her bed after a month that a pretty little girl detained her there. We have had such a set of sunshine and good weather that we have been charmed to the Forest and are there still, and nothing but the good news of your being ashore in Old England will bring us home.'[13]

Perhaps Pepys' heart glowed even more at the note which the young wife, pretty Sarah Houblon, added to her father-in-law's letter. 'I could chide and call names,' she wrote, 'but that words are too small a revenge; therefore I am resolved blows shall end our quarrel, especially since you are turned soldier.* Therefore come home quickly that your sorrow may be over as well as Mrs Hewer's;'† – she spelt it Huer – 'I wish her age may get over hers so easily as your ill nature will help you out of yours.' Then she told him of her sister Dolly's 'pretty dafter', and prayed her dear Samuel to furnish himself with plenty of his favourite chocolate to keep himself warm when he returned to England. 'Here is all in health, men, women and children and servants, who spend mighty time in their devotions for your safe return. Your friend Thomas never hears you mentioned without lifted-up eyes. Adieu.'[14]

On the 13/23rd February, Pepys reached Puerto de Santa Maria again. Thence he despatched a note across Cadiz Bay to Mr Hodges asking him to get Sir John Berry, then at anchor in the harbour, to send his barge to fetch him. He had urgent business of the King's, he explained, to discuss with him next day at Hodges' house. For in his last letter Dartmouth had told Pepys not to hesitate to take any man-of-war that would bring him quickly to Tangier. No business that any captain might pretend to could be of greater service to the Crown than that.

Yet when next morning Pepys crossed the Bay, where four English men-of-war were lying, he found that Sir John had no intention of honouring Dartmouth's order. Instead he produced an order of the Admiral's giving him and his fellow captains leave to remain at Cadiz until the fleet arrived.‡ They were there to make money shipping plate to England, not to ship an impatient bureaucrat to Africa.

---

* She spells it 'solger'.

† Old Mrs Hewer, Will's aged mother, who kept house for him.

‡ In his original letter of January 11th, old style, Dartmouth expressly asked Pepys to spare one commander who was his particular friend in order to give him a chance of making a fortune. 'As Atkins has drawn the order no commander's name need now be added, so that you may apply it to whom and when you please. But remember Harry Williams is my old friend, and since he is in hopes of making his fortune I would not injure him.' Lord Dartmouth to S. P., Jan. 11th, 1684. *Howarth*, 166.

The *Deptford* ketch happening to come at that moment into the Bay from Tangier, Berry suggested that Pepys should return by her. As she was packed with soldiers this proposal did not at all appeal to him. But he gave no answer, merely sending Berry Dartmouth's original order and leaving it to him as senior officer at Cadiz to execute it in whatever way he liked.[15]

The result was that a few hours later young Captain George of the *Deptford* ketch presented himself at Hodges' house, 'very readily in appearance' but in fact doing all he could to discourage Pepys from sailing, hinting darkly at adverse winds and the possibility of being two or three days at sea and so missing the fleet. No doubt he was well aware of the late Admiralty Secretary's distaste for rough weather. 'And indeed', Pepys recorded, 'I stomached being so used, but glad I had this instance in my own case of what I am collecting about this business of money. And so without giving any plain reasons for it, forbore to make use of him and would not go. Nor could George well have gone with any ease to me, having a whole company of soldiers from Tangier on board him, a pestered small ship and in want of water.' In such conditions Pepys would certainly have been sick.

As it was, it was George who was sick. Unable any longer to conceal the ill-effects of his previous night's debauch with Kirke, Berry and Killigrew, he was forced to rise hastily from the table in the middle of dinner. He spent the afternoon on Pepys' bed in a fit of *delirium tremens*.[16]

During his last days in Spain, while he awaited the arrival of Dartmouth and the fleet from Tangier, Pepys occupied his time collecting the views of the English merchant colony on the state of the Navy. Two days after his return to Cadiz, he took a jaunt with Hewer and Hodges in Berry's barge to Puntales Castle and thence across the inner bay to dine at the White House, a pleasure resort on the Isla de León much frequented by the English. On the way, Berry, who was still feeling the results of Monday night's debauch, opened his heart about the carriage of money and goods in the King's ships, declaring that when he was in the Straits – it had been during Pepys' reign at the Admiralty – he had never carried a single bale. He had even, he said, rejected a petition from the united merchants of Cadiz and a clear £300 profit sooner than wait a fortnight for the arrival of the treasure fleet. Which, Pepys thought, was very remarkable.

Yet now, half a dozen years later with a Flota again in the Bay,

British naval commanders were neglecting every duty and crowding into the port like flies to get a share of the profits of shipping bullion to England. Captain Williams, towards whom Dartmouth had asked Pepys to be particularly considerate, had already loitered round Cadiz for two months, until the merchantmen he was supposed to be convoying home had chosen to risk capture at the hands of Sallee pirates rather than wait any longer. So unconscionably had some of the captains behaved in the pursuit of this unseemly business that they had defeated their own object, many merchants now preferring to send their valuables in unprotected trading ships sooner than entrust them to officers so rapacious and unreliable. One or two commanders had actually obtained cargoes by fraudulently announcing that they were sailing direct for England when they were under orders to proceed in a contrary direction. As a result, Berry lamented, more than a quarter of a million of pieces-of-eight which would otherwise have been carried home by the fleet were at that very moment being put aboard the *Andalusia* merchantman. And this in spite of the war with Sallee.[17]

At the White House, further instances were afforded of the condition of the Navy. First there was the not very edifying spectacle of young Captain George trying to recover his drink-shaken nerve and stomach by swaying unsteadily across the garden. Then at dinner Hewer told the story of Captain Priestman's forcible seizure of two black seamen out of a merchantman and his threat to sell them unless her owners would pay the wages of two of their hands who had deserted to his ship. And a young naval officer almost caused a riot in the presence of the diners by striking a Spanish Master with his stick – an act which, in a land where an affront to a man's dignity was regarded as worse than murder, might have ended in international complications, had not Berry and Pepys intervened in time. The Navy was not making the name of England either liked or respected.[18]

Returning in the barge, with Cadiz glittering before them like a city of crystal, the talk drifted to the way in which Herbert had feathered his nest while in the Straits. He seems to have made a practice of exacting 50 per cent, and sometimes as much as 75 per cent from his captains on the profits of their 'good voyages' in return for his sending them with bogus orders to convenient stations. As a result the Mediterranean fleet had degenerated into a kind of private trading corporation presided over by a master-racketeer flying the King's flag. Herbert had even employed a merchant as his factor to visit the ships and make up accounts and bills of lading with his captains. Yet this was the man who had been recalled home, not to be cashiered as Pepys held he deserved, but to be made a Commissioner of the Navy he had disgraced, and who now – though Pepys had still to learn it – had just been appointed Rear-Admiral of England.

Pepys asked how long this business of Admirals sharing their captains' profit had been going on. Berry thought it had begun during the command of Admiral Allin, afterwards Comptroller of the Navy, and that Spragge and Narbrough had continued it, though confining their 'rake-offs' to discreet presents. But Herbert had outdone them all, insisting on a regular commission from his commanders on all trading and allowing them nothing for expenses or unforeseen losses incurred in the King's service. 'Upon the whole,' was Pepys' summary, 'it is plain that this business of money runs through and debauches the whole service of the Navy, and is now come to the highest degree of villainy and infamy, and nobody considers it.' He omitted to add that in a Service starved by jealous Parliaments and with pay often years in arrear, the temptations that confronted naval officers were very great.[19]

At dinner next day at Mr Hodges', where Berry was one of the guests, the subject – one suspects at Pepys' contriving – was raised again. Berry was the readier to talk about it at a table full of English merchants because of his indignation at their sending home so much of the Flota's bullion by the *Andalusia*, which during the past few days had shipped 80,000 pieces-of-eight, or nearly twice the sum put aboard his own *Henrietta*, a far more powerful ship. When Pepys asked the reason Berry replied with dark looks that it no doubt proceeded from the merchants' resentment at the misconduct of the King's captain, for otherwise they would entrust their bullion to a ship of the line sooner than to a merchantman. But Hodges did not think it was due to any ill will; they merely preferred an armed merchantman, who after all was strong enough to beat off any Sallee-man, because they knew that their money would thus be brought straight to the Thames without extra charge or trouble, whereas the fleet might be detained at Plymouth or Portsmouth. Berry was still complaining when Captain Jacobs of the *Andalusia* came in to tell the company that he had taken in all he intended, had locked his hatches and would be gone by the first fair wind.

Since there was always the chance that Pepys might one day return to Derby House;* and as the opportunity of such an audience did not occur every day, Berry continued to range freely over the faults of the Navy. He even criticized Dartmouth, expressing astonishment at his failure to court-martial Aylmer and Shovell for the affronts they had so meekly suffered from the Spaniards. He recalled how, before he left England, the Admiral had promised the King to restore the discipline of the Navy, terrifying the gentlemen commanders by his threat to do so at a Council of officers at Portsmouth. Yet he had since done nothing, but left the young libertines to do as they pleased. And when expostulated with, he only replied that he could not afford to make himself enemies to no purpose.[20]

Berry also complained about a recent order of Dartmouth's to end the squabbles of his captains for precedence while employed on roving commissions. This had laid down the right of the senior captain on any station to fly a broad pendant save when there was an express commission to the contrary. The consequence was that every commander now put the King to the charge of a broad pendant whenever he encountered a younger captain than himself. Pepys could not agree with Berry's exaggerated view of this harmless and sensible order. His own indignation was reserved for the fact that such a rule should be looked upon as either new or necessary, since it had been the practice of the Service from time immemorial.[21]

After the guests had gone, he remarked to his host that he believed that what Berry had said of his own conduct in refusing merchandise was true enough. 'But indeed at the time he durst not do otherwise, for it was in my time and I did limit them and see that they kept to their orders.' It was one of the reasons why the gay young captains so much disliked him. Hodges told him how every day they came to him and his fellow merchants with scandalous tales of one another, every one calling his brother officer fool and knave behind his back, and fawning for orders like the humblest factor.[22]

From Sir Martin Westcombe, the English Consul, Pepys learnt

* The Admiralty Office, see *The Years of Peril*, 92.

much more that he dreaded to hear of the state of the Navy. He obtained from him some useful papers on the subject to take back to England. One of them related how the abominable Herbert had announced before a great company just before prayers on a Sunday morning, that he should think it no sin to lie with a woman on his deathbed if he had the strength to do it. Pepys with his sober Puritan background would never have made such a remark. Yet he might have remembered that in his own thirties, though a married man, he had quite cheerfully seduced the wives of men who depended on him for promotion and livelihood, tousled a surprising number of young women in coaches, taverns and even in the sacred precincts of the Navy Office, and visited a bride on the day after her wedding 'to have a bout with her . . . to see how she finds marriage'. And Herbert, who at least had the excuse of being on a dull foreign station, was no older than Pepys had been at the time he did these things, while many of his captains were younger.[23]

A farewell visit to the Cartuja, a present of petrified stone and a sight of the sick and dying seamen of the Flota being carried through the narrow streets of Cadiz concluded Pepys' somewhat disappointing experience of Spain. The sad spectacle reminded him how unfortunate the Spaniards had always been in their naval undertakings. 'Never let me forget', he noted, 'to improve the present state of the Spanish Navy all flowing from their neglect of seamen, and doing all by the gentlemen, and all that for money or friends and not for their qualifications.' It was a lesson which he hoped to apply elsewhere.[24]

On February 21st, old style, Lord Dartmouth, his work at Tangier done, anchored with the fleet in the Bay of Bulls to take in water before sailing for England. Pepys packed his baggage, swollen by the presents he had bought for his friends at home and a quarter cask of sherry from Mr Canham of Sanlúcar for himself, and bade farewell to his kind hosts. Rather to his distress they insisted on making up a little more money for the *Grafton* to carry to England as a special compliment to Lord Dartmouth and her captain, Sir William Booth. Then on his fifty-first birthday, after a holiday that had been prolonged for two months beyond the three weeks originally granted, Pepys rejoined the fleet.[25]

For three more days they lay in the Bay taking in water. On the 25th Pepys was present at a Council of War convened to try two seamen who had run away from one of the ships. Afterwards he witnessed the brutal, though customary, punishment of flogging the offenders round the fleet. He could not help wishing that the court-martial had been called in to punish more powerful sinners – Shovell and Aylmer, for instance, who were still swaggering about unrebuked, or Captain Layton, the poor prisoners' own commander, whose barbarous treatment of his men seemed to him a crime against the Service. As the terrified wretches were rowed to their own ship to be flogged, the whole crew came running to the side crying out that they would gladly be flogged too if they could be redeemed from serving under such a captain – a man, Pepys noted savagely, who not only treated them with unreasoning cruelty, but cheated them of their victuals merely to pamper a worthless wife that made him a cuckold every day.

Next morning, February 26th, the fleet weighed from the Bay of Bulls, nineteen men-of-war with twelve merchantmen in company. After standing off the coast for a few hours, while stores were put aboard the six small frigates which were to remain behind in the Straits, Dartmouth set sail for England. It was then seven in the evening.[26]

4
The Great Storm

' "Wouldst thou" – so the helmsman answered –
"Learn the secret of the sea?
Only those who brave its dangers
Comprehend its mystery." ' *Longfellow*.

Early in the afternoon of the first day at sea it came on to blow so hard that the main topsail of the flagship was torn from the yard. By nightfall it was driving with such strength from the south-west that the crew could hardly maintain a pair of low sails. During the night disaster followed disaster: at three in the morning the *Grafton*'s mizzen was split and ninety minutes later the mainsail. Orders were then given to lay the ship's head to the southward, while the men bent a new mainsail and mizzen. In the broken grey of the morning Cape Spartel and Africa could be seen looming out of the clouds, while of the fleet that had stood two days before out of the Bay of Bulls, only a solitary ship remained tossing and labouring to leeward.

During the day the fleet was gradually reassembled, the *Grafton* beating up and down making signals, while lame duck after lame duck came under her stern to report damages. In the afternoon Dartmouth came to an anchor once more in the desolate Road of Tangier, sending his smaller vessels into the Straits to shelter under Gibraltar.

'Consider', Pepys noted on his tablets, 'the mighty care of an Admiral for a whole fleet, as in our case that came all well about thirty-five ships, men-of-war and merchantmen, over night from Cadiz, and in one night all parted by foul weather, ... many missing, some drove into the Straits, and ourselves and the rest all with loss of masts or sails or rudder or something or other.' One loss, at least, might have been averted. Sir John Wyborne of the *Happy Return*, one of the soberest commanders in the fleet, had for some time past complained of a defective rudder, asking leave to go to Cadiz for its repair. But Dartmouth, who by now regarded all requests of this kind merely as excuses for making money, refused it, having reserved that privilege for some of his own friends. He had even cautioned Wyborne, a poor and honest man, not to be in so much of a hurry to get rich. In that terrible night's storm the *Happy Return* had lost her anchor and might easily have foundered – 'A pretty instance', was Pepys' comment, 'of the fruits of this money business.'[1]

During the next four days while the fleet was refitting, Pepys had the mournful satisfaction, whenever driving clouds of rain and the motion of the ship allowed, of gazing on the ruins of Tangier. Piles of blackened stones and gaping holes in the hillside, out of which the Moorish sentries could be seen peeping, was all that was left of that once thriving Vanity Fair. Ensign Phillips, the young engineer, sketched it for him in water colours – a sombre study in greens and browns, solitary under the wintry sky.[2]

On March 3rd, though a fresh gale of wind sprang up from the south, there was sunshine and the promise of spring in the air. That afternoon the men hoisted the yards and topmasts. The ships were unmoored ready to put to sea. Next morning at five, a week after leaving Cadiz, the fleet weighed anchor and stood out to sea again with a fresh southerly wind.

While the ships were spreading their sails to the north and the familiar landmarks of the Bay slipped slowly past them and fell away imperceptibly to stern, Dartmouth gave Pepys his own views on the deplorable state of the Navy. Being little more than a passenger in the fleet, he explained, it was of small use for him to create trouble for himself at home by curbing the young, licentious captains. And yet no one knew better than he how necessary it was to have this business of Cadiz and its golden lure brought to an end. He therefore begged Pepys to join with him when they got home in getting the old Admiral's Instructions corrected and enforced. He spoke with contempt of Herbert, who had often not slept aboard his ship for months while he pursued his unsavoury vices ashore. He was even a traitor, having in betrayal of his patron, the Duke, corresponded with Shaftesbury and dismissed his chaplain for not drinking the great rebel's health, swearing in his usual foul-mouthed way that he did not care who was uppermost so long as he was provided for. Pepys was only too ready to agree with Dartmouth: of all men living, he recorded, Herbert was the only one he knew without a single virtue to compound for his vices.

These quarter-deck meditations were interrupted by the growing discomfort of the ship as she encountered the roll of the open Atlantic. By eight o'clock the wind had shifted back into the west. At noon, after plying all morning to windward, the fleet was about five miles N.E.N. of Cape Spartel, contending against a sea that grew hourly worse. By dusk the Cape was nine miles away. All night the *Grafton* and her consorts battled with great seas where more than a century later the supreme naval victory of England was to be fought and won. Dawn was on the waters when the flagship, unable to weather the foul ground of Cape Trafalgar, went about and stood again to the southward.

That evening the fleet abandoned the attempt. At seven o'clock the ships anchored in twenty-three fathoms of water under the familiar shadow of Cape Spartel. Here they waited until March 8th for the gale to abate.[3]

Pepys spent the unwelcome days off that gloomy coast meditating on the unpredictable nature of a sailor's life. 'Surprise at sea by cross winds', he noted for his future *navalia*, 'carrying you back again, more than at land.' How little was this understood by landsmen – by the average Englishman. 'Our want of a prayer for a good wind do enough show how little our churchmen make it their business to go to sea. Which may serve also to improve the description of the dangers and illness of a sea life, whereas they ought the first to look after the wonders of God in the deep. And here comes in the story of Harman's chaplain asking what he should do to be saved, and Solomon's magnifying the mystery of a way of a ship in the sea.'

So ran the tenor of Pepys' thoughts as he jotted them down in rough shorthand on the crowded pages of his little memorandum book. All these instances, of which he was now both spectator and victim, of the maddening contrariness of the sea and the mischances suffered by ships emphasized how important it was that their commanders should be qualified by training, experience and rigid discipline for their work. He thought of the Admiral's vast responsibilities and how necessary it was that they should be discharged by adequate hands. He recalled what Dartmouth himself had said of the insufficiency of Sir William Booth, whom he acknowledged as the best man in England to command a flying squadron of frigates but one far too inexperienced in navigation and seamanship to be captain of a great vessel that needed skilful handling. With the growth in the size and complexity of ships-of-war, the education of naval officers had become a national necessity.[4]

What happened after the fleet again put to sea on the 8th proved it the more clearly. The great gale of March 1684 – one of the worst in the memory of even those stormy seas – continued to rage, with low clouds and horizontal rain driving in on the crest of giant waves from the westward. On the morning of the 11th, the mainyard of the *Grafton* cracked near the slings, leaving the crew struggling all day in the swell until by evening, having put a fish upon the yard and woolded it, they were able to reset the mainsail. Two days later, after a terrific battle under low sails against a great sea from the N.N.W., the mainyard broke again only half an hour after the men, relying on a temporary slackening of the gale's fury, had set the main topsail. This second disaster was due, Pepys noted, to the unseamanlike way in which the spikes had been driven in to fasten the fish upon the yard after the previous break.[5]

As it was they were three days repairing the damage while the flagship made what way she could under a foresail, fore topsail and staysails, with a main topsail for a mainsail. All the while the fleet was labouring in titanic seas, driven far to south and west of its proper course and in hourly danger of being forced on to the pirate coast of Morocco. To make matters worse supplies were running low, and the seamen who had long been on short victuals were faced with the triple perils of starvation, shipwreck and captivity. On Sunday, March 16th, the day on which the mainmast was at last mended, Pepys noted that he and his companions were actually farther from home than they had been three weeks before when they sailed from Cadiz. 'It is by our experience to be observed that no force of timber, plank, iron or cordage is to be relied on against the sea ... This voyage has shown me at once all the elements dangerous to us, and this in a dark night in danger of famine and upon an enemy's shore.' The 'us' is an unconscious symbol of Pepys' self-identification with the service.[6]

Slowly the fleet edged its way towards the north. To get home more quickly Dartmouth, in perpetual fear lest the King and Duke should be induced by his enemies to disown him in his absence, left Killigrew behind with the transports and heavy ships and went ahead with the frigates. He and Pepys comforted themselves with the reflection that it was better to serve such princes as theirs who understood the sea and could appreciate a seaman's difficulties, than those who had to depend entirely on the representations of landsmen. Off Cape St Vincent the storm lashed itself into renewed fury, parting three of the frigates in the darkness from the main fleet. In the morning after that awful night another frigate was seen to be labouring in distress, and it was presently learnt that that good old seaman, Captain Wilde of the *Oxford*, who had long been failing, had died in the night. They buried him the same evening with the solemn rites of the sea, the guns sounding mournfully as the gunner's mate of each ship took the time from the half-minute glass before him.[7]

During the days that followed, while the fleet fought its way northward, Pepys talked much with the ship's officers about the affairs of the Navy. Sam Atkins, his old clerk, now acting as joint secretary to Lord Dartmouth, told him how openly the captains despised their orders, each man saying that it was better to get a few thousand pounds by a 'good voyage' in defiance of orders than to obey them, when at the worst the only punishment would be dismissal from an uncertain employment. Once rich, for all they cared, the Service might go to the devil. Atkins cited the case of Captain Russell, who had made a vast fortune by ignoring all Pepys' rules, and could now never be tempted to sea again, though the best gentleman commander in the fleet.*[8]

Another instance of the crying need for a more regular discipline at sea was afforded by one of Pepys' shipmates. This young gentleman, a son of Sir Joseph Wetwang, had been Lieutenant of the *Happy Return* until, after repeated offences of insubordination and drunkenness, he had been permitted by Dartmouth, an old friend of his father, to resign in order to escape the consequences of his behaviour. 'Consider', Pepys recorded grimly, 'if this be good in law, what use the Laws Martial can be of to the discipline of a fleet, if it shall be in the power of any delinquent to avoid justice by flinging up his commission.'[9]

In his anger at the slackness and corruption of the Service he had formerly controlled, Pepys, it may be argued, was being less than just to the young sea officers whom he so bitterly condemned. After all they were fighting men, rough and ready as fighting men have

---

* Nine years later he commanded the Grand Fleet at La Hogue.

need to be in a primitive world, and seamen living the harsh, monotonous life of the sea far from their homes and little supported by their superiors in England. They had to look after themselves for there was no one else to do so. And in their corruption and their spirit of rebellious independence, they differed little from many of their countrymen on shore. The English of the seventeenth century loved liberty, hated restraint and, when they found themselves in a position to line their pockets at the expense of the Crown, never showed the slightest compunction in doing so. Why should their younger sons and brothers, cooped in small ships in remote exile under a foreign sun, show any more?

Pepys was a man of the pen, little accustomed to danger or monotony, a bureaucrat with a passion for rules of his own devising, a great condemner of the human failings of others, though one who had done very well for himself in his own time. He was growing old and, many must have thought, curmudgeonly. But his anger was not caused solely by the time-long corruption and laxity that seems to us the common air of his age. For he stood, as it were, on the threshold of his own sacked and broken house. If his past life had had any significance, it was that in his five years at the Admiralty he had achieved the unachievable and had driven corruption and laxity headlong out of the chief of the state services. He had given the Navy of England what he had hoped would prove a permanent rule and harness. And now, after five more years of the inept control of his successors, everything he had striven for had vanished as though it had never been. In this he was like the man in the poet's mirror who sees his life's work broken. He did not see it so unmoved.

Nor was his indignation only that of a mortal thwarted. Almost alone among the men of his century Pepys grasped what the sea might come to mean to his country. More than Raleigh before him or Halifax in his own day, though with only a tithe of their eloquence, he comprehended the future of England. The winds and tides that cradled her spoke to this landsman of her destiny. When most of his contemporaries were expending all their powers in contending for particular forms of government and worship, he was scanning the horizons which have since grown familiar. Beyond the island mists, yet within reach of a little people of five or six millions, could they but be made to realize it, lay the shadowy outlines of a wealth and power such as no race had ever before enjoyed in the history of the world. Bondsman of the pen and ledger as he was, comfortable materialist in peruke and fine linen, Samuel Pepys was yet sustained by vision. There was only one means by which that vision could be made a reality: the precepts he had spent his life in framing, and their observance by those who wrought the nation's destiny at sea.

It was this inner conviction that justified Pepys' indignation against the men of Tangier, though in later years many of them, schooled by his hard rules, were to do their country good service. He could not rest so long as the regulations on which he knew his dream depended were hourly flouted. He questioned Atkins about the keeping of ships' journals, a formality on which he had always been careful to insist in his days of power. Atkins told him that captains seldom now bothered about them but left all to their clerks. Herbert in particular made sport of the practice, declaring publicly that he had never kept a journal in his life and never would. What the devil, he asked, was the use of remembering where the wind was when it was past? He did not even know the names of the ropes on his own ship so that he was perpetually having to bid his men 'Haul up that whichum there!' usually with some lewd jest to disguise his ignorance. It was so in everything he did.[10]

Such was the result, Pepys reflected, of the fatal distinction between gentlemen and tarpaulins. These young men with their fine clothes and Court ways, who looked to Herbert as their natural leader, and drank, diced and whored in the face of the whole fleet, set a standard which better men were forced to follow, turning swaggerers and ruffians, drunkards and spendthrifts that they might be thought gentlemen.

As Pepys looked out on the waste of waters, such distinctions seemed meaningless. 'I may challenge the best gentleman that is', he wrote with a touch of that sardonic philosophy which adversity always brought out in him, 'that I will whisper something in his ear (let him tell me his father and mother's descent but for three generations backward) that he will desire me to hold my tongue, if he values the imputation of bastardy, disloyalty, knavery, mechanicry or poverty.' In a ship the ordinary gradations of society were levelled to a bare, swaying deck, on which man stood a poor, forked creature, with nothing but his skill in seamanship to secure him from the terror and immensity of the seas. And save for that skill nothing else mattered at all.

Pepys had too much respect for birth and breeding not to wish to see those who possessed them in the Navy. But first they must submit themselves to the stern training that alone could turn them into seamen. It was hard to expect a nobleman or courtier to make the sea his trade and share the conversation and company, diet and clothes of a rude sailor. 'Nor can he be neat and nice', he reflected sadly, 'to make love in the fashion when he comes among the ladies.'

It was, indeed, the very tastes and inclinations of fine gentlemen that seemed to have banished all honour and decency from the Navy. Every captain now intrigued, cheated and quarrelled to get money to maintain his expensive vices, a tenth part of which would make ten plain tarpaulins and their families happy who were now ready to starve. And for every penny the individual gained by such means, the King paid twice or threefold.[11]

There was only one remedy. The opportunities for making easy fortunes by carrying plate and merchandise that tempted courtiers and titled adventurers into the Navy must be taken away. And they must be replaced by regular, adequate salaries, such as could enable honest men to keep themselves and their families decently without having to cheat the Crown. 'Let the business of carrying money', Pepys wrote, 'be taken away, and that will of itself take away the difference of gentleman and tarpaulin, for it is only for the sake of that that the difference is made and kept up.' Henceforward there should only be one distinction, that of rank, awarded after adequate training and experience. In all else those who served the King at sea should be brothers. In his egalitarian plea, so easy to comprehend in our day, so hard in his, the great Secretary of the Admiralty reached back to Drake, forward to Nelson.[12]

Poor sailor as he was, Pepys, not without a certain unromantic heroism, continued to pursue his historical studies on the rolling deeps off the Portuguese and Spanish coasts where in time to come those dispensations of Providence which he coveted for his country were to be won by the broadsides of the men his rules had schooled. He pored over Hakluyt's *Voyages*, wondering as he did so at the strange indifference of an island people who had left the chronicling of its sea annals to a poor country parson. More than ever his reading prompted him to practical ends: 'puts me again in mind of

Sir W. Ralegh's advice for the laying down the discipline of the sea in writing as that of the land has by divers been done'. As he gazed at the encircling horizon and all the untamed wildness it enclosed, he recurred to his oft repeated question whether the Dominion of the Seas claimed by the English had ever yet meant anything more than a mere negative freedom from pirates. In this element even the smallest mastery of wind or tide was an achievement calling for a vast accumulation of human thought and power. Turning over the pages of his Bible he noted that in Deuteronomy xxx. 12, and Romans x. 6, going over the sea was reckoned of equal difficulty with going up to Heaven.[13]

The last week of March offered further proof of its difficulty. On the 23rd a fresh gale of wind and rain set in, and by evening the men were forced to hand the topsails. Next morning the starboard clew of the *Grafton*'s mainsail gave way, compelling the captain to lower the main yard a-portlands and square the mainsail. While a new mainsail was being set the pendant of the yard broke as a great sea poured over the decks. Six men were washed from the yard, three of them being drowned. As darkness fell on the relentless Atlantic the gale still blew with undiminished fury. 'I know nothing', wrote Pepys, 'that can give a better notion of infinity and eternity than the being upon the sea in a little vessel without anything in sight but yourself within the whole hemisphere.'[14]

He knew now the dangers of the sea and understood its mystery. To the poor, illiterate and desperate men, brought into its service by harsh necessity, his heart went out in almost fierce sympathy. 'Let me also taste their beverage', he wrote in his memo book, and the entry, one feels, was made with affection. They and their like were the ministers of the work to which all his experience and study were prompting him. And the hard trade which they adopted for lack of any other means of livelihood, they struck to in the end out of love, 'with a resolution to live and die in it and so make it their interest to make themselves masters of it by learning and doing and suffering all things'. By such indomitable instruments something great might one day be achieved.[15]

All this Pepys talked over with Dartmouth as they sat in his cabin or paced the quarter-deck while the *Grafton* bore them across the Bay to England. The Admiral as usual was full of fears both for his own future and for that of his country. Now that his work was done, his apprehensive, melancholy nature made him view the evacuation of Tangier as a disastrous mistake. With the end of the English outpost in north Africa, the King of France could make himself master of the Mediterranean and by an alliance with the Moors destroy our trade with the East, overrun Flanders and Holland and finally, with the Channel ports in his hands, make a direct attack on England. That this was his object seemed clear from his grandiose and costly plans for increasing the French Marine. Dartmouth therefore proposed that he and Pepys, before it was too late, should think seriously what could be done to save the Navy.

Pepys shared the Admiral's views on the ambitions of France and still more those on the need for England to look to her moat. But he was less gloomy about the future. Even in the Mediterranean, once the abuse of Good Voyages had been put down, all that had been lost might be recovered. In an interesting talk with the engineer, Beckmann, he had recently discussed the possibility of replacing Tangier by Gibraltar, where his own brother-in-law Balty had for some time past been keeping English naval stores. More than any other place, Beckmann said, it would give England command of the Straits. It could be captured without the loss of a single life, and afterwards fortified for a mere trifle against all the fleets and armies in the world. Lest Spain should take fright or any other nation be tempted to act first, Pepys and Beckmann had agreed to keep the project to themselves.* They would not even mention it to the King.[16]

With Dartmouth and Booth Pepys discussed those leading reforms which he knew were necessary if the Navy was to be preserved. Nothing could be done until discipline was restored by the prohibition of 'good voyages', a sufficient system of pay and allowances and the regular inspection of ships' journals at the end of every voyage. The distinction between 'gentleman' and 'tarpaulin' must go, and an end be put, by the publication of an official Navy List, to those squabbles for precedence between captains that so lowered the dignity of Britain in foreign ports.

Above all the inept rule from above which had prevailed since the politicians had driven him from the Admiralty in 1679 must be

---

* Twenty years later and a year after Pepys' own death, it was carried out, since when England has kept a permanent footing, if not always a fleet, in the Mediterranean.

brought to an end. There was no possibility of eradicating abuses so long as the fleet was controlled by land 'Admirals' who were ignorant of all that belonged to the sea. 'Do an oyster gape and shut according to the tide when it is out of water?' Pepys asked among his naval queries: 'if so, a better oracle for the sea than any of our present Commissioners of the Admiralty'. Under their shameful negligence the very officers of the Navy Board – formerly good and experienced men of his own choosing – had become as lazy and corrupt as themselves.[17]

One sinister figure above all had to be fought and destroyed – the one-eyed Arthur Herbert. He was now a Commissioner of the Navy and Rear-Admiral of England, ranking only under the titular Vice-Admiral and royal bastard, the young Duke of Grafton. He stood high in the favour of the King and Duke of York, and enjoyed the reputation of a daring fighter and a successful leader of men.

But Pepys was not afraid of Herbert. He had taken his measure and was ready for a fight with him. All the time he had been away he had been collecting evidence of his corruption, immorality* and contempt of discipline. Over all the seas to the southward from Cadiz to Algiers the reputation of the man hung like a curse. The brutish slave-traders of the pirate cities of north Africa shuddered at his name, for his cruelty exceeded even their own. Whispers had reached Pepys of how he had starved hundreds of his prisoners to death to obtain the money allowed him for their victuals. And those all-recording notebooks duly contained a special reminder to investigate Herbert's official accounts. For there, Pepys reckoned, he might light on something worth discovering.[18]

To exorcize this evil creature's influence he and Dartmouth resolved, by hook or crook, to bring back the Duke into the Navy. And though they did not yet know it, the time was ripe, for the long unpopularity of the heir presumptive was waning at last before one of those revulsions of feeling so natural to England where sooner or later everything inclines towards a mean. Only under the protection of a Prince of the Blood would it be possible to withstand the powerful interests that were destroying all that

---

* For a characteristic story of this told by Pepys in language too graphic and direct for printing, see *Rawl. MSS. C.* 859, f. 112.

was now left of the Navy. Together the two men agreed to tackle the royal brothers when they got home and show them the necessity of it.[19]

But they had still to get there. Throughout March the gale continued to blow with scarcely a break. It was not till the 29th that the fleet, now only six ships strong, reached the entrance to the Channel. At six that morning they took soundings in seventy-five fathoms. At two in the afternoon they sounded again, having sixty-five fathoms, peppery sand and small white shells. Yet, so defective were their charts and so vague and contradictory the notions of navigation in those days when no means was known of fixing longitude, that still no one seemed to know exactly where they were or what course they ought to pursue. Some held that they were to the west of the Scillies, some to the east, while others were positive that they were in imminent danger of running on to the coast of France. And when next morning, which was Easter Day, the wind came fair and the sun revealed to the look-outs the Lizard and the cliffs of Cornwall, the storm-belated voyagers were amazed.

Pepys, improving even that shining hour, could not help noting how quickly the attitude of the navigators changed. 'We are very solicitous in our disputes and opinions touching our draughts and log lines and things', he wrote in his note book, 'when we are at a loss for our ways, finding or suspecting faults in every one of them, and comparing one man's notes and books and notions with another's, which, if we could improve by comparing and drawing inferences from, when the issue has decided which is wrong and which is right, would be of good use. But soon as ever we see land all difference is forgot, or any desire of recording the truth, but on the contrary, everybody endeavours to make himself be thought to have been in the right, and not thinking also that they shall ever come to the same loss in the same place again. Hence it comes that the science of navigation lies so long without more improvement.'[20]

Between six and eight in the evening the fleet anchored in Plymouth Sound. Mr Blathwayt, the Secretary-at-War, was waiting there with orders to land one of Kirke's battalions and take on board the garrison of Plymouth for transport to the Thames: the King's ships at sea were now so few that the government could not afford to waste such an opportunity. While this was being done next day, the ships were re-victualled. Pepys, gazing at leisure on the misty shores of his native land, still leafless after the coldest winter within the memory of man, occupied his time by making notes on the fortifications of Plymouth.[21]

As the wind was favourable Dartmouth, who was almost beside himself with anxiety to lay his report before the King, gave orders to sail for Spithead at the earliest possible moment. At four in the afternoon on the 31st the *Grafton* weighed and turned out of Plymouth Sound. But despite the Admiral's repeated signals, not another ship stirred from her moorings, each captain pretending some excuse to procure himself another evening ashore. All night the flagship lay by and waited while the wind wasted. At dawn only one vessel was in sight. Yet when Pepys spoke to Dartmouth about this shameful business, the Admiral could only bewail his misfortune in commanding a fleet where any disciplinary measure must produce a swarm of enemies backed by his own chiefs, the politicians at the Admiralty. Only the return of the Duke of York to the Service, he repeated once more, could set things right. At that moment Pepys may have doubted whether even the Duke would be strong enough to mend things.[22]

Two days later he bade farewell to the fleet at Spithead. What he had now to do for the Navy, if it could be done at all, must needs be done on shore behind the doors of an office. With Henry Shere to bear him company he posted from Portsmouth up the London road. Next day after dining at the 'Red Lion' at Guildford, he reached London and, going straight to his friend, Sir Leoline Jenkins, the Secretary of State, placed in his hands the anxious, impatient letter which he carried from Dartmouth to the King. A few minutes later he was standing bareheaded in the Royal Bedchamber.[23]

5

Recall to the Admiralty

'Seest thou a man diligent in his business? he shall stand before kings.'
Proverbs xxii, 29.

Pepys, who had at last grown a very wise man, did not assail his sovereign's ears with the protestations with which the anxious Admiral had armed him. It was impossible, he afterwards told Dartmouth, to describe the King's impatience at the slightest suggestion of his having ever doubted his faithfulness and diligence, 'his last word being that I might assure you that, however some persons might be impertinent enough to use a greater liberty of talk elsewhere, none to this hour had ever taken upon them to say one word to your prejudice to him'. And the Duke, who came in during the interview, Lord Sunderland, the Secretary of State, and Lord Rochester, the First Lord of the Treasury, whom Pepys saw afterwards, were equally reassuring. It seemed that all Dartmouth's fears had been groundless. Harbord and the rest of his 'little enemies', whatever they might secretly desire, had not dared to open their mouths. For since the failure of the Rye House Plot in the previous summer the Whigs had been going downhill apace.

From the royal presence Pepys went to Lady Dartmouth, whom he found with her family in good health. Then, late as it was and tired though he must have been after his journey, he sat down and wrote a long letter to his anxious chief. In the midst of it, he was interrupted by a message from Lady Williams, bringing him news of the sudden death of Lord Brouncker, and desiring his immediate advice as an executor of his will. He went at once, for whatever the nature of her former relationship with his old colleague, time had transformed the 'painted lady' of eighteen years ago with 'her talk, conceitedness and her impudence' into a friend. And Brouncker's passing broke another link with the far days of the Diary and Seething Lane. A few days later he followed him to the grave in the little church of St Katherine's near the Tower.[1]

Yet even the loss of this ancient associate coming at such a moment seemed to point towards the pole to which Pepys' every thought now turned. The Navy was in dire need, and he knew that he alone could save it. Brouncker's death left a vacancy on the Admiralty Board. It was one that he might fill. Then, if Shere could be substituted for the incompetent Brisbane as Secretary, they might together put some life once more into the Service.

So at least it seemed to Dartmouth, who wrote hopefully from the Downs, propounding his plan to Pepys. He felt the more enthusiastic, being then hotly engaged in an epistolary battle with Brisbane and their Lordships of Derby House, who had just insulted him by sending orders direct to one of his captains. 'Playing of tricks with me', he called it, 'endeavouring to lessen my command.' He loosed his pent-up feelings against the hated 'land Admirals' in one tremendous broadside, sending a copy of it to Pepys to show the Duke. Hewer, who was still with the fleet, was enchanted with it: 'a disrespect and breach of the discipline of the Navy in the highest nature has provoked my lord to resent it', he told his old master, 'in such a letter as, though the style will not be well pleasing to them, will make them sensible of their error or ignorance, and learn them how to behave themselves better towards a person of that worth and knowledge as Lord Dartmouth is.'[2]

For the moment Pepys' official ties were at an end. His services during his eight months' absence were rewarded by a payment of £992, calculated at the rate of £4 a day for 248 days, which included his Spanish holiday. He was now free to spend his time as he chose – a comfortably-off virtuoso of middle-age with a host of friends and all the pleasures of London at his call.

But these no longer sufficed him. His gaze was now riveted once more on the Navy and nothing could distract it. That the Service to which he had given his best should be so neglected and betrayed, angered and hurt him as much as Scott's personal attack on his own life and honour had done. The shorthand notes on naval needs and abuses which he had made at sea were continued on shore. All who could add to his knowledge and store of sea ammunition were attacked with eager questions; Deane, Dr Gale and Sir Peter Pett found themselves in turn taxed for their expert contribution. 'Here is Mr Pepys come who will be the proper subject of your naval addresses in the future,' wrote Robert Southwell to Sir William Petty, directing that great man's new 'fit of the double-bottom' to where he knew it would be welcome. And even though this ended in disaster like all Petty's attempts to build a double-bottomed boat, Pepys was sympathetic and even enthusiastic. That any eminent civilian should concern himself in sea matters was to him a cause for delight, and almost for personal self-congratulation.[3]

Others not directly concerned with the Navy, but who had learnt to honour its former administrator, rejoiced at his return to England. Evelyn turned from the paper which he was preparing on the effects of the late winter on vegetation* to welcome him, helped him to procure a set of the *Philosophical Transactions of the Royal Society* for his library, and invited him to view an eclipse of the moon from Mr Flamsteed's observatory at Greenwich. In return Pepys lent him Mr Burnet's new book on the theory of the earth, now published for the first time in English† – a loan which quickly bore interest in the sage of Deptford's uninvited but no doubt welcome observations on this admirable piece of reading – 'The whole hypothesis so ingenious and so rational, that I both admire and believe it at once. I am infinitely pleased with his thoughts concerning the Universe (intellectual and material) in relation to this despicable molehill on which we mortals crawl and keep such a stir about, as if the Τὸ Πᾶν (this All) were created for us little vermin.'[4]

Yet by the time good Mr Evelyn had finished his encomium, only a very detached philosopher could have thought of Mr Pepys as vermin. For all that Pepys had canvassed in his quarter-deck talks with Dartmouth had come swiftly and unexpectedly to pass. In the middle of April the 'land Admirals' were still drawing their salaries in idleness, while Herbert was promoted to the vacant permanency on the Board caused by Brouncker's death. A week later they were in the street. Before the end of the month that whiggish and somewhat bilious observer, Narcissus Luttrell, whom Pepys perhaps occasionally encountered on his rambles round the book barrows, was noting sorrowfully in his journal that his Majesty (whom he cordially detested) had been pleased to recall his letters patent to the Commissioners of the Admiralty. And, what was worse – though in this Luttrell was partly misinformed –

* It had been so hard that as late as May a country gentleman complained that it was impossible to secure even a sprig of rosemary for a funeral. *H.M.C. Fleming*, 194.
† There is a copy in the Pepys Library.

to constitute his Royal Highness the Duke of York (whom he loathed still more) Lord High Admiral.[5]

It had all happened with staggering suddenness. After a brief indisposition following his first arrival in England, Pepys had carried a petition from the Clothworkers' Company to Hampton Court, where during the Court's summer sojourn at Windsor the Friday meetings of the Privy Council were held. Afterwards he was publicly presented to the King by the Duke. Something, it was whispered, was in the air. A few days later, back in London, he received by Lord Dartmouth's hands an urgent summons to Windsor.

Here he was asked by his sovereign to resume his former charge at the Admiralty.* For, convinced that the country was now ready for it, the King had decided to take the Navy out of the hands of politicians and dissolve the Admiralty Commission. The nominal charge he resumed himself, entrusting its general supervision to his brother, though, in accordance with the letter of the Test Act, without his old title of Lord High Admiral. The virtual administrative control went to Samuel Pepys. On May 12th Evelyn, returning from Deptford to London, found the greatest of the national services once more directed by those competent to do so. Everyone, he wrote, was glad of the change.[6]

Naturally no one rejoiced so much as Pepys. The office to which he had been so suddenly called was a more important one than that which he had held under the Admiralty Commission of 1673. It was constituted for the first time by letters patent under the Great Seal by the simple but proud title of Secretary for the Affairs of the Admiralty of England. The salary was £2000 p.a. – the equivalent of at least £10,000 p.a. in modern money.† It had formerly been only

* In his *Memoires touching the Royal Navy,* written five years afterwards, Pepys gives the date of his recall as May, but from an unpublished letter of May 19th to a friend in Spain, in which he speaks of being detained at Windsor several weeks longer than he had expected (*Rawl. MSS. A.* 190, f. 74), as well as from Luttrell's entry, it appears to have taken place at the end of April. His official salary, however, did not begin till May 19th (*Rawl. MSS. A.* 177, f. 125), the date of the patent revoking the Admiralty Commission of 1679 (*Pepysian MS.* No. 1867, *Naval Precedents,* 169).

† This included a commutation of the invidious fees for Passes which Pepys received during his first Secretaryship, though not of the Admiralty fees for new appointments which he retained. He was also entitled to an allowance for house rent and travelling. The scale of salary placed the new appointment in the first rank of the great offices of State. *Rawl. MSS. A.* 177, ff. 125, 127.

£500 p.a. Yet by far the greatest significance of the change to this ageing man of many friends and tastes was that it gave him the chance of re-creating his life's work. That which had been so tragically interrupted by the political upheaval of 1679 could be begun again.[7]

In those opening days of his mission, envisaged under the grey walls or walking on the lawns of Windsor, Pepys took stock of the task before him. What he found was not encouraging. When he had been driven from his post he had left to his successors a fleet of 76 ships at sea and 12,000 men in pay, equipped for war and with stores enough to set out the remainder in any emergency. Now, apart from a small peacetime establishment of a score of frigates and two or three fireships, manned by just over 3000 men, the Navy had ceased almost to exist as an effective force in the affairs of Europe. For the rest of the fleet, after five years of neglect, was literally rotting in harbour. So hopelessly was it out of repair that, according to its own Surveyor, it could not even be made to float without a preliminary expenditure of about £120,000. The Navy debt had increased from £305,000 to £384,000. And the stores were almost empty.

Yet this was not all. No one knew better than Pepys what had befallen the discipline of the Service. All the rules he had established had been forgotten. While vast sums had been squandered or pocketed by venal officials, the offices he had created to check corruption and extravagance had been abolished in the name of economy. The Navy was being run as a gigantic swindling concern by those who should have been its trustees, from the well-connected commanders who quarrelled among themselves as to which should enjoy the illicit benefits of the next 'good voyage' to the store-keepers and petty clerks who picked the Yards bare. To such a pass had the wasted years of control by ignorant politicians reduced Pepys' administrative machine. To set it once more in motion, to overcome inertia and expel vested interest demanded the labours of a Hercules and the wiles of a Ulysses. The former Pepys had always been ready to give. But what of the latter?[8]

The dark years spent beneath the shadow of Scott and Lord Shaftesbury had taught Pepys wisdom. He began gradually. His first orders, issued on May 23rd, were little more than friendly

notifications of his presence to returning captains.* He told them
that he had been recalled by a gracious sovereign. But, as a modest
hint of what they must presently expect, he also enclosed a copy of
the rules which Dartmouth had issued at Tangier for regulating the
formalities of salutes and precedence.

Towards the end of June Pepys made a further cautious move. He
addressed to the members of the Navy Board a request for a 'true
and strict report of the state of the Navy', an inventory of its ships,
artificers, stores, works in hand and debts. In the King's name he
directed them to continue to meet from day to day 'without
intermission' until the task was finished. He also asked them to
explain how it was that, though the supplies allowed them for
materials had been recently halved by an economizing Treasury,
they had only discharged 200 of the 1500 workmen maintained in
idleness in the dockyards. Here was a note that had not sounded in
naval ears since the spring of 1679.[9]

Yet whatever was to be done, could not be done in a hurry. The
most at the moment that Pepys could wheedle in ready money from
the First Lord of the Treasury was £12,000. That £49.7s. of this was
allotted to passing his own patent may be taken as a sign that the old
Adam was still alive in our hero. He meant to better the world but,
till he was able to, he took it as he found it. Absence from office had
not made him forget the useful art of looking after himself.[10]

We see him doing so, peering over his shoulder at the rough notes
he made in his pocket-book that June. On his return to London, this
comfortable, weather-beaten gentleman of fifty-one, with the soft
rounded features of well-living projecting complacently and unde-
afeated from under his great wig and the dark furrows made by
strife, labour and experience, accepted the honours which his many
friends and the powers of this world were now ready to accord him.
Great peers like Lord Ailesbury – that pattern of old-world loyalty –
begged him to visit them, the Clothworkers' Company besought him
to serve on a committee for setting up King James I's statue in the
Royal Exchange, and congratulatory messages on his recall to the
glories of Derby House flowed in from every corner of the British

---

* 'I am heartily glad to hear of your safe arrival after so long absence and desire
your letting me hear from you again so soon as you come to Portsmouth that I may
move for further orders for you, which you may expect very soon after.' *Pepysian MSS.
Adm. Letters*, x, 3.

world. Even distant New Hampshire, through its Governor's well-turned phrases, swelled the laudatory chorus.[11]

As soon as he got back to London from Windsor, Pepys made a round of his old friends – his generous bail, Peter Pallavicini, and the ever-beloved James Houblon; official colleagues like Blathwayt of the Army Office and his fellow diarist, Sir John Reresby, now Governor-elect of York; Parrey, the Clerk of Christ's Hospital; Leyenbergh, the Swedish Resident, with whom he had once nearly fought a duel; and the great merchant prince, Sir John Buckworth, who had come of the same homely fen stock as himself. He visited the shops, which for so long had been deprived of his wonted custom, took his Spanish books to Mr Scott to be bound, bought some little handkerchiefs, nose pincers, a short peruke, Dugdale's *Monasticon* – antique Popery in these changed times was becoming quite a fashion – Mr Boyle's latest scientific work and that elegant publication, *The Rules of Civility and Complaisance*, had his seal cleansed and chose himself a gold pen, a silver ruler and a set of silver standish glasses. In short he sampled again the seemly pleasures of the town.[12]

Yet as if to remind Pepys in his hour of triumph of the nightmare shadows of the past, there flitted across the stage of his life at this moment the shade of John Joyne, at whose suggestion he had once crouched behind the panelling of a Strand tavern to overhear the bawdy jests and treasonous oaths of the murderer Scott. This honest survivor of the brisk days of informing and counter-informing had since given up any half-hearted attempts to practise his craft of watchmaking and abandoned Paris for his native country. Pepys' return to the Admiralty naturally presented itself to him as a golden opportunity. He appeared hat in hand at the door of Derby House with a request for a loan of £20. It was granted. These phantoms of the past were best exorcized quickly.[13]

For the rest one could fix one's eyes firmly on the present, so real and substantial, with Lord Chief Justice Jeffreys scarifying traitors with forfeited charters and monstrous fines, and the good Duke, after all his buffetings, moving god-like and disdainful of penal laws by his brother's side. Mr Evelyn's grandson at Oxford, a most promising young gentleman and still only very imperceptibly a prig, expressed the sense of these things in a panegyric of fifty-four verses which he sent to Pepys to forward to the heir presumptive. Gone was

the shameful Admiralty Commission, the last pool of corruption left
behind by the retreating tide of Whiggery:

> Only one thing was left unfinish't yet,
> at once our joy and safety to complete,
> which our great pilot saw and straight commands
> the fleet be rescued from unskilful hands.

And though in the privacy of his study in Will Hewer's house in
York Buildings the Secretary of the Admiralty may have reflected
that the great pilot had been rather long about it, there was no
gainsaying the happiness of the parting shot which this hopeful
youth directed with such neat precision at the persons of the
retreating Commissioners:

> Men born t'improve some little country seat
> have souls too narrow to direct a fleet.

No one, it was plain, but great York and Albany could do that –
always assisted, of course, by Mr Pepys.[14]

The summer of 1684 was marked by scorching heat and a drought
as unprecedented as the harsh frosts of the previous winter. Every
morning Pepys would descend the steps beneath Inigo Jones' stone
water-gate and glide under an Italian sky, past the gardens and
buildings of Northumberland House and the royal Palace to Westminster Stairs, where he would step aloft to Derby House, the
administrative quarter-deck, as it were, of the King's Navy. Here,
with his clerks writing in echelon in the great room next door, he
would transact the old familiar business which for him, despite the
lapse of years, time had turned to routine. He sent off the *Dartmouth*
frigate on the Iceland convoy and the *Henrietta* yacht to fetch a
British ambassador from Dieppe, issued orders to have a young
gentleman examined for a lieutenancy – for the rules of the past were
once more beginning to hold – and granted or refused leave to the
officers of the fleet. Wherever this was asked for on grounds of
sickness, he demanded a physician's certificate – a rule that he
applied with democratic impartiality to everyone from the maimed
seamen who served in the King's ships as cooks to the Commissioner
of Chatham Yard. He also took care to see that every vessel was
supplied with a chaplain duly certified by the Bishop of London.
And in the intervals between these activities he bent that untiring

and omniscient mind of his to studying a new proposal for expelling worm from ships' timbers.[15]

Gently but surely the quickening touch made itself felt in every part of the sluggish body naval. To Captain Gifford of the *Mermaid*, whose youthful insubordination Pepys had more than once grimly noted during his late voyage, he wrote with a suave persistence that stirred that youthful commander to a most unwonted activity. 'I am to pray you', Pepys was presently able to reply to this reformed character, now hastily fitting out his ship for sea, 'to continue your diligence towards her despatch, and your accounts to me of the day's progress made in it. As to the delay given to her by the negligence of your purser, I have sent to him about it, and pray you to acquaint me if he continues to give you occasion of further complaint and I will immediately inform his Majesty of it and move him for another to succeed him.'*[16]

No part of the charge entrusted to him was too small for Pepys' attention. That every man's duty should be done to the King and right to all men had long been his own working motto: he intended to make it once more the Service's. He gave no mercy to those who relied on their official immunity from the legal processes of their creditors and so brought the Navy into discredit. A captain who had tricked the Lisbon merchants of their goods and stuffed his ship so full of merchandise that there was no room left for his officers' baggage, was amazed to receive from Derby House a peremptory communication which struck at the very foundations of his irregular, extravagant life:

I send you hereinclosed a paper put into my hands this morning from one Anne Lacock by way of complaint against you for non-payment of the sum of six pounds, which she says you have owed her this six years; and am to desire your giving me some account of it, that in case she should petition his Majesty or Royal Highness for leave to arrest you, I may be able to do you and her right to them. Pray return the enclosed with your answer.†

In the same way the purser of the *Mordaunt* was briefly informed that unless he attended the Admiralty at eight o'clock in the morning on

* S. P. to Capt. Gifford of the *Mermaid*, July 1st, 1684. *Pepysian MSS., Adm. Letters* x, 44.

† S. P. to Capt. Wren of the *Centurion*, June 30th, 1684. *Pepysian MSS., Adm. Letters* x, 42.

the following Monday to explain why he was withholding £10 from a creditor, the latter would be given immediate leave to arrest him.[17]

Naturally no one felt the change at the Admiralty more than the Officers and Commissioners of the Navy Board. Under the rule of the 'land Admirals', even such experienced administrators as Sir John Tippetts and Sir Richard Haddock had sunk into a state of coma, their only remaining concern being to draw their salaries and perquisites and leave that troublesome thing, business, to their clerks. Pepys, who had been an officer of the Navy Board himself, could not acquiesce in this view of their functions. They now found themselves being constantly called before the King or Duke, at whose side they were only too sure to encounter the small upright figure and enquiring face of the Admiralty Secretary. At his instance they were subjected to long and embarrassing inquisitions from the Lords of the Treasury about the fate of the monies that had passed through their hands. And every time Pepys went to Windsor, which was at least once a week, they could count on receiving next day a maddening letter informing them that his Majesty had enquired with fresh earnestness after the despatch of their promised Report on the State of the Navy.* Indeed the frequency with which that easygoing monarch figured in his little sea secretary's correspondence at this time would probably have greatly surprised him had he known of it.[18]

While Pepys was the cause of such disturbance in others, he himself suffered disturbance. In the early morning of Wednesday, July 9th, the house in Buckingham Street which he shared with Will Hewer and his mother was nearly consumed by fire. A dozen houses in York Buildings were burnt and the rest only saved by the arrival of the Guards and the drastic blowing up of Lord Willoughby's house above the Thames and No. 13 next door, furniture and all.† No. 12, open once more to the river, escaped by a hair's breadth. Some of Pepys' and Hewer's household goods, stolen in the general confusion, were less fortunate. Hewer lost a large table-watch in a shagreen case made by John Strelby of Greenwich, a load-stone case

---

* 'the importance of which will excuse the frequency of my solicitations.' S. P. to the Navy Board, July 15th, 1684. *Pepysian MSS., Adm. Letters* x, 58.

† By a curious coincidence our informant is Robert Harley who refers to the fire in a letter to his father and who twenty years later was himself to succeed Pepys at No. 14, where he entertained Swift while Prime Minister (*H.M.C. Portland* III, 381).

and a miniature in a silver-gilt case. John Walbanke, the clerk, was also unlucky, losing pictures, books and bedding. It was Pepys' fourth experience of that ever-lurking, sudden menace to the seventeenth-century Londoner's security. 'I thank you kindly', he wrote in reply to a colleague's anxious enquiries, 'for your compassion to me upon occasion of the late unhappy fire, and bless God I am no greater a sharer in the calamities it brought, though I am very far from being free.'* In that sudden moment of midnight panic all his most cherished belongings, including his papers and books, had been bundled together, and were now in indescribable confusion. And for a few days his grip on the collars of the idle relaxed, while he busied himself with briefing and instructing Counsel for a hearing which he and his injured neighbours had procured from the King against the owners of the waterhouse with its tall smoking chimneys and high wooden tower whence the fire had come.[19]

By the beginning of August Pepys had made sufficient progress in setting the rusty wheels of naval administration to work again to be able to pay a visit to the ships and dockyards. For some weeks he had been writing over the heads of the somnolent Navy Board direct to the dockyard officials, asking for accounts of expenditure and estimates for repairs. Their replies had not been reassuring. He was now to see the worst for himself. On August 12th he accompanied the Duke, his son-in-law, Prince George of Denmark, and Dartmouth down the river by yacht to Sheerness. Hence they took coach to Chatham Yard.[20]

The state of the great ships was more deplorable than anything Pepys could have conceived. There they lay, the very flower and heart of his cherished Navy. Dutch guns could have done no more to them than the neglect and corruption of the politicians. Their buttocks, bows and quarters were soft with decay, their tree-nails burnt and rotten, the planks started from their transoms and ready to drop into the water. Some were in actual danger of sinking at their moorings. Patched with canvas and shotboard to hide their nakedness, they reminded Pepys of the battered ships he had so often seen returning from battle. Yet the only battle of their brief, bloodless history had been that which he himself had waged on the floor of the House for their laying down. Such seemed the end of the stately

* S. P. to Sir J. Godwin, July 16th, 1684. *Pepysian MSS., Adm. Letters* x, 60.

ships of the line which he had conceived and planned to give his
country an enduring ascendancy over her rivals and the permanent
command of the seas. His dream had dissolved into dust – literally
dust, powdered fine like a coating of sand over the rotting sides that
could not even be breamed without imminent danger of taking
fire.[21]

Yet it was not in Pepys' nature to despair. In the third week of
August he 'made a step down' to Portsmouth, travelling post that he
might reach it on Monday evening. He spent all Tuesday inspecting
the crumbling ships in the dockyard and conferring with Sir Richard
Beach, the Resident Commissioner, and leaving before dusk the
same night in order to report to the King at Windsor first thing next
morning. For a man of what was then accounted more than middle-
age, he was showing remarkable vitality. Under a necessity most of
that summer of 'running almost daily' between Windsor and
London, he still somehow found time and energy to compose a Latin
inscription for an old acquaintance in Norfolk, to correspond with
Lord Chief Justice Jeffreys about the fanatics – the 'Malevolent
Party', as he called them* – who were said to be conspiring new
rebellion in that county,† and to take his place on the new Court of
Governors of St Thomas' Hospital.[22]

At the beginning of September, he was back at Portsmouth, this
time in attendance on the King and Duke, who had driven over from
Winchester where the Court was enjoying its autumnal holiday.
Here, among some other sights good and bad, but mostly bad, Pepys

---

* S. P. to Sir T. Allin, Aug. 26th, 1684. *Pepysian MSS., Adm. Letters* x, 106.
  † 'My Lord,

After congratulating your lordship, your safe return from the North, this serves
only to give court to a letter, this day come to my hand out of Suffolk from Sir Thomas
Allin. It coming to your Lordship through my hand arises not from my being in any
wise interested in the subject of it (as being wholly a stranger to the country) but the
particular correspondence happening between us as old fellow officers of the Navy. So
much intimation I have nevertheless of its contents as gives me occasion only to say
that the old known loyalty of Sir Thomas Allin will not suffer me to doubt the
integrity of his intentions and advice in it towards the King and his Government.

I humbly kiss your Lordship's hands and am,
    my Lord,
        Your Lordship's most faithful and obedient servant,

                                                        S. P.'

S. P. to Lord Chief Justice Jeffreys, Aug. 26th, 1684. *Pepysian MSS., Adm. Letters* x,
106.

had the misfortune to see the captain of the *America* 'overcharged with drink'. It was a spectacle he did not readily forget. For the next few months his correspondence is full of references to the battle he now set himself to wage against intemperance. 'Till that vice be cured', he wrote, 'which I find too far spread in the navy, both by sea and land, I do despair of ever seeing his Majesty's Service therein to thrive, and as I have given one or two instances of my care therein already, so shall I not fail by the grace of God to persevere in it as far as I am able till it be thoroughly cured, let it light where it will.' A little later he was able to introduce a system of fines to the Chatham Chest for all instances of drunkenness on service. For repeated offences he recommended dismissal from the Service, on the grounds that 'he whose debauchery renders him unfit for any one charge in the Navy, renders himself by the same means unfit for every other'.[23]

The commanders of the King's fleet were rediscovering in more ways than one that the Secretary of the Admiralty had an inconveniently pertinacious memory. Nor was his temper too easy. 'It gives me pain', he assured one captain who had asked to be sent on some special voyage, 'when I find his Majesty's commanders arguing with him about what work they shall be set upon, as if his Service in general (while so many others want it) were not thank-worthy unless they may be appointed to this or that particular part of it.'*[24]

It must have been an outlet for his feelings that autumn to issue a royal warrant, countersigned by himself, to his adversary Herbert, ordering him to submit an account of the slaves he had captured (and, as Pepys happened to know, starved) two years before.† This was a real triumph, for it was a little transaction of Herbert's which everybody but he had overlooked. The bold young libertine of an Admiral was still the Duke of York's favourite and strongly entrenched at Court. To Shere, Pepys confided his private view of Herbert's much cried-up command in the Straits – 'a most crying sin and shame', even to the corrupt purchase of a scandalous peace from the Moors when they were on the point of being forced to sue for it. For once Pepys had given a dog a bad name, nothing would content him but hanging it.[25]

---

* S. P. to Capt. Tyrrell, Aug. 26th, 1684. *Pepysian MSS., Adm. Letters* x, 105.
† *Rawl. MSS. A.* 177, f. 142. See also f. 150.

Yet beneath the severe and self-righteous demeanour which he resumed on returning to office, Pepys had another side to show to those who approached him with proper care and humility. A poor lad, who had missed his ship, waited with his anxious parents at the Admiralty to beg forgiveness, and received it readily enough, together with a note from the great Secretary to his captain at Spithead:

I understand by the friends of this poor youth that his not being ready time enough to return on board you before your leaving the River arose from their (not) being furnished with necessaries to send him to sea with. It is a pretty modest youth, and one of whom I remember you gave me a very good character when last at sea. Wherefore pray, as late as it is, find him a berth with you this voyage . . .*

Pepys had not forgotten the days when he himself had been poor and humble. And his heart went out to youth, for in spite of everything there was something in him that was still young.[26]

At the end of September, on the day after the Court returned to Whitehall for the winter, Pepys made an important move. He had been contemplating it ever since he returned to office. Having secured the royal authority, he transferred the Admiralty office from Derby House to his own home at No. 12 Buckingham Street, which he now took over from Will Hewer.† The move was quickly performed. The last official letter went out from Derby House on September 25th; the first from York Buildings on the 29th. It was a change which saved Pepys an unnecessary daily journey. More important it enabled him to resume his former practice of sleeping beside his business, which it demanded, without removing from the quiet haunt above the water-gate which he had come to love. It also enabled him to live there at the King's expense.[27]

* S. P. to Capt. Tyrrell, Sept. 1st, 1684. *Pepysian MSS., Adm. Letters* x, 144.

† One of the volumes of Pepys' letters at the Bodleian (*Rawl. MSS. A.* 190) is entitled 'Sept. 20, 1684. The first half of my freshest papers of all sorts, public and private, lying before me at my removal from Derby House, requiring my first attention and despatch.' The parish rate of £4 p.a. for No.12 Buckingham Street, hitherto paid by Will Hewer, was in 1685 raised to £4. 10s. and paid until 1688 by 'Esq. Pepys'. The house with its beautiful seventeenth-century oak staircase still stands, though it is its neighbour No. 14, a building of much later date, which is marked with an L.C.C. plaque commemorating Pepys' residence. (See pp. 181–2, and *L.C.C. Survey of London* xviii, Part ii (*Strand* 1937), 65–6, 69–74.)

For the next four years, in many ways the most formative in its whole history, the heart of the Navy was in York Buildings. In the tall, book-lined rooms with their glimpses of quiet street and river, Pepys conceived, pronounced and recorded the rules which time and the long momentum of work and precept were to make alike the routine and the spirit of a great Service. To obey orders punctually and without question and to hold the Regulations of the Admiralty as more sacred than the Ten Commandments, to do one's duty for one's bare wages without cavil and in the face of death, and to lay one's all in the keeping of the Navy in the belief that somehow in this world or some other the Service would care for and vindicate its own; such was the creed which the little scribe in the great wig taught the fighting men of the Stuart Navy. In this, unsympathetic as it seemed to the chaotic and tempestuous individualism of the seventeenth century, lay devotion, inspiration and the joy of sacrifice. Unguessed-at by its creator a course was being charted that led through the shoals of Quiberon and the deeps of Trafalgar to sea dominion and empire. As Pepys dictated to his clerks the strong rules he had framed, he was unconsciously writing a chapter in the future history of his country.

In some dim, indefinable way his contemporaries were aware that this autocrat of the pen and sand-box, who bore no titles and pursued his dry-as-dust labours with such gusto, had in him something of greatness, and honoured him accordingly. Even the scribbling fraternity recognized it: an aspiring author in the September of 1684 dedicated a pamphlet to him on the advantages that would ensue to British trade by opening the Scheldt. And far away in the south seas a shipload of English pirates, led by young William Dampier, coasting the wild Patagonian shore and discovering (or imagining they discovered) a wooded island with a fine natural harbour, named it at the instigation of their Master, William Ambrose Cowley, 'Mr Secretary Pepys' Island, in honour of that great Patron of Seamen, Samuel Pepys Esquire'. A far more distinguished honour came to him in December when at their annual meeting the philosophers of the Royal Society elected him their President.[28]

Yet this great man was not without many humble employments. He sent out the little *Kingfisher* to Rye Bay 'to improve the present season in the taking of fish' for the royal table, prepared lists of ships

for the herring and Turkey convoys and did what he could to help
John Joyne again by lending him £10 to experiment on an instrument for finding the longitude. He also looked about for a place for
Balty, now deprived of his employment by the evacuation of
Tangier, and attended to the education of Samuel Jackson. 'I have a
nephew, my own sister's son,' he wrote to the captain of the *Phoenix*
frigate, then fitting out for a voyage to India in the service of the East
India Company, 'a boy of between 15 and 16 years old, who I have
for some time bred in town to writing and arithmetic in order to the
making him a seaman, it being my purpose to bind him apprentice
to some Turkey or East India merchant. For though he is the nearest
of kin to me of any relation I have next his mother, yet I'll make a
seaman of him so that . . . he shall be able to earn his living that way
as much as if he had not a farthing to trust to. For which reason I
don't intend to enter him into the King's service, but breed him as I
think I have heard you say you yourself were . . . first in the
merchant's . . . The truth is, he is in his nature very good and well
inclined, but heavy and backward in his learning.' Anxious to take
so good an opportunity as Captain Tyrrell's voyage, Pepys asked
that his nephew should be employed as an ordinary cabin boy,
taught to work and obey orders to 'put a little briskness into him'. If
the captain agreed he should be sent down to Portsmouth by the
next coach. 'The youth is healthy and strong', he added, 'though not
so forward and pregnant at his books as I could wish.'*[29]

Jackson duly went, shivering in the Portsmouth coach on the first
Thursday in November. He took with him a seaboy's dress and
equipment, purchased for him in some haste by Pepys' old friend
and former clerk, Richard Gibson. The whole transaction seemed to
afford the Admiralty Secretary a good deal of quiet satisfaction. The
lad's sea-sickness would soon wear off, he wrote philosophically, as
he concluded with the Chairman and Governors of the East India
Company the terms upon which the *Phoenix* was to be engaged in
putting down the interlopers who infringed their monopoly.[30]

The approach of a new year saw Pepys once more at the familiar
task of preparing and presenting estimates. On October 31st he
drew up his Memorial for the Privy Council, proposing an establishment of 3000 men for the next thirteen lunar months. It was all that

---

* S. P. to Capt. Tyrrell, Nov. 1st, 1684. *Pepysian MSS., Adm. Letters* x, 174–6.

could be looked for in the existing mood of the Treasury. Yet even this humble figure proved too much for the feeble energies of the Navy Board. As Christmas approached Pepys addressed letter after letter to Sir Richard Haddock, the Comptroller, asking him and his fellow officers for the figures which they no longer seemed capable of supplying.[31]

For the moment the question of money was the key to all Pepys' cherished reforms. Without it he could do nothing. 'No good husbandry or saving can be too great,' he wrote, 'or, I fear, great enough to enable the King (as the state of his treasure seems at this day to be) to answer the many other and great occasions of expense necessarily requiring regard to be had to, even for the preservation of his Navy from ruin.' Commenting on the unaccountable increase in the charges for moorings, he poured out his heart in an indignant letter to the Commissioner at Chatham:

I cannot enough express to you the astonishment I am under to find so monstrous an imposture put upon the King far above twenty years together, to the costing the Crown by a moderate valuation above £100,000, without having so much as one word offered or pretended to be offered by the Officers of the Navy, and more especially the Surveyor, in justification of it ... I say I am put beyond all measure of wonder to think that so chargeable and visible a mismanagement should be introduced, continued and still maintained without one syllable rendered either in defence or excuse of it, but that which certainly could never be given by men who put any price upon the reputation of being thought either sincere or prudent in the management of such a trust ... namely that they found it so (though at the same time some of them do well remember when it was otherwise) and were unwilling to alter it. I may perhaps appear to say this to you in too earnest a style, but I must confess to you I cannot think of it with so little indignation as to be able to mention it more gently, especially when I consider of what value £100,000 would be to the King and his crown at this time in the business of the Navy.*[32]

The bitter season of storms, snow and frost that so dramatically succeeded the hot dry summer of 1684 proved too much for Pepys' health. During the last days of November he wrestled with a cold, trying every remedy for it – orange-water and treacle for hoarseness, anchovies and oil for coughing, and Goa powder mixed with eight or nine drops of balm of Gilead on a lump of sugar, 'a sovereign healer'

* S. P. to Sir J. Godwin, Jan. 10th, 1685. *Pepysian MSS., Adm. Letters* x, 267 (partly printed in *C.P. MSS.* 1, 115).

before retiring at night. But it was not till he gave in and took to his bed – a surrender that followed a miserable trip down the river to Tower Stairs in pursuit of the procrastinators of Seething Lane – that his physicians were able to make any headway.[33]

While Pepys was coughing and sneezing over the inexplicable estimates of the Navy Board and pressing its reluctant members for details, he was preparing to defend himself from what seemed to him an outrageous attack from that very quarter. For, threatened by the publicity which his just indignation had aroused, those responsible for the neglect of the thirty new ships were spreading it abroad that their condition was solely due to the defective materials out of which they had been built. As the Scandinavian and Baltic timber and plank used in their construction had been purchased under Pepys' immediate direction, this constituted precisely the kind of attack on his personal honour to which he was peculiarly sensitive. His mind recurred to similar insinuations in the past, such as those he had had to rebut about those early presents from Sir William Warren, the timber merchant, now, poor man, fallen from his former greatness and immured by his creditors in the Fleet prison.[34]

As usual on such occasions Pepys refused to take detraction lying down. He marshalled his full forces against his accusers. Knowing what a powerful appeal to national prejudice was contained in the implication about the purchase of foreign timber, he wrote to the Master Shipwrights in each of the Dockyards asking them to give their reasons for the decay of the ships and precise details of their defects and needs. The public, as his accusers were well aware, was far too ignorant of naval matters to realize that for many purposes in the construction of great ships no English timber large enough was available. Pepys was determined to enlighten it. All this led to an acrimonious correspondence between the Navy Board and the shipwrights, to whose technical knowledge he repeatedly appealed to confute the ignorance and supineness of their official superiors. The conclusions arising from it were reported verbally to the King in a private interview on December 2nd by the Admiralty Secretary (who with his cold must have had a very red nose and bleary eyes at the time). A month later, on New Year's Day, 1685, he presented them in a more permanent form beautifully bound in black morocco bearing the royal arms and majestically entitled: 'The State of the

Royal Navy of England at the Dissolution of the late Commission of the Admiralty, May 1684.'*[35]

But the King never read it. The bitter mid-winter of 1684–5 saw the climax of the great tide of loyalty to the Crown which had set in with Charles' dramatic victory over Shaftesbury four years before. Pepys, who had stood fast by the throne in its darkest hour, bore a part, though a more modest and discerning one than that of some, in the transports of that final triumph of the old Cavalier Party. At the turn of the year he busied himself with Sir Christopher Wren on behalf of the Clothworkers' Company in suggesting final improvements to the statue of the King's grandfather which Grinling Gibbons had made for them to fill a niche at the Royal Exchange: it would be best gilded, they decided, like the other statues, for that 'adds a lustre to them'. And he permitted his copyist, Paul Lorrain, whose inexpressible loyalty was possibly not unmingled with a hope of clerical preferment, to dedicate to him an anagram on his Majesty, beginning:

He's God on Earth, an Angelic blessing of the land.†[36]

Yet for all this loyalty a term was set. While Pepys waited for the royal comments on his masterly report on the Navy, made arrangements for the Duke of York's coming visit to Scotland and kindly interested himself in the recapture of a negro slave of Sir Phineas Pett's who had been so ungrateful as to run away to sea, the cruel cold of that winter was proving too much for the King. On Sunday, January 25th, Pepys dictated a précis of his somewhat exacting views on the rights of foreign flags to salutes in their own ports,‡ and

---

* *Pepysian MS.* No. 1534.

† 'For this and some other composition in a similar strain', commented a disgusted Whig, 'the writer was preferred to the dignity of Ordinary of Newgate.' *H.M.C. Rep.* 8 (*Ashburnham*, 7).

‡ '*The Rules about Salutes at this day Established and Observed by the ships of the King of Great Britain with respect to those of foreign princes.*

In the harbours or roads of foreign princes . . . the Commanders of his Majesty's ships are to send ashore to inform themselves what return will be made to their salutes. And in case of good assurance given that they shall be answered gun for gun, they are then to salute . . . But if not, they are in no wise to salute that place . . .

In case of ships of his Majesty carrying his flag, his Commanders are (before saluting) carefully to inform themselves how flags of the same quality of other princes have been saluted there, and to insist upon being saluted with as great respect and advantage as any such flags have been in that place . . .

afterwards recreated himself against his Monday labours by perus-
ing Dr Gale's learned comments, half in English and half in Latin,
on the various uses of the word *Maremium* and the carriage of the
Byzantine fleet overland in the year A.D. 877. A few hundred yards
further down the river, his sovereign, if Evelyn is to be credited, was
spending his Sunday in the midst of his concubines – three ageing
ladies whom he had known thirty-nine, twenty-five and fifteen years
respectively – in a scene of profuse gaming, luxurious dallying and
profaneness. It was the last earthly Sabbath but one that he was to
spend in this or any other way.[37]

A week later, propping his feet up as was his wont on the icy
window for his morning shave, Charles was stricken with a sudden
fit of apoplexy. At the close of an anxious day Pepys announced the
news to the fleet, as also of the King's providential recovery:

For the preventing your being under any uncertainty touching what I fear
you may otherwise have differently reported to you . . . his Majesty, after a
most surprising and dangerous fit of apoplexy or convulsion after his rising
from bed this morning, is (blessed by God) entirely recovered from the fit,
and it's to be hoped may be preserved from any returns of it.

'God grant us his perfect recovery,' he added piously, 'and we, by a
faithful and loyal discharge of our duties, to deserve the blessing.'*
It was nearly midnight before he felt able to leave the Palace and
return to York Buildings.

Hopes proved liars. Next day the royal audience of the Navy
Board in the Treasury Chamber which Pepys had arranged did not
take place, nor the next day, nor the next. The bright flame of life
which had guided Charles through his many trials was flickering
and failing. In those last agonizing hours, Pepys was among the
throng who pressed all day in and out of the royal bedchamber and a
witness of the confused ministrations which the doctors forced on the
dying man. In a flash of insight he noted it in his minute book,

---

Upon their meeting with any of the ships of war of the French King from Cape
Finisterre farther on in all the seas, as well in the ocean as Mediterranean, they are
expressly required neither to give any salutes to, nor . . . require any from them.

By his Majesty's command,
S. P.'

Pepysian MSS., Adm. Letters x, 301–2.
  * S. P. to Capt. Tevanion, Feb. 2nd, 1685. *Pepysian MSS., Adm. Letters* x, 302.

relating what he saw to the subject of all his thoughts and labours: '. . . the lamentable condition I see the poor King in when in his epilepsy, through the awkwardness and private interest and punctilios of his people about him, (rendering him less happy than any his meanest subject) is a proper instance for explaining the condition of the Navy while under the inspection and conduct of hands too big for it.'[38]

Death took the King on Friday. Next day, Pepys in the midst of a thousand scenes of change, mourning and tumultuous hopes, wrote to his naval correspondents to tell them of the great occurrence that had revolutionized his world. His old patron, the Duke, was now, as he put it, 'in a more transcendent capacity'. Nearly a quarter of a century had passed since the day when on the deck of the *Naseby* James had first called him by his name and promised him his future favour. Since then Pepys had seen him in every vicissitude: exile, proscription and peril of death. Now what had seemed inconceivable had come to pass, and James was King.[39]

6

A New Reign

'I have been reported to be a man for arbitrary power, but that is not the only story that has been made of me. I shall make it my endeavour to preserve this government both in Church and State as it is now by law established.' *King James II's Accession Speech to the Privy Council.*

Though the ports were closed and the troops stood to arms, the old fear that the dreaded accession of a Catholic King would plunge the realm into civil war proved groundless. After a few hours of alarm, all was seen to be tranquillity and loyalty. King Charles had left his kingdoms to his brother in peace. The new sovereign, with the austere dignity of one who had known unjust persecution, informed the Privy Council that he would respect the laws and liberties of his subjects. It was generally felt that the country and Church were safe in the hands of a prince who, whatever the limitations of his character, had never been worse than his word. That he should publicly attend Mass in the precincts of Whitehall was unfortunate, but it was only to be expected. Things, reasonable men reflected, might so easily have been worse.

The change of sovereign was, of course, accompanied by a change of Ministers. The High Tory, Rochester, became Lord Treasurer and the 'trimmer' Halifax was promoted to the impotent splendour of Lord President – a virtual removal from power which no one much regretted, for that fastidious nobleman suffered from Pepys' dangerous complaint of being always in the right and was consequently much disliked. On the whole the tendency of the new government was towards outward solemnity and respectability. The buffoons and profaners who had flourished under the good-natured Charles were banished the Court, and, if there was less laughter in high places, there was a great deal more ceremony and order. All this was naturally pleasing to Pepys. The only exception – and it was an unfortunate one – was the further preferment of Admiral Herbert. But even this, it was rumoured, was qualified by a rider from his pious sovereign that he should live with his wife and cease to blaspheme in front of his father.[1]

Pepys remained where he was, though with greatly enhanced dignity. No new Lord High Admiral or Commission being appointed, he was left the unchallenged administrative head of the first Service in the State. In its hierarchy only the King was above him. Within four days of Charles' death, he had the satisfaction of reading his volume on the state of the Navy to his new sovereign, or rather half of it. For James postponed the rest of the treat for a day or two, and then had the Secretary of the Admiralty, who must have felt very well satisfied with the transaction, read it all over again to himself and the Lord Treasurer. There for the moment, however, the matter rested, for the King had many other affairs to occupy his thoughts.[2]

In the intervals of another shocking cold, which stopped him even from speaking, Pepys resumed the ordinary routine *minutiae* of the Navy. Such were the punishment of a pilot who had run a ketch on the Whiting Sand, the escort of an Indian Prince round the dockyards 'with all the civility that becomes a man of his quality',* and the investigation of a broil in which Atkins' old friend, Captain Vittles, now Master Attendant at Chatham, had been hit on the head in a convivial moment by an inferior officer.[3]

Had Pepys wished it, it is likely that a still higher position could now have been his for the seeking. Better than anyone in England, the new King knew him for what he was – a man of unshakable loyalty, unrivalled industry and ability. A Secretaryship of State, great wealth and a title were all probably within his reach. He left them unsought. He had something more important to do. To his honour this man, who in his youth had loved the pomps and vanities of this world more than most, used his hour of utmost opportunity only to advance the work to which he had dedicated himself. He did not even trouble to take out a patent to renew his appointment and safeguard himself from future trouble. He just went on with his task. He could have done his country no higher service.[4]

People, of course, were quick to recognize Pepys' changed position. They saw him as one who stood at the King's left hand, giving counsel and having command. Thus Thomas Baker, Consul at Tripoli, desiring to be recalled from his tedious and dangerous

---

* S. P. to Capt. Vittles, Feb. 24th, 1685. *Pepysian MSS., Adm. Letters* x, 344.

employment, made his first application to him. True to his principles, the Secretary of the Admiralty replied that the business of
placing and removing Consuls was foreign to his province. He
added, however, that he had laid his wishes before the King and
obtained the desired consent.[5]

Another application was made to Pepys a few days after the start
of the new reign. Twenty years before an old Commonwealth
seaman, who had become involved in a dispute with the law, had left
his native land and taken service with the Dutch. In the course of
that service he had done his own country a terrible injury by piloting
his paymasters over the shoals of the Thames and Medway to where
the finest ships of the English Navy were lying unmanned and
defenceless at their moorings. Few men had better cause to remember that hour of national humiliation than Pepys, for he had been
Clerk of the Acts at the time: fearful lest the mob should avenge the
flames of the Medway by making a bonfire of the Navy Office, he
had sent his wife flying into the country to bury his savings in his
father's garden at Brampton.

King Charles had had good cause to remember the incident too.
His own people never quite forgave him for having permitted it to
happen. Nor has posterity done so. It was with more than common
magnanimity, therefore, that he pardoned Captain Robert Holland
for his fatal act of treason. The old mariner, who had since served
the sea under many flags, could not forget the generosity of the
sovereign whom he had so injured. Towards the end of 1684 he
obtained leave from the Danes, in whose service he was now
commanding a ship of the line, and returned to England with a
project for destroying the Dutch fleet. Once before during the third
Dutch War he had offered it to the government. But an attempt to
apply it in the Schoonvelt in May 1673, just before Pepys first came
to the Admiralty, had failed through a fault in timing on the part of
the English Admiral.

Hearing rumours of a new Anglo-Dutch war Captain Holland
had come to offer the project again and his own services in carrying it out. Misfortune had dogged his steps. Shipwreck on the
way and then King Charles' illness and death delayed his chance
of presenting it. Now his leave was at an end, and the rumours
of war likewise. Before he returned to Denmark he placed his
plan in Pepys' hands. He knew that it would be safe there and

used, should the occasion ever arise, to his country's best advantage.*

It was a daring project, and one worthy of the man who had conceived, however fatally for England, the most remarkable naval feat of arms of his age. It was the practice of the Dutch, Captain Holland pointed out, to bring down their north Holland and Amsterdam squadrons each spring over the Wieringen Flats without guns or provisions. These were only taken on board in deep water. By taking advantage of the prevailing westerly winds of April, it would be possible for a flotilla of, say, ten warships and six fireships, drawing not more than twelve foot of water, to enter the Zuider Zee by the Vlie or Texel and so destroy the greater part of the Dutch fleet while still unarmed. That done the victors would command all the Zuider Zee from West Friesland to Holland. Nor would they stand the least danger of being attacked by the rest of the Dutch fleet in the open sea. If desired, they could garrison Texel or Wieringen island permanently. The ships to do the business could be secretly built as if for the coal trade, or hired from Denmark. If there was any difficulty as to manning, seamen in plenty used to navigation in shallow waters could be hired from Bremen, Hamburg, Lübeck, Rostock and the north German towns from whence the Dutch habitually recruited their fleet. The same plan could be used against the French at Dunkirk, Bordeaux or Toulon or the Spanish at Cadiz. His own life and services, should they be required, Captain Holland offered with it.[6]

But these were times of peace, and in the spring of 1685 the chief concern of Englishmen was not to harass their enemies but to crown their King.† They did so on April 23rd, St George's Day, and Pepys as one of the Barons of the Cinque Ports took a gratifying part in the ceremony. He did not have, as at the last coronation twenty-four years before, to rise before dawn and creep by stealth into the Abbey. Instead he entered Westminster Hall at the seemly hour of eight and took his place in the procession with the great Lords of State. And as foremost Baron of the Cinque Ports he bore the left-

---

* The story of this strange episode in English naval history, till now unknown, will be found in *Rawl. MSS. A.* 189, ff. 251–4.

† 'Your letter of the 21st finds me at a time of so much hurry re: the King's Coronation which is to be solemnized to-morrow that I can only welcome you home.' S. P. to Capt. Wren, April 22nd, 1685. *Pepysian MSS., Adm. Letters* x, 440–1.

hand front pole of the royal canopy and so – only a foot or two from his sovereign and just ahead of his old Tangier friend, Dr Ken, now Bishop of Bath and Wells – marched from the Hall into the Palace Yard, where once, a young clerk in the Exchequer, he had scurried on petty errands. But that one brief glance is all we have of him, stiffly marching among his peers along the blue carpet that covered the cobbled stones, through the Gatehouse and along the great Sanctuary to the west end of the Abbey.

The auguries of the coronation were somewhat disquieting. At one point in the service the crown tottered precariously on James' head: at another the canopy that Pepys was helping to carry broke above the royal person. And when the Tower guns broke into the thunder that told the listening people that the King had been crowned, a gust of wind rent the standard above the White Tower. Yet these were more remembered in after years than at the time, when, judging by the verse and prose that depicted the day's events, the onlookers, as is usual at coronations, were too much dazed by the pageantry to be critical about points of detail. One poet, apostrophizing the resplendent beings who filed past him, was so overcome at the sight of the Queen, who was carrying the equivalent of about a quarter of the annual naval estimates in jewellery, that he seems to have lost the use of his senses:

> She was so proper and complete
> That (as she walked along the street)
> Her gait made all beholders gaze . . .
> I lent mine ear and heard them sing
> A simphonia to the King,
> And every fish from shrimp to whales
> Danced jigs and played them with their tails.*

It was a happy conceit and one which the Secretary of the Admiralty, walking soberly but nobly by with his silver stave and its tinkling bells, might even have taken as a kind of compliment to himself.

When the long service was over, Pepys took his part in the traditional banquet in Westminster Hall. He had no need now to

---

* *Bodl. Rawl.* 537. A Description of the Ceremonial Proceedings at the Coronation of their most Illustrious, Serene and Sacred Majesties King James II and his Royal Consort Queen Mary.

scramble, as he had done a quarter of a century before, for some poor rabbits from the feasting Lords, but sat down himself – a part of that 'brave sight' – at one of the topmost tables with the two Archbishops, twelve other prelates, twelve Judges and his thirty-one fellow Barons. Here, with his hat upon his head and to the accompaniment of music by Purcell and Locke, he feasted off hot larded leverets, beef-à-la-royal, Batalia pie, soused carps and wild pigeons, lobsters, pickled oysters and periwinkles, and more other noble dishes than could be catalogued in half a dozen pages. It is scarcely surprising that next day all the official letters he dictated to his Majesty's officers and commanders were embellished with a reference to the preparations he had been 'obliged to make for yesterday's great solemnity'.[7]

The glories of the day did not end with daylight. At night the river beneath Pepys' windows broke into flame with what a contemporary journalist who was present described as 'those miraculous and highest strains of art, the Coronation Fireworks. London seemed to have disembogued and emptied its inhabitants into the boats and on the shores of the Thames, the prospect of Frost Fair reviving in those endless multitudes that crowded and covered it. The tide was out, which happened well for the rabble, of whom many else would have been drowned by accidental slips and press of the people, which now were only dirtied; squibs, rockets, serpents and what else of fireworks the boys and rabble could reach to were the divertisement and dread of the people till the long-wished hour arrived.' And when at nine-thirty or thereabouts their Majesties with a numerous train of nobility came into the Galleries of Whitehall, and a hushed silence followed the cheering that greeted them, all London gasped as the fireworks with 'a horrid impetuosity and noise' and a 'stupendous torrent of fire' rose into the sky. As another eye-witness put it,

> The frightened Gods thinking their skies on fire
> For safety to the farthest Heavens retire.

Fortunately Pepys did not feel it necessary to exercise a similar discretion and was careful to preserve a reproduction of the scene among his collection of prints.[8]

In all this splendour and gladness there was one flaw. A short while before the coronation that staunch old Anglican, Mr Evelyn, was grieved by the unwonted spectacle of open preparations to beautify the Popish Oratory at Whitehall and of Romanists swarming at Court, with greater confidence, he noted, than had been seen in England since the Reformation. In the coronation itself there was a significant omission from the traditional ceremonies: the King did not take the Sacrament. Pepys, who preferred to keep his eyes on the Navy, took little note of these things. But shortly after the festivities were ended his Majesty was graciously pleased to show him, 'with the veneration given to relics', a gold chain and crucifix over six hundred years old which had been found in Edward the Confessor's monument in the Abbey while it was being cleaned for the coronation. However pleasing to a virtuoso, it must to a subject and office-holder have been a somewhat embarrassing spectacle.[9]

'The business of the coronation being now over', Pepys wrote on April 27th to the Navy Board, 'and with it the interruptions . . . to his Majesty's bringing other matters of public concernment to determination, and among them several particulars of importance relating to the Navy, which have been for some time and are still depending, he is pleased to appoint to-morrow in the afternoon about 4 o'clock for your joint attendance on him at the Treasury Chamber at Whitehall.'* It was time to resume work.[10]

To the Admiralty routine the summer of 1685 added labours of another kind. On May 19th Pepys resumed his old task of representing the Navy in the House of Commons. A General Election, the first since 1681, had followed the Coronation. It was favourable to the Court and tory interest, the electioneering tactics which Shaftesbury had evolved being now used with devastating effect against his own party. Pepys was returned both for Sandwich and Harwich. At the former place, of which he had recently been given the Freedom, he was elected unanimously by all who were qualified to vote under the new Charter. But the victory being slightly tarnished by an adverse and illicit poll taken by the disfranchised electors, Pepys chose to sit for his old constituency.[11]

Six years had elapsed since, after vainly trying to defend himself against the false accusations of Scott and James, Pepys had passed amid the execrations of the mob from St Stephen's to the Tower. Now the wheel of fortune had come full circle. On the day after he took his seat again in the House, the most sinister of his former

* S. P. to Navy Board, April 27th, 1685. *Pepysian MSS., Adm. Letters* x, 444.

adversaries, Titus Oates, underwent the first instalment of the awful sentence which the Courts had meted out to him. As he was whipped at the cart's tail from Aldgate to Newgate, even his brazen courage and impudence failed him. But though his agonized roar could be heard resounding above the shouts of the people, he survived.[12]

Three days after Parliament met, news reached London that the whig Earl of Argyll had landed in Scotland from Holland and that the Covenanters were in arms. The King came down to the Lords in person. The Houses, reversing '41 and '79, voted that they would stand by their sovereign with their lives and fortunes. Pepys was already at his desk writing to the ports to mobilize his scanty ships. Apart from a fitful watch kept by the *Kitchen* yacht off the Dutch coast, which he had ordered a few weeks before, the Navy had been unable to oppose the invasion. Such were the financial straits of the government* that the total effective force in home waters at that moment consisted of two frigates, with three others in harbour just returned from abroad, five others waiting orders to sail on distant voyages and two more fitting out.[13]

Happily rebellion was far away in the remote fringes of the western Highlands. As soon as troops and ships had been despatched to the north, King and Parliament settled down to the normal business of the session. Pepys, as an old hand whose parliamentary experience now went back a dozen years, not only represented the government in naval matters, but took a considerable part in the routine work of the House. He served on Committees for considering laws expiring or in need of renewal, for naturalizing French Protestants, and for expunging republican resolutions from the Journals of the last two Parliaments. For this last he was particularly well fitted, having borrowed the Journals some years before to take copies of such entries as referred to the Navy and his own prosecution. In face of those delaying and passive tactics which his collecting instincts always inspired, Mr Joddrell, the Clerk of the House, had had quite a struggle to recover the precious volumes.[14]

The principal business of the session was to supply the King with

---

* On Jan. 16th Pepys had written sadly of the great want of money he had found in every part of the Service. In March the wages of the yachts' crews alone were £15,294 in arrears. *Pepysian MSS., Adm. Letters* x, 272, 457.

money. It was seven years since any Parliament had voted the Crown a penny. The Navy was nearly £400,000 in debt and its Stores were almost empty. Fortunately for the work of restoration which Pepys had to do, the new Parliament was of a complexion very different from that of its three predecessors, and promptly proceeded to settle a revenue on King James greater than that enjoyed by any of his ancestors.

For the first time since Pepys' return to the Admiralty a programme of naval reconstruction became a practicable possibility. But even before he could bend his mind to it, a startling event made its necessity obvious to every Englishman. For some time past the government had been receiving mysterious tales of the Duke of Monmouth's activities among the republican exiles in Holland. It was one of Pepys' duties as Secretary of the Admiralty to transmit these to the fleet. On June 2nd he sent an express to the Downs to inform the captain of the *Oxford* that news had reached the King that Monmouth had bought two ships; he warned him to keep a close watch on the Dutch coast. A week later Captain Skelton of the Portsmouth guardship was ordered to put to sea to look out for 'a certain ship carrying 32 guns with about 150 men of several nations, and having in his stern the picture or figure of the sun rising out of the clouds. The said ship', Pepys continued, 'having been lately bought by the Duke of Monmouth at Amsterdam for the transporting of men and arms to some part of the coast of England in order to the beginning some commotions here answerable to the rebellion in Scotland by Argyll, which ship if it shall be your fortune to meet . . ., it is his Majesty's pleasure that you endeavour by all acts of hostility to reduce, sink or otherwise destroy.'* By June 11th, faced by this new threat, Pepys had managed to gather together a dozen frigates of varying sizes, while six more in harbour were being hastily got ready.[15]

How little Britannia with such a petty trident ruled the seas soon became known. On the morning of the 13th news reached London that Monmouth, with a small nucleus of republican desperadoes and a large store of arms, had landed two days earlier at Lyme Regis. (It was here that five years before the informer Scott had been so busy telling stories of the young Duke's legitimacy.) Pepys at once

* S. P. to Capt. Skelton, June 9th, 1685. *Pepysian MSS., Adm. Letters* xi, 37.

despatched orders to all ships within reach to proceed to Lyme Bay and attack the invaders. To every letter he added a *God-speed* of his own devising: 'wishing good success in a juncture and main affair of so much moment to the King and his government'.[16]

Such for two days and nights was the burden of Pepys' correspondence, as he exhorted his sluggish subordinates to bestir themselves in their royal paymaster's business. His task was now twofold: to destroy the invaders' transports before they could get away, and to prevent any other vessels from Holland coming to their aid. In both he was successful. By the 23rd he was able to congratulate Captain Trevanion on having captured the rebel ships and their arms. Though the Navy had failed to prevent Monmouth's landing, it at least had made his escape impossible.[17]

What remained to do was the work of the land forces. With the rest of London Pepys heard the royal train of artillery under his good friend Mr Shere thundering over the cobblestones towards the western road. For the next three weeks, with his unconscious genius for mirroring the chief occurrences of his age, Pepys in his letters to the watching ships provided a running commentary on events in the West.

The changing hopes and fears of that brief, tragic rebellion as experienced by one waiting news in the capital are recorded day by day in the pages of the Admiralty Letter Book. On June 16th the invasion seemed already defeated. 'Since mine by express to you yesterday', Pepys reported, 'nothing new has happened but the news of the Duke of Monmouth having made a small sally in the night out of Lyme and surprised a small party of the Militia about five or six miles off in their quarters, where they made shift to kill a brother of Colonel Strangways in his bed, but was soon beaten back to the town in disorder, where the Duke seems to be shut up without any appearance of his being ever able to go further into the land.'*[18]

But Pepys was wrong. A week later the story had taken a new turn. The rebels were now at large wandering about the country, and gathering recruits from the Protestant peasantry of the West. They had taken Taunton and Bridgwater, had threatened Bristol and were now believed to be marching on Exeter. Thither, in great

* S. P. to Sir R. Beach, June 16th, 1685. *Pepysian MSS., Adm. Letters* XI, 61.

haste, Pepys despatched Admiral Herbert in command of the naval forces, to assist the Duke of Albemarle in defence of the city.

But good news from Scotland discounted the bad from England. There the rebels were dispersed and Argyll captured. When his captors remarked that it was to be expected that the King would one day revenge himself on the Dutch, the whig Earl replied heartily that he both believed and hoped so – believed because they had assisted him so much and hoped because they had not done so more. Pepys, reporting this conversation, added a hope that the Duke of Monmouth would soon meet a like fate such as would cause him to alter his style. And when he did so, he assured Sir Robert Holmes, those ill-advised enthusiasts who had flocked to his mock-regal banner would also receive their recompense, 'not doubting but that the King will in a little time be in a condition both to reflect upon the lists, which I find sent him in from divers places, of those that have served him as the Lymingtonians have done, and to give them their just reward for it'.* Pepys' old acquaintances, Lord Chief Justice Jeffreys and Colonel Kirke, were soon to help fulfil this pious prophecy.[19]

June went out and July came in, with London still full of drums and trumpets and expectant rumours. On the 1st, Pepys, who by now had got twenty-six miscellaneous ships of war out to sea, instructed Herbert to watch for a vessel of Monmouth's reported in the Bristol Channel. It was probably, he warned him, carrying arms to the rebels, as well as 'to the helping their leader to his escape when that shall come to be his fortune to need'. The invaders were still dodging in the enclosed grounds of the West which prevented their being attacked. But what could not be done by open fighting would presently be effected by hunger. The news from Scotland was splendid: Rumbold had been hanged and Argyll had either lost his head or was to do so that day.[20]

It was at half-past eleven on the morning of Tuesday, July 7th, that Pepys, in a hasty postscript to a letter to Captain Fazeby, was able to give 'the first notice of the happy news just now brought to the King of the total defeat and rout given to the Duke of Monmouth's army yesterday upon a moor within two miles of Bridgwater, his Foot being all cut off or taken, his Horse fled . . .

* S. P. to Sir R. Holmes, June 25th, 1685. *Pepysian MSS., Adm. Letters* XI, 86–7.

The Duke of Monmouth, who fought very stoutly at the head of the Foot is escaped, at least does not yet appear whether dead or alive.' There only remained now to keep a sharp watch at sea for the fugitives, they, 'praise be God, having nothing left them to save themselves by but flight or the King's mercy'.* Neither was to avail them.[21]

Two days later, at the end of a letter of congratulation on his vigilance written by royal command, Pepys reported the final triumph to Herbert. 'I doubt not but you have heard before this the tidings of that last instance of success to the King's arms and cause which was left us to ask of God Almighty for him, namely the taking of the Duke of Monmouth.'† Some, who lacked Pepys' simple faith in his master's goodness, may have felt that it might have been better if the Almighty had denied the King this final triumph and allowed the handsome, foolhardy youth to have been knocked on the head in the battle that ended his career. Others felt uneasy at the increased prestige of a standing army under a papist King who had never been defeated and had never been known to compromise. He had less cause to do so now than ever.[22]

Pepys himself had suffered too much from Monmouth's black-guard partisans to feel many qualms about his end – an event which took place inexorably on Tower Hill on the 15th after one tantalizing and fruitless interview between the doomed Duke and his uncle. Afterwards the rising artist of the day, a young German named Godfrey Kneller, who had just finished painting Pepys' city friend, Sir John Buckworth, limned the severed head. It was all that remained of the beauty and tragic futility that had been James, Duke of Monmouth.

Monmouth did not perish alone. His unlettered followers were handed over to Lord Chief Justice Jeffreys and Colonel Kirke and his Tangier lambs. Their cruelties did more harm in a fortnight to their master's cause in the West than the whig intrigues of seven years. But to Pepys, and to many simple loyalists who thought like him, the Bloody Assize seemed no more than the just punishment for treason. He therefore felt no scruples in backing the petition of a sea captain for the grant of a thousand rebels for transportation to

* S. P. to Capt. Fazeby, July 7th, 1685. *Pepysian MSS., Adm. Letters* XI, 125–6.
† S. P. to Rear Adm. Herbert, July 9th, 1685. *Pepysian MSS., Adm. Letters* XI, 138.

Virginia or the Indies, 'there to be treated according to their deserts'. Before approaching the fountain-head of mercy, however, he enquired 'what sort of usage these fellows are to receive, whether to be sold entirely, as blacks are to slavery for their whole lives, or how long . . . that the King may understand both the value of the benefit he is to give Captain Barnaby, and whether the terms upon which these prisoners are to be sold be such as stands with his Royal Intentions to have them punished by'.* There was a hard knot somewhere in Pepys' heart: he was a man of his time. The lives and happiness of a rabble of unknown west-country peasants who shared the political principles of Shaftesbury and John Scott weighed nothing with him when set in the scales against the claims of a deserving naval officer.[23]

Yet even Pepys' loyalty could not save him from an awkward encounter with a suspected person. On July 8th, the day after the news of Sedgemoor reached London, he entertained a country kinsman – possibly Thomas Pepys of King's Lynn – to dinner. With him had come a young Norfolk attorney who had just married his daughter. A few days later Pepys received a letter from the Mayor of Dover about a mysterious stranger called Samuel Forster, who had been detained under the emergency orders forbidding unlicensed persons to leave the country. For it appeared that, lacking a warrant from the Secretary of State's office, the absconding gentleman had unaccountably attempted to secure a passage to France by making use of Pepys' name and even claiming his relationship.

Pepys was greatly puzzled. 'Very unwilling I should be', he replied to the Mayor, 'to disown an acquaintance, much less a friend or kinsman that has need of any just service from me. But at so suspicious a time as this I must take leave to forbear the owning or giving protection to any whose name like that of this gentleman I am wholly a stranger to. Not but that it may very well be that I may be related to one of that name, as being a name of too good credit for me to disown kindred with. But at present I cannot recall any such, and therefore . . . I shall desire, before this gentleman receives any benefit from the using of my name, he will be pleased to inform me a little more particularly touching himself, who is he, from whence he set out, and . . . whither he is going and on what occasion.'†

* S. P. to Sir W. Pole at Bristol, July 29th, 1685. *Pepysian MSS., Adm. Letters* xi, 209–10.

† S. P. to Mr Tiddeman, July 17th, 1685. *Pepysian MSS., Adm. Letters* xi, 158–9.

Imagine, therefore, Pepys' surprise when he learnt by further letters from Dover that the prisoner was the young gentleman who had so lately dined at his house and had married his fair cousin. 'I should no more have thought on him for a man likely to be in custody at Dover for endeavouring an escape beyond sea,' he protested, 'than I should have thought of the man (whoever he is) that I shall next meet in the street. For I could never have imagined that a young fellow, an Attorney-at-Law newly come out of the country in the term-time from his wife and family, that had never known what it was to travel [but] between Norfolk and Westminster Hall, should be brought by his father-in-law (whose daughter, my kinswoman, he married) to dine with me upon the Wednesday without one word of anything but business to be done in the country at their return home, should within three days after mount himself for Dover and there pretend himself bound for Paris and from thence for the Emperor's army in Germany; and this with so much haste and privacy as from want of passage from Dover to leave his horse there and try by stealth to find it at Folkestone; and this with so much confidence as to make use of my name for his protection, without saying one word that his father-in-law or wife are privy to his going, but rather on the contrary seems in his letter to expect that I should conceal it from them.'

'Sir, pray give me leave', Pepys concluded, 'to desire your letting him understand what I here write to you, and that though I have no reason to believe that his errand abroad has any relation to state matters, yet I cannot but think his manner of proceeding in this matter is such as must imply something very evil on his part with relation to his family or clients, or something or other that he is afraid to answer for; and that therefore he is not to expect my troubling myself at all about him but leave him to stand or fall by his own innocence, intending to take the first opportunity I have to send the letters he has wrote to me to his wife that she and her friends may know what is become of him. And this is the last trouble I shall give myself about him.'* For it was not to be expected that so

* S. P. to Mr Tiddeman, July 21st, 1685. *Pepysian MSS., Adm. Letters* xi, 174–5. I do not know who Samuel Forster was. It is curious, however, that five years before a certain C. Forster, a relation of Sir Timothy Tyrrell's, was active in supplying information about Col. Scott's life in Paris. Pepys heard, however, Forster was 'a very debauched, idle rascal' and therefore forbore to make use of so 'scandalous an evidence'. *Rawl. MSS. A.* 194, ff. 97v–98.

good a man as the Secretary of the Admiralty should protect the unrighteous.[24]

'The dust being now laid which was raised by the late troublesome rebellion,' he wrote to Sir Robert Holmes on July 28th, 'a man may hope to look about again, and among other things enquire after his friends.' The ordinary routine of the Navy began anew, and the Secretary's letter book was filled again with correspondence on such matters as the best way of keeping ships' biscuits from perishing, the provision of a yacht to take the French ambassador to Calais and another to carry the Duchess of Portsmouth with her numerous company, servants and baggage to Dieppe. For under the new dispensation the 'chargeable ladies about Court' were no longer in favour.

Nor were those who deviated a hair's breadth from the path of strict discipline. Pepys had occasion before the month's end to administer a severe rebuke to one of the captains who refused to pay the duty on some wine found in his yacht by the Customs authorities on the grounds that it was for his own drinking. 'His Majesty,' he wrote, 'was pleased to express his dislike of such proceedings and commanded me to make the same known to you . . . and further to observe to you that his Majesty will not allow such a liberty in any of the captains . . . but expects on the contrary a willing submission in all of them to his Officers of the Customs who ought to be countenanced on all occasions by his other servants in the execution of their duty.'* The ideal of the English civil servant of the future was already taking shape under Pepys' hand.[25]

If he was teaching his subordinates to render honour where honour was due, he was coming in increasing measure to receive it himself. It was to his judgment alone that the King during that summer entrusted the examination of a private bill touching the affairs of one of his most loyal and noble subjects – a remarkable instance of the royal trust.† And on July 14th, for the second time in his life, he became Master of Trinity House. He was the first to be chosen as such under its new Charter. As this document, an enormous one which Pepys himself had drafted, could not be got ready by Trinity Monday, the Installation was postponed until the

---

* S. P. to Capt. Fazeby of the *Henrietta* yacht, July 21st, 1685. *Pepysian MSS., Adm. Letters* xi, 174.

† For changing the settlement of the Ailesbury estates. See *Ailesbury* i, 111–12.

20th. In the presence of the young Vice-Admiral of England, the Duke of Grafton, Lord Dartmouth, and a large and distinguished company, Pepys was acclaimed Master and patron of English navigators and seamen. At Deptford Church the learned Dean of Worcester, Dr Hickes, whom Pepys had specially selected for the honour, preached on the triple virtues of Unity, Charity and Seamanship.* Afterwards they all took barge back to London, sitting down, eighty at a table, to a great feast in the new Trinity House. Mr Evelyn, who seldom missed these entertainments, carefully recorded the scene.[26]

This was not the only honour conferred on Pepys that summer. On May 30th he was made a Deputy Lieutenant for Huntingdon-shire by the Lord Lieutenant, the old Earl of Ailesbury. About the same time Moses Pitt, the bookseller, dedicated a new work to him – a set of *Six Dialogues about Sea Services between an High Admiral and a Captain at Sea* written by Nathaniel Boteler, a retired naval comman-der. This was followed by the dedication of another book, the narrative of Thomas Phelps' sufferings as a slave among the Barbary Moors and of his remarkable escape. Pepys had been instrumental on Phelps' return to England in introducing him to the King, and the grateful seaman in his preface apostrophized the great Secretary. 'None will ever dare to dispute the truth of any matter here delivered when they shall understand that it has stood the test of your sagacity. Sir, your eminent and steady loyalty, whereby you asserted his Majesty's just rights and the true privilege of your country in the worst of times, gives me confidence to expect that you will vouchsafe this condescension to a poor yet honest seaman who have devoted my life to the service of his Sacred Majesty and my country; who have been a slave but now have attained my freedom, which I prize so much the more in that I can with heart and hand subscribe myself, Honourable Sir, your most obliged and humble servant.' It was a long road that Pepys had travelled since the day when, a shy

* 'I . . . do desire your giving yourself the trouble of waiting upon Mr Dean Hickes with your desire and mine in the name of the whole Corporation that, if it may stand with his leisure and convenience, we may receive the favour from him on Monday next; acquainting him with the general and usual subject of our spiritual entertain-ment on that occasion, namely Unity and Charity, with what he shall see fit to mix with it relating to our function and trades as seamen.' S. P. to Sir R. Haddock, July 16th, 1685. *Pepysian MSS., Adm. Letters* xi, 154. Hickes' dissenting brother had been in arms for Monmouth and was a victim of the Bloody Assize.

young landsman, he had first stepped aboard little Captain Country's ketch to wait on his patron Mountagu in the Sound.[27]

But Pepys was never for long allowed to forget that he was human. Here indeed was the sheet-anchor of his sanity and common-sense. Though he took his place with his mace-bearers in the great chair at the Royal Society's horseshoe table and made the captains of the fleet wait on him hat in hand at eight of a morning, he was not without reminders of how different his state had till lately been. From the Gatehouse prison and like places of confinement, he still received periodical communications from the watchmaker, John Joyne. On more than one occasion he paid the fees for his release. He had had no dealings with Joyne of which an honest man had any cause to be ashamed, yet there were episodes of the past, harmless but humiliating, which he preferred to keep quiet. Besides he was sorry for Joyne, who though a rogue had once done him considerable service.[28]

The autumn of 1685, with Argyll and Monmouth out of the way and an adequate revenue settled by a loyal tory Parliament on the Crown, witnessed a growing interest in the state of the battle fleet. In August the Court moved to Windsor, where Pepys as usual was forced to spend a good deal of time, and in the following month to Winchester. Thither after dinner on September 16th, the Secretary of the Admiralty with his friend Evelyn set out in Mr Short's hackney coach drawn by six horses – the whole hired by the Crown at a cost of £22. 15*s*. – with the intention of attending the King on a visit to his ships and dockyards at Portsmouth. That night they reached Bagshot, where before supper at their inn Evelyn took a brief walk through the forest to visit his old acquaintance, Mrs Graham, a former Maid of Honour. He found her children running in and out of their sick brother's bedroom that they might catch his smallpox – a primitive form of vaccination in which the two travellers were much interested. Next day, setting out early, they reached Winchester.

They discovered the King at the Deanery discussing with Bishop Ken the strange miracles performed in Spain by the Saludadors. Pepys, who during his visit to Spain, it will be remembered, had inspected the Saludadors for himself and pressed one to get into an oven so vigorously that the fellow had finally confessed that the whole thing was a fraud, afterwards told his fellow philosopher that his royal master had been imposed on. 'But', he added, 'I did not conceive it fit to interrupt his Majesty who so solemnly told what they pretended to do.' For there was a point at which a too zealous insistence on truth became unprofitable. It was better for a prudent and loyal subject to listen in respectful silence to his sovereign's stories about the cures performed by his late royal brother's blood and his intentions (which did him credit) of having all the negro slaves on the plantations immediately baptized.[29]

Next morning early they set out for Portsmouth. Pepys and Evelyn preceded the King, driving through the wooded Hampshire countryside and noting with interest the preparations made for the royal progress – the country people in their best clothes crowding the hedges and the Mayor and Aldermen of Portsmouth with their mace waiting by the roadside a mile out of the town. Through narrow streets lined with soldiers they made their way to God's House, where the King after inspecting the yards and fortifications sat down with his company to dinner. Evelyn was much impressed on this occasion by his sovereign's minute care for his fleet and dockyards, predicting that his 'infinite industry, sedulity, gravity and great understanding and experience of affairs' would materially enhance his people's welfare. Their cup of happiness would be full, he held, were his Majesty to be converted to the national religion.[30]

But of this ultimate miracle there was at present little sign. Shortly afterwards Pepys, visiting Windsor, found his Majesty in a particularly gracious mood, ready and even anxious to talk on other matters besides the affairs of the Admiralty. His familiar discourse, which turned on such pious topics as the long-retarded conversion of Lord Arlington and the power of the Catholic Church to grant dispensations, so emboldened Pepys that he took his courage in both hands and begged his Majesty to tell him whether there was any truth in what was being whispered about the deathbed conversion of King Charles II. Alarmed at his own presumption, he beseeched his Majesty to pardon him if he had unwittingly touched upon a subject which it did not befit him to mention.

But the King, who knew his little Secretary's loyalty, became more gracious than ever. With the utmost ingenuousness he told him that his royal brother both was and had died a Catholic. Then, beckoning mysteriously, he bade him follow him into his closet. Opening a cabinet he pulled out some papers, which were written in the late King's hand and contained several arguments against the doctrine of the Church of England, charging her with heresy, novelty and fanaticism. When Pepys had read the original, his sovereign crowned all by handing him a copy attested in his own hand and which he offered to lend him.

Pepys was almost beside himself with excitement. As soon as he was able he bade his two dearest friends, Evelyn and James Houblon, to dinner, and when the meal was over led them into a private room and showed them the precious document. Evelyn, the best scholar of the three, noticed that the contents were no more than the usual arguments used by proselytizing Roman priests against the Church of England. But Pepys was able to assure him that they were unquestionably in the late King's writing. On the whole Evelyn decided that they must have been copied in the royal hand from some priest's papers.

None the less he was deeply impressed by what he called 'his Majesty's free and ingenuous profession of what his own religion is, beyond concealment upon any politic accounts. So I think him of a most sincere and honest nature, one on whose word one may rely, and that he makes a conscience of what he promises, to perform it. In this confidence I hope that the Church of England may yet subsist, and when it shall please God to open his eyes and turn his heart (for that is peculiarly in the Lord's hands) to flourish also.' For Mr Evelyn was one of those rare and happy souls who saw the Anglican Church not as a comfortable and convenient compromise, with a decorous liturgy, assured power and comfortable benefices, but as the sacred ark of the Covenant. 'In all events, whatever do become of the Church of England, it is certainly of all the Christian professions on the earth, the most primitive, apostolical and excellent.' One sometimes gets the feeling that the more worldly Pepys, good churchman as he was, was not quite so sure of this.[31]

There were certainly many Englishmen who did not share Evelyn's tolerant views about the religious beliefs of their sovereign, but who hated and feared them. Across the water his cousin Louis was using tyrannic power to waste and destroy the French Protestants. Nor were certain scenes enacted in England that autumn reassuring – the savage sentences on the poor Protestant rebels,* the

---

* 'The country looks, as one passes, already like a shambles.' Sir Charles Lyttelton from Taunton to Lord Hatton, Oct. 7th, 1685. *Hatton* ii, 60.

execution of one old woman for sheltering a fugitive and the burning of another, the elevation of Judge Jeffreys, reeking with the blood of western peasants, to the Lord Chancellorship. To a generation brought up on the crude woodcuts and harrowing tales of Foxe's *Book of Martyrs*, there was a savour of Smithfield in the air. Most ominous, perhaps, of all was the edict forbidding the customary bonfires on Guy Fawkes Day. 'What', asked Evelyn, 'does this portend?' Many Englishmen had a shrewd suspicion.[32]

But Pepys was not troubled; he had other matters, more important as they seemed to him, to look to. Such leisure from the cares of the Navy as he had, he preferred to devote to his friends rather than vex his mind over public affairs that did not concern him. We see him that autumn visiting old Mrs Hewer at Clapham, corresponding with Evelyn about antiquities and the higher principles of domestic economy, and entertaining Sir Robert Southwell's fourteen-year-old son, Ned, during the latter's frequent hours of vacation from school. 'I can't but thank you', he wrote to his old friend in the country, 'for the acquaintance you have recommended me to; and yet I am ready to wish sometimes you had let it alone. For I can't put a book or paper into his hand out of a desire to entertain him but he makes me sweat with one confounding question or other before I can get it from him again; even to the putting me sometimes to more torture to find the gentleman a safe answer than ever Sacheverell or Lee did. Only to-day (I thank him) he has used me very gently upon occasion of two papers I got him to read to me, the one an account I have lately received from Algiers of the whole proceedings, by way of Journal, of the French fleets there; the other the Statutes designed by Sir William Boreman for the government of his new Mathematical School at Greenwich in imitation of that of the King's at Christ's Hospital. Wherein, asking our young man his advice, as Sir William Boreman does mine, he has given it me with great satisfaction without putting me to any pain about it; only I have promised to carry him down with me next week, when I shall be desired to meet the Founder upon the place. And indeed it is a deed of the old man's very praiseworthy.'

'And for the young one', he ended, with a blessing to Southwell's whole fireside, 'you may be sure I'll keep him my friend, as you counsel me, for fear of his tales. For o' my conscience the knave has discovered more of my nakedness than ever you did, or my Lord

Shaftesbury either. In a word, I do most heartily joy you in him, and (as evil as our days are) should not be sorry you could joy me in such another.' For Pepys, never more charming than in his love of 'freshe younge things', must have had his lonely hours. It is perhaps not fanciful to suppose that he sometimes wished he had a son.[33]

Yet in another sense Pepys had sons enough. His were the King's ships and all that belonged to them, and they craved more love and devotion from him than any mortal child could have done. And in the autumn of 1685 they gave him plenty of trouble. In October he issued elaborate instructions for the guidance of the guard-ships that reveal how much thought and labour he was giving to every detail of the neglected economy of the Navy. Henceforward their standing rigging was to be set up and kept constantly in good repair, six months' boatswains' and carpenters' sea-stores for every ship placed in some convenient spot ashore, and every ship to be graved once a year. All captains were to sleep on board and set a quarter of their ship's company to keep watch at night, complements were to be maintained and absence without leave strictly forbidden, and due care taken 'for the putting out all fire and candle, and that no person whatsoever be permitted to lodge below the gun deck'. And once a week every ship's company was to exercise with small arms under the corporal.

Similar rules were promulgated for the management of guard-boats protecting the ships in harbour. Twenty were to be maintained permanently at Chatham and twelve at Portsmouth. These were to be manned from the guard-ships and act under the orders of the captain of the guard-ship on monthly duty. Every night a guard-boat, known henceforward as the scout-boat, was to take its turn on patrol, commanded by a gunner, manned by a coxswain and ten rowers, and armed 'with six half-pikes and six firelocks, with powder and bullets suitable to them'. Rowing exercise was ordained for all men employed on guard-boats at least once a month. It was the duty of the boat 'upon the scout' to visit every ship in harbour, boarding her if not hailed by her, seeing that all fires and candles were out by eight at night and reporting 'any disorder on board any ship by drinking or otherwise'. She was to challenge all passing vessels at night and to 'look into creeks and other places where any boats may probably be harboured, as well for the preventing any thievery or embezzlement as any surprise by an enemy'. Any danger or accident was to be notified to the guard-ships and other guard-boats by a prepared system of signals. The captain of the guard-ship in charge was to keep a journal of the guard-boat's proceedings and forward it to the Comptroller at the Navy Office each quarter.

For everything in the Navy, from great to little, Pepys was devising a rule. In some notes made by him during a visit to Chatham at the end of October he recorded his opinion that 'our expenses and wantonness in our ships' boats is very chargeable and troublesome to the King. Were it not better done', he asked, 'to have a certain size, figure, kind and value of ornament for every sort of boat of every rate, well digested and established as a standing rule not to be departed from?' The question was most characteristic.[34]

There was a still more vital one waiting an answer. It had waited for five years, and if final ruin were not to befall the English Navy it could wait no longer. The battle fleet was gradually sinking at its moorings. On October 16th Pepys sent orders to Shipwrights' Hall summoning its members to join with the King's shipbuilders in an urgent survey of the great ships lying at Woolwich and Deptford. On the last day of the month he was with Lord Dartmouth at Chatham. In a few notes he indicated the vicious circle which was keeping the English battle fleet in a state of ruin from which recovery would soon be impossible. 'The Master Shipwrights', he wrote, 'do now plainly each for himself lessen their estimates and reports of the defects of their own ships, thereby to hide and prevent the observation of their own ill works, reserving themselves to get the same done unseen when their ships come under repair. The Navy Office do also industriously demand below the truth, and then afterwards, when the ships come under their hands to repair, say that the work upon further survey appears worse than they expected. By which means the King is always in the dark, and they at liberty in their demands.'*[35]

None the less a remedy was to be found.

---

* 'Notes at my late being at Chatham.' Oct. 30th, 1685, compiled on Nov. 27th, 1685. *Rawl. MSS. A.* 464, ff. 112–13.

7

The Special Commission

'They drew the naughty shipwrights up with the kettles in their hands,
And bound them round the forecastle to wait the King's commands,
"Since ye have made your beds", says he, "ye needs must lie thereon;
For the sake of your wives and little ones, good fellowes, get you gone."

When they had beaten Slingaway; out of his own lippes
The King appointed Brigandyne to be the Clerk of his ships;
"Nay, never lift up thy hands to me – there's no clean hands in the trade,
But steal in measure", says Harry our King, "there's measure in all things
    made".'

Kipling.

Early in November Pepys received a communication of supreme importance from Sir Anthony Deane, the great shipbuilder whose early career he had made. Since the tragic days of the Popish Terror, Deane, who had suffered proscription and imprisonment by his side, had been employing in private practice the brilliant talents which he was prevented from giving to his country. No one in England knew more of the art of marine construction than he or had played a greater part in the building of the thirty ships eight years before. It was to Deane, therefore, that Pepys had turned that autumn when the improved finances of the Treasury, following the parliamentary session, for the first time made a programme of wholesale rebuilding possible. Given an annual sum of £400,000, Pepys asked him after his visit to Chatham, what could he do to restore the fleet?

Deane wasted no time. He realized as much as the Secretary the urgency of the work. 'For if', he wrote, 'the Navy which is the strength of the nation shall fall under such a degree of decay as to fail us in case of any sudden attempts from our neighbours, at whose pleasure it lies to . . . break the peace any day of the year, we may repent overlooking this great work when it may be too late.' The words, for all their clumsy phrasing, express an unchanging principle of the national polity. He recalled, not without bitterness, how eight years before, when Pepys and he were in the Service, the whole fleet, save for thirteen ships, had been ready for war. Now by the

Navy Board's own admission it would take three years at least before a single ship of the line could be got to sea at all. 'There is nothing', he ended, 'but our long acquaintance and freedom with each other could permit me to take this liberty . . . If anything I have herein offered shall administer matter of advantage to the King's service or satisfaction to yourself, I have all that I aim at in it and shall take great pleasure therein. But if his Majesty shall think either this Proposition or my service of any use or advantage to him, I hope the great pains, care and charges I have been at for these last six years to make myself master of methods to make good such a proposition may meet with such suitable rewards and encouragements as a service of so great importance to his Crown and dignity may deserve.'* For having fifteen children to provide for, Deane could not afford the luxury of being an altruist.

In the proposals which accompanied his letter, Deane analysed the state of the Navy. Of the ships of the line – nine 1st rates, fifteen 2nd rates and thirty-nine 3rd rates – there was not one but stood in need of repair. The entire battle strength of the nation was laid up. Even of the 4th rates or large frigates – prototypes of the modern cruiser – only twelve out of forty-five were fit for sea. Apart from these the total force available consisted of five 5th rates, seven tiny 6th rates, two fireships, a sloop and ten yachts. Of a total of a hundred and seventy-nine ships, a hundred and forty-two were crocks.

Striking as these figures were, they were no more so than the scheme which Deane drew up to remedy them. For an annual sum of £400,000 – actually less than what was at present being wasted by the Navy Board – he offered, not only to equip an adequate peacetime guard with an establishment of 4000 men in winter and 6000 in summer, but to repair the entire fleet within three years. To achieve this, he would require regular weekly payments secured on the Customs. And he stipulated that he and whoever were joined with him to carry out his plan should have power to 'put vigorously in execution the standing Instructions and Orders that have from time to time been made for the well governing the Navy, and . . . to suspend any officers that shall be found either to break or neglect complying with the said Instrument'. They were to have authority

* Sir A. Deane to S. P., Nov. 4th, 1685. *Rawl. MSS. A.* 464, ff. 88–91.

to give rewards not exceeding a total of £2000 p.a. to officers who showed conspicuous merit, to discharge idle workmen and to vary the employment level at the dockyards as they chose.

The plan would not have been Deane's had it not ended with a characteristic passage of defiant self-justification. 'But it may be objected that . . . if the proposer can do such great service for his Majesty now, why did he not do it when he was in his late Majesty's service? To which he makes this short reply . . . that from his single care and industry in the place he served, he saved his Majesty above one hundred thousand pounds, and had saved the further sum of one hundred and fifty thousand pounds more if either his repeated advices or letters upon that occasion had taken effect with those whose duty it was to have preserved his Majesty's treasure therein.'[1]

Such was the genesis of the famous Special Commission. At the time he received this communication from Deane Pepys was pressing the Navy Board for a final estimate of the exact time and cost of repairing the fleet. During the next few weeks he was prevented from pursuing the subject by his attendance in Parliament which reassembled on November 9th.

In the Commons Pepys defended the naval administration with his customary vigour. This was easier than it would otherwise have been owing to the fact that the opponents of the government based their attack mainly on grounds of religion. There was not one officer in the Service, Pepys was able to reply, who had not taken the Test. As to Monmouth's expedition a nation could always be invaded whatever the size of its fleet, if the invader enjoyed good fortune. The conception of a blockade was still beyond Pepys' mental reach or the practicable ambitions of a seventeenth-century Englishman. Meanwhile, he told the House, since Parliament had voted a supply, a thousand men were working daily on the ships in the Yards. He did not add that under the direction of the Navy Office their labour was proving almost wholly useless.

It was not a comfortable session. The best that could be said for it was that it was soon over. Monmouth's Rebellion had left behind it one national nightmare in the shape of an enlarged and now apparently permanent regular army. And the King's desire to help his fellow Catholics was fast creating a worse one – the popular fear of the papist officers who would one day, it was believed, command it. James' honest but tactless references to them in his opening speech caused a loyal but strongly Protestant Parliament to appeal to the Law against its sovereign. This created a tory dilemma of the first magnitude. The dilemma increased when it became clear that the King was a better Papist than Tory, and that the Cavalier principles which he had once seemed ready to die for in the last ditch were less dear to him than the approval of his confessors. The Commons voted him supplies but refrained from thanking him for his speech. The Lords asked that the laws against Catholic office-holders should be put into force. No one was surprised when on November 24th the King prorogued the Houses.[2]

With Parliament out of the way the Secretary of the Admiralty was free to devote his whole mind to the great work of saving the fleet. On November 26th the Navy Board submitted its latest estimate of £132,112 spread over two years for repairing the rotting timbers of the thirty ships and completing the three new 4th rates under construction. With this document, touching in its ingenuous-ness, Pepys made great sport. In the last sixteen months, he pointed out, the Navy Officers had only completed £25,000 worth of estimated work; why should it be supposed that under the same hands the work should go any faster in the future than in the past? At the present rate of progress, on their own showing, five years at least must elapse before the fleet could be ready. And in the meantime the ever-growing rate of decay would have far out-stripped the repairs.[3]

Pepys had made up his mind to act by himself: there was no other way. Just before Christmas he subjected Meeres and Lesly, the purveyors of the Navy, to a close examination as to the amount of large English plank available for the work of repair. From their answers it was clear that there was very little. And it was equally plain that no timber that was not bought at once could be seasoned in time to be of the least use in the work of reconstruction if the fleet was to be saved from imminent destruction and the nation from the evils that must follow.[4]

On December 23rd Pepys therefore wrote over the heads of the Navy Board to the Master Shipwrights and Clerks of the Cheque at each of the five Yards. From the former he asked for particulars of all ships docked and repaired during the year and from the latter a detailed schedule of wage bills during the past two quarters. The returns were to be rendered by January 1st. With these Pepys knew he could pulverize the figures submitted by the Navy Board. That some might regard such details as beneath the dignity of a Secretary of the Admiralty did not worry him in the least; he had not been Clerk of the Acts for thirteen years for nothing. And he sat down with Samuel Atkins to prepare the great oration in which he would explain his proposals to the King.[5]

He completed it on the last day of the year. The notes from which to deliver it he wrote in his own hand,* and from these rather than from the printed narrative which he compiled for his justification in later years we may learn the real form and manner of what was to prove the most momentous discourse of his life. For by it he saved the fleet which he had helped to create and which one day was to change the fate of Europe and the future destinies of the world.

On January 1st, 1686, he delivered it at a 'solemn hearing' in the presence of the King and the Lord Treasurer. He opened with the usual unembarrassed assertion of his claim to be the Service's advocate: 'the length', he said, 'of my experience beyond anybody else's in the Navy entitles me to this liberty, improved by the use made of my leisure during my five years recess in looking through the whole in all its parts, so as I could never have done had I continually remained under an obligation of spending my whole time upon one part.' He followed this bold start with a tactful and characteristic reference to his principal auditor: 'I need not open to the King anything of the importance of the Navy of England that he has so often hazarded his life for.' For Pepys was pleading now, not to a tumultuous Parliament, but to an absolute monarch with money in his purse. How the 'poor wretch', Elizabeth, and his father the tailor, and his brothers and sisters playing with him long ago in St Bride's churchyard, and Downing's clerks and the old gang at the Exchequer, would have gaped to hear him!

Then he spoke with indignation of the state of the Navy as he had left it in 1679, with its stores full and the thirty great ships fast building, comparing it with the 'deplorable degree of calamity' in which he had found it on his return. And this despite all the ready money which the naval administration had had at its disposal for the work, including the extra £160,000 which King Charles had added

* 'Notes for my Navy Discourse to the King and Lord Treasurer, 31 Dec. 1685.' *Rawl. MSS. A.* 464, ff. 168–99.

out of his own purse to the grants voted by Parliament for the original building programme in 1677. Some of the ships had not been so much as graved during the whole of his five years of absence. Since his return the King, the Lord Treasurer and he himself had done everything possible to put things right; neither money, men nor materials had been spared. Yet if anything things had got worse.

For, though an interminable correspondence had been going on between Admiralty and Navy Board for the past eighteen months about the repairs of the battle fleet, and large sums had been provided for that purpose, not a single foot of large-size timber or plank for carrying out the work had yet been contracted for. And though since his own return to office more than £90,000 had been supplied for labour and materials, the Navy Board, with scarcely anything to show for it, were still demanding the sum originally asked for as though nothing had been expended at all. 'The defects of the fleet', he asserted, 'are hitherto grown upon our hands faster than we have repaired them.'

Then he spoke of the causes of those defects. They were purely personal. Though once good men, and some of them of his own former choosing, the members of the Navy Board had been so long spoiled under an ignorant Commission of 'land Admirals' who could not distinguish between their doing right or wrong, that they had become completely useless. They left everything to their clerks, shirked meetings and were grown indifferent to reproach. And here Pepys reminded the Treasurer how he had charged them publicly with their neglect and not even received a reply. Their habitual negligence had lost them all credit and authority, and their subordinates despised them. They were divided by openly expressed differences and party fanaticism. He did not suspect their loyalty, but no disloyalty could have brought the Navy to a swifter or more complete ruin.[6]

The King was deeply impressed. Perhaps he was aware of the contents of a New Year's gift which his Secretary-at-War, William Blathwayt, had that day given the Secretary of the Admiralty – a detailed calculation of the size and cost of the Dutch naval establishment for the year. For with eight ships of the line at sea and 8440 men in pay, it was more than twice as large as his own summer guard. And James was already beginning to have occasional doubts of his Dutch son-in-law, the cold, ambitious, ever-calculating Prince of Orange. He gave Pepys orders to put the gist of his speech into writing, with his views as to what could be done to right matters and by whose hands.[7]

This document was ready by January 26th – a Memorial and Proposition to the King, Pepys called it. Three days later he gave it to his sovereign in the presence of the Lord Treasurer and saw them both read it 'with extraordinary instances of satisfaction and concurrence'. He was not displeased with it himself.

It began with a comparison of the state of the Navy in May 1679 and May 1684, very much, of course, to the disadvantage of the latter. Since then it had become, if possible, worse. The Stores were almost empty, and at the moment of writing only a single 5th rate could be fitted out for sea in under two months without borrowing from the Harbour Guard. 'In a word, after the utmost effects of the efforts now used . . . assisted by money and workmen to the full of their demands . . . it is most manifest that . . . the decays of your fleet do grow upon your Officers' hands faster than the cure.' As an example of their supineness, Pepys mentioned that Falkland, the Navy Treasurer, had not adjusted his accounts for the past five years.

There followed the Proposition. Based on Deane's plan of November 4th it claimed that with £400,000 p.a., supplied in regular quarterly payments, it would be possible to meet the ordinary overhead charges of the peacetime Navy on shore and in harbour, maintain a squadron of one ship of the line and nine frigates in the Channel as well as the ships already in the Straits and Indies, and by the end of the year 1688 repair the battle fleet. This programme was to include the completion of the three new 4th rates on the stocks and the building of two additional ones every year. The figures – which Pepys appended, including £133,023 for repairing the ships in harbour, £85,510 for furnishing them with stores, £36,000 for the new 4th rates, and the balance for the ordinary charges of the peacetime establishment – exceeded the total of £400,000 proposed by £90,787. Yet this he held could be made up by good management if the payments were only made punctually.

His revolutionary plan Pepys justified in his grandest manner. 'Though the general and habitual supineness, wastefulness and neglect of order universally spread through your whole Navy . . . seem to render any peremptory undertaking herein (from me at least) very unsafe, if at all justifiable; yet so much am I acquainted with the power of industry and good husbandry, joined with knowledge and methodical application (no two of which seem at this day stirring together in any part of your Naval Service) that, after weighing every article of what I am by your Majesty's command now going to offer you, I am satisfied that your Majesty may reasonably expect the services mentioned.' And the event was to prove Pepys right.

It was one thing to state his project: it was another to carry it out. For this Pepys proposed a Special Commission to take over the duties at present exercised by the Navy Board and carry out those more extraordinary ones called for by a great emergency. Its members were to have, not only a practical knowledge of every branch of naval administration and a mastery of accountancy, but, as Pepys put it, 'vigour of mind joined with approved industry, zeal and personal aptness for labour', combined with 'an entire resignation of themselves and their whole time to this your service without liableness to avocation from other business or pleasure'. In short a whole Commission of Samuel Pepyses was to be found to save and restore the Navy.

The King gravely approved. Pepys was instructed to prepare a Commission 'conformable thereto'. Without a moment's delay and with the same zest and vigour that he had employed over a quarter of a century before to secure the Clerkship of the Acts and an official residence for himself and his wife, he threw himself into the business of preparing the Commission and putting it into execution. The deadweight of inertia and self-interest which for so long past had impeded naval reform suddenly began to move as it encountered the force of that strong and unrelenting pressure. Something was about to happen at last.[8]

On February 5th Pepys was back at the Palace with the first draft of his proposed Commission. He had based it on one of James I's reign used in an earlier attempt to restore the Navy after a period of decline. After explaining its general nature to the King and the Lord Treasurer, he got his favourite young clerk, Josiah Burchett – many years later to be his successor at the Admiralty – to read it aloud to them. This completed, he received their authority to settle the details with the Attorney-General.[9]

Of these transactions, as of many of the most important events of his life, Pepys kept a journal – 'My Diary relating to the Commission constituted by King James the Second, Anno 1686, for the Recovery of the Navy', he called it. Day by day, in bare but essential outlines, he recorded in dictated longhand the progress of those fast-driven negotiations which put into operation the Special Commission. On Sunday the 7th, two days after his draft received the royal approval, he was at work collecting his Commissioners. His choices, already named in his earlier Memorial to the King, were Anthony Deane, Will Hewer, Sir John Berry, Captain Shales, his brother-in-law Balty St Michel, and three members of the existing Navy Board, Sir Phineas Pett, Sir John Godwin and Sir Richard Beach. Of Deane he had written that his talents were so much superior to all he had ever met in the Navy, that they could not be dispensed with. To him, as the man needed above all others, he wrote in the most flattering terms summoning him to an interview with his sovereign next day.[10]

To Pepys, in his simple and complete self-identification with the Navy, it must have seemed bewildering that his friend should have refused such a call. But, since his retirement, Deane had built up a private practice more lucrative and secure than anything the public service could offer him. As he explained to Pepys in a letter of February 11th, he had a family of fifteen children, 'and not', he added hopefully, 'without expectation of more'. He also – though he did not mention this – had considerable interests in London house property.* The gracious observations of his Majesty, therefore, made comparatively little impression upon him. This was awkward in every way, because Deane, as well as being the joint originator of the whole scheme and a man of an industry and integrity almost equal to Pepys', knew far more about the thirty new ships and the means of saving them than anyone else living. To make matters worse another of Pepys' intended Commissioners, Captain Shales, declined also sooner than relinquish his exceedingly remunerative office of Purveyor General of the Army.†[11]

Despite these disappointments, Pepys pressed eagerly forward

* He had been one of the three speculators who had bought York House from the ruined Duke of Buckingham and developed it as York Buildings. *L.C.C. Survey of London* XVIII, Part II (*Strand*), 51.

† Shales' subsequent financial history and the scandals connected with the commissariat of William III's army in Ireland three years later, suggest that Pepys was mistaken in his man.

with the preparation of the Special Commissions. After much pursuing of the Attorney-General, who may very well have felt that the law business of the nation was more urgent than that of an impatient bureaucrat, he persuaded him by February 26th to agree to the final draft. Next day he had the Commissions engrossed for the King's signature. There then followed a maddening delay from Saturday till Wednesday afternoon when the King and Lord Treasurer were both at sufficient leisure to give Pepys the necessary audience.

When the King had approved and signed the Commissions Pepys broke the news of Captain Shales' refusal and suggested Mr Maddox as the fittest man to take in his place. But the Treasurer, who was not over happy at the prospect of having to pay both the old Principal Officers and Commissioners and the new, suggested one of the former, Sir John Narbrough, as a measure of economy.

Pepys acquiesced, but went on to raise the more important subject of Sir Anthony Deane whose letter he read them. The King and Treasurer were in a quandary, for they were confronted on the one hand by the Admiralty Secretary's unanswerable insistence on Deane's indispensability and on the other by Deane's delicately veiled but absolute refusal to undertake the work at a salary of £500 p.a. With the politician's facility for declining issues, they compromised by telling Pepys to write to Deane and offer him the privilege of carrying on his private practice while serving the Crown at the same time. This he did that night after attending a Council meeting of the Royal Society, telling his old friend that the King was well aware that with his industry and skill he could employ his time more remuneratively than by compounding it for a bare salary. The royal suggestion, he explained, was that he should so arrange his private affairs as to retain the profits of them while drawing his official pay. 'By which this £500 p.a. will be an entire addition to your other present income, be it what it will.'[12]

As Pepys had perhaps feared, this compromise did not commend itself to Deane, who, however tiresome he might be occasionally, was a scrupulously honest man. He replied that, though the father of so many could have little pleasure in refusing an extra £500 p.a., he could not deceive his Majesty by taking his money on terms inconsistent with the work expected of him. As shipwright of the new Commission his whole time would be required if the Navy was to be saved from ruin. And this in justice to his family he could not value at less than £1000 a year.[13]

This letter Pepys communicated next morning to the Lord Treasurer. At his request he took Deane round that same afternoon to his lodgings at Whitehall, where Lord Rochester tried to argue with the obstinate shipbuilder and ended by losing his temper. It was Rochester's way when he did so to swear like a cutter. 'My Lord', Pepys recorded in his journal, 'expressed his dissatisfaction with Sir Anthony Deane's backwardness and standing upon terms with the King with a degree of heat that I was sorry for, as being what was too much to be offered to anybody that was not then in the King's pay, and much more to him that I knew the King could not be without, had he asked ten times as much.'*

Next day, Sunday, March 7th, was a day of crisis. In the morning, before going to church, Pepys spent an hour closeted with the Lord Treasurer: they finally agreed that Deane's letter should be shown to the King. This was done on Tuesday, when Pepys got him alone in the Queen's Bedchamber. To convince him of the impossibility of finding anyone who could take Deane's place, he offered to prepare a list of all the leading shipwrights in the country with their qualifications or lack of them. And with this end in view he made him promise an audience on his return from hunting on Thursday afternoon.[14]

As soon as he got home Pepys settled down to his list. No one in all England knew better than he how to draw up a damning document, and he never achieved a more devastating one. Ruthlessly and categorically each of the master shipwrights, naval and civilian, was subjected to a thumbnail character sketch showing how unfit he was for his trade. Nor where so much was at stake was Pepys the man to restrain his language or to boggle at calling a spade a spade.

With the official shipwrights he made short shrift. Sir John Tippetts' 'age and infirmities arising from the gout (keeping him generally within doors or incapable of any great action abroad) would render him wholly unable to go through the fatigue of the work designed for Sir Anthony Deane of visiting and rummaging the yards, offices, ships and works', Sir Phineas Pett was 'in every

* *Pepysian MS.* No. 1490, pp. 14–15.

respect as the first', and Mr Lee, the Master Shipwright at Chatham, had never built a ship in his life and was remarkable for nothing except his gout. The others were dealt with likewise. The best of them seemed to be the Master Shipwright at Portsmouth, Mr Betts, who at least had built several good ships but was 'illiterate and not of countenance, method or authority sufficient for a Commissioner of the Navy'. Mr Lawrence was 'a low-spirited, slow and gouty man . . . illiterate and supine to the last degree'. As for John Shish, the Master Shipwright at Deptford, he was just 'old Jonas Shish's son, as illiterate as he . . . low-spirited, of little appearance or authority . . . little frugality'. His father, he added, was 'a great drinker and since killed with it'.*

Their assistants were worse. Mr Stiggant was only a boatbuilder, Mr Harding a very slow man of no learning authority or countenance, and Mr Barham above three-score years old, a person without spirit or method and a fanatic into the bargain. The private shipbuilders were little better and as useless. Pepys disposed of them without mercy, especially with Jonas Shish, brother of John, who like the rest of his family was 'illiterate, low-spirited and of no countenance for supporting such a charge', and had never built a warship in his life.[15]

This strenuous libel the Secretary of the Admiralty prepared himself to deliver to his sovereign on the evening of Thursday, March 11th. He must, one fancies, have taken a pretty delight in it. Fearing, perhaps, that the Lord Treasurer might induce the King to prejudge his case, he only notified that statesman on the morning of the royal appointment. He did so in a short, formal note in his grandest manner:

My Lord,
    Your Lordship will be pleased to know that the King has assigned this evening (after his return from hunting) for my rendering him an account of something he expects from me towards his coming to a determination in the business of Sir Anthony Deane, with his commands to me to advertise your Lordship of this his appointment.

---

* 'The Characters (as they have been carefully and impartially collected by Mr Pepys) of the several Master Shipwrights.' *Pepysian MS.* No. 1490, pp. 143–52. A characteristic specimen was 'Mr Pett. One that loves his ease, as having been ever used to it, not knowing what it is to work or to take pains. Bred always in the King's service within doors, and very debauched.'

I am
> My Lord,
>> Your Lordship's most obedient servant,
>>> S. Pepys.*

The Lord Treasurer retaliated by failing to appear. But Pepys, after waiting vainly for him that night in the ante-chamber, got his way next morning, when he cornered both him and his sovereign in the royal Closet and triumphantly presented his list. There was no further resistance. Deane was to have his salary and Pepys his way. By dinner time he was able to announce his victory to Deane and Hewer, the two men whom it most concerned and whom of all the world he trusted best.[16]

The week-end of March 14th saw the climax of Pepys' struggles. On the Saturday morning he took Deane to the Palace to kiss the King's hand, and afterwards in the Treasury Chamber received the Lord Treasurer's apologetic explanation that his 'earnestness' – for such he called it – of the previous Saturday arose from no unkindness but solely from his fear that his master's Service would be wrecked by the great shipwright's reluctance to return to it. On the same day royal warrants were issued to the Attorney-General to prepare the patents for the first batch of Special Commissioners. And on Sunday Pepys carried Will Hewer to his sovereign's bedchamber to an interview at which the kindest things were said, as they were also at the Cabinet meeting in the afternoon, when Pepys' final Commissioner was ushered into the presence. This was no other than Balty St Michel, who after many vicissitudes as soldier of fortune, secret-service agent, Muster-Master, Store-keeper and Victualling Agent, and beggar, now found himself after two years of unemployment rocketed into the lofty position of Special Commissioner of his Majesty's Navy at the dockyards of Deptford and Woolwich. For in accordance with a decision to have a resident representative at each of the chief ports, Sir Richard Beach was allocated to his old station of Portsmouth, Sir Phineas Pett to Chatham and Sheerness, and Balty to the Thames.[17]

The remaining member of the old Navy Board had still to be disposed of. The preliminary negotiations had been kept a secret. Now suddenly these easy-going officials found themselves presented

---

* March 11th, 1686. *Pepysian MS*. No. 1490, pp. 153–4.

with a *fait accompli*. Sir Richard Haddock, who had been Sandwich's flag-captain at Solebay and a Navy Commissioner since 1673, was the first to hear of it. On the morning of the 17th he appeared at York Buildings, alarmed and indignant. Getting nothing out of Pepys but a lofty and general assurance that the worst was true, he hurried to the King with angry complaints of his being undone. It was not an auspicious interview. Next day, a chastened man, he was back at the Admiralty imploring his good friend the Secretary to pardon him for his past trespasses against him. Pepys assured him that these had never weighed with him a jot and that he was still to be employed in the Service, adding that no other prince in Europe would have kept him there after such mismanagement.[18]

When the sleepy lords of Crutched Friars realized that it was their work and not their salaries which were in danger, they cheered up vastly. For the King and Pepys were just enough to remember that, whatever they had become under the rule of the late Admiralty Commission, they had once been good men. They were to be retained to adjust old accounts and carry out routine work of a subordinate kind. With this they were content. Tom Hayter, the Comptroller's Assistant, who in the old days of the Diary had been one of Pepys' clerks, who owed his whole fortune to him and who had repaid him during the Popish Terror by slavish subservience to his enemies, came cap in hand to ask his pardon 'for anything wherein he had given me occasion of being dissatisfied with him'. 'Which I told him', Pepys recorded in his diurnal, 'whether there were anything or no, or I had any resentments thereof or not, ought not, nor never did nor should operate at all with me in any matter where the good of the King's service is concerned. And therefore told him his Majesty's gracious intention of keeping him still in his pay as at present, where I had done him no ill office. But that his Majesty had not yet fully determined upon the work he would allot to him; but that I supposed he was indifferently disposed to whatever his Majesty should require from him. Which he readily and thankfully agreed to.'* Pepys was right. So long as they had their pay, Hayter and his like did not mind what they did.[19]

One at least of the Principal Officers of the Navy had always moved in a higher political and social sphere than that of his

* Saturday, March 27th, 1686. *Pepysian MS*. No. 1490, pp. 35-7.

colleagues. Readers of the Diary will recall the feelings of awe with which Pepys had first encountered Sir George Carteret, the Navy Treasurer, whose fine ways seemed so far above those of the Comptroller and the Surveyor and whose son had even married Lord Sandwich's daughter. Later the Navy Treasurership had been held by the proud cavalier, Sir Thomas Osborne, who had used it as a jumping-off ground for the peerage and the highest office in the State.

Pepys regarded this office as beyond his cognizance. But the present occupant, Lord Falkland, and his predecessor, Edward Seymour, the great west-country magnate, had neglected it so shamefully that he felt himself obliged to draw up a special Memorial on the duties of the Navy Treasurer. In it he recalled the complete disregard for the Lord High Admiral's Instructions of 1671 both by Falkland and Seymour. The latter, who had combined his care of the naval finances with the Speakership of the House of Commons, had not even bothered to attend a single meeting of the Navy Board during his eight years of office.*[20]

This document Pepys presented to the Lord Treasurer on the last day of the month, asking him to attend the King at the earliest possible moment in order to place it in Falkland's hands. Rochester, who was on the point of leaving town for his Easter vacation, pleaded for a respite. But as soon as he was back in the first week in April and the royal preoccupation with sacred matters permitted the resumption of business, Pepys pressed home his attack. On the night of Sunday, April 11th, he had the happiness of summoning Falkland to attend the King next afternoon at Whitehall. Here in the presence of his sovereign and Lord Rochester, Pepys lectured the crestfallen Navy Treasurer on the duties of his office, adding a list of recommendations which he had made to ensure their future performance. The King added a few words of his own and 'with great kindness and plainness, too, opened the importance of his compliance strictly in his attendance at the Board and giving his whole time to the business'. All of which Falkland thankfully and submissively received, as indeed he had to, even Pepys' shattering proposal that his official residence at Deptford should be handed over to Balty. At the end of this painful interview, the poor gentleman, who, it

* *Rawl. MSS. A.* 464, ff. 95–101.

appeared, 'had been for some time in physic and water drinking for the gravel', confided to Pepys that his neglect had been largely due to 'the ill-treatments which he had received from Sir Richard Haddock'.[21]

Meanwhile Pepys had been hurrying through the last formalities required for the opening of the new Commission. On March 17th – a day on which he also found time to preside at the Royal Society's Council meeting for the third week running – he secured the royal signature to a warrant to pay the Commissioners' salaries. The drafts for their patents he carried in person to the Attorney-General's clerk, Mr Johnson, at the Temple in whose hands he left them. Three days later he penned an advertisement for the *Gazette* inviting landowners to fell trees suitable for compass or knee timber or plank. He also ordered an immediate survey of the Stores. On the same day he entertained the members of the Special Commission to dinner in York Buildings and treated them afterwards to a two hours' speech on the work before them. And on Monday the 22nd their proceedings were opened at St James' Palace by the King delivering to them 'a very earnest, plain and serious discourse' on their duties, which Pepys, who had drawn it up, had just finished reading over to him in his Bedchamber. As the passing of their patents was held up by the continued absence from town of the Attorney-General, a temporary warrant was issued next day authorizing them to act. On the 26th, after a speech from the Lord Treasurer promising punctual payments of ready money and his help in their great and arduous task,* Pepys brought the old and new Commissioners together and read them their preliminary instructions. 'With which,' he concluded, 'after several interchanges of friendly discourse between them together, and more particularly the old ones with myself, without any show of disagreement or reluctancy in their obeying the King, I left them to their work.'[22]

But in his haste Pepys unwittingly broke the laws of the Medes and Persians. For on the 28th, by presenting to the King for his signature the Bills which the Attorney-General had at last prepared, he infringed an ancient administrative monopoly of the

---

* '. . . Saying that he believed it to be the greatest task that ever any man undertook.' *Pepysian MS*. No. 1490, pp. 32–3.

Secretary of State. On April 2nd, he learnt that Mr Bridgeman of the Secretary's Office had put a stop to the passing of the patents.

Pepys, though he privately noted that he could justify what he had done on the score both of precedent and reason, wasted no time in making his apology. 'I understand from the Signet Office', he wrote to Bridgeman, 'that my too great intentness upon the despatch of the Navy commissions has betrayed me into the mistake of tendering to his Majesty the Bills for his signing, which ought not to have been done by any other hand than one of my Lords, the Secretaries of State. But when I have said to you (what few else I believe can) that neither the King's nor Lord Admiral's hands were ever worth a penny to me in fees for all the commissions and warrants that have passed mine for the Navy in 25 years' service, nor never shall, I do not think I need to make any other excuse than that which is indeed the true one for this mistake: namely an over-care for the hastening of these commissions without the due heed had to this particular in the forms of doing it. Which (as you see needful) I entreat you to say on my behalf to my Lords, to whom I would most unwillingly give any occasion of thinking me forgetful either of the dignity or rights of their Office. But having said this, the importance of the despatch of these commissions makes me beg you to let me know how in the absence of my Lord President this slip is to be now rectified, whether by my waiting on you to the King about it or having the Bills new writ over . . . for your taking the King's hand to them. For whatever it is that will be most satisfactory to my Lords, I will take care to see done. But pray favour me with your directions herein as soon as you can, the whole business of the Navy awaiting its despatch.' For Pepys, who had so great a feeling for the forms and rights of power when exercised by himself, knew how to respect it in others. 'I am in my 'pothecary's hands this morning,' he added, 'which prevents my present waiting on you, but shall be in condition of doing it at what hour you please in the afternoon.'*[23]

Pepys was wise to mention his own indifference to fees. The stop put to the passing of the patents was raised as soon as the Secretary of State's fees had been paid, 'the fear of losing which', he noted, 'I find after all to have been the only occasion of that stop, and not the

---

* S. P. to Mr Bridgeman, Easter Tuesday, April 6th, 1686. *Pepysian MSS., Adm. Letters* xii, 46–7.

point of jurisdiction or strictness of method to be preserved'. Yet it was characteristic of him that he should draw up an elaborate list of instances in which the rights of his own Office had been invaded by past Secretaries of State.* To this he attached a detailed list of Admiralty fees for the past twenty years showing how reasonable they were compared with those of other Offices and how much they had been reduced during his time. Thus a naval captain paid only £2 in fees for his commission, while an army captain, who held a far less important command, had to pay £5 to the Secretary of State and another £1 to his clerks. And a lieutenant in the army paid exactly four times as much as his naval counterpart. Counter-attack was always the soul of Pepys' defence.[24]

After a four months' campaign Pepys had attained all his objectives. The patents passed the Great Seal on Saturday, April 17th. Deane, Narbrough, Berry, Godwin and Hewer took over from the former Navy Board the sole work of building, repairing and equipping ships and Yards, the recruiting and payment of officers, seamen and workmen, and the making of surveys, estimates and contracts. They were to appoint regular days for public meetings at the Navy Office every week, 'to cause a strict, methodical and perfect survey' of all ships and stores, to keep accounts and prepare estimates, to contract for materials and acquaint themselves with the state of the market by inspecting the weekly Customs House returns, to keep a strict check on the receipts and issues of naval stores, to supervise the duties of all subordinate officers and to make themselves jointly responsible for their fulfilment. Above all they were 'to apply themselves with the utmost thoroughness, diligence, efficacy and good husbandry' to the repair of the ships in harbour, and 'to have a more than ordinary regard . . . to the recovering (as fast as may be) the lost discipline of the Navy and the encouraging and establishing of sobriety and industry', visiting all cases of drunkenness and debauchery by immediate suspension. For these purposes they were to reside constantly at the Navy Office. The remaining members of the old Navy Board, Haddock, Tippetts and Sotherne, were turned out of their houses to make way for them, but were allowed £80 each towards the cost of new quarters on Tower Hill. The three of them were to be employed with the Navy

* *Rawl. MSS. A.* 171, f. 82.

Treasurer in winding up their own past and exceedingly confused accounts. All Commissioners, old and new, except Deane, were to be paid £500 a year with allowances for travelling and expenses.[25]

On Monday the 19th Pepys met them by appointment at the Navy Office, where he formally read them their General Commission and Instructions. When old Haddock ventured to offer a criticism, he was told that it would be time enough for that when they had mastered them. 'Which was yielded to,' Pepys noted, 'and I left them to proceed by themselves. And thus the whole matter is finished. God grant it good speed.'[26]

The world saw all this as a great personal triumph for the Secretary of the Admiralty, as indeed it was. 'It is done at Pepys' request wholly,' wrote a courtier, 'and his creatures placed in it, Sir Anthony Deane, Eure etc.' 'The Navy Commission is all altered and modelled according to Pepys' design,' another reported. And the world, being the world, supposed that he was making a remarkably good thing out of it and much regretted that it was so difficult for honest gentlemen of aristocratic connections to get themselves posts in so lucrative a service. For the Navy since the meeting of Parliament seemed to be rolling in money and most of it was thought to stick, in the manner of that age, to Mr Secretary's fingers.* Even his proudly displayed list of establishment fees was used against him in the town's malicious talk. 'I know the griping temper of both him and Eure,' a disappointed suitor wrote, 'and what rates every poor bosun pays for what he has purchased with his blood and many years' hardship.' For there were some who had not forgotten the cruel libel of 'A Hue and Cry after P. and H.' of seven years before.[27]

During the winter and spring that saw the launching of the Special Commission, Pepys' ordinary avocations went on much as usual. He still had to bear the administrative burden of an interminable war against the Sallee pirates. It was his business to maintain the squadron serving in those seas. In doing so he helped to establish what was henceforward to be a cardinal principle of British sea policy, the use of Gibraltar in place of Lisbon as the base and 'seat of

---

* 'Phil has many wonderful kind expressions from the King, so that I imagine some room in the Navy (where they roll in money) might be found; so I advise you to solicit hard and court kindly. Sure Pepys would value Lord Ossory's recommendation at no mean rate, though Eure and he together neglect all where money chinks not.' (. . . to John Ellis, April 6th, 1686. *The Ellis Correspondence* (1829) I 93–4.)

naval action in the Mediterranean'. The great rock was still in Spanish hands, nor was Pepys destined to live to see it in those of his country. But he paved the way for Rooke's inevitable achievement of 1704 by a stealthy process of infiltration. By his instructions Jonathan Gauden, the Mediterranean victualler, was empowered 'to make presents to the Governor and officers of Gibraltar as there shall be found occasion for the procuring their assistance in the better carrying on his Majesty's service'.*[28]

Otherwise the routine of Admiralty pursued its normal course. Pepys encouraged the industrious, checked the overweening and impetuous, and rebuked the idle. When the King's favourite officer, Sir Roger Strickland, a Catholic, elected to leave his command in the Downs and come up to town without permission, he was favoured with a sharp rap over the knuckles from the Admiralty. Nor did his subsequent complaint at such unfriendly treatment gain him anything. 'I beg you once for all to be assured', he was dryly informed, 'that I both have and will ever on all occasions acquit myself both towards you and every gentleman that has the honour of serving the King with all the personal respect that I am able to express consistent with the greater duty I owe to the King's Service and the recovery and preservation of that discipline therein that for some time has been wholly overlooked. So that if you shall at any time find ought coming from me on that score that may be uneasy to you (such as that which you gave me occasion of mentioning touching Commanders-in-Chief departing from their posts without any knowledge given thereof . . .) I shall depend upon your excusing it as that which the duty of my place will not allow me to overlook.'† Gradually, in a short-tempered and intensely individualistic age, Pepys was building up a technique of official rebuke – aloof, dispassionate and unanswerable.[29]

So likewise when young Mr Batten, the Clerk of the Survey at Portsmouth, presented, unasked, to his sovereign a collection of Tables and refused to accept any criticism of their youthful errors, the sharp voice of the autocrat of York Buildings might have been heard dictating that icy rebuke which still reproves from the faded page of the Admiralty Letter Book:

* *Pepysian MSS., Adm. Letters* xi, 509.
† S. P. to Sir R. Strickland, January 28th, 1686. *Pepysian MSS., Adm. Letters* xi, 555.

I cannot but again tell you that I am entirely a friend to your industry and so would not say anything in discouragement to it . . . This only in truth of friendship I must take the liberty of saying to you, that, by the time you shall have conversed in the world and business as long as I have done, you'll find it of much more use to you rather to distrust than to presume too easily upon the sufficiency and unanswerableness (as you term it) of your own conceptions. The errors visible in your Collection of Tables presented to the King and my Lord Treasurer (and of which I thankfully acknowledge your giving me a copy) being such and so many as . . . would have required your committing them to the overlooking of some friend, and particularly Mr Surveyor, your master, whom I doubt you omitted among those most knowing officers you speak of, before you had exposed them, especially with so much self-satisfaction as you appear to raise to yourself from them, as I may hereafter have opportunity between ourselves of showing you.*[30]

To those who did well Pepys could speak in another tone. When his bluff old acquaintance, Captain Vittles, and Mr Trevor patched up their unseemly quarrel and agreed to abide by his arbitration, he praised them warmly for having behaved 'as just and prudent men and as servants of one royal Master'. He was always glad to encourage legitimate aspiration – provided it was modest and did not puff itself up unseemly – even when the applicant was unknown to him. 'I am beholden', he wrote to the Colonel of the Duke of Norfolk's Regiment, 'to an extraordinary accident for the coming to the knowledge of what I am owing to you for your favour to me in behalf of a young man, my namesake, though otherwise wholly unknown to me, whose fortune it seems has led him early to the sea and thereby given him some expectations of having it made useful to him by means of the post wherein I have the honour of serving the King in the Admiralty. And thereupon, I understand, he has found ways of applying to you for the favour of discharging him from the relation he has to yourself under your command in order to the bringing him within reach of mine . . . If you shall please to think his desire excusable, and that . . . his behaviour under you has deserved that favourable character which the world tells me you are pleased to give of him, I shall then add my request to his.'† It is noticeable that in his correspondence with his fellow public servants, Pepys was wont to employ the kind of language that the accredited representative of one sovereign power uses towards that of another.[31]

* January 5th, 1686. *Pepysian MSS., Adm. Letters* XI, 530.
† S. P. to Col. Sallesbury, March 23rd, 1686. *Pepysian MSS., Adm. Letters* XII, 32.

Youth he was always ready to befriend. Captain Fowler of the *Happy Return* carried to sea with him two of his young protégés – a younger brother of Mary Skinner and a son of Sir John Holmes, who for his mother's sake as well as that of the dead Admiral his father, Pepys did his best to save from his own vices. These were the cause of a great deal of trouble to all concerned: 'such', Pepys wrote to Captain Fowler after hearing of them from the young gentleman's mother and uncle, 'as in my life I never yet heard of, to the making them as well as myself despair of his ever being reformed if it be not by the severity which they hope you'll . . . give yourself the trouble of ordering him to be treated with during their voyage'.* Sooner than hear of young Skinner falling into the same debauched habits, he added, he would rather he were knocked on the head or flung into the sea.[32]

Just occasionally Pepys' own past impinged on his irreproachable and stately present. There was Bagwell, for instance, the carpenter of the *Prince*, whose career he had always so prudently assisted and whose wife, no longer wanted as of old, had taken to haunting the doorstep of York Buildings in pursuit of every new appointment that seemed tenable by her husband. Such conduct, whatever compensation it might once have brought in its train, was now unpleasing to Pepys. He even wrote to Bagwell to tell him so:

Mr Bagwell,

I am your friend and always have and will be so, your service to the King well deserving it. But I cannot pretend to be able to do everything that is desired of me, even by those that do deserve it well, there being a much greater number desiring and waiting for employment than the Navy can find opportunity of satisfying. And when opportunities do fall, I would not have it thought that the disposal of them lies in mine or any other's hand but the King's, upon my showing him the several testimonies which each man brings of his abilities and their qualifications.

And hence it is that I advised Mrs Bagwell, as I do everybody else, not to lose their time in attending, at least upon me, because that occasions them but an increase of expense in staying in town and does them no advantage after once they have informed me in their case and request. Which is the reason that the greater part of his Majesty's favours of this kind are done to persons that know nothing of it till word is sent them of its being done. This I thought fit (out of my old friendship to you which I have no reason to

* S. P. to Capt. Fowler, December 22nd, 1686. *Pepysian MSS., Adm. Letters* xi, 501–3.

alter) to say to you for removing the apprehension you seem to be under of my backwardness to do you kindness on occasion of the late vacancies of a Master Shipwright's and Assistant's place . . .*

'A letter of kindness', Pepys described this missive. The same benevolent motive, he maintained, underlay his refusal to lend Joyne more than another £5; such help would merely encourage the importunate watchmaker to remain idle and stop him from applying himself to his trade. The proper place for the past was the past.[33]

One ancient obligation had always had an awkward way of intruding itself at inconvenient moments – the promise made twenty years before to pay his predecessor, Thomas Povey, half the profits of his Tangier Treasurership. On several occasions Povey had dunned him for an account, though never with much success. As a matter of fact for the past six years the Treasurership had been held by Hewer. This, however, did not stop that unbusinesslike fellow, Povey, from putting in a claim, not only for the old arrears owed him by Pepys but for half of Hewer's profits as well. He wrote what could only be regarded as a most insulting letter, asking for a statement of all sums received since the last time of accounting, and complaining that he could get no satisfaction from Hewer whose tenure of the office, he maintained, was solely for Pepys' ease and convenience. Twenty years had now passed since he and Pepys entered upon a solemn contract, based upon valuable consideration and on a friendship which had continued with every familiarity until he had demanded his just rights. And Povey went so far as to point out how unlikely it was that the profits of the Treasurership, which during the two years ending 1668 had brought in £1100 over and above the official salary, should afterwards have become so negligible as to excuse even the formality of an account.

Pepys did not answer. Two months later Povey appealed to Deane as a fair-minded man and a friend of both to mediate between them. He complained bitterly of the way he had been ignored. 'Common civility returns an answer in matters of lesser moment and common justice expects a probable reply . . . It is not the least of my grievances that I am slighted as impertinent. Contempt, neglect or superficial evasions, or obstinate or affected silence, were never

* S. P. to Mr Bagwell, January 7th, 1687. *Pepysian MSS., Adm. Letters* xi, 531–2.

excusably admitted in conversation, much less in business, to be a decent way of proceeding, especially with one not much inferior to them, though not in so thriving and swelling a condition as themselves.'* Yet it does not appear that the poor man ever received any satisfaction.[34]

For Pepys had far outdistanced the formerly elegant and envied Povey. Once, long before, he had written in his diary after dining with 'extraordinary cheer' at Povey's house, how 'in a word, methinks, for his perspective upon his wall in his garden, and the springs rising up with the perspective in the little closet; his room floored above with woods of several colours, like but above the best cabinet-work I ever saw; his grotto and vault, with his bottles of wine, and a well therein to keep them cool; his furniture of all sorts; his bath at the top of his house, good pictures, and his manner of eating and drinking do surpass all that ever I did see of one man in all my life'. The boot was now on the other foot, and it was the prudent Mr Pepys who had become possessed of these princely things.[35]

Nine times that winter this 'thriving and swelling' man took the chair at the Royal Society.† In the summer he gave his *imprimatur* and his name to the title-page of the greatest scientific book ever published, Dr Isaac Newton's *Principia*. For he was no longer a mere amateur virtuoso: he was become a patron of virtuosos. Evelyn described how dining at Pepys' fine house in York Buildings he witnessed a wonderful experiment made by one of his fellow guests, who pouring a very cold liquor into a glass and super-fusing on it another, produced a white cloud, then boiling, divers coruscations and flames of the fire mixed with the liquor. 'Which being a little shaken together, fixed divers suns and stars of real fire, perfectly globular, on the sides of the glass, and which there stuck like so many constellations, burning most vehemently and resembling stars and heavenly bodies, and that for a long space.' It seemed, Evelyn thought, to exhibit a theory of the eduction of light out of chaos and the gathering of universal light into luminous bodies. 'This matter, or phosphorus, was made out of human blood and urine, elucidating the vital flame or heat in animal bodies. A very noble experiment!' It was so now with everything about Mr Pepys.[36]

* T. Povey to Sir A. Deane, April 8th, 1686. *Rawl. MSS. A.* 179, f. 40.
† On November 30th, December 2nd, 16th, 1685, and January 13th, 27th, February 3rd, 10th, 17th, and March 24th, 1686. *Journal Books of the Royal Society*.

He was at the very summit of his earthly power and glory. He stood at the King's right hand, ruled the Navy and saw his ventures prosper. He was Secretary of the Admiralty, Master of Trinity House, and President of the Royal Society. His confidential clerk, Will Hewer, who had once slept in his attic and done his chaws, was now a man of vast wealth, a great financier and Master of the Clothworkers' Company; his poor brother-in-law, Balty, a Special Commissioner for the Navy. His private house was the Admiralty of England. By the measure of this world Pepys had arrived.

8
The Great Secretary

'This High Dignity was lately executed by Commissioners . . . But their Commission being at length dissolved, the execution of their office was committed to the care of his then Royal Highness the Duke of York, now King of England, since when it has been executed by the indefatigable care and pains of that most ingenious and expert person, Samuel Pepys Esquire.' Dr Edward Chamberlayne, *Angliae Notitia* (16th ed. 1687). The Admiralty.

Yet across the bright course of Pepys' success there lay a shadow. Of his own fidelity to his master, the King, there could be no question: he was bound to him by the ties of ancient service, common enthusiasm for a great work and the plain loyalty of an obedient subject. That James was a Catholic was to him no valid reason for his withholding the minutest part of his whole-hearted service. Duty, patriotism and love of his work all combined to make Pepys' path a straight one – unswerving obedience to the gracious master who trusted him and who loved his Navy almost as much as he did himself.

But to Englishmen who did not possess Pepys' passion for order and rule in secular affairs and his liking for tolerance in those of the spirit, allegiance to a Catholic King was no easy matter. Even the most loyal had been nursed in a faith whose very essence was a loathing for what was held idolatry and priestly despotism – the forms and ideals of the Roman Church. The Anglican Tories, who had rallied to the defence of the throne against Shaftesbury's triple assault by republican, non-conformist and atheist, had been ready to accept the royal supremacy in religion. But when that supremacy was seen to be a mere channel for the more ancient dominance of a foreign priesthood their loyalty was shaken to its foundations. For James' piety grew with the years, and the Closet, the Chapel and the Bedchamber were alike seen to be crowded with priests and confessors. In the great Cavalier revival of the early sixteen-eighties, Englishmen had shown their willingness to kneel to the throne. But when its sacred occupant was observed to be kneeling also, with his back to his subjects and his face to a painted altar set up by the Bishop of Rome, what then?

James himself had his own view of the situation, and one which he was always ready to expound. During his brother's reign, he explained, he had risked the loss of three crowns for the sake of his religion. Now that God had blessed his fidelity by giving him the regal power, he felt bound to use it for the maintenance and advancement of his religion, which stood in the greatest need of his aid. This was difficult to answer, for by the law of England Catholic priests were liable to a horrible death and even laymen were subject to penal taxation and deprived of all the most cherished rights of citizenship. The Roman rites and beliefs were ceaselessly held up to obloquy in the public pulpits and insulted by the ignorant and brutal mobs. How, James asked, could he as an honest man be expected to stand by and not use his power to protect those of his subjects who were being persecuted merely because they shared his own Faith? And how as a King expect his authority to be observed when his Creed was branded and ridiculed by those who ate his bread and owed him allegiance?

Though to the defeated republicans and the ignorant and bigoted bulk of the population who loathed Popery for the joy of hating, all this meant nothing, to the better and more thoughtful Protestant English there was a great deal in the King's argument which it was impossible to answer. They had called him to the throne to save the realm from anarchy and their estates and Church from spoliation. They could not grumble because he used his power to protect the religion which he had openly professed in the days of exile and proscription. The dominant tory and Anglican interest had therefore begun the reign by accepting an illogical situation as best they could, swearing allegiance and even expounding a mystic philosophy of non-resistance to a King whose Faith their laws and religion condemned and trusting to his royal promise and good sense to preserve their own Church in its monopolistic integrity while he did what he could to mitigate the harsh lot of his own.

Had circumstances not been against them it is just conceivable that this tremendous compromise between diametrically opposing ideals might have succeeded. After all the scene of the experiment was England. But three circumstances were adverse. These were the international situation, the state of the succession and the royal temperament. The former made itself felt from the first moment of the reign. It was all very well for a Catholic King to preach tolerance to Protestant England when across the Channel his cousin and nearest ally, the Catholic King of France, was subjecting his Protestant subjects to one of the most cruel religious persecutions the world had ever seen. In the autumn of 1685 Louis had revoked the Edict of Nantes, the charter by which a former French sovereign had guaranteed the immunity of the Huguenot community from persecution. Englishmen, whose jealous Protestantism had been nursed on tales of the Massacre of St Bartholomew and the wood-cuts of grilling co-religionists in Foxe's *Book of Martyrs*, were now treated to the spectacle of thriving and respectable French Pro-testants hunted from their homes by dragoons, chained to galleys under the Mediterranean sun or flying penniless and homeless to England,* while their children, torn from them, were driven by priests to Mass. In the ensuing uproar the royal sermons in favour of tolerance fell on somewhat deaf ears.

Whatever James' ultimate intentions, such a moment was one that called for the greatest forbearance and tact. These were qualities he did not possess. Instead of accepting the *status quo* until the panic caused by his ally's cruel display of zeal had died away, he publicly pressed forward every measure that could alleviate the lot and advance the influence of his fellow Catholics. Had there been no ill-feeling towards the Roman Church, the stream of promotions that now came the way of its adherents, the swarm of alien priests at Whitehall, and the conversions in high places, all of them loudly acclaimed by the triumphant proselytizers, would have aroused opposition. As it was, they produced a panic. The tory tide that had still been flowing strongly at the King's accession suddenly stopped. By the spring of 1686 the ebb had set in.

The King, blind though he was to public opinion, had some excuse for his precipitancy. He was already in his fifties, a far more advanced age than it is accounted to-day. His eldest daughter, the heir presumptive, was married to a Protestant prince who had allied himself with all that James most hated. Unless he could firmly establish civic and religious freedom for his persecuted co-religion-ists in the few years of power God gave him, it would be taken from them again by the accession of the wife of William of Orange.

* James, who was shocked at his cousin Louis' intolerance, gave them £1500 out of his privy purse and ordered a collection to be made for them throughout the kingdom. *Ailesbury Memoirs* i, 103.

Unhappily, spurred on by his priests, whose very circumstances deprived them of all knowledge of the Protestant English, and by his own arrogant and impatient temperament, he imagined that he could best accomplish this object by riding roughshod over the laws and prejudices of his subjects. In this the poor, gullible man was encouraged by the worst and most treacherous minister any King ever had to advise him – the enigmatic Lord Sunderland who, from being his former enemy, exercised an ever-growing ascendancy over him, luring him on to blind and rash courses that alienated him from his best subjects and proved his ruin.[1]

So it came to pass that the good rules and strong and honest administration which Pepys was so industriously introducing into the English governmental system were in danger of appearing to his countrymen more in the nature of a tyranny than a boon. Though they created an executive instrument giving hitherto unguessed-at opportunities to England, they were associated with regal power which protected a hated religion and insolently dispensed with ancient laws to do so. They depended for their existence on the will of a sovereign who increasingly based his authority on the subservience of venal judges and the might of a professional army. English religion and liberty were alike ranging themselves in the forces gathering in the path of Pepys and his King.

But in the spring and summer of 1686 Pepys still paid little regard to the growing strength of the Opposition. He had his work to do, and that was enough. On April 22nd he marched the now thoroughly contrite members of the old Commission into the King's presence to thank him for his continued favours and acquaint him that they had taken a house on Tower Hill in which to perform their business.* Five days later he escorted his sovereign and the Special Commissioners round the empty Stores and docks at Chatham, where the great ships lay rotting at their moorings, their planks patched with old boards and canvas, their buttocks blistered by the sun and their holds with toadstools growing in them as big as one's

---

* A last despairing attempt was made by Sir Richard Haddock to avoid the loss of his house at the Navy Office, but Pepys, on being tackled by the Lord Treasurer whom Haddock had inveigled into pleading for him, replied firmly 'that there was a necessity for it . . . , it being indispensably necessary that the Secretary of the Office must reside there, as the Clerk of the Acts did, and always had done'. *Pepysian MS.* No. 1490, pp. 58–60.

fist. All the time, while the Commissioners tramped round the derelict battleships and the King probed the mouldering timbers of England's defences with his own hand, Pepys kept up a running lecture on the causes that had brought them to this pass.

Afterwards there was a solemn conference in the house of Mr Gregory, the Clerk of the Cheque, attended by the King, Prince George of Denmark, the Duke of Grafton, Lord Dartmouth, Rear-Admiral Herbert and the Special Commissioners. Here his Majesty listened to a further speech from the Secretary of the Admiralty on 'the universal supineness of his officers'. This was followed, as Pepys in his record of the expedition described it, 'with a proof of it the same evening beyond all expectation or imagination upon our seeing him aboard his yacht in the evening bound for London, and we back again from below Gillingham up the river in a violent storm of rain all that evening and night, without one port shut upon any one of the ships in our passage but what we had by hailing caused to be so, . . . neither shipwright nor assistant nor any other officer minding it . . . Nothing being more evident than the evil that this negligence has brought upon the Navy by ships being kept with their ports either always shut in dry weather or open in wet, to the occasioning that succession of heat and moisture that has ruined them . . . This seems to give a perfect consummation of the late business of our Navy settlement by the King's becoming an ocular witness of the necessity of it from the state of his ships.'[2]*

This trip to Chatham was followed by visits to the other Yards. At the end of May, Pepys accompanied the King and the Special Commissioners to Portsmouth; in June he was at Chatham again: and in August, when the King went on a progress in the West, back at Portsmouth. On these expeditions he seems to have travelled in some style, judging by his subsequent claims for expenses. The two days' visit to Chatham worked out at £31. 12s., those to Portsmouth at £15. 8s. and £20† – no trifling sums in the money values of the time. From the same accounts we know that he was much that summer at Windsor in attendance on the King; between June 6th and September 26th he travelled there twenty times with his young clerk, Josiah Burchett. In addition there were occasional journeys to

* Tuesday, April 27th, 1686. *Pepysian MS.* No. 1490, pp. 66–71.
† *Rawl. MSS. A.* 177, f. 134.

Hampton Court to attend meetings of the Council which were held there weekly during the King's summer sojourn at Windsor. And when at the Office he was accustomed to begin his day's routine before eight.*[3]

The wet summer of 1686 saw the Special Commission fairly launched on its work of restoration. It witnessed also two other of Pepys' triumphs – his vindication from the charge of having built the thirty new ships of inferior foreign timber and his famous 'Establishment in lieu of Plate Carriage'. Almost the first official act of the Special Commission was to confer with a delegation of leading Thames shipbuilders convened by Pepys. Their testimony established it beyond question that for vessels of over 300 tons burthen Prussian and Bohemian plank was cheaper, more reliable and more enduring than English. This was officially confirmed by the Privy Council on October 8th, when the King after studying the evidence declared himself 'convinced of the safety, benefit and present necessity of making use of plank of foreign growth'. The onus for the state of the thirty ships was thus officially laid where it belonged – on the old Navy Board. What was more important, the royal declaration left the Special Commission free to purchase the large timbers of the Baltic, which were so urgently needed for the work of reconstruction. In this as in so much else, Pepys was a pioneer, applying the results of scientific investigation to the conduct of public administration. It is among the major achievements that constitute his claim to be regarded as the father of the modern Civil Service.[4]

Even more far reaching in its results was the issue on July 15th of 'His Majesty's Regulation in the business of Plate Carriage, etc, with his Establishment of an Allowance for their tables and other Encouragements to his Sea-Commanders'. This great measure was the direct fruit of Pepys' voyage to Tangier and Cadiz and of what he had seen there of the system of private trading in the King's ships. It was twofold in its scope, depriving naval officers of the power of offending while providing them with regular allowances to place them above the reach of temptation. Henceforward no captain was to carry plate, bullion, jewels or any other species of merchan-

---

* 'It would be a particular favour to me if you could . . . give me an opportunity of conferring with you here upon Monday morning next about 8 of the clock, or as much earlier as you please.' S. P. to Mr Bowtell, May 22nd, 1686. *Pepysian MSS., Adm. Letters* XII, 105.

dise without a written warrant under the royal hand, upon pain of being immediately discharged and rendered incapable of future employment. The same prohibition was extended to the carrying of passengers, saving only 'our subjects redeemed from slavery, shipwrecked or taken at sea out of foreign ships'. Any profits made in violation of these orders were to go to the Chatham Chest for maimed seamen.

As with all Pepys' administrative rules, provision was made to enforce them. On arrival at a foreign port every captain was to notify the Secretary of the Admiralty by the first post home, continuing to supply him with accounts of his proceedings and abstracts from the ship's journal by every post so long as he remained there. To safeguard against loss or pretended loss of correspondence, a copy of every letter and abstract was to be deposited with the English Consul. Other provisions were inserted for regular transmission to the Admiralty of copies of all orders given by Admirals and Commanders-in-Chief to their subordinates. At the end of every voyage, ship's journals were to be forwarded at once to York Buildings for inspection. In the rules which Pepys prepared for erring captains there were no loopholes.

While he discouraged and punished the bad, he encouraged the good. The King's Regulation established a system of rewards and allowances to compensate commanders for the loss of irregular perquisites and enable them to support their position with comfort and dignity. Over and above their pay and the existing victualling allowances,* every captain was to receive a table grant proportionate to the importance of his command. Thus the present pay of £273. 15s. p.a. of the captain of a 1st rate of the line was to be supplemented by an additional £250, and the £136. 10s. of the captain of a 4th rate or cruiser by another £124. 5s. To appreciate how much more liberally Pepys and his sovereign interpreted the needs of serving officers than later administrators, it is necessary to multiply these sums at least fivefold and to recall that income-tax did not exist. The table grant was to commence on the day on which the ship was reported as fitted for sea and ready to execute her sailing orders.

Provision was also made for dividing the value of prizes between

* £12. 3s. 4d. a year. *C.P. MSS.* I, 212.

captains and crews. Insistence on rule and precedent was to be accompanied by special rewards for 'signal instances of Industry, Courage, Conduct or Frugality'. Pepys' impress was stamped firmly and, as time was to prove, permanently on the discipline of the Navy. The profession which before 1686 could breed a Herbert as its shameful exemplar, purified and redeemed was in the next century to give Britain a Vernon, a Hawke, a Jervis and a Nelson.[5]

This historical reform was explained to an assembly of naval captains by the King himself in its author's presence at Windsor in the summer of 1686. For many months after Pepys' correspondence was full of reminders of its existence. Before every voyage a formal notice was despatched to every captain together with a copy of the new Regulations:

This serves to convey to you his Majesty's written orders pursuant to his resolutions lately opened to yourself (among other Gentlemen Commanders . . . then attending his Majesty at Windsor) touching the business of plate carriage and his Establishment of an Allowance for Tables and other encouragements. Whereof wishing both to his Majesty and you the satisfaction graciously intended by him therein, I remain, etc.*

With this notice Pepys always enclosed the formal certificate of the ship's readiness for sea, which a commander had to complete, sign and return before his table allowance became payable.[6]

In this year all the birds that Pepys had roused during his Tangier voyage came home to roost. In April his earlier Establishment of May 1676 – now long neglected – for Volunteers and Midshipmen Extraordinary was revived as an encouragement 'to families to better quality . . . to breed up their younger sons to the art and practice of navigation'. The most careful rules were laid down to govern their service, both as to the number that could be carried in any ship and their own behaviour on board. Pepys believed in catching his future Admirals young. Volunteers were not to be admitted over the age of sixteen. They were to receive a small allowance in addition to their victuals as ordinary members of the ship's company, and were to be content 'with what accommodation

---

* S. P. to Captain Killigrew of the *Dragon*, Captain Hosier of the *Saphire*, Lord Berkeley of the *Charles* galley, and Captain Gifford of the *Mermaid*, Sept. 16th, 1686. *Pepysian MSS., Adm. Letters* XII, 248.

shall be afforded them'. In return for these privileges they were to study and practise 'the art and duty of a seaman' in a lively hope of further favours to come. Those who had formerly served as lieutenants or commanders, but for whom no present employment offered, might be admitted as Midshipmen Extraordinary on production of a certificate of good behaviour signed by their former captain. Midshipmen Extraordinary unlike Volunteers were to be granted an allowance for a servant according to their quality. But no Midshipman was to receive any pay before he had delivered to the Secretary of the Admiralty 'a perfect journal, fairly written, kept and signed by himself, expressing in distinct columns the place where the said ship shall have been each day at noon, the daily change of the wind, and all extraordinary accidents happening in the voyage'. Pepys' passion for naval education had not grown less with the years.[7]

Another Establishment of the same kind was promulgated in the autumn for Boatswains' and Carpenters' Sea Stores. Till now such stores had been issued in a haphazard and, as well may be imagined, exceedingly expensive way 'at the pleasure and discretion of inferior officers in the yards'. This, Pepys and the Special Commission resolved, could continue no longer. Henceforward elaborate regulations were laid down governing 'the qualities, quantites and proportions of each distinct species of stores' to be supplied to every rate of ship according to the length and nature of its voyage. In the same way the old rule about the use of the King's flag was reissued and strictly enforced, and all breaches of it sternly punished. An instance of this occurred in the autumn, when news reached the Admiralty that the private packet boats plying between Holland and England were taking the outrageous liberty of hoisting the King's Jack as soon as they got out of the Thames. Having caused Mr Skelton, the royal Envoy Extraordinary at the Hague, to investigate the matter, Pepys did not rest till he had brought the offenders to a reckoning.[8]

The summer of 1686 produced the usual minor incidents between Great Britain and the rival naval powers of France and Holland, the long drag of the frigate war against the Sallee pirates, and the alarms caused by the appearance of some Algerine men-of-war in the Channel. One of them, after capturing several foreign prizes, put into Harwich to refit, relying on the late treaty of peace and alliance between England and Algiers. Her presence there was a great embarrassment to the Government, for the local authorities, at a loss what to do with her, yielded too readily to an insular instinct to clap her dusky crew into jail and seize her cargo. Pepys intervened and instructed the Mayor of Harwich to supply the needs of the stranger at moderate rates, 'they being the King's allies', but to rescue, firmly but tactfully, any English slaves found among the crew. 'I am apt', he wrote, 'to believe the King will not think it anywise fit that, having had the fortune to be brought near their own country, they should be continued and carried out again in that condition, but . . . will rather find some other way to have their ransom paid in case their own friends are not able to do it.'*

The subsequent negotiations brought the captain and master of the Algerine to London, where they were interviewed by the King and Cabinet. The Sunday evening's entertainment which their visit afforded was described by Pepys with obvious enjoyment in a letter to Mr Sandford. 'They appeared very much unprepared either what to ask in reference to themselves (the young one, who is a seaman, insisting upon a supply of stores, while the old one who is a soldier would allow that they wanted nothing but provisions and a pilot) or what to grant in reference to the King's demand of his subjects, their slaves.'† In the end the matter was referred to the arbitration of a London merchant experienced in such matters. Meanwhile the Commander-in-Chief in the Straits was instructed to represent the inconvenience of the whole irregular business to the Dey of Algiers. The affair was finally closed by a promise from that friendly despot that any of his captains henceforward entering the Channel should be promptly and pacifically hanged.[9]

Occupation of a less exciting nature was afforded that summer at York Buildings by an elaborate survey, carried out in conjunction with Trinity House, of the encroachments made by private trespassers on the banks of the Thames between London Bridge and Cuckold's Point, and by the examination of plans for a public hospital for relieving old and bringing up young seamen – the germ of the royal foundation at Greenwich in the next reign. The Victualling Commissioners, to whom during Pepys' absence in Tangier the feeding of the Navy had been entrusted by the late

---

* S. P. to Mr Sandford, Sept. 30th, 1686. *Pepysian MSS., Adm. Letters* XII, 274–5.
† Do. Oct. 5th, 1686. *Pepysian MSS., Adm. Letters* XII, 285.

Lords of the Admiralty, found themselves subjected to his searching scrutiny.* For Mr Secretary, however severe and occasionally unfair to highly placed commanders and officials, always looked with a jealous eye on every tendency to starve the plain sailor of his just portion.[10]

A slightly comic element made its appearance about this time in the Admiralty Letter Books with the rival claims of two ingenious projectors, each of whom had invented a new sea-pump. Sir Samuel Morland, who had been Pepys' tutor at Cambridge, had in the course of years acquired almost a monopoly of government inventions, though he had somehow contrived to remain in a state of perpetual and clamorous impecuniosity which no reward could long alleviate. He was now challenged in his most sensitive part, the naval pump, by a persistent and avaricious baronet from the far end of Scotland named Sir Robert Gordon who submitted a pump of his own to the Admiralty. At first there was some difficulty in making this engine work, and then only with such a noise as to be almost unbearable. Indeed during the summer of 1686 Sir Samuel Morland formed the habit of attending its trials, which took place in the early hours of the morning in St James' Park, in order to see it fail.

But on a further trial at the beginning of November Sir Robert's pump proved so unexpectedly successful that Morland was driven hastily to invent an entirely new one of his own. This he submitted after a few days with a long letter to the King claiming that it was cheaper and more lasting and able to be worked by fewer hands than any 'other pump whatever, though all the engineers in the world should contrive together to contrive it'. He accordingly offered to submit it to a trial with any other chain pump and Sir Robert Gordon's in particular. The plans of this wonderful machine and the correspondence to which they gave rise were all passed to Pepys, who for several weeks suffered many explanations from his old tutor. He was also the ultimate recipient of the petitions which Morland was in the habit of slipping into his sovereign's hands as he passed down the corridors of Whitehall. These generally took the form of peremptory demands:

1. That this may be the last trial, and a final end put to all disputes.

* *Rawl. MSS. A.* 171, f. 86.

2. That your Majesty will send positive orders to Sir Robert Gordon to forbid him to imitate any part of my last engine or model, particularly the drum capstan, but above all the counterpoise . . . , being the principal part of my invention whereby I pretend to outdo him or others . . .

3. That when he has finished and fixed his engine, he may have order to quit the place, and I free liberty to go and set up an engine to be tried together with his, that so I may not be disturbed as I was before the last trial by both Sir Robert and his workmen and treated with very undecent language . . .

4. That your Majesty will speedily order me a reimbursement of the £200, I being in very great want of it.*

In the end it was found necessary to set apart two separate ships for the scene of these experiments owing to the suspicions entertained by the rival inventors of each other's honesty.†[11]

The controversy was still raging in the following spring, though by that time with such advantage to Sir Robert that poor Morland spoke of committing suicide. The scene of battle had now shifted to York Buildings and the Navy Office, which were perpetually bombarded with requests from the successful inventor for rewards and the defrayment of his expenses. To secure these, Sir Robert even tried to bribe Pepys, explaining with the innocent effrontery of his race that the £1000 which he had expended on his invention had hitherto prevented him from making a suitable acknowledgment. He added that one of the most acceptable features of the royal bounty when it came would be that it would give him the chance 'of requiting in some measure those obligations I lie under by the constant trouble you were pleased to give yourself'.‡ 'Sir,' replied the great Secretary, 'I am obliged to you for your courteous expressions . . . But (as I said to you on the like occasion the other day) I . . . assure you that I never yet suffered myself to rob his Majesty of any part of the thanks due for his favours to private persons and will not begin to do otherwise in the case of Sir Robert Gordon. To whom if I have in any wise been serviceable, I think

* Nov. 19th, 1686. *Rawl. MSS. A.* 189, f. 53.

† 'After mature deliberation I do humbly beg that Sir Robert may have free liberty to carry aboard the ship that very individual Engine which he . . . showed you and the Committee and with which he so much triumphs. And that he be permitted to set it up in what part of the ship he pleases. For my part I am not envious in the least either to see it tried or to see the inside of it till the trial is over.' Sir S. Morland to S. P., Dec. 10th, 1686. *Rawl. MSS. A.* 189, f. 60.

‡ Sir R. Gordon to S. P., May 16th, 1687. *Rawl. MSS. A.* 189, f. 131.

myself abundantly rewarded for it by the industry I have seen him use to render himself so to the King, my master.' And he enclosed a warrant for £318 on the Treasury, or about a third of the sum which the baronet had claimed. Within a fortnight he was receiving complaints from Captain Shovell about the pump's imperfections.[12]

At the end of the first six months of the Special Commission's existence, Pepys and its members attended the King and Lord Treasurer in the Treasury Chambers to report progress. Though they had been compelled to add a supplementary £23,081 to Pepys' original estimate, they had already accomplished much of which they could be proud, and were. On taking over the work of the old Navy Board in April they had found 'nothing a'doing in the Yards' beyond some leisurely repairs to two ships of the line. They had now gone so far as to put all thirty new ships out of any danger of sinking. Moreover they had issued and were enforcing orders that would prevent their ever falling again into so lamentable a state, the result, as they stated, of 'an unpardonable degree of negligence and ignorance'.* At the Yards they were employing once more the full complement of workmen without resort to the press-gang or any interference with the work of the ordinary shipbuilding yards. They had contracted for £90,000 worth of goods. By Lady Day 1687, they reckoned, they would be able to set to sea, if need be, a fleet of sixty-five vessels, including three 1st rates, seven 2nd rates, twenty-one 3rd rates – that is thirty-one ships of the line – and twenty-five 4th rates. The success of the first stage of their work had exceeded everyone's wildest hopes. It was no wonder that the King praised them. Yet to Pepys' experienced eye it was plain that the bulk of the work was being done by two only of their number, Will Hewer and Anthony Deane. For all his careful choice of them and 'daily eye and hand upon them', the rest, 'what with the laziness of one, the private business or love of pleasure in another, want of method in a third', had already proved themselves little more than passengers.[13]

Possibly the swift success that attended the Special Commission on the Navy had some influence on the royal decision to set up another and more questionable Commission. During the summer of 1686 two great political questions were put to the test – could the King as statutory head of the national Church use his supreme

* *Rawl. MSS. A.* 189, f. 308.

ecclesiastical power to benefit a religion antagonistic to that Church, and could he as ruler of the State use his prerogative to suspend the Law? To attain his ends – the emancipation of the Roman Church in England – he attempted both. Feeling as a Catholic unable to exercise in person the ecclesiastical rights vested in the Crown by the English reformers of the sixteenth century, he resorted to an Ecclesiastical Commission of subservient prelates and lay politicians, presided over by Lord Chancellor Jeffreys, to silence criticism of Rome in the Anglican pulpits. At the same time, by dismissing several of the more independent judges* and replacing them by more complaisant lawyers of his own choosing – one of them, curiously enough, a brother of Milton the poet – and then bringing a test case against a Catholic office-holder who pleaded the royal dispensation for his breach of the Test Act, he secured a judicial *obiter dictum* in favour of his right to dispense with the penal laws against his Catholic subjects.

What King James' Protestant subjects thought of these events was becoming every day more clear. The Judges on circuit were received with conspicuous coldness by the Anglican gentry, while the Catholic chapels of the foreign ambassadors were insulted by the mob. At one of these the hot-headed apprentices pulled down a cross and, affixing it to the nearest pump, paid mock obeisance to it. They would have no wooden gods worshipped in their city, they cried, as they laughed and hallooed around it. And when the flustered Lord Mayor arrived to restore the peace, he was greeted with scornful shouts of 'What! is the Lord Mayor of London come to preach up Popery!' It made things very awkward for the authorities.[14]

Through these gathering clouds, Pepys pursued the tenor of his way – a very great man. His power was patent to all, and it was not the less respected because he scrupulously refrained from using it in whatever did not concern his own business. In the Navy and all that appertained to it his word was law. His influence was exercised in a thousand unobtrusive ways, and nearly always in useful or kindly ones, whether it was to get the Astronomer Royal to defend a treatise on Navigation that was being unjustly criticized, or to secure the payment of past debts to the half-ruined Victualler, Sir Dennis

* 'Our Judges sit very loosely upon their benches.' April 17th, 1686. *Ellis Correspondence* i, 104.

Gauden, or to champion, at Mary Evelyn's request, the cause of a too blunt tarpaulin captain who had fallen foul of a Court lady while transporting her home from her husband's embassy in Constantinople. 'But this mishap', Pepys warned Captain Fowler after he had secured the King's pardon for him, 'you will not be able to avoid no more than anybody else that has a quarrel with a fair lady, that her report will prevail among the ladies, whatever it does elsewhere. As an instance of which you must know that my Lady Trumbull has had such impressions made upon her concerning you from the account she has met with of your goodness knows what usage to my Lady Soames, that you may as well expect to persuade a child to meet a bulbeggar in the dark as my Lady Trumbull to venture herself in a ship with Captain Fowler. So that the King has been prevailed withal to appoint another ship for that voyage and (as far as I can judge) I don't think you have any reason to be sorry for it, nor consequently (seeing that it is over) to give yourself any more care about the differences between my Lady Soames and you, the King not having been pleased upon all this noise to express any change of his opinion touching your capacity of serving him as a seaman. And for a courtier I don't think he ever took you for any or thought the worse of you for not being one.'* It was the wife of Pepys' old Tangier acquaintance, the timorous Doctor, now knighted and made English Ambassador to the Ottoman Porte, who was so reluctant to entrust herself to the honest captain.[15]

Not that Pepys, though ready to overlook the lack of a courtier's gallantry in another, was ungallant himself. One of his many minor acts of kindness that year was to place a yacht at the disposal of Nell Gwynne, now fallen from her former state and fast nearing her end. And he was both a courtier and a virtuoso. He corresponded with Sir Christopher Wren about an old sail which he lent to help his friend Signor Verrio paint the ceiling of the Chapel Royal,† and took a great deal of trouble to procure specimens of the vegetables and plants of New England to please that prince of gardeners, John Evelyn.[16]

As in the past Pepys' influence was at the disposal of his friends and relations in the Service, provided always that they merited it.

* S. P. to Capt. T. Fowler, Dec. 22nd, 1686. *Pepysian MSS., Adm. Letters* xii, 406–7.
† He was careful to choose one that would 'not be at all the worse . . . by its being spotted or smeared with the painter's oil colours'. *Pepysian MSS., Adm. Letters* xii, 244.

That, however, was essential: no degree of kinship could excuse a breach of duty. When his humble cousin, Thomas Alcock, carpenter of the *Elizabeth*, was accused – it transpired falsely – of embezzlement, the grim Admiralty Secretary let his superior know: 'by God's grace if you find the least umbrage of a miscarriage of the same kind in him he shall soon make a vacancy instead of filling one'. In the winter of 1686–7, he had three youthful protégés at sea, Samuel Jackson, young Holmes, now in the East Indies, and Peter Skinner. The last, who was master of the same flowery pen as his elder brother, was always thanking his patron for his favours. They included, it appeared, not only instruction in navigation, but a view of the world and Captain Fowler's fatherly chastisements: 'I desire your Honour's excuse for the weakness of so green a youth, . . . but hope time and your Honour's patronage and encouragement will spring forth a more fragrant fruit in him.' Pepys' experience of Mary Skinner's feckless brethren can hardly have encouraged him to share these hopes.[17]

His other and younger nephew, John Jackson, now aged 15, was not intended for the sea. In June 1686 Pepys entered him as a Pensioner of Magdalene College, Cambridge, under the tutorship of Mr Millington – an act of piety which the Master of the College gratefully described in a letter of appreciation as 'crediting us with the education of your nephew'. John Jackson himself paid tribute to his uncle's kindness in a Latin epistle written in a large flowing hand beginning '*Vir Noblissime et Amplissime!*' The reports of him were most satisfactory: 'innocent, modest and diligent', was the Master's exordium, while his tutor described him as 'very tractable and docile, endued with solid parts and good memory'. The Jackson estates at Ellington still occupied a good deal of Pepys' scanty leisure: in November 1686 some of the leases fell in and he was asked by Peterhouse, the landlords, whether he wished to renew them. It was characteristic of his method of evading inconvenient issues that he delayed for so unconscionable a time before committing himself to a definite answer that the college was driven to expostulate.*[18]

---

* 'The 18th of the last I writ to desire you to write your mind to the College about Ellington lease, but hearing nothing since, I fear that might fall short, which makes me give you the trouble of this, the Master and Fellows daily expecting your resolution. £500 will be the least they will take. This is all . . .' W. Spenser, Bursar of Peterhouse, to S. Pepys, *circa* January 8th, 1687. (The letter is undated, but bears a London postmark of Jan. 10th.) *Rawl. MSS. A.* 189, ff. 302–3.

As though the concerns of his own younger kin were not trouble enough, Pepys continued to care for the children of his friends. When Ned Southwell finished his education in London at Christmas, Sir Robert, his father, wrote gratefully from King's Weston to his old acquaintance and fellow civil servant thanking him for all the wise and loving service he had done the boy: 'I do acknowledge them to be very many and more perhaps than you think I know.' And thereafter Pepys followed his pupil's career with eager interest. 'If country wishes and country gratitude could do you any good', Sir Robert told him, 'the young man and I will be answerable for your welfare. He is going to Oxford till Michaelmas next, having met with a tutor to our mind who then intends to leave the place. 'Tis one Mr Lane of Merton College who intends to follow the Civil Law and in the interim to pour in logic as fast as his disciple can swallow. From thence I intend him for Lincoln's Inn and to take his fortune in the Law. I had thoughts of travel and preparations for the like service his father trod. But the ground being grown too slippery . . . , let us venture him into Westminster Hall, where the cats fall always on their legs.'*[19]

The slippery ground to which Southwell referred so ominously was caused by the increasing tempo of the King's religious policy. Determined to emancipate his Catholic subjects at the earliest possible moment, and believing compromise to be weakness and weakness ruin, James was now proceeding ever more swiftly down the perilous path of dismissing his Anglican and high tory Ministers and replacing them by those – the representatives of a tiny minority – who shared his desire for toleration. In the autumn five Catholic peers, who had suffered with him under the Popish Terror, were admitted to the Privy Council. At Christmas the champion of the cause of Anglican exclusiveness, Lord Treasurer Rochester, was given the option of entering the Catholic communion or laying downt the white staff. He chose the latter, and the Treasury, like the Navy and the Church, was put into Commission with a Catholic, Lord Belasyse, among its members. The King explained to his brother-in-law that it was not lack of trust or of gratitude that caused him to dismiss him, but the impossibility of carrying through his policy of suspending the Test Act and the oaths of religious

* Sir R. Southwell to S. P., Jan. 15th, 1687. *Rawl. MSS. A.* 189, f. 331.

conformity under a Minister who regarded their continued existence as the keystone of national polity.

To the ordinary Anglican loyalist it seemed as if the solid earth was crumbling away. 'I could not have believed', wrote Evelyn who watched the Jesuits in their rich copes officiating at the altar at Whitehall, 'I should ever have seen such things in the King of England's Palace, after it had pleased God to enlighten this nation.' A month later, in the January of 1687, the good man was in despair at what he saw: 'Popish Justices of the Peace established in all counties, of the meanest of the people; Judges ignorant of the Law and perverting it – so furiously do the Jesuits drive, and even compelling Princes to violent courses and destruction of an excellent government both in Church and State . . . The Lord Jesus defend his little flock, and preserve this threatened church and nation!'[20]

9

His Orders Hold

'So this man – prescient to ensure,
(Since even now his orders hold)
A little state might ride secure
At sea, from foes her sloth made bold.'
Kipling, *Pepys Tercentenary Poem.*

The common people had a ruder way of expressing their disgust.
When a new Catholic chapel was opened in the City and, in defiance
of law, thrown open to all and sundry, the Lord Mayor, fearing the
wrath of the London mob, which, as a contemporary put it, had 'as
weak a pretence to prudence upon such occasions as any mobile in
the world', sent his officers to lock the doors. For this he received a
public reprimand in the Council, and the chapel was reopened
under protection of the Militia. Whereupon there appeared on
Sunday in time of service 'a heedless pretence' who stood about the
place, we are told, 'laughing and staring. An officer bade him go out
since he appeared not by his behaviour to be of that religion. He said
he would not go out, and if they said much to him, he would break
their crosses and juggling-boxes down, whereupon a riot seemed to
form.' The interrupter without difficulty evaded the half-hearted
attempts of the authorities to arrest him, and, lying in wait after
service for the priest, gave him a thrashing and threw him into the
gutter. And though the Lord Mayor was brought again before King
and Council and the City threatened with military occupation if it
could not keep the peace better, it made no difference to the attitude
of the untutored populace. For the rude and valiant natives of this
intolerant island were clearly of the opinion that the Bishop of Rome
had no jurisdiction in the realm of England.[1]

This was the period of what became known as 'closeting', when
the King in his zeal made a practice of withdrawing into his private
closet with the functionaries of Church and State, and there frankly
discussing with them, high and low alike, his revolutionary plans for
equalizing all creeds before the Law. If they replied that their
scruples must prevent them from obeying the royal will in a policy

directed towards removing the penal laws and the oaths of conformity, they were told that the state of their health or the King's service necessitated their retirement. Pepys, who was never a zealot for any one creed or dogma and whose own sufferings under persecution had given him views on toleration far in advance of those of most of his contemporaries, had no quarrel with his sovereign's desire to end the era of persecution. He was only restrained by his sense of caution. But as it was not his way to allow prudential motives to interfere with the discharge of his official duties, and as he never meddled in politics outside his own department, he remained at his post, advising his master in all matters appertaining to the sea and keeping quietly outside the little inner ring of zealots and careerists who, under Father Petre and Lord Sunderland, were egging on the King in his desperate race to jostle his subjects out of their deepest prejudices and habits of thought.

To those of his fellow officials whose religious views or fears disabled them from accepting the course of events with his own calm detachment, Pepys extended all the help he was able. When his colleague, Sir Phineas Pett, was threatened with the withdrawal of the royal support at the forthcoming parliamentary election, he boldly stood up for him at the next Cabinet meeting. And his influence was such that he was able to quiet his Majesty's scruples as to Pett's ability to serve him. It was this generous and Christian readiness to use his hard-earned influence not to advance himself further but to help those who were in the shadow that caused him to be solicited so often in this troubled time. Sir Matthew Andrews, his fellow Governor of Christ's Hospital, turned out of the Commission of Peace after nineteen years' service, and Captain Langley, deprived of the Mayoralty of Harwich, were among the many who sought his aid.[2]

Early in the New Year a more serious offender against the overriding royal will wrote to Pepys in a sad dilemma. It was his old red-nosed friend, Dr Peachell, Master of Magdalene, Cambridge, who had had the misfortune to be chosen Vice-Chancellor at the very moment that the King had resolved to apply his dispensing power to the Universities in order to secure the admission of deserving Catholics to Fellowships and degrees. As Oxford and Cambridge were the corner-stones of the Anglican hierarchy and the exclusive nurseries of those who moulded public opinion from the pulpit, this was a serious matter. In an agony of mind poor Peachell related what had happened: how the King had been pleased to direct a letter to him as Vice-Chancellor to admit one Francis Alban, a Benedictine monk, without administering the statutory oaths; how, unable to decide whether it was better to disobey the King's letter or his laws, he had prayed God to direct, sanctify and govern him in the ways of His higher laws. For a smack of the old pre-Restoration piety of phrase still hung about Peachell for all his love of the bottle. Now, feeling it 'unmannerly to importune his Sacred Majesty' further and 'strain his friends against the grain', he had decided to obey his conscience, incur the King's displeasure and cast himself upon his princely clemency.

But such martyrdom did not come easily to the good Doctor. 'Worthy Sir,' he told his old pupil, ''tis extraordinary distress and affliction to me after so much endeavour and affection to his Royal person, Crown and Succession, I should at last by the Providence of God be exposed to his displeasure. But I must commit myself to the great God and my dread Sovereign, the Law and my friends, none of which I would have hurt for my sake, but desire all favour and help they think me capable of without hurting themselves. For if I do ill, 'tis not out of malice but fear of the last judgment, and at the worst through involuntary mistake. Sir, I am sorry I have occasion to give you this information and trouble. But you will pardon, I hope, if you cannot help.'[3]

Pepys could not help. But when Peachell came to London in the spring to explain his refusal to the Ecclesiastical Commissioners, he refused to cold-shoulder him and earned the unhappy man's gratitude for the frank and friendly way with which, when all were shunning him, he greeted him in the royal Withdrawing Room. But more than that he could not do. Deprived of his Vice-Chancellorship, suspended from his Mastership, Peachell was dismissed by Lord Chancellor Jeffreys with a terrifying admonition 'to go away and sin no more'.[4]

'The Laws of the Land and the oaths we lie under are the fences of God's church and religion,' Peachell had written in his agony, 'and I cannot suffer myself to be made an instrument to pull down those fences.'* Many an honest Englishman felt the same. But when in the

---

* Dr J. Peachell to S. P., April 23rd, 1687. *Rawl. MSS. A.* 189, f. 145.

spring of 1687, the godless Rear-Admiral of England, Arthur
Herbert, pleaded his conscience as a reason for refusing to promise
the King his support for his attack on the Test Act, it was plain to
the discerning that the time had been reached when it was no longer
to a prudent man's advantage to obey the King. But possibly
Herbert's dismissal was the result not so much of his hitherto
unsuspected religious scruples as of Pepys' report on his financial
misconduct during his Mediterranean command. It appeared that
he owed the Treasury over £4000 and was entirely unable to account
for the slaves whom he had starved and sold.* And a further
enquiry, instigated by the King, had been ordered into his accounts
as Master of the Robes.[5]

It is just possible that in this uncertain time Pepys may have toyed
with the idea of apostasy. Among his friends were such devoted
Catholics as Lady Throgmorton and Lady Tuke, and at the Pearses'
house he sometimes used to meet the learned Dr Philip Ellis,† who
later became Roman Catholic Bishop of Aureopolis and the King's
Agent at Rome. But his sympathy for his royal master's professed
ideal of religious toleration needs no such improbable supposition to
explain it. It was in keeping with the whole bent of his mature mind.
Among Pepys' papers of this year are some private theological
writings of Sir William Petty, procured for him by his friend
Southwell, and to which we know that he attached particular
importance. They incline towards freedom of conscience and absolute equality for all Christian sects before the Law. 'As to con-
troversies,' ran a passage in one of them, 'he thinketh it safe and
decent to hearken to them who sit in Moses' chair, and that every
soul be subject to the higher powers, and that two or three met
together in the name of God do make a competent church, and that
Vox populi is *Vox Dei*.' It is not unreasonable to suppose that these
were also the religious views which Pepys in his middle-age, and
after his long and harsh experience, had come to accept. They are
certainly not the tenets of the Catholic Church. But they tally almost
exactly with certain of those which Pepys' old acquaintance of
Seething Lane days, William Penn the Quaker, now in high favour

_____

* *Rawl. MSS. A.* 177, ff. 140–1.

† Ellis' relations were always expecting to see him with 'some badge of a more
eminent character, as a gold cross before or scarlet skull-cap behind'. *Ellis Correspondence* I, 239.

at Court and unworthily suspected of popery elsewhere, was so industriously preaching to an unconverted England. They are those which future generations have come to accept as rational and wise.[6]

That Pepys, therefore, raised no conscientious opposition to the King's policy, however ill-timed he may have thought it, and that he entertained at his house men who did their best to further it like the time-serving Bishop Cartwright of Chester, is no proof, as some have supposed, of lack of courage or religious conviction on his part. It is almost certain that he believed his master's immediate and declared object to be a right one, though he may well have doubted the practicability of his methods.[7]

Nor can fear of losing his post have been any reason for his acquiescence, for in the winter of 1686/7 he was far from well, believed a collapse of his over-taxed powers imminent and looked forward to an early release from office. Repeated pains in his kidneys made him afraid of a return of his old disease, the stone. A little before Christmas he told Balty not to rely on his continuance in high place for much longer. 'It was not without very much ground that in one of my late letters of general advice to you, I cautioned you against depending upon any support much longer from me, I then feeling what I now cannot hide; I mean that pain which I at this time labour under (night and day) from a new stone lodged in my kidneys and an ulcer attending it, with a general decay of my stomach and strength that cannot be played with long. Nor am I solicitous that it should.' And he cautioned his brother-in-law to beware of improvidence, lest the long friendship he had shown him should be wasted and his family be left once more at the mercy of a cruel world.[8]

Pepys' fears for his health proved for the present groundless. The stone subsided, and during the next two years he suffered from little more than a rheumaticky shoulder and the old trouble with his eyes. But his fears of Balty's reckless extravagance were speedily justified. Before the end of January he had to intervene to save him from arrest at the suit of a lady creditor who was dunning him on the score of a fine saddle long unpaid for. In his reply to Pepys' letter of reproach, Balty paid an eloquent tribute to what he called his 'great goodness and kindness in stopping the clamours of that nasty woman about the saddle' but dismissed it none the less as a small matter, to be explained by his large family, his former

unemployment 'and many other grievous causes'. 'It is therefore', he
went on, 'extreme grievous to me to have from such a blessed person
such an expression as in the beginning of your said letter . . . And
although you are pleased to say that you hear of my continued
extravagant expenses, I hope it is but the effect of your generous and
kind conjectures, being confident that . . . none but the blackest
envy and malice (on which curses attend) can accuse me.'*

Pepys replied with sorrowful dignity. His brother-in-law, he well
knew, was incorrigible:

Brother,
I have received your letter of the 24th and have said my say. Upon your
own head be it if in deceiving me you at length find the effect of it to the ruin
of your family. I am sure I have nothing to lead me to these jealousies
concerning your conduct but my fears on their and your behalf . . . Nor have
I my information but from them that bear you good will; besides that your
running on the score of this saddle seems very little to consist with the good
husbandry you would be thought to walk by. But I have done; and shall be
glad to see you, and without anger as you call it, though it deserves another
name; it is being too painful a thing to write at all, and much more upon a
subject so unpleasant to me as this is.†[9]

Only a fortnight after the despatch of this solemn document Pepys
learnt from Balty's clerk that his master was in trouble again. This
time it was undeserved misfortune. 'This afternoon about one, his
lady fell in travail, and was about two delivered of a son; but the
birth of the child became the death of the mother, for within a
quarter of an hour after, her soul expired; and hath left a husband
and numerous family bleeding under (I think) the saddest accents of
sorrow I ever saw.' The poor, neglected woman had had her revenge
at last.

Pepys comforted his brother-in-law by return with the stately
condolences of the seventeenth century. He took the occasion to add
some further good counsel, which Balty's clerk, who lacked nothing
of his employer's eloquence, acknowledged with fitting humility and
gratitude. 'He returns your Honour millions of thanks for your great
kindness and generous favours . . . which he will own to his life's end
and endeavour strictly to observe and obey those excellent advises

* B. St Michel to S. P., Jan. 24th, 1687. *Rawl. MSS. A.* 189, ff. 224–5.
† S. P. to B. St Michel, Jan. 27th, 1687. *Rawl. MSS. A.* 189, f. 225.

you are pleased to administer; which having said, a deluge of tears again overwhelming him, could add no more.' Balty himself was able to write a few days later; he should, he assured his protector, to his life's end study to obey his commands and follow every one of his counsels. 'I am, Sir, stopped with a torrent of sorrowful lamentation, for, oh God, I have lost, oh I have lost such a loss that no man is or can be sensible but myself. I have lost my wife, Sir, I have lost my wife; and such a wife, as your Honour knows, has (may be) not left her fellow.'* Poor Balty's recognition of the fact seemed a little tardy.[10]

February 1687 saw another of Pepys' friends in trouble – not from the loss of a wife but from taking one. Sir Samuel Morland, who was wont to alleviate his recurrent insolvency by the rapidity with which he invented some new wonder – his latest was a naval gun-carriage – suddenly embarked with reckless haste on a novel method of bettering his condition. 'Being', he told Pepys, 'almost distracted for want of monies, my private creditors tormenting me from morning to night and some of them threatening me with a prison . . . there came a certain person to me whom I had relieved in a starving condition and for whom I had done a thousand kindnesses, who pretended in gratitude to help me to a wife who was a very virtuous, pious and sweet dispositioned lady and an heiress who had £500 p.a. in land of inheritance and £4000 in ready money, with the interest since 9 years, besides a mortgage upon £300 p.a. more, with plate, jewels, etc.' This catalogue of charms turned out a complete fraud, for the lady proved no better than the generality of her kind and, indeed, rather worse, for besides being penniless she was a whore and diseased at that. All this, as he poured it out in his letter to his worldly-wise friend at the Admiralty, he had discovered too late: by charms or witchcraft he had been 'led as a fool to the stocks and married a coachman's daughter, not worth a shilling and one who about nine months since was brought to bed of a bastard'.

Thus, in addition to being practically bankrupt, poor Morland had become the jest of London. Having laid his sad case before the Spiritual Court, he begged Pepys for the sake of old acquaintance and Christian charity to speak to the King and get him to move his proctor on his behalf. 'A flood of tears blind my eyes and I can write no more.'[11]

---

* B. St Michel to S. P., Feb. 14th, 1687. *Rawl. MSS. A.* 189, f. 316.

Pepys did what he could and consulted the Judge of the Admiralty Court. But he found that the opinion of the town was against his foolish tutor, and that there was little chance of finding any legal ground for nullity. Six months later, in November 1687, Morland was besieged in the poor hut in which he sheltered near Hyde Park gate by 'rude fellows' with orders from his wife's proctors to take him alive or dead. In the following spring he was being dogged by bailiffs on the score of her debts. Throughout the sordid affair Morland turned perpetually to Pepys to help him, until the lady's brazen and open adultery at last gave him the freedom of divorce.[12]

Morland was far from being the only person who came to Pepys for help. Some of the greatest in England did so. The University of Cambridge, threatened with the embarrassment and scandal of a State lottery in the town, besought his intervention: so did Oxford when the Stationers' Company tried to deprive it of its ancient privilege of printing Bibles. Nor did they appeal in vain. In such matters the despotism of King James could generally be tempered a little by the good sense of his friend, the Secretary of the Admiralty. Sir Robert Southwell, at whose instance Pepys secured the release of a poor Huguenot seaman from a French galley, thought him the most powerful man in England, 'and perhaps in the world', he added, 'when I see who, against his will, you could force to be guilty of one good action. Whether Father le Chaise' – King Louis' Confessor – 'will not stick on your skirts for this odd prank, I leave you to consider.'[13]

His old companion and rival, John Creed, desiring to be an Elder Brother of Trinity House;* Lord Chancellor Jeffreys, who signed himself his most entire affectionate friend and servant and wanted a post for a protégé; Dr Mills in search of a Prebendal stall; Evelyn troubled by the smell of the mud in the Deptford docks; Sir William Petty anxious for the royal sanction for the publication of his studies on statistics and political economy, all turned to Pepys. 'I thank God', was Petty's grateful verdict, 'that his Majesty appointed you

---

* 'It coming with some reluctancy into my mind that I am still (almost to ridiculousness in so much seniorities) but a younger brother in Trinity House, I soon thought of one that could with great ease remedy it.' J. Creed to S. P., April 1687. *Rawl. MSS. A.* 189, f. 98.

to examine these my opinions.'* When Bolingbroke became First Lord of the Treasury the ladies of Covent Garden are said to have cried out in jubilation, 'Five thousand a year, girls, and all for us!' Learned men had similar reason to rejoice when Pepys was in power. Dr Nathaniel Vincent had only to ask to receive twenty-five guineas that he might enrich his 'little study' with an expensive work of reference. Even a female poet – a poor widow – who enclosed her verses and a litany of her wants† did not go away empty. And the Fellows of his old College at their audit dinner feasted by Mr Pepys' grace on a doe from the royal forests.[14]

The learned recompensed the great Secretary by flattering him. More than one author that year dedicated his book to him – Dr Richard Cumberland his work on Jewish Measures, charmingly inscribed 'for that good affection being begun in your youth thirty years ago in Magdalene College', Captain Greenville Collins his Chart of Harwich and its adjacent coasts, Nathaniel Vincent his *Conjectura Nautica* and Francis Willoughby his *Historia Piscium*. As President of the Royal Society Pepys bore the cost of sixty of the plates of this last work, and the Society graciously ordered 'that a Book of Fishes of the best paper, curiously bound in Turkey leather, likewise five others bound also' should be presented to him. (One of them he sent to his old tutor, Mr Hill, in Holland.) And the greatest of all seventeenth-century scientific works, Mr Newton's *Principia*, went out to an awed but puzzled world with his name as *ex officio* licenser, on its title page:

Imprimatur, S. Pepys, Reg. Soc. Praeses. Julii 5 1686[15]

Yet Pepys was greatest by far in his capacity as plain Secretary of the Admiralty. Thence all his honours sprang. What he had won by virtue of penmanship, method and precedent he continued to maintain by these weapons. Among certain notes in his own hand, written about this date and entitled 'Momentalls', is an entry which showed how zealous he still was to enhance the stature of his office:

* 'The matters pretend good to all the King's subjects and the means propounded are of an high extraordinary nature, and therefore should be exposed to public view . . . If you cannot understand them alone, they are not fit for the public and must be made plainer.' Sir W. Petty to S. P., Sept. 8th, 1687. *Rawl. MSS. A.* 189, f. 19.

† 'And pardon this from one who being like one near drownding catches at the most likeliest support to convey me to shore.' Anne Murcott to S. P., May 7th, 1687. *Rawl. MSS. A.* 189, ff. 49–51.

Lord Admiral's Duty.
  Secretary Admiralty and his office to be certain, depending on the Crown, not the Admiral, and his work and duty adjusted.*

Nor would he tolerate any suggestion that he did not personally supervise the work of his office even in its most minute part. When at the end of 1686 one of his senior clerks, Walbanke, died, and his old friend, Mrs Pearse, the Surgeon-General's wife, sought the vacant post for her son, Pepys addressed to that young gentleman a letter which summarized his reaction to any suggestion that one of his subordinates could in the smallest degree be indispensable. Not having seen the light before, it is worth perusal as a perfect expression of that high bureaucratic pride which was so characteristic a part of Pepys' legacy to the Civil Service of his country:

Mr Pearse,
  Pray (whatever be the issue of your present desire) don't forget the right you have to be always welcome to me . . . Wherefore don't any more treat me as you have done now at that distance that does not become me to receive from one that I esteem so nearly as I do you.
  . . . I am far from forgetting the proposition made earlily to me by my excellent Lady, your mother . . . in prospect of Mr Walbanke's death. Nor have I escaped many solicitations . . . since yesterday morning, not only from the Navy Office but from potent hands at Court, both the one and the other grounded upon a mistake people had been led into of Mr Walbanke's mighty sufficiences by his being admitted to be indeed the do-all to the late Commissioners at Derby House. Whereas I never thought fit to rely on his clerkship for the drawing up of one letter or paper of moment in my life, nor have felt any want of him during his long absence, poor man, by sickness at a time wherein matters of more importance to the Crown have been transacted in reference to the Navy than ever passed this office since England had a Navy. Not that he wanted talents very useful in their kind relating to the keeping of the books, marshalling the papers and examining of passes and divers other things wherein time only had made him fully master of the methods of the office, and he his brother by his continually employing him for many years under him. So that the affairs of this office are no more affected by his death than they would, were he still alive or had never been born.†[16]

Every month that Pepys sat in his office at York Buildings frowning his disapproval at any deviation from his rules – his

* *Rawl. MSS. A.* 171, f. 89.
  † S. P. to J. Pearse junior, Dec. 16th, 1686. *Rawl. MSS. A.* 189, ff. 261–3.

portrait painted about this time by Godfrey Kneller reveals the frown as an apparently permanent feature of his expression* – those rules became more firmly established in the professional consciousness and habitude of the Service. Every captain at his potent bidding now sent to the Admiralty before each voyage his Certificate of Readiness for Sea, at each port of call his Abstracts and when the voyage was over his Journal. For only when these were received regularly were wages and allowances paid. After a while observance of these formalities began to become second nature – the administrative and liturgical ritual, as it were, of the Navy.[17]

Like the men of the past who founded the great monastic orders whose history he so loved to study in his leisure, Pepys' plan was to make a rule for all things, great or small. From that unresting brain came a perpetual flow of rules of every kind: for a clear method of dividing prizes between officers and seamen, for pensioning naval widows and orphans,† for regulating the issue of rum and brandy. A rule now became sacred because it was a rule and not merely on account of its intrinsic importance; it was only to be broken when the unforeseeable necessity of the King's Service made it imperative to do so. Its wisdom was not to be called in question.

Nor was its enforcement by Pepys' office to be regarded as a matter of personal grievance or affront by those holding the King's commission. 'Sir,' he wrote to the captain of the *Assistance*, who had complained about his allotment of guns, 'I have received yours of the 6th inst. And though it be what nothing but your own saying so would have made me believe, yet because you have said it, I will believe that you did not know there was any Establishment of Guns in the Navy, that the number and nature thereof to each ship were not reduced under a known and regular Establishment. But I must beg you to alter your mind so far concerning me as to think that I can do my duty to the King in taking notice (as he both commands and expects it from me) of all things wherein the discipline and good order of his Navy is concerned, without the least want of good will and respect to the persons to whom the same relates. This, I assure

* Yet in a painting of him in my possession sent to Sir William Booth in the closing years of Pepys' life, the frown has vanished and the softer lines of youth have revived in the mellow twilight of retirement.

† In all wars, and not merely, as formerly, in those against the Dutch and Algerines. *Pepysian MSS., Adm. Letters* xiv, 2, 27, 53.

you, is true in your particular case, to whom I will be found so on all occasions. And I am sure I have been as forward to do all offices of kindness as you (by a mighty mistake) would seem, from this honest freedom of mine in the execution of my duty to the King, to collect the contrary. Which if everybody should do, to whom on like occasions I never fail to exercise the same necessary and friendly liberty, I should have a weight upon me much less easy to bear than all the work of my office besides.'* For step by step in days when gentlemen drew their swords at a verbal slight, Pepys had to educate his high-spirited contemporaries in the formalities and ungrateful necessities of official correspondence. He did so with all the courtesy that was compatible with unswerving firmness.[18]

There was no avoiding Mr Pepys' way. If an officer, however highly placed, had occasion to come up to town on his private occasions, he must apply to the Admiralty for the King's formal consent.† He was expected to do so in a set petition, stating the exact reasons for which leave was needed and the number of days required. It all sounds so natural and normal to us: it did not seem so to the men of that time. Once a captain, unaccustomed to the new regime, arrived unexpectedly in the Downs from the West Indies, having abandoned his station in a pet after a quarrel with the Governor of one of the islands. The letter in which Pepys informed the offender of his horror and of the impending certainty of an enquiry and court-martial is a little epistolary masterpiece:

Sir,
    I have received yours of the 2nd inst. from the Downs, and cannot but congratulate you your safe arrival there with one of his Majesty's ships, though I must own myself wonderfully surprised with the tidings of your being there. Nor is his Majesty himself (to whom I immediately communicated it) less earnest to know the true grounds of it, which both for his satisfaction and your own justification it will be necessary that you enable me without delay to give him. For the coming home of a ship from a station to which she was purposely and at great charge sent . . . will necessarily call for some good reasons to justify it . . . His Majesty has been pleased to tell

---

    * S. P. to Capt. Wright, Aug. 9th, 1687. *Pepysian MSS., Adm. Letters* xiii, 243.
    † 'Sir. I received yours of the 9th inst., and did immediately move his Majesty in your desires herein for leave to continue in town ten days longer on score of your health, which he was very graciously pleased to grant, as you will find by the enclosed warrant. To which, praying you to be referred, I remain, Your most humble servant, S. P.' S. P. to Sir R. Strickland, March 12th, 1687. *Pepysian MSS., Adm. Letters* xiii, 6.

me that he will have the matter fully enquired into, as becomes a proceeding extraordinary . . .*

'I thank you', he added, 'for the account you give me of that which you call a fiery vapour falling upon you, the effects whereof are very wonderful and indeed not at all less surprising than your being here to relate them.' None knew better than Pepys how to rebuke ignorant presumption with a velvet touch.[19]

He knew, too, how to rebuke it in the great. The rules he enforced to preserve the respect due to the King's flag were flaunted in the spring of 1687 by the papist Sir Roger Strickland, who had now succeeded Herbert as the royal favourite in the Service. With the high temper of his ancient race, Strickland had set his heart on flying a Vice-Admiral's flag during a voyage to the Mediterranean in which he was acting as second-in-command to the young Duke of Grafton, and this though only a small force of frigates was employed. This Pepys sternly opposed until he learnt that the King in a weak moment had been induced by Strickland's importunity to promise it. He thereupon withdrew his opposition but wrote that officer such a letter with the coveted warrant as must have turned his triumph to rage:

I am loath it should be thought possible that any degree of friendship or other consideration whatever could prevail with me to mislead his Majesty by one word of mine to the granting a thing so extraordinary, so irregular, and unjustified by any practice past, and unlikely to be ever imitated in time to come, as this which you have thus contended for of having two of the top flags of England exposed to sea in view of the two greatest rivals of England for Sea Dominion and Glory (I mean the Dutch and French) with no better provision for supporting the honour thereof than six ships, and two of them such as carry not above 190 men and 54 guns between them. And this too obtained through mere force of importunity by one who but in September last charged Captain Priestman with turning the King's flag into ridicule in putting up but an unusual swallow-tailed pendant.

Lest the royal favourite should charge him with disloyalty to his master's wishes, the uncompromising Secretary went on: 'However, as much as I do with this my usual plainness unbespeak the thanks you might otherwise conceive due to me on this occasion' – one

* S. P. to Capt. St Loe of the *Dartmouth*, March 22nd, 1687. *Pepysian MSS.*, *Adm. Letters* XIII, 22–3.

fancies that Pepys must have smiled as he postulated this improbable contingency – 'this much I shall take to myself of the merit of having done you justice therein, that from the instant his Majesty was first pleased to tell me of the promise he had been prevailed with to make you touching the Flag, showing me at the same time his being not at all less sensible than myself of the irregularity of the thing so granted, I have never made it my part officiously to inculcate anything to him that might interrupt the resolution he had thus taken in your favour, as well remembering that his Majesty is master of his own orders and can as well dispense with as make them and, above all, that it is a virtue much more becoming a Prince to do violence to himself by dispensing with an order than grieve a good servant by a breach of a promise.'* And he ended this stinging communication by advising Strickland to thank the King for the privilege but to refrain from using it.[20]

The same jealous vigilance for the King's honour characterizes Pepys' correspondence in another much-disputed matter – the immunity of naval officers and officials from arrest for debt. He would neither allow the King's prerogative to be overridden by insolent bailiffs and creditors, whom in any case of contempt he summoned to York Buildings to explain themselves, nor his justice to be called in question by any avoidance by public servants of their private liabilities. Those who tried to do so were quickly undeceived, their papers being endorsed by a curt 'Left to the Law' in the Secretary's hand. Nor would he tolerate in the Navy the practice, tacitly allowed in every other branch of the public service, of payments by incoming holders of offices to their predecessors. He himself, he once stated, might have made £40,000 by such an abuse of the King's favour, and he would never concur in suffering others to do what nothing could tempt him to do himself.[21]

For the essence of Pepys' rules was that no one was allowed to break them. One of his finest letters of this period is that to the two naval officers he most cared for and trusted, Sir John Berry and Sir John Narbrough, reproaching them for having given an old friend a Lieutenant's Commission contrary to the regulations laid down in his Establishment of 1677.† Least of all would he allow any

---

* S. P. to Sir R. Strickland, July 5th, 1687. *Pepysian MSS., Adm. Letters* XIII, 276–9.
† July 21st, 1687. *Pepysian MSS., Adm. Letters* XIII, 205. See Appendix A.

deviation in his own office from the rectitude he enforced on the Service. When in the summer of 1687 his favourite clerk and disciple, Josiah Burchett, confidant and companion of all his recent journeys and an inmate of his household, offended against his stern regimen, he was summarily dismissed. Nor could all Burchett's repeated entreaties turn Mr Secretary's heart. 'I know well enough', the young penitent sadly confessed, 'that whatever you do, you do by the rules of justice.'* Sometimes it seemed to those about him that this great man was too severe and unbending.[22]

But Pepys' task was to build a vessel stout enough to withstand the changing waves of individual feeling. And all its hundred and one urgent needs of the moment, as well as its greater ones of the future, were his care. His lot it was to send out squadrons and appoint captains, to confer with the Navy Office and supervise the Special Commissioners, to enquire into complaints and punish offenders, to reward the diligent and arbitrate in disputes. The applications for yacht-passage across the Channel, the appointment of properly qualified chaplains to every ship, the leakage of British seamen through the inducement held out to them by the shipping agents of foreign states, were alike his concern. Nothing was too small for his eye. Seventy-six pages of one of his many volumes of administrative papers, now preserved in the Bodleian Library, are concerned with his own personal examination during 1687 of the wrong suffered by the purser of the *Suffolk* at the impetuous hands of the Master Attendant at Chatham, his old acquaintance, Captain Vittles.†[23]

The principal naval events of the year 1687 were the presence of the Algerine fleet in the Channel in June, the Duke of Grafton's voyage to the Mediterranean and the despatch of Sir John Narbrough to the west. The first was occasioned by a naval war between Algiers and England's ancient rivals, the Dutch. The presence off the British coasts of African corsairs, rendered desperate by poverty, caused great anxiety to the government. When they first appeared

---

* J. Burchett to S. P., Aug. 8th, 1687. *Rawl. MSS. A.* 189, f. 1, printed in *Howarth*, 181–2. In after years Burchett was to become what was virtually the first permanent Secretary of the Admiralty, MP for Sandwich, which he represented in Parliament for half a century, and the historian of the Navy.

† *Rawl. MSS. A.* 177, ff. 1–76. The award was promulgated on Jan. 4th, 1688, over two years after Vittles had struck John Trevor over the head with a boat-hook for attempting to go on shore contrary to his orders.

Pepys thought it almost inevitable that some untoward act of 'that heady and faithless people',* as he termed them, would lead to a rupture. Afraid of the loss that would follow to the Levant and Turkey merchants, he warned James Houblon to look to his trading ventures. But by the exercise of considerable tact on the part of all concerned, the danger was averted, though not before British sea-going opinion had been outraged by large numbers of derelict and rifled Dutch ships driving helplessly about the narrow seas. At one time Pepys had had to address a severe rebuke to the officers of Pendennis Castle who, regardless of the treaties with Algiers, seized and jailed the crew and confiscated the powder of an Algerine prize driven into Falmouth by stress of weather.

The most delicate situation of all arose in the middle of June, when Sir Roger Strickland was ordered to sea with a hastily collected squadron to perform the double function of preventing the Algerines from returning with any British subjects who might have been captured from Dutch ships and of enforcing a salute from the French fleet, which was hovering in the Channel under Monsieur de Tourville in search of escaping Huguenots.† For a week or two the country was on the verge of war. Fortunately both tasks were accomplished without resource to blows. It was quite a little triumph. Pepys himself secured the release of some unfortunate French Protestants who had been captured by the Algerines while crossing in a Dutch vessel to Holland. They dared not, he told the Admiralty Judge, claim their privilege as French subjects to secure their release for fear King Louis should compel the Algerine Government to deliver them 'from their captivity in Africa to a more severe one under himself at home'.‡ Pepys even succeeded in persuading his sovereign to stretch the laws of denizenation by claiming them from the Moors as British subjects.[24]

After this unwelcome incursion, the Duke of Grafton, who was about to sail with the new Queen of Portugal to Lisbon, was instructed to extend his voyage into the Mediterranean. The visit of

* S. P. to J. Houblon, June 4th, 1687. *Pepysian MSS., Adm. Letters* xiii, 116–17.

† '... which squadron will I doubt not (with God's assistance) suffice to support his Majesty's honour in these his seas against anything that shall be offered in diminution of it by Monsieur Tourville, it being his Majesty's expectations that his honour be asserted, and is in no doubt but it will effectually be so.' S. P. to Sir R. Strickland, Sunday night, June 12th, 1687. *Pepysian MSS., Adm. Letters* xiii, 136.

‡ S. P. to Sir R. Raines, June 7th, 1687. *Pepysian MSS., Adm. Letters* xiii, 128–9.

a British fleet had a sobering effect on the authorities at Algiers and secured a confirmation of existing treaties. The expedition was chiefly notable for being based strategically on Gibraltar, whence Pepys victualled and controlled England's distant ships. He had some fears lest the place might be taken by the French, who had also established a victualling station there, before his chance should come to seize it for England.[25]

The expedition to the west was of a different kind. For some time past there had been talk of fabulous treasure in a Spanish wreck which had lain for nearly half a century near the shoal of Bahama off the coast of Hispaniola. A small stock-company of Gentlemen Adventurers, including the Duke of Albemarle – son to the stout old fighter of Pepys' youth – and Sir John Narbrough, had sent out two small ships to investigate. Early in June 1687 they returned to England with the first instalment of the treasure amounting to over a quarter of a million – equal in those days to a fifth of the national revenue. Few, if any, like enterprises can ever have yielded so rich a return: it is reckoned that the shareholders received £10,000 for every £100 invested. And the remainder of the treasure was still to be reclaimed. On Tuesday, June 14th, the four chief partners waited on the King and Council in the Treasury Chamber at Windsor, where Pepys in attendance took notes. It was agreed that the government should lend them a fully-manned and equipped frigate for a year and the services of Sir John Narbrough to command it, in return for a fifth of the treasure if under £150,000 and a third should it prove more.*[26]

In the autumn Narbrough sailed for the West Indies. He was followed a few weeks later by the Duke of Albemarle who was sent out as Governor-General of Jamaica to consolidate the trans-Atlantic empire fast forming in these islands and along the eastern shores of North America. Much about the same time Pepys was employed in working out plans for a further western expedition to suppress the English pirates, who despite many efforts to bring them under the heel of authority were still spasmodically terrorizing the Spanish Main and South Seas to the profit of the colonies but the scandal of the civilized world. He reported that a force of five frigates manned by 725 men at an annual cost of £33,930 would be needed if

* *Rawl. MSS. A.* 189, ff. 370–8.

the work was to be done properly.* Many years later he entertained
– with great pleasure – one of the most famous of the pirates whom
he was seeking to destroy as an honoured guest at his house in York
Buildings. From the other side of the globe his correspondents sent
him news of England's growing concerns in India, where a tiny
squadron under his friend Sir John Wyborne was assisting the East
India Company to put down the interlopers.[27]

Though the old problem of money still made itself felt, the mists of
imminent bankruptcy which had darkened the path of every naval
project through all Pepys' twenty-seven years of experience were at
last beginning to lift. Save when a temporary stop was caused by the
change at the Treasury at the beginning of the year, the cash
payments required for the work of the Special Commission continued regularly at the rate of £7000 a week. Early in the year
additional sums of over £40,000 were allowed for new storehouses
and dry-docks at Chatham and Portsmouth. The Navy debt,
reduced by over £300,000, stood in January 1687 at no more than
£171,836. 2s. 9d. The repairs of the battle fleet were pushed rapidly
forward, and during the summer four new frigates were launched.
Soon the country would have a Navy which could bid defiance to,
and perhaps master, any in the world.[28]

* *Rawl. MSS. A.* 198, ff. 15–16.

10

Recreations of a Virtuoso

'We eat with great pleasure, and I enjoyed myself in it with reflections upon the pleasures which I at best can expect, yet not to exceed this; eating in silver plates, and all things mighty rich and handsome about me. A great deal of fine discourse, sitting almost till dark at dinner, and then broke up with great pleasure, especially to myself.' – *Pepys' Diary*, Nov. 28th, 1666.

King James the Conqueror had made up his mind to conquer England. His father had died because he could not make up his mind, and he was not going to fall by the same mistake. His whole life had shown him the advantages of being resolute. He had spent the first years of it in civil war and exile, yet had returned triumphantly with his brother to England without yielding an inch of principle. Later, to the terror of cowards and trimmers, he had openly declared his reconciliation to the Catholic Church and had again refused to compromise, with the result that, after a further period of persecution, proscription and exile, he had seen his enemies defeated and ruined and all that he had so courageously stood for universally acclaimed. Since his accession he had smashed Monmouth, Argyll and the Whigs, had set the Navy on its feet and doubled the size of the army. If the Cavalier Party and the Anglican Church, who had once stood by him, now chose to stand in his way, so much the worse for the Cavalier Party and the Anglican Church.

Protected from the salutary sting of criticism both by his position and the bent of his temperament, and spurred on by his priests and the inexperienced Catholic politicians at his side, James seemed to have no doubts. He had tamed warlike and covenanting Scotland; he could tame England. His third kingdom, Ireland, being predominantly Catholic, needed no taming. The armies he was raising there under the papist Lord Deputy, Tyrconnel, could be used later if any of his English subjects were so foolish as to imitate Monmouth. Right and reason were clearly on his side. As a devout Catholic it was his divine mission to help the faithful men and women who had stood fast by their Faith under the persecutions of the cruel laws which were now administered in his name, to relieve them from humiliating disabilities and to give them their share in the civic privileges of their country. As a just sovereign it was his duty to give all his subjects of whatever creed the right to worship God in their own way and to utilize their talents regardless of discriminating oaths and tests. And if some of them opposed freedom of conscience for their own selfish reasons, he must enforce that freedom.

In the course of the three years of his reign, therefore, the King performed a complete *volte-face*. The Tories and high Churchmen, who before his accession had been his best friends and were now passively resisting his repeated wishes for the abolition of the religious tests, should be given a taste of his displeasure. The persecuted non-conformist minorities whom he had formerly defeated with their aid should be raised from the dust and given executive office with the despised Catholics. The second anniversary of his accession was marked by a widespread pardon of forfeitures and penalties incurred by Dissenters and Whigs, and the promise of liberty of conscience to all. Meanwhile the tory press was muzzled and the chief tory magistrates of London replaced by Whigs and Dissenters. In April, after Parliament had been again prorogued for a further six months, a royal Declaration 'for a general toleration of all religions' was issued, suspending the penal laws and dispensing with the oaths and tests for admission to civil and military office.

Throughout the summer of 1687 the new policy was pursued relentlessly. *Mandamus* letters were sent to both Universities for the admission of papists to degrees and Fellowships: those who opposed the royal will were suspended like the laws. A crop of conversions to the Catholic Faith in high places followed. 'All goes redwise', was the catchword of the hour. The man in the field and the street watched with horror the growing size of the King's army, the great summer camp at Hounslow and the admission of Catholics to high military office. Even the frowning guns of the Tower of London were now placed under the orders of a papist.

Yet so long as the penal laws remained on the statute book, the King was aware that the whole fabric of toleration and religious equality which he was trying to create rested precariously on the royal prerogative. Should anything happen to him, and his Protestant daughter and her sombre Dutch husband inherit his power, the old, harsh laws would again be enforced. If his system was to endure they must be repealed without delay. A tory Parliament had refused to do so, and had since been prorogued. A non-conformist

Parliament might act differently. A non-conformist Parliament there should be.

The closing years of Charles II's reign had shown how easily the electoral machinery of the country could be altered to return a Parliament of a new complexion. The same methods were now employed to reverse the policy of those years and ensure that the electoral corporations, which had returned Whigs in 1681 and Tories in 1685, should in 1688 return a solid *bloc* of enemies to the Anglican monopoly. On July 2nd, 1687, the existing Parliament was dissolved. At the same time steps were taken to replace the tory office-holders in the counties and parliamentary boroughs with new men favourable to the royal policy and to alter the constitution of the electoral corporations. What *Quo Warranto* had done once, *Quo Warranto* should do again.[1]

In the late summer of 1687, the King made a Progress through the western midlands to prepare the ground for the revolution he was planning. He began by a visit to Portsmouth on August 16th. Here Pepys attended him while he inspected fortifications, discussed plans for new forts and tested an engine of Sir Samuel Morland's. Two days later, on his return to London, the Secretary of the Admiralty was summoned to join the Court again at Bath. Hence he accompanied it to Gloucester, where he transacted Admiralty business on the 23rd – Sam Atkins had been left in charge at York Buildings – and on the following day to Worcester.[2]

At this point Pepys' brief part in the royal Progress came to an end. He was probably not sorry, for his chief friends in the place – Dr Reynolds, the Bishop, his 'cousin Nan', wife of the Cavalier Fisher who entertained him,* and the learned Dean, Dr Hickes – being all Tories, were all out of favour. Hickes, who read the King an Address in the name of the Dean and Chapter, was not so much as answered. The only people in the most royalist city in England who appeared to be in his Majesty's good graces were the Presbyterians.

Pepys' method of dropping out of the Progress was characteristic. 'To tell you the truth,' he explained on his return, 'I was got with Mr Dean of Worcester into the Library among the manuscripts and pored away my time till (at my going out) I found nobody left in the

---

* After his return to London Pepys made a note that he must remember to thank her for her hospitality. *Rawl. MSS. A.* 186, f. 233.

town but myself.'* Leaving the Court to pursue its missionary
pilgrimage to Chester, he returned to London and his own business,
stopping a night at Oxford on the way and sending from his inn to
Merton College for young Ned Southwell whom he just missed. He
was back at the Office on the afternoon of the 27th.[3]

With every year Pepys was growing more of a philosopher. When
the disturbing pressure of outside politics became too great he drew
himself more closely into the inner citadel of his work and his love of
study and scholarship. Among what he described as his 'By-Notes
Private' for that winter is an entry which reveals that in the midst of
business and civic alarms he was pursuing his researches for a life of
Lord Sandwich. Other evidence shows him still accumulating
information for his history of the English Navy, 'with hopes', he told
an informant, 'to ease posterity for my time of the difficulties that my
predecessors have left me under to recover any certain knowledge of
the history of theirs'.† All historical learning was grist to his mill:
that year he added to his library an index of the letters and
manuscripts of the Reformation belonging to the Dutch Church in
London.[4]

The library continued to grow. It was already passing out of the
stage required by a cultured gentleman for his private reading into
that of a remarkable collection of rare and beautiful books and
manuscripts. In the shops of Little Britain – that 'plentiful and
learned emporium of authors' – the virtuosos of the later seventeenth
century were wont to gather to examine the latest sheets from the
printing presses and discuss them with those 'knowing and conver-
sable men', the booksellers. In such company the small erect figure
and dark features of the Secretary of the Admiralty must often have
been seen: here, whenever his naval occasions permitted, he would
buy a Turkish history, a volume of Scottish Ballads, Dean Hickes'
latest book or a Greek folio for his cousin Gale. His favourite
bookseller was Robert Scott, the king of Little Britain, who loved, as
he told him, to find a perfect book for him. When Scott acquired a
copy of the 'old Ship of Fools in old verse, yet so very fair and perfect
that seldom comes such another', he let Pepys have it for eight
shillings, though it had never been sold before under ten.[5]

---

* S. P. to Mr Munsteven, Aug. 27th, 1687. *Pepysian MSS., Adm. Letters* XIII, 255.
† S. P. to Sir A. Deane, March 12th, 1687. *Pepysian MSS., Adm. Letters* XIII, 15.

Pepys was not only a collector of books. Anything rare and curious interested him, provided the sum demanded was not too princely. In October 1687 he was offered a complete set of Roettier's medals for £42 by a friend. He made enquiries about the globes of the great Dutch master, Blaeu, whose masterpieces, the finest of their kind in the world, had been since his death in the hands of Joannes van Keulen* the Amsterdam globe-maker. Demanding only the very best, he ascertained that a globe of 26 inches diameter with fannered frame could be bought for 250 guilders or £22. 14s. 6d.[6]

Pepys could afford these luxuries now, for his fortune was greatly increased by the emoluments of his Office. On November 19th he accounted for £2622 received in fees for passes during the past three and a half years, leaving a residue of £4378 due from the Crown to bring his salary up to the agreed £2000 p.a. For this sum a royal warrant was issued to the Navy Board. It did not include the Admiralty fees for new appointments, which ranged from £5 for Master Shipwrights, Storekeepers and Clerks of the Cheque, to 10s. for Midshipmen, Volunteers and Chaplains. It would probably be no exaggeration to say that Pepys was enjoying the equivalent of a modern income of well over £10,000 p.a. free of tax, with all his expenses including the rent of his house paid.

Yet when his fortune is compared with that of his friend, Sir Stephen Fox, who as Paymaster to the Army extorted a King's ransom from the nation† and laid the foundations of a great house, one is struck by Pepys' moderation. He might have made himself one of the richest men of his time. A quarter of the State's expenditure and an even greater proportion of its patronage passed through his hands, and in his own department he was absolute master. He preferred to be modestly comfortable, surrounding himself with the beautiful things of which he made himself the custodian and trustee for posterity. The public's money he enjoyed by spending it on the public's occasions better than anyone else could have done.[7]

In the early months of 1688 such time as Pepys could spare from affairs of State was occupied in the business of moving his home and

---

* Spelt by Pepys' informant, Mr Faseley, 'Coulen'. *Rawl. MSS. A.* 171, f. 4.

† '. . . whose employment was valued at £10,000 p.a.' *Reresby,* 401.

office from No. 12 to No. 14 Buckingham Street, of which he took a
lease for himself and the Admiralty from Will Hewer.* No. 14 was
the finest house in York Buildings, newly completed at the south-
west end of the street on the site of Lord Willoughby's burnt-out
mansion. It thus fronted both street and river, standing almost
immediately above the beautiful stone water-gate past which the
waters of the unembanked Thames still flowed. Between it and the
river wall was a walk planted with trees where Pepys and his
neighbours employed an honest gardener.†[8]

The outside of the house Pepys beautified at the King's expense.
Over the main door facing the Thames he had a shield carved by
Mathias Fletcher, Master Carver of the Deptford Yard, containing
the Lord High Admiral's anchor with the imperial crown and
ciphers, eight feet deep by six broad and costing £30. Above them he
had displayed the Royal Arms set in the midst of the pediment,
fifteen feet long and nine in height and costing £73. 15s. so that all
the boats on the river could see who and what dwelt within. To
enhance the effect he had them gilded and coloured.[9]

Pepys took a good deal of trouble in furnishing his fine house. He
got Houblon to negotiate the purchase of £80 worth of tapestry for
its walls; after much ado the great merchant secured two pieces of
eight by four ells at 25s. 6d. an ell, a reduction of twenty-five per
cent on the usual price – 'a pennyworth', as he called it. The office
also came in for attention: before the move Pepys had made a
general review and arrangement of his loose papers, and the shelves
of the presses which lined the walls of the clerk's office were now
filled with neatly docketed bundles.‡ To these were added as soon as
he was established in his new quarters a splendid collection of maps
and plans, which were sent down from Whitehall by the King in
parcels – a Spanish map of Africa, charts of the Philippines, Java,
Japan and the East Indies, a print of Speed's of the Earl of Essex'

* The house still belonged to Hewer at the time of his death in 1715. (*L.C.C. Survey
of London* XVIII, Part II)*Strand*), 71 *n*.) Its assessed rental in 1696 was £200 p.a.

† To S. P. from Peregrine Bertie, May 23rd, 1688. 'About the Walk and Trees in
York Buildings.' 'Mr Pepys. This is to let you know that Mr Euers did imploy the
bearer, John James, to look after the trees and walk, and many of us did give our
consent to it. And if he has not offended you, I should for my part be glad he
continued in his place, for he is an honest man and fitter for that employment than
any.' *Rawl. MSS. A.* 179, f. 78.

‡ For a list of these see *Rawl. MSS. A.* 186, ff. 4–5.

attack on Cadiz, a map of Sebastian Cabot's, a draft of the pinnaces belonging to Henry VIII's fleet and much else. They were intended to adorn the Admiralty, but somehow most of them found their way ultimately into Pepys' private collection.[10]

Over his household Mary Skinner appears to have presided in some capacity not quite clear: it is not even certain whether she was living with Pepys or not at this time. She is certainly mentioned on more than one occasion as concerned in his domestic arrangements. In a letter to the Governor of Barbados written in March 1688 Pepys acknowledged 'the fruit which my friend Mrs Skinner has received of your kindness to her at my instance, whereof she is most sensible'.* Those were the days 'when keeping was in the fashion', and friendship as between man and woman was a wide term. Mary Skinner cannot have been wholly in charge for him, for in the fall of 1685, he had sought a professional housekeeper. Mrs Evelyn, a great authority on such matters, claimed to have found an ideal one: 'such a one as I am sure so good a master deserves . . . She is very neat, an excellent housewife, not ungenteel, sightly and well-behaved, yet of years to allow the necessary experience and prudence to direct in a family and preserve respect.'† In the end Pepys, perhaps wisely, had chosen a protégé of James Houblon's, a Mrs Fane, whom that discerning merchant had known 'from her bib upwards'.[11]

Mrs Fane had all the virtues save one. She was knowing, faithful and vigilant, a strict home-keeper, which much endeared her to Pepys, and an excellent sick-nurse. But she was also a shrew with a bitter tongue that at times made the household in Buckingham Street very far from the peaceful place that Pepys would have it. After eighteen months of her despotism, he put his foot down and dismissed her. There followed an uneasy interregnum of a few weeks during which he hastily summoned one Judy Robbins from Chatham, though whether the same Mrs Robbins, daughter to old Delks the waterman, with whom he had toyed so voluptuously in his office one August twenty-two years before, history, discreet Muse, does not relate. The lady came, for she could not bear, she said, to hear what ill-carriage his honour Mr Pepys had received from his servants. But lameness and increasing years had rendered her less

* S. P. to Col. Steed, March 31st, 1688. *Pepysian MSS.*, *Adm. Letters* XIV, 102.

† To S. P. from Mrs Mary Evelyn, Nov. 29th, 1685. S. J. Davey, *Catalogue* (1889), Item 2889.

stirring and serviceable in the managery of a house than once she had been, she explained. Mr Homewood, Clerk of the Survey at Chatham, to whom Pepys had written to enquire about her, informed him privately that, though she still answered the character of a careful, diligent and housewifely person, she would probably be unable to stay as he had reason to believe her secretly married to the gentleman whose house she kept at Chatham.[12]

The crisis ended in Mary Skinner's persuading Samuel to give the bitter-tongued Mrs Fane another chance. Mrs Edwards – the Jane Birch of former days – was unable to aid him in this emergency as she had often done in the past, since she was now looking after Will Hewer's new house in Villiers Street a few yards away. She seems to have still had a good deal of influence with her old master, for it was through her that the clerk Josiah Burchett, still unforgiven, made a last despairing effort to recover his favour.* His 'good old Mistress' he called her. Her son, Samuel, then aged 15, was one of the forty children from the Mathematical School who were presented to the King on January 1st, 1688, by the Lord Mayor in the presence of Pepys and his fellow Governors of Christ's Hospital.[13]

One familiar inmate was lacking now from his home – the gentle singing master, Morelli.† On his father's death he had left Pepys' protection and returned to Hainault to look after his mother and sister and his little estate. He had found the former dead and the latter wasted by Louis XIV's wars of conquest. Hearing that his Britannic Majesty was about to form a chapel of musicians, he had written to his old patron to beg him to secure his admission. But on his return to England Pepys refused to see him. It seemed that the

* See a letter in Burchett's beautiful sloping writing of April 23rd, 1688, and addressed to Mrs Edwards at Mr Hewer's house in Villiers Street in York Buildings. 'Mrs Edwards. Though I have many times of late attempted to cast myself at my honourable master Mr Pepys' feet to beg his pardon and compassion, yet whenever opportunity offered itself, the fear that seized me rendered me wholly unable to do it. I am afraid his Honour thinks 'tis pride that keeps me from it, but God knows 'tis so far from that that I would gladly do anything that might procure me but never so small a portion of his favour, it being the only thing that can make me happy in this world. For my devotion to his service is such that 'tis not in my power to seek after anything else. Whereby I am reduced to so poor a condition that 'tis next akin to starving . . . For God's sake be my solicitor.' *Rawl. MSS. A.* 179, ff. 20–1.

† There is an interesting reference to Morelli in Roger North's autobiography as the 'Italian' singing master who taught North's pretty cousin to master 'that puzzling instrument, the lute' and to sing to her own accompaniment 'after the Italian manner'. R. North, *Lives of the Norths* (1890 ed.) III, 29.

young man, greatly improvident, had contracted a secret marriage and concealed the fact. This was an offence which the autocrat of York Buildings found it particularly hard to forgive. Possibly it was with a favourite servant.[14]

In York Buildings Pepys entertained his friends and took his seemly pleasures. The sound of music so familiar to No. 12 now came nearer to the waterside: passers-by on the river must have often heard it of an evening borne to them from the tall balconied windows whose silver sconces twinkled at them through the leaves. Pepys loved to give his guests a concert. In the April of 1687 Evelyn listened to the famous singer Cifaccio, esteemed the first in Europe, performing before a select company at Admiralty House, extending and loosing his notes with incomparable softness and sweetness, though for the rest, the fastidious gentleman noted, he found the Signor 'a mere wanton, effeminate child, very coy and proudly conceited'. It was certainly a feather in Pepys' cap to have secured him to grace his private concert, for Cifaccio disdained to show his talent to any but princes. Lady Tuke had beguiled him into coming by telling him that her friend, Mr Pepys, was a great lover of music and had the best harpsichord in England, which, Evelyn recorded, 'he touched to his voice rarely well'. (Lady Tuke was careful to caution Samuel not to offer the great man a present as some had had the presumption to do.) Cifaccio was so impressed by this that he brought the incomparable Baptist* along with him to play this noble instrument.[15]

Pepys delighted to be thus at ease with those he loved. Perhaps he was happiest of all when he could entertain James Houblon on a fish day to a dish of ling and a merry afternoon of good talk and banter, or spend a cool summer's evening with him on the river – 'when we may despise the sun'. The stately pair loved to stroll under the trees of St James' or drive together in Pepys' coach in Hyde Park. The comradeship between these two – bureaucrat and merchant, Tory and Whig, Englishman and Huguenot – grew with the years. 'If I hear not from you by pennypost', wrote Houblon in one charming note, 'I'll not fail you at your house at seven in the evening tomorrow, when you shall dispose of me as you please, as you always shall and of all that I have.' The whole Houblon family was included

---

* '. . . that excellent and stupendous artist.' Evelyn, *Diary*, Jan. 28th, 1684.

in the friendship: in the summer of 1688, Samuel gave a favourite riding pad to Wynne Houblon, the husband of his beloved Sarah. 'I don't extremely wonder at the greatness of your noble present, 'tis so like Mr Pepys,' the gratified man replied. 'But Sir, not to detain you too long from your extraordinary affairs, permit me to entreat you to consider a little farther before you part with so good a servant as your horse may be to you.'[16]

Another friend, almost equally beloved, was Sir Robert Southwell. From his Gloucestershire home, King's Weston, he wrote often to his old colleague: 'we are here among the trees and sometimes joining our heads to understand the useful things of this life'. One of his letters, just before Christmas 1687, brought the sad news of the death of another friend, the much admired Sir William Petty, whose writings, theological and economic, Pepys so carefully enshrined in his collection.* Death was already growing busy among his circle of friends; good, kindly-faced Sir John Buckworth, his fellow fenman, went the same December, and in the next July Sir Dennis Gauden, the Victualler, whose father had given him his first pair of silver flagons nearly a quarter of a century back.[17]

Presents still came for Pepys, though of a different kind. Will Howe – 'that pretty and sober fellow' now grown into a colonial Judge† – sent him sweetmeats and refined sugar from Barbados, where he was a councillor and a great man. Lady Wyborne sent from Bombay‡ a velvet carpet and her husband a fine plain cane, a jasper antonia stone and fifteen little birds for Pepys' aviary; the purser of the *Charles* galley at Gibraltar a 'present of sweet waters' comprising 'two half chests of flourences, two boxes of essences and six flasks of orange-flower water'. From Ireland came a gift of usquebaugh, and from Jersey red-legged partridges and barrels of pickled carp; 'the only things', the donor, Sir Philip Carteret explained, 'this poor island can afford which are not in greater

---

* He did not, however, include Petty's solitary essay in verse; the lines he wrote to his six-year-old daughter:

> 'My pretty Pusling and my daughter Ann
> That shall be countess, if her pappa can.
> If her pappa cannot, then I make no doubt
> But my little Pusling will be content without.'

† *Pepysian MSS., Adm. Letters* XIV, 106.

‡ 'For swearing, lying, backbiting and all manner of villainy, it very much outdoes Tangier.' Sir J. Wyborne to S. P., Jan 14th, 1687. Smith II, 64.

plenty in England', adding that not all the birds and fish in the island would be enough to do Pepys honour.* He asked him to present a few of the former to the King if he thought them worthy of his acceptance.[18]

Carp and partridges were not the only things Sir Philip – kinsman to Pepys' old friend and patron, the Navy Treasurer – sent him. In the letters that accompanied them were answers to questions that the Admiralty Secretary had put to him about the naval and military strength of France: how Monsieur Vauban, the great engineer, had been visiting all the harbours of Normandy and Brittany and what vast works were being set in train at Granville. It looked like a threat to the Channel Islands. News of much the same kind was reaching Pepys from other sources. For England's southern neighbour was dreaming of universal empire. Thoughtful men everywhere feared that her armies would soon be set in motion against Rhineland and Netherland and her new navies put to sea to challenge command of Mediterranean and Channel.[19]

But James II of England, unlike his subjects, had no fears of France. No sovereign, as Ranke said, was ever less concerned with the balance of power. For support in domestic crisis, should his bold projects miscarry, he looked for help to his Catholic cousin, King Louis. If a European conflagration was again to come – and all Louis' motions made it imminent – the Crown of England was more likely to side with France than against her. Besides, England had a naval and commercial rival of older standing than France, against whom King James had twice led her fleets and Pepys seven times set them to sea. To many older men, who then as now viewed the world through the eyes of their youth, the Dutch still seemed the natural foes of England.† It was only the younger generation who could fully realize that what Holland had once been it would never be again,‡ and that it was with France that their country would have to reckon in the future.

* Sir P. Carteret to S. P., Nov. 3rd, 1686. *Rawl. MSS. A.* 189, f. 235.

† So to the elder statesmen of the early seventeenth century Spain still seemed England's eternal enemy, to those of the nineteenth France, and to those of our own day Germany.

‡ In March 1687 Pepys received information from Amsterdam that since the last war the Dutch had lost almost their entire Baltic trade to England, and that they now only sent 80 ships to the Levant where before they had sent 200. *Rawl. MSS. A.* 189, f. 292.

A faithful servant of King James could be excused for regarding
the Stadtholder of the United Provinces as a man to be watched and
feared. For, though his nephew and son-in-law, he was the champion of all those who opposed the religious and political aims of the
King of England. If there was to be an alliance against France,
William would be its mainstay: if there was to be foreign support for
the political malcontents in Britain, William would be behind them.
Already Holland was sheltering rebels like Locke and Burnet as in
the past it had sheltered Shaftesbury, Monmouth and Argyll. It was
natural, therefore, that the Secretary of the Admiralty should keep a
careful watch on its coasts and harbours, though he also did so, as
we have seen, on those of France.[20]

There was no doubt that the Dutch were making preparations. As
early as March 1687 Pepys was informed by the Marquis d'Albeville, King James' Irish envoy at the Hague, that at Amsterdam the
butter-boxes had four lines of thirteen vessels each, all in good
condition and ready to sail at two days' notice. Many of them were
ships of the line. The magazines and stores were full and all the
shipyards busy.[21]

They were busy in England too. Throughout the year 1687 and
the ensuing winter the Special Commission, its burden borne by
Hewer, Deane and Pepys – its 'worn, unassisted Secretary', as he
afterwards described himself – went vigorously ahead with its work.
Already the end was in sight. By the spring of 1688 the greater part
of the battle fleet, given up for lost three years before, had been
repaired. To maintain it in good order an additional dry-dock was
being built at Portsmouth capable of receiving the largest ships of
the line and measuring 250 by 68 feet with a depth of 24 feet 3
inches. New storehouses were already built or rising in all the
dockyards, and the stores and magazines filling fast. 'Mr Pepys',
wrote his neighbour, Lord Ailesbury, 'put the ships and docks in the
greatest order beyond what can be expressed.' Another year and the
work of restoration would be complete. By the Christmas of 1688
Pepys hoped to be able to make the King a present of the finest
fighting fleet England had ever known.[22]

He was laying plans for the distant future too. Among the State
papers of the year 1791 is a letter written at the instance of that
formidable administrator, Sir Charles Middleton, afterwards Lord
Barham, referring to an important proposal for improving the

durability of ships which he had found among the official correspondence of over a century before. It appeared that in 1687 Mr Secretary Pepys, who had been beguiling his leisure hours by reading Dr Plot's *Natural History of Staffordshire*, had been struck by a passage describing the method of felling timber in that remote country. This differed from that in use in the royal forests of the south, where the trees were cut in the spring as soon as the sap was up and subsequently bark't as they lay prostrate. But it seemed that the wise men of Staffordshire from time immemorial had bark't their trees in the spring and left them standing throughout the summer to fell them in the late autumn when the juices that bred worm and decay were no longer active and the cut saplings able to endure without decay as long as the heart of the tree.

In reading this passage Pepys recalled that King Charles I's *Sovereign of the Seas* had been built of northern timbers, and that to this fact 'that extra degree of lastingness' observable in some of her beams (for the ship was still in commission after half a century's service) might be imputed. Accordingly he got Dr Plot, who was a fellow member of the Royal Society, to prepare a paper for the royal eye on the most seasonable time for felling timber* – as he did another on the corrosion of guns and the decay of cables and hawsers – the result of a visit paid by this ingenious philosopher to the Yards at Chatham. He then instructed the Commissioners of the Navy to take the first opportunity of experimenting on these lines. For by industry, method and constant endeavour it must be possible, Pepys held, to bring the Navy to such a state of perfection that it would surpass all others and be susceptible of no further improvement.[23]

Yet in the last resort the Navy like everything else that belonged to England was dependent on the King's policy. And by the end of 1687 it was clear that the royal hand on the helm was heading the ship of State towards the gathering storm.

* It was entered in the *Philosophical Transactions of the Royal Society* in January 1691. See A. Wood, *Athenae Oxonienses* (1721 ed.) II, 1122.

The Gathering Storm

'In power, as in most other things, the way for Princes to keep it, is not to grasp more than their arms can well hold.' – Halifax, *The Trimmer*.

Pepys' plans, like other men's, were at the mercy of his fellow mortals' folly. Great events, moved by causes which he could not control, were about to sweep his schemes into dusty pigeon-holes and his name, for a while, into limbo. The opening of the year 1688, which was to bring his reform of the Navy to completion, saw Louis XIV pressing his cousin James to aid him in his European ambitions in return for the assurance of ultimate help from France if his own perilous projects in England went awry. Once again the joint enemy was to be Holland, whose destruction was to coincide with the establishment of toleration in England. It was to Holland that Pepys had just hopefully sent his younger and cleverer nephew, John Jackson, to complete his education.*

Louis was on the verge of embroilment with the Dutch over the rather dubious affairs of his ally Denmark. He wanted James to use his fleet in conjunction with his own to prevent a junction of the Dutch and Swedish fleets against that country. This was a great deal more than James was prepared to do, for he knew that his own battle fleet was not yet ready for a naval war. Nor had he any desire to repeat the errors of 1672. The most he would agree to was to fit out a small squadron in the spring to make a joint, though pacific demonstration with the French fleet. This would serve as a warning to the Dutch, who had angered him both by opposing English commercial claims in the East Indies and by delaying the return of certain English regiments which he had lent his son-in-law. They were also giving shelter to many of his own rebellious subjects, including Pepys' old adversary, Harbord.[1]

In the routine of the Admiralty, therefore, a hint of warlike preparations began to appear during the opening weeks of 1688. Old

* 'By-Notes Private 1688.' *Rawl. MSS. A.* 186, f. 233.

ships were examined for conversion into bomb vessels and the size of the Channel Guard was slightly increased. Pepys, submitting the usual annual project, made provision for a force of 4035 seamen. They were to be disposed in one 3rd rate, nine frigates and three yachts in the Channel, a guard-ship each at Portsmouth and Sheerness, two frigates in the Channel Islands, eight in the Straits, one in Ireland, two in Virginia and three in the West Indies. The total did not include the ships lent to the East India Company. At the same time the Catholic Sir Roger Strickland was raised to Herbert's vacant place as Rear-Admiral of England, though to Pepys the new appointment can scarcely have been much more welcome than the old. Shortly afterwards orders were given to set out twenty ships for sea.[2]

These preparations were soon magnified in Holland, where they were quickly followed by retaliatory and far more warlike measures. The Dutch burghers were seriously alarmed. For the first time William of Orange saw a possibility of enlisting the aid of his fearful and jealous countrymen in a crusade of armed intervention in England to secure his wife's inheritance. At that moment he learnt that that inheritance was fatally threatened. The people of England learnt it also. The Protestant succession to the throne, which had reconciled them to the present but temporary evil of a Catholic King, was in danger. The Queen was reported to be pregnant.[3]

It was William's chance and he knew it. Cold and unamiable, he had the essential element of greatness that seizes opportunity without flinching. If he could conquer England and turn her latent powers against France, he could straddle across Louis' march to world dominion. Beyond the waters of the North Sea the rough, boisterous, ruddy-faced people who had sent his grandfather to the scaffold and had twice exiled his father-in-law, were now looking to him as their only hope. Somehow, before Louis flung down the gauntlet to Europe and the armies of the great captains poured into the Netherlands, he must cross those waters.

In England a chill filled men's hearts. If a son was born to King James and lived, he would be brought up a Catholic and rule after his father. The Catholic prelates and the Jesuit Fathers who swarmed at Court, the papist lords who sat on the Council Board, the papist officers who swaggered at the head of the regiments and companies of a standing army, would remain. Presently the talk of toleration would die away, what had happened in France would happen in England; religious liberty under a Catholic King would give place to priestly edicts, the jails of the inquisition and the shouts of papist dragoons. The fires of Smithfield would be lit again.

This was the moment, while William's agent, Dyckvelt, was almost openly canvassing the malcontent magnates of England, that good King James chose to cross the *t*'s and dot the *i*'s of his religious policy. With a folly all his own he re-enacted his Declaration of Indulgence, suspending the penal laws and the oaths of admission to civil and military office, and commanded that it should be read in every Anglican pulpit. It was promulgated on April 27th; it was to be read on the last two Sundays of May and the first two of June. The pill of religious equality was to be forced down the throat of the Church of England once and for all. It was bitterly cold, with raging easterly winds prolonging winter throughout April. And all the while multitudes of flying Huguenots, horror stricken and bereft of all they had, continued to pour into the country.[4]

The news from Holland grew more insistent: the ports were unusually busy. Even the king became suspicious. But with the facile optimism of an essentially weak man, he refused to let his mind dwell too much on the Dutch preparations. He gave order, however, at the beginning of April that the Navy Office should prepare victuals for an extra thousand men against emergencies. Pepys himself saw to its execution. Yet on the day that the Declaration of Indulgence was promulgated the gravity of the news from Holland was such that he sent secret instructions to the acting Commander-in-Chief in the Downs written in his own hand. It looked to him, and for a moment his master too, as though the Dutch might be planning a sudden dive at his great ships at Chatham to rob him of all he had wrought so hard for during the past two years. They at all costs must be saved.[5]

Pepys acted with his usual energy and speed. On April 30th he instructed the Special Commissioners to hasten the despatch of the ships fitting out. On May 1st he sent them to Chatham to discuss with the chief officers of the Ordnance measures to secure the battle fleet. Finding the fortifications, which were the charge of the Ordnance Office, much neglected, they recommended that they should be at once repaired and a boom and chain got ready to close the Medway at Upnor Castle. But they held that the most effective defence would be the immediate commissioning of all 3rd and 4th rates, manned by a force of 8000 men, to encounter the Dutch at sea.[6]

These resolutions Pepys laid next day before the King. They were received with little enthusiasm. To the royal mind, once more reassured by the false, beguiling Sunderland, too much alarm at Dutch preparations seemed to imply a distrust of his policy. After all they could scarcely be regarded as dangerous unless England herself were growing restive. This was exactly what James, protected as he was by God and the whole hierarchy of Heaven, was resolved not to believe. Besides, alarmist measures would be expensive and not only upset all the careful estimates which had been made for restoring and maintaining the Navy, but trench on other branches of the royal revenue. As it was, the pay of the Yards was in arrears. There were many in the royal entourage of priests and backstair politicians who did not like Pepys and thought he served the King too well.* They knew of better ways of spending his money than on ships and dockyards.[7]

James, however, did promise his old servant that he would himself visit Chatham in the following week and discuss with his principal officers of the Navy and Ordnance what might best be done to guard against accidents. On hearing the news Deane, always a little prone to extremes, became enthusiastic. 'Happy the people of England', he wrote, 'in a Prince so understanding matters of this nature as, of himself, to come to such resolutions as, in all human probability will be found the best and safest for securing his navy and justifying yourself hereafter should any accident happen thereto, which God forbid.' Yet Pepys, though he would have been the last to admit it, may well have had his doubts.[8]

On the afternoon of Monday, May 7th, he and Hewer took coach for Chatham, with Samuel Atkins in attendance. For the next few days Atkins, probably at his chief's suggestion – for it was the kind of occasion in which Pepys, recalling the events of 1667, saw the need

* 'Though it might reasonably be expected your long and faithful service to the Crown, without getting from it either estate or honour, might justly deserve from all a good esteem and value, yet, sir, (as I have often taken the boldness and freedom of telling you) you are not without enemies which think you serve the King too well.' Sir A. Deane to S. P., May 4th, 1688. *Rawl. MSS. A.* 186, ff. 245–6. Printed in Smith II, 122.

of vindicatory evidence – kept a diary.* 'We set out after 3', he wrote 'and arrived at Chatham Dock by 8, nothing passing that evening but walking about the Yard.' The Navy Commissioners had already preceded them there.

Next morning at Sir Phineas Pett's house Pepys, formally presiding, asked Deane to explain the position to the rest of the Commissioners. It was their duty, they were informed, to secure the great ships in Chatham harbour and Gillingham Reach, but to remember that their sovereign did not wish to incur the expense of setting them to sea, since he did not believe the Dutch to have any hostile intent, 'it being not their interest to exasperate either him or the people of England'. While this official view of the situation was being debated, word was brought that his Majesty had arrived at Strood and was just taking barge for the Dockyard. After requesting Pepys, therefore, to open its proceedings in the royal presence, the meeting adjourned to dine while it still had the chance. As the recording Atkins put it, 'we all went to the Hill House to eat a bit to be ready to wait on the King.'

At one o'clock James landed at the Dockyard gate and at once went to Sir Phineas Pett's house. Here he mounted his horse and inspected a regiment of infantry which had been drawn up along the brick wall at the back. After viewing the new wharves and storehouses, he returned to the house, where, 'having eaten a bit standing and drunk a glass of wine',† he repaired to the Banqueting House in the garden. In these *alfresco* surroundings Pepys, in the presence of the Prince of Denmark, Lord Dartmouth, Deane, Berry, Tippetts, Hewer, Haddock, Booth, Sotherne and Pett, reported the discussions of the morning. But it proved too late to come to any resolution that day, and when Pepys had finished his speech, the King left to inspect the new batteries down the river and spend the night on his yacht.

On the following day, Wednesday the 9th, the King went over the yards and ships. He also examined the famous New England tree,

* 'Sir A. D. and Mr Hewer, their Minutes of the Proceedings at Chatham at his Majesty's visiting his Yard and Ships there, May 1688, in order to the consulting for the safety of both upon intelligence received of Sea Preparations extraordinary reported to be then making in Holland, with the different advices offered to the King thereupon and Issue of the whole.' *Pepysian MS.* No. 2879, *Miscellanies* XI, 913–26.

† To save the Resident Commissioner expense he had thoughtfully decided to take his meals on board his own yacht. *Pepysian MSS., Adm. Letters* XIV, 156–7.

thirty-nine inches in diameter, which was being made into a mainmast for the *Royal Sovereign*. Afterwards in the Banqueting House in Pett's garden, he announced his decision to the assembled company, now increased by the arrival of Sir Roger Strickland and the young Duke of Grafton. He proposed to fit out two more 3rd rates only and three 4th rates, to be manned for economy's sake with the lowest complement of men practical. The remainder of the 3rd rates would be moved above Upnor Castle. The 1st and 2nd rates were to stay where they were.

His Majesty having made known these frugal resolutions, nothing remained but to discuss the best way of preserving the great ships in the circumstances. It was resolved to sheathe them with three or four strakes of milled lead between wind and water, the King pointing out that a bullet might pierce but could not splinter such a protection. Deane stressed the importance of guarding against any decay of their timbers through lack of air. Pepys took the opportunity to mention the business of flags, which was then occupying a good deal of his thoughts, and read 'very distinctly over the table' (one suspects, looking straight at Strickland) a paper he had prepared on the subject. His Majesty graciously remarked that it would increase the honour of Admirals when it was clearly known who was Vice-Admiral and who Rear-Admiral. After that Pepys went on to speak about naval salutes and the extravagance they occasioned in wasting powder and needless drinking of healths, but was finally stopped by the King who remarked that it was late and adjourned further discussion to 'a more solemn meeting in London'. For news had reached him that the pregnant Queen had been taken ill.[9]

After the King's immediate departure for London, Pepys, Deane, and Hewer went down to Gillingham Reach to view the great ships. Here on board the *Britannia*, the finest of all the many ships they had given the Navy, they sat down to a treat of cold meats and a bowl of punch. Then they viewed Gillingham Fort, where they found only one man on duty and the state of the platforms and gun-carriages such, 'as is better to be silent than to say anything as to their condition'. Afterwards they walked back to Chatham through the woods. There was a touch of idyll in it – the three old friends, mirrored in Atkins' laconic journal, going home together in the calm of that May evening, their work, though they knew it not, almost done.[10]

It is the last time we shall see Pepys in his glory, before his world

breaks in storm. His royal master's word was still law and his
realm inviolate, and he the chosen and unchallenged ruler of the
naval administration. At York Buildings all mankind stood before
him cap in hand. Even the King's son, Mr FitzJames,* learning his
trade as seaman with Captain Lloyd of the *Sedgemoor* at distant
Gibraltar, complimented him with a gift. It was to Pepys that the
ambitious came when that spring Sir John Godwin's death left a
Naval Commissionership to be filled: among others Sir Edward
Dering, recalling that he was still owed £8000 by the government
for ancient contracts, and Captain Vittles, 'with moderate hopes of
having discharged myself in my trust hitherto with a strict integrity
and duty'.† The Service was learning at last to speak Pepys'
language.[11]

It had reason to. His orders held. No longer could a captain
hope to trade for months at a stretch at the King's expense: the
jealous eye of the Admiralty followed him in all places. Captain
Killigrew of the *Dragon*, commanding the squadron operating
against Sallee in Morocco, must have wondered that the little
autocrat of York Buildings should know every movement of his
ships. A commander who dared to poke his nose unauthorized into
Cadiz or Lisbon was quickly apprised of his crime; the barren rock
of Gibraltar was the only harbour now allowed to the captains of
the once envied Straits squadron. The naval age of gold had given
place to one of iron.

An officer could not even drink like a gentleman; when he did so
he was tried by court-martial. 'I did believe myself', wrote one
gallant captain who had so offended, '(and have been taken notice
of by persons that inhabit both on shore and sea) to have lived a
very retired life, and sometimes in two months together never was
in a public house, and then upon some occasion extraordinary. Yet
I fall into faults, although the original of this was the King's service
(to my expense). If being a true penitent for my fault can make any
atonement with his Majesty for me, I am sure I am. And to
demonstrate that I am so, I shall avoid all manner of society where
wine, punch or other liquor may give cause of suspicion that a man
may be in error of having drunk too much. For I am resolved as

---

* Younger brother of the Duke of Berwick. *Pepysian MSS., Adm. Letters* xiv, 16.

† 'I do with all humility and resignedness of mind offer myself to your Honour's
judgment and favour.' March 9th, 1688. *Rawl. MSS. A.* 186, f. 6.

long as I am in his Majesty's service to avoid all sorts of strong drink, either in public or private, for his Majesty's frown to me is death.'* He probably meant Mr Secretary Pepys'.[12]

If Pepys could frown, he could also bless. The widow and child of Captain Fowler, dead in the performance of his duty, felt the effects of his kindness when they received a gratuity from the Crown together with an additional £10 contributed out of the Secretary of the Admiralty's own purse. A host of poor and needy folk besieged York Buildings with letters and more personal solicitations. Those who were prepared to earn their living by honest work, however humble, knew that Pepys would be their friend. Some of them were his own kinsmen, like young Samuel St Michel, whom he presented to the King and for whom he secured a berth in a ship of the line. But though he was his nephew and godson, the boy had first to establish his worth by serving a sixteen months' apprenticeship in navigation in the *Fubbs* yacht. Among other applicants were two Pepyses who, though not of his kin, presumed on their names to ask his favour; proving deserving of it, both received it.[13]

The young as we have seen were always sure of his affectionate if severe interest. That July he got Signor Verrio's son a place as volunteer on board the *Bonadventure*; the same good offices were at the disposal of many other hopeful youths. He knew that they could be formed for his stern, beneficent purposes and England's if the Service could have the moulding of them while they were still pliable. There were occasions, though, when he thought them too young. 'In friendship to you,' he wrote to an old acquaintance who had asked for a volunteer's place for a son, 'I can't omit to observe some apprehension I have that the King will think 12 years, which you say is his age, as much too early for a child to set out to sea as anything above 16 too much.'† The King's thoughts, it should be remembered, were a time-honoured euphemism by which Pepys indicated his own.[14]

That the King had other thoughts which were not those of Pepys or any other sound-headed Englishman was a misfortune that could not be helped. For that unhappy prince, with his eyes shut to all that was happening both in his own realm and the world outside, and his

* Capt. Sir William Jennens to S. P., Feb. 26th, 1688. *Rawl. MSS. A.* 186, f. 8. See also *Pepysian MSS., Adm. Letters* xiv, 27, 37, 54, 93, 121.

† S. P. to T. Tiddeman, Feb. 9th, 1688. *Pepysian MSS., Adm. Letters* xiv, 35.

ears closed to every counsel but that of the Palace priests, was rushing headlong on disaster. All his hopes were now set on securing the election of a new Parliament in which the Cavalier and Anglican party which had once been his mainstay should have no part. In every Corporation Tories were being expelled and Dissenters and Papists put in their places. Judges, Lord Lieutenants and the Archbishops were instructed to interrogate their inferiors as to their willingness to comply with the royal wishes at the forthcoming election. Those who refused were to be punished.[15]

Unlike most of his countrymen Pepys had never felt fear or dislike of the King's desire for religious toleration. He did not even quarrel with his claim to suspend the Penal Laws. 'Very fit it is', he wrote of his sovereign's breach of one of his own sacred regulations for the Service, 'that the King should be at liberty to dispense with as well as to make his own rules.'* Yet he could not fail to feel alarmed at the way in which the most deep-rooted, popular prejudices were being disregarded and the affections of the most loyal subjects recklessly alienated. At the end of March worthy Mr Loton, Chaplain of the Ordinary at Chatham, was threatened with summary dismissal because he had not shown himself sufficiently active in advocating the repeal of the Test Act and Penal Laws. John Loton, who had held his post with distinction for over a quarter of a century, was an old and honoured friend; many years before Pepys had presented him with a stone tablet of the Commandments for his church. He now intervened on his behalf, vouching for his loyalty and guaranteeing that, whatever his private views, Loton would support the royal candidate at Chatham in the event of a parliamentary election. But the order to read the Declaration of Indulgence in the pulpit was too much for Loton's overstrained conscience, as for many another clergyman's. His refusal to do so placed it beyond Pepys' power to help him further. Loton explained to him that it was founded on considerations that admitted of no further compromise. 'I presume Mr Crewe will be glad of this opportunity to make a second attempt on the Navy, and I cannot reasonably expect your Honour's protection. God's will be done! I must choose suffering rather than sin, and will, by the grace of God, always walk by this rule, that popularity shall never corrupt my loyalty nor loyalty my

* S. P. to Mr Gregory, Aug. 9th, 1687. *Pepysian MSS., Adm. Letters* XIII, 247.

conscience. I will first give to God the things that are God's, and then to Caesar the things that are Caesar's.' A little later, and in a more worldly but less popular cause, Pepys was to prove that the same rule was his.[16]

Clergymen far more important than Mr Loton found the royal instructions to read the Declaration too much for their consciences. The reading was ordered to take place on Sundays, May 20th and 27th in London and Westminster, and June 3rd and 10th in the country. It was almost everywhere disregarded. The lead in disobedience was given by the Bishops, formerly the most loyal of the King's subjects. On Friday the 18th of May seven, including Archbishop Sancroft and Pepys' friend, Dr Ken, now Bishop of Bath and Wells, met in Lambeth Palace and drew up a petition to the King begging him to withdraw his orders, since obedience to them must involve a breach of the Law. This document, signed by all, was taken the same evening by six of them to the Palace and presented to the indignant monarch, who could see in it nothing but downright mutiny. His view of it was confirmed by the simultaneous appearance of the offending petition in print. That same night it was sold in the streets and thrown broadcast on coffee-house tables. James felt, and not without justification, that the petition, so damaging to his credit and prerogative, was intended not so much for his own eyes as for those of his subjects.[17]

It was resolved therefore to prosecute the seven signatory Bishops for publishing a seditious libel. On the 8th of June they were summoned to the Council Chamber. Pepys was with the Lords of the Council who sat at that historic board. The proceedings were conducted by the King and Lord Chancellor Jeffreys. After many minutes of angry questioning the Archbishop and his colleagues admitted their signatures. They were then informed that a criminal information would be exhibited against them in the Court of King's Bench. When, like the true and obstinate Englishmen that they were, they refused to enter into recognizances, they were committed to the Tower. Among those who were present at the Council was Father Petre, the King's Confessor, the most hated man in the kingdom. All down the river, in Macaulay's classic phrase, from Whitehall to London Bridge, the barge that bore the Bishops to their gentle martyrdom passed between lines of boats, while every roof was crowded with a multitude of sympathetic watchers.

The Law, in the hands of Jeffreys and the Judges, had broken the power of English provincial self-government; it would now, the King hoped, shatter the resistance of the Church. Behind it lay the threat of the army, encamped in its thousands on Hounslow Heath, armed with terrible and as yet untried engines of destruction and reinforced daily by drafts of what seemed to the English vile papist savages from the bogs of Ireland. From all over the country came tales, wildly exaggerated, of their excesses in private houses or on the highway. The nation was ready to believe any rumour against those who possessed the three supremely unpopular attributes of being at once Irish, Catholics and soldiers. Nor could all the King's careful orders for the strict maintenance of military discipline reassure an alarmed and outraged opinion.[18]

Pepys, playing his small part in this imbroglio, appeared for a moment in the full limelight of national publicity.* On June 29th the Bishops were brought to trial in Westminster Hall. The Hall was packed with the English aristocracy, now united by the jealous national religion against their sovereign and resolved to see their champions set free. Outside a vast and noisy crowd waited in its turbulent strength. It was like some great sporting contest staged before the excited gaze of a nation.

From the first the government was seen to be struggling against a force beyond its control, like men in some frail skiff trying to weather an overwhelming sea. The Lord Chief Justice and his three brethren, dependent servants of the Crown as they were, made no pretence of their fearful deference to the popular clamour. The Attorney- and Solicitor-Generals spent many hours attempting to prove the elementary and universally accepted facts of publication and delivery, and were forced, amid shouts of laughter from the contemptuous nobility, to call official after official to prove what everybody in England knew. All the great men of the Bar were briefed for the Bishops, led by Pepys' old chamber-fellow of Cambridge days, Sir Robert Sawyer, the ex-Attorney-General. They included a former Chief Justice of the King's Bench, the same Pemberton who had been so unsympathetic when Deane and Pepys had appeared before him nine years before. Against them the newly

---

* So also did Will Hewer whose name appeared on the panel of the Jury. *Ellis Correspondence* II, 2. But though his name did so, Hewer himself did not. *Verney Memoirs* (1925) II, 457. Possibly Pepys got him excused on the plea of naval urgency.

appointed Attorney-General, Sir Thomas Powis, and the Solicitor-General – the renegade Whig, Sir William Williams – seemed men of straw.

To prove publication of the Bishops' petition in Middlesex, the chief officials who had been present at the Council meeting were called. The fantastic legal quibble seemed likely to non-suit the Crown even before the real case had begun to be argued. For, though the Bishops' admission of their signatures was shown, publication in Middlesex was at first made to depend on the production of a witness able to swear that he had seen the original delivery of the petition. As no one had been present but the King himself, who could not be called, this was impossible. The Crown's only chance was to get someone who had attended the Council meeting to testify that on that occasion the Bishops had admitted that the petition before the Board was that which they had delivered to the King.

The three Clerks of the Council, Blathwayt, Bridgeman and Sir John Nicholas, were called in vain. None of them could recall an admission which had never been made for the simple reason that it had not been doubted for a moment by anyone. After the triumphant shout that followed the Crown's third failure, the Solicitor-General lost his temper and cried out, 'Here's a wonderful great rejoicing that truth cannot prevail.' Then, recovering himself, he added, 'There's Mr Pepys, we'll examine him.'

The little man, all straightforward dignity, was duly sworn. The Lord Chief Justice took personal charge of him, remarking, 'Come, I'll ask the questions. Were you at the Council Board when my Lords the Bishops were committed?'

Mr Pepys. Yes, I was.

L.C.J. What were the questions that were asked either by the King or by my Lord Chancellor?

Mr Pepys. My Lord, I would remember as well as I could the very words; and the very words of the question were, I think, *My Lords, do you own this paper?* I do not remember anything was spoken about the delivering, but I believe it was understood by everybody at the table that that was the paper that they had delivered.

L.C.J. Well, have you done now? (The question was directed to the Attorney-General.) But to satisfy you I'll ask this question. Was this question asked, Was this the paper you delivered to the King?

Mr Pepys. No, my Lord.

Attorney-General. Pray, sir, do you remember whether the King himself asked the question?

Mr Pepys. You mean, I suppose, Mr Attorney, that these were the words, or something that imported their delivering it to the King.

Attorney-General. Yes, Sir.

Mr Pepys. Truly, I remember nothing of that.

Solicitor-General. Did you observe any discourse concerning their delivery of it to the King?

Mr Pepys. Indeed, Mr Solicitor, I did not.*

Unlike the other witnesses, Pepys made no attempt to evade the simple truth to win the goodwill of either King or nation. But like them he had to run the gauntlet of the mob as he came and went.[19]

Next morning, amid thunderous cheering, volleys of gunpowder and pealing bells, the excited populace took the acquitted Bishops to themselves. That night the Pope was burnt in effigy in the streets and many Catholics assaulted. On the same day the chiefs of the proud aristocracy who for the next century and a half were to rule England despatched to William of Orange, with whom they had long been in secret correspondence, their formal invitation to invade England at the head of a Dutch army. It was carried by the late Rear-Admiral of the kingdom, Arthur Herbert, disguised as a common seaman. Beneath the surface of national life revolution had begun.[20]

For nothing but a revolution could now do the business of Protestant England. William had no longer even the shadow of a right to intervene in his father-in-law's kingdom. Three weeks earlier his wife had ceased to be heir presumptive to the throne. In the early hours of Sunday, June 10th, a month before her time, the Queen had given birth to a male child. Pepys, announcing the great news to Sir Roger Strickland shortly after two that morning, wrote of the newcomer as being 'in all the circumstances of health, full growth, and whatever may encourage us to expect his long life as well as pray for it'.† Less loyal souls felt differently. The fertility of Mary of Modena had entailed a Catholic dynasty on a militant Protestant nation. The Popish Terror of a decade before was coming again.

* Cobbett and Howell, *State Trials* xii, 350, and F. Hargrave, *State Trials* iv, 363.
† S. P. to Sir Roger Strickland, June 10th, 1688. *Pepysian MSS., Adm. Letters* xiv, 222.

Fear and lies as ever went hand in hand. Though the natal chamber at St James' had been crowded with a numerous concourse of both sexes, many of them were Papists, and few of those, who by virtue of their constitutional station should have attended, were present. The Archbishop of Canterbury was in the Tower, the Princess Anne at Bath, the Princess Mary in Holland, and most of the great Protestant Lords in disgrace. It was at once bruited abroad, and by some of the highest in the land, that the unwanted child had entered the Palace in a warming-pan. The bawdy lie was soon the jest of every tavern and coffee-house. The official celebrations of the birth, though followed with interest in Rome, were received by the English with little enthusiasm. At Gloucester the Mayor was forced to commit the churchwardens because they would not ring the bells.[21]

But the Navy was still a law to itself. Pepys himself drafted the order for celebrating the Prince's birth in the fleet. Here at least, whatever the attitude of the fine gentlemen commanders, the personal loyalty of the tarpaulins to their former Admiral made the news sure of a welcome. Among the ships of war in the Downs there was probably more goodwill to the Crown than anywhere else in the kingdom: even the army at Hounslow cheered the acquittal of the Bishops.[22]

The last days of May and the first of June, bringing new rumours of fleet movements in Holland, witnessed a further concentration of 4th and 5th rates in the Downs. On June 14th Strickland was reported to be in command of 'more than 20 nimble frigates and fireships well appointed and daily expected to be joined by others of yet greater force from the River of Thames'. To fit them out Pepys and Deane worked the clock round. 'I am really weary', wrote the latter from Chatham on June 1st, 'it being now 12 at night, having not been in bed ... above five in twenty-four hours since my departure. Yet I shall think it no trouble if it content my great Master; otherwise no wealth would tempt a man to deal with so many vexations from ignorance, negligence and sloth.'* Other vessels were getting ready at Portsmouth; it was said that there would soon be 6500 sailors in pay, more than double the normal peacetime complement. In the meantime Strickland was ordered to

* *Rawl. MSS. A.* 186, f. 206.

shadow the Dutch fleet should it put to sea. On the 18th Pepys instructed him to send out relays of 'small nimble frigates' in pairs to cruise 'about the back of the Goodwin' and off Orfordness. They were 'to speak with all ships passing those ways, and to gain what intelligence they could of the number, force and motion of the ships of any foreign Prince or State'.[23]

But the battle fleet – the three score or so of great ships that in the last resort would have to do the King's business – remained in harbour. The men who should have manned them were scattered through the merchant marine, in foreign service or thronging the seaport steps and waterways where the effects of the Service's discipline and tradition never touched them and where they were subject to all the impressions of popular rumour and opinion.* Herein lay the supreme lesson of seventeenth-century naval history, that the silent pressure of sea power could only be exercised when the Grand Fleet was in being. Till a revolution in national finance and opinion should make that possible, permanent naval supremacy there could be none. Yet all else requisite for that supremacy was already achieved. The revolution alone was needed.

For, thanks to Pepys, Deane and Hewer, the work of the Special Commission was almost finished. The Navy was now sustained by discipline, wise rules for every occasion and a growing tradition of service. And, lying silent at their moorings, were fifty-nine ships of the line of battle, all but a dozen or so of them with their repairs completed and ready to be commissioned whenever order should be given and men be found to man them. By June 20th Pepys was able to present a plan, already discussed in the spring with his royal master and Lord Godolphin, for restoring the Navy to its old constitution of Principal Officers and Commissioners, leaving the invaluable Deane as Inspector-General of Works and Stores, and William Hewer of Accounts.† It was resolved that the Special Commission, its purpose accomplished, should be dissolved before the end of the year.[24]

Meanwhile on the continent of Europe, as in England, the clouds grew more lowering. King Louis and the Emperor were marching to war. In Rhineland and Flanders, German and Frenchman, Pro-

---

* 'Drums are beating up about Wapping for seamen, but few come in.' *Verney Memoirs* (1925) II, 460.

† *Rawl. MSS. A.* 170, ff. 215–16.

testant and Catholic would soon be embattled in a conflict that threatened to end in the universal hegemony of the Lilies. The Dutch, knowing that they soon must be embroiled and dreading an alliance between England and France which James refused either to own or deny, were uniting behind their Stadtholder in his daring project of intervention. In England jealousy of the French and a deep-seated belief that the coming struggle would decide the future of Protestantism in the world were also drawing men nearer to Orange and further from the pro-French affinities of their King. The birth of the Prince of Wales and the invitation of the aristocratic chiefs in England decided William. '*Nunc aut nunquam*', now or never, he is said to have murmured. He was aware that his time had come.[25]

The strengthening of the English Channel Guard in June, itself the result of warlike movements in Holland, was attended by still greater activities on the part of the Dutch. But, faced by an increasingly complex situation, James only vacillated. At one moment he accepted King Louis' offer of a French fleet to co-operate with his own against the invaders; a few days later, fortified by official denials from the Dutch ambassador, he dismissed William's project as unthinkable and refused his cousin's offer with pride. The erratic movements of his ships indicated the changes in the royal mind. On the 2nd of July Strickland was ordered to Solebay. A few days later he was recalled to the Buoy of the Nore. On the 18th the King – according to some accounts to appease an incipient mutiny caused by the saying of mass on the flagship* – visited the fleet and took pains to ingratiate himself with the sailors, 'behaving with great affability and taking notice of every particular officer'. He did not know that certain of the gentlemen commanders, through the agency of Pepys' old enemy, Edward Russell, were already in secret communication with William. On the 21st Strickland was again ordered to sea.[26]

About the same time came news of the loss of an English admiral, who was neither a papist like Strickland nor a traitor like Herbert or Russell though an attempt had been made about this time to seduce him from his allegiance. Narbrough's expedition to the West Indies

* . . . 'The true cause was to appease the seamen, who were ready to mutiny upon occasion of some sea captains using mass openly on board.' (*Reresby*, 503.) There is no confirmation of this in Pepys' papers.

in search of treasure had ended in sickness and death. Characteristically, though stricken down by fever, he had refused to sail for home until he had recovered a lost anchor. Samuel Jackson, serving aboard his ship, described the event in a letter of July 20th to his uncle Pepys. The young man was plainly touched by his Admiral's tragic end in that far place after his work was done – 'as though fate', he wrote, 'had decreed him to lie there'. So was Pepys, who mourned him, 'not for private friendship's sake only, (tho' that be very great) but for the sake of the King and his Service, in which (without wrong to anybody) I do not think there does survive one superior, if any one equal (all qualifications considered), to Sir John Narbrough'.*[27]

Narbrough's death was a real blow to the Navy, which in the coming months was to have need of a man of his resolution and experience in sea command. On the very day that the news of his death reached London two of the most distinguished officers of the Service, Sir John Berry and Sir William Booth, became involved in a most unseemly broil while paying the Yard at Chatham. Pepys was abroad with his cousin, Dr Gale, taking his Saturday evening's recreation, when Berry in a sad heat arrived at York Buildings to speak with him. Finding him out he unwisely carried his angry tale to the King, who ordered the Admiralty Secretary to make an official investigation of the whole affair.

Pepys' task was the more unwelcome since both Admirals were his personal friends. According to Berry, Booth had pricked as absent from duty a valued purser, on a false charge of Captain Vittles' clerk – one 'little better than a madman'. When he protested, he had been treated 'with very scurrilous language' before the clerks. Booth denied this. It was, however, quite certain that the incident had not ended before one Admiral had called the other a 'lump of flesh'. At this Berry, who was notoriously stout, had shouted 'Get out of the room, get out of the room', and had finally left it himself in a fury, threatening to appeal to the King.†

Booth's version of course was different. He had been presiding at the pay since seven in the morning – without so much as a break for dinner – when at four in the afternoon Berry, who should have been

* S. P. to Capt. Smith of the *Falcon*, July 19th, 1688. *Pepysian MSS., Adm. Letters* xiv, 278.

† *Rawl. MSS. A.* 177, f. 78.

there all the while, stumped into the room and, turning his back on him, proceeded without a word of apology or explanation to enquire what was the matter with his purser. And on being informed, he had cried out that that was all nonsense for he was an honest fellow, and without more ado had directed the clerks to pay him. At which 'extraordinary proceeding of Sir John Berry', Booth declared, 'I must confess I was provoked to an unusual degree of passion and did flatly oppose Sir John Berry . . . peremptorily insisting (by virtue of the place I was then in) upon the payment of the mulct . . . I finally broke off the dispute and according to my duty in that place caused the defalcation to be made . . . Which done, and that being all which Sir John Berry seemed concerned for, he withdrew, leaving me to prosecute the remainder of the King's business alone, which I did with the same quiet and satisfaction to all wherewith I had before done it.' Booth admitted, however, that he had been 'transported to such a degree of passion' that he had told his fellow Admiral to hold his tongue. In the circumstances, Pepys, who took shorthand notes of the evidence, was forced to recommend that both officers should be temporarily relieved from duty.[28]

For a few weeks in the second half of the summer of 1688 there was a marked slackening in the tempo of public affairs, and warlike preparations were suspended. The infatuated King, who through all the alarms of the year had continued to correspond amicably with his son-in-law, again refused to believe the existence of the treacherous project now openly whispered in every coffee-house and market place. Instead he turned his gaze from the armaments of his neighbours to the morals of his subjects. A proclamation directed as much against the rich as the poor — a particularly injudicious exercise of tyrannical power — was issued against debauchery.* The nation was to be made worthy of the divine blessing so recently and, as it seemed to James miraculously, vouchsafed it. On July 17th a magnificent celebration of fireworks was held on the Thames before a concourse of 100,000 spectators in honour of the Prince of Wales and his entry into a world which in seventy-seven rather weary years was to offer him few such courtesies.[29]

By the end of the month Strickland's fleet was back in the Downs.

---

* 'It curbs even our loose houses and regulates our very sleeping; and the good wives are well-wishers to it, for that it obliges men and masters to keep good hours and go to bed betimes.' *Ellis Correspondence* ii, 14.

On August 1st Pepys under orders from the Palace wrote that his
sovereign would not require any greater force at sea that year.
Money was tight, and there was some difficulty about paying the
Yards. At Chatham Deane was industriously putting the finishing
touches to the work of the Special Commission: 'I can truly say', he
wrote to Pepys, 'that I never took more pains nor was more zealous
to make a good issue than in this journey all my life, and hope it will
end well, it seeming a pleasure to rid the business off-hand.'*[30]

It almost seemed at that hour as though the chief remaining
naval business of the year would be to wind up the Commission,
re-appoint old Sir Richard Haddock to the revived Comptrollership
of the Navy and choose a new Victualling Comptroller in his place.
Phineas Bowles, the former Storekeeper at Tangier, was seeking the
post: his family, he explained, was a large and chargeable one, and,
Pepys, on his frequent journeys between London and Windsor, was
much solicited by this needy official. Sir William Warren was also
after the job. The great timber merchant, who had first wooed Pepys
with a silver dish and cup a quarter of a century back, had now,
what with 'misfortunes and losses by fires ashore and ships at sea',
lost almost his entire estate. 'Yet, Sir,' he assured his ancient friend,
'my spirits are not so low, nor my condition so bad, as to seek a place
for the salary's sake. I have been bred in business at home and
abroad, and always very painfully industrious therein for near 40
years. But now since my late misfortune by fire (which in a few
hours consumed all I had) I am for want of business become as a fish
out of water. And I should be the veriest fool in nature if I expected
ease and rest in the place I offer at, having seen, for about 20 years
together, your unwearied diligence day by day (and most part of the
night also) in all your stations, and all under you, together with
those you have chosen out, as Sir Anthony Deane, Mr Hewer, Mr
Hayter, etc. who I hear have come into their employ as well by your
kindness as their own great merit.'†[31]

But if the opening days of August 1688 seemed to promise quiet, it
was a promise quickly belied. The hush was one of expectancy only,
for the curtain was ready to rise on the drama which had been
preparing for so long. All the protagonists were pursuing their

* Sir A. Deane to S. P., Aug. 3rd, 1688. *Rawl. MSS. A.* 186, f. 171.
† Sir W. Warren to S. P., Aug. 20th, 1688. *Rawl. MSS. A.* 179, f. 68. See also *Rawl.
MSS. A.* 189, ff. 100–1.

respective plans, and the clash between them could no longer be delayed. Abroad Louis was preparing to extend his boundaries. Europe was arming to resist him and William of Orange assembling his ships and troops for his dash on England while there was still time. If he were to wait till Louis turned his legions towards Holland, he must needs wait for ever. Meanwhile the Dutch ambassador continued to deceive James, and James to deceive himself as to his son-in-law's intentions.[32]

In England men waited breathlessly. All who had any stake in the Protestant Reformation – the nobles and gentry who held abbey lands, the clergy of the threatened Established Church, the populace who hated Rome – looked to William. The King looked as resolutely away and pinned all his hopes on the general election for which he had so long prepared and which, he was assured, would secure him what he so ardently desired – an anti-Anglican Parliament to remove the stigma of the penal laws from the statute book.[33]

Between these contending forces stood Pepys, completing the last touches of his work of restoring, consolidating and disciplining the Navy. Soon he was to feel their shock and be drawn into the whirlwind. In the second week of August he had a foretaste of what was to come, for Deane received warning from Harwich that there was a conspiracy among their constituents to supplant them at the last moment by others because they were believed to have promised to vote for the repeal of the Test Act.* After all Pepys had done for Harwich, this was a bitter pill to swallow.[34]

There was a worse shock in store, both for him and his master. On August 16th, he left London at six in the morning to attend the King at Windsor. That day an account, too alarming to be ignored, arrived from the English agent at the Hague of William's preparations – of 23 ships of war at Amsterdam already rigged with topmasts, 11 more at Helvoetsluys fitting out with all possible speed, and others in the same advanced state of preparation elsewhere – in all 90 ships, great and small.† Pepys received confirmation of this news from Captain Faseby and from his old tutor, Joseph Hill, who in a letter written from Rotterdam on August 19th, dwelt on two

* *Rawl. MSS. A.* 179, f. 179.
† *Rawl. MSS. A.* 186, ff. 57–60, 84.

mysteries, Mr Newton's *Principia*, 'which is understood by few but deservedly admired by all that understand it', and the activity of the Dutch fleet, whose purport seemed far more intelligible to the lay mind.[35]

12

Invasion

'O, why does he stay so long behind?
Ho! by my shoul, 'tis a Protestant wind.'

Lord Wharton, *Lilliburlero*.

The Admiralty could disregard the preparations on the other side of the North Sea no longer. On the night of August 17th Pepys countermanded the orders, issued in a calmer hour, for the fleet to sail westwards, and instructed Strickland to remain in the Downs 'in the best readiness that may be for the execution of any orders'. Three days later all leave was stopped and partial mobilization ordered. All available frigates were to be concentrated in the Downs, six ships of the line fitted out for sea at once, and the 5th rates in harbour converted into fireships. All, as Pepys put it, was 'to be dispatched as for life and death'. Smacks were hastened down the river for scouting, frigates ordered to cruise off Orfordness and the Goodwins, and the *Mary* yacht sent scudding over to Holland to find the whereabouts of the Dutch fleet.[1]

Pepys, dictating letters in the office at midnight, sitting with the King in Cabinet* or hurrying between London and Windsor,† was the nerve centre of the naval mobilization. He was once more performing the task he had first essayed a quarter of a century before and had learnt to do better than anyone else in the world. By his side, as permanent chief of his London office, was Samuel Atkins, who once had faced death for his sake. Down the river his long-tried aides, Deane and Hewer, first chosen by him in the far days of his

---

* 'I so far concurred with you touching the importance of its consequences to the King at this juncture that I have made it my work this evening to communicate the same to him by reading it openly in his presence at a meeting of the Cabinet at my Lord President's.' S. P. to Sir R. Strickland, Sept. 25th, 1688. *Pepysian MSS., Adm. Letters* xv, 40–1.

'. . . having much business against the Council and the Cabinet that will be after it, which I fear also will sit late (as for some time it has continually done)'. S. P. to W. Hewer, Sept. 27th, 1688. *Pepysian MSS., Adm. Letters* xv, 55.

† See Appendix D.

administrative youth, were doing all that masters of their profession could do. The latter, writing to him from the Admiralty at midnight on the 23rd, described how he had left Deane at Chatham at eight the previous evening, reaching town at four in the morning, and had since been drafting orders all day long for getting out the ships, paying a flying visit in the afternoon to Woolwich with Balty St Michel to hasten on the work there.

To Pepys it must have seemed as though all the doubts of the past twelve months had been suddenly resolved. Now that actual invasion was threatened there could no longer be any question of divided loyalties. His master was in danger and needed the services of all his subjects, 'it being', he told a colleague, 'the time in our whole lives wherein the same can be of most use and importance to him'.* It never even occurred to his simple loyalty that it would be possible to fail that test.[2]

Not every Englishman possessed his single-hearted faith. Many saw in William's threat a hope of deliverance; most did not know what to think. One well-informed and communicative gentleman, not altogether misreading his age and his fellow men, went so far as to disbelieve the whole story, asserting that the rumours of invasion were put abroad by the Army Secretary in order to pocket the fines of officers who ignored their recall from leave.[3]

Though even as late as mid-September James, still over-persuaded by Sunderland and the lying assurances of his son-in-law and the Dutch ambassador, could not bring himself to believe that William would dare to land at such a season, and it was the fashion among the courtiers to make fun of such anxious patriots as Pepys, the possibility of invasion was at last beginning to be taken seriously. On Sunday, August 26th, an important conference was held in the royal closet at Windsor. In addition to the King and Mr Pepys, there were present Lord Dartmouth, Sir John Berry, Captain John Clements and three Elder Brethren of Trinity House, all experienced seamen. It was resolved to reject Sir Roger Strickland's advice to base his squadron on the Gunfleet on the grounds that it was an ill Road at such a season and that, if the wind should hang easterly, he would only be driven up the river by the Dutch. Instead he was to

* S. P. to Sir P. Pett and Sir W. Booth, Aug. 26th, 1688. *Pepysian MSS., Adm. Letters* XIV, 370.

leave the Downs at the first opportunity and place himself between the North Sand Head and the Kentish Knock, there to continue under sail by day and to anchor by night. Should the Dutch slip by him down the Channel, he was to follow them as far as the Scillies and, at any attempt to land, 'to proceed hostilely upon them'. Should they bend their course into the Thames he was to follow them there also, endeavouring to get the wind of them. Only in the event of a westerly wind was he to return to the Downs.[4]

During the closing weeks of August and the first three of September mobilization went forward by cumulative steps, as the fears of the Court grew, waned and grew again. Down by the waterside and on Tower Hill the drums beat for volunteers, and at the ports the carpenters broke the Sabbath with hammering, and the press-gangs waited for incoming merchant ships. 'The King our master', wrote Pepys on September 3rd to the Commander-in-Chief at Gibraltar, 'has now for about fourteen or twenty days been greatly awakened, and indeed little less than surprised by a sudden and most extraordinary preparation in Holland for some immediate enterprise at sea by an endeavour of fitting forth all at once the greatest part of their biggest ships from all their provinces, and this with a degree of industry (by working day and night, even by candlelight) that has not been exceeded, if equalled, in the most pressing times of war, and this at a season of the year so unapt and unacquainted with preparations of this kind'. Thanks, however, to the counter measures taken by the English naval administration, there was reason to hope that 'by God Almighty's ordinary blessing with the concurrence of the season we may at last reckon ourselves safe against any extraordinary mischiefs that might be otherwise apprehended from so unusual a proceeding and insult from a neighbour in alliance'.* But he added that, though there might be no attempt at invasion for the moment, the complexion of affairs at home and abroad was such that there was little hope of being able to survive the next spring without a rupture.[5]

God Almighty's blessing, judging by the subsequent course of events, was less responsible for such safety as England enjoyed than Pepys' labours. These were attended by many difficulties of which

* S. P. to Capt. Killigrew of the *Dragon*, Sept. 3rd, 1688. *Pepysian MSS., Adm. Letters* XIV, 385–7.

the most serious were an almost universal shortage of men – intensified by the simultaneous recruitment of the army and James' reluctance to use the press-gang* – and inexplicable delays by those responsible for sending down guns and provisions. Lesser trials were the vagaries of the Post Office, which kept Pepys' midnight messengers hanging about for hours while its horses were being saddled. He met them all by cheerful and unflagging industry and by a serene loyalty that was an example to the whole Service.[6]

In such a time of emergency there was no room for exclusions or for such peddling distinctions as had been depriving the public of good servants on the score of religion and politics. Sir Phineas Pett was permitted to remain at his post at Chatham, and his gout – a royal euphuism for unbending Protestantism – was conveniently forgotten. Booth and Berry returned to their Commissionerships and received commands at sea as well. Even Josiah Burchett was allowed to return to the Service, though not to the Holy of Holies above the Watergate which he had desecrated. Instead of an infinity of applications for a handful of places, there was a post henceforward for every qualified man. Yet Pepys' rules still held, for all who aspired to commissions had to show that they had been examined according to his regulations.[7]

Still the King, despite all the dangers that surrounded him, held to his perilous course. While time was yet left to him, his confessors and his conscience alike told him, he must do God's work, overthrow the Anglican monopoly, establish the freedom of the Roman Church in England and the lawful succession of a Catholic line. The nonconformist Parliament which was to secure these blessings was summoned to meet in November. Those who by their long loyalty to the Crown had earned the hatred of the 'dissatisfied Party' – now rendered powerful by the King's favour – were those whose seats were hardest to hold. 'I would be very glad to be serviceable to you and in you to the King in this affair as I could,' Pepys wrote to Sir Phineas Pett who had appealed for his help at Rochester, 'but am a little doubtful whether I can be able to attend you at the election, as having one of my own to look after, and at this time a very busy Office.'† He himself, his freehold at Harwich in danger, was forced

---

* On Sept. 18th the fleet was reported to be 6000 seamen short of its complement, though this was probably an exaggeration. *Ellis Correspondence* II, 191.

† S. P. to Sir P. Pett, Sept. 22nd, 1688. *Pepysian MSS., Adm. Letters* xv, 30-1.

to look round for an alternative seat. He accordingly asked his old friend Sir Robert Holmes, in the Isle of Wight, to keep a 'berth' for him there, where Hewer also was to be provided for. Holmes replied that he would gladly do so if he could, but begged him to let the King know of the troubles in the island itself. For here also the malcontents, encouraged by the King's folly, were growing daily bolder: 'I was never so afraid as I am at present,' he wrote, 'for fear of those devils falling upon me.'* In the meantime Pepys did his best to strengthen his hold on Harwich by getting the Customs House removed to that place from Ipswich. In the interstices of naval business he even found time to spend some hours closeted with the Customs' officials explaining to them how much the removal would benefit the trade of the country, not to mention the purses of 'the worthy gentlemen, our good friends of the Corporation'.[8]

It was not surprising that in that strained and cloudy time Pepys' temper grew a little acrid. The effects of it were felt by his negro whose debauched course of life had long been ruffling the ordered serenity of York Buildings. Such a degree of roguery had this troublesome black buck come to – 'lying, pilfering, drinking, taking tobacco in his bed and being otherwise mischievous beyond the powers of good or bad words, whipping or fetters to reform him' – that early in September Pepys came to the conclusion that he was too 'dangerous to be longer continued in a sober family'. Upon which Mrs Fane, the housekeeper, who more than agreed with him, in her furious resolve to rid the house of poor Sambo before he did some new mischief or other, got Henry Russell, the Admiralty waterman, to bundle him without a word of explanation aboard the *Foresight*, then fitting out in the River for another voyage to the West Indies. To his great annoyance, Pepys was subsequently forced to explain matters to her bewildered captain. The offending negro, he requested, should be kept to 'hard meat' till he could be disposed of 'as a rogue' in some plantation, the cost of his entertainment being deducted from the sale price and the proceeds invested in whatever Captain Stanley thought fit. 'Praying you in the meantime that you'll commit it to somebody to keep a strict hand and eye upon him, suitable to the cautions I have before given you of him.'†[9]

* Sir R. Holmes to S. P., Sept. 3rd, 1688. *Rawl. MSS. A.* 179, f. 44.

† S. P. to Capt. Stanley of the *Foresight*, Sept. 11th, 1688. *Pepysian MSS., Adm. Letters* xiv, 407–9.

Before the end of September even the King was growing aware of the sinister nature of the forces that were threatening him. Every day brought tales of new defections to William. In the London streets medals of the petitioning Bishops and prints of army officers who had protested against the inflow of papist recruits from Ireland were selling like hot cakes. On the 20th James, who had been down the river to Chatham and Sheerness to view the fortifications and naval preparations, was brought back post-haste to London by news from Holland which it was no longer possible for him to disbelieve.* He is said to have turned white and speechless at the proofs of his son-in-law's treachery. Already, he was informed, the Dutch fleet was getting aboard the last requisites for an invasion – wheelbarrows, shovels, saddles and bridles. And, bold in the extreme as such a venture seemed at that season of the year, at any moment the invaders might appear off the English coast.† Evelyn, arriving from the country, found the Court in such a panic as he could scarcely credit.[10]

These alarms were followed by new orders for mobilizing the Navy and Army, and at last by a revolutionary change in the government's policy. To the bewilderment of the nation the ship of state was seen to put her helm about and go round to the opposite course. Frightened by the way events were shaping, entreated by the remaining Tories who still clung to him, and with even Sunderland and Jeffreys now counselling surrender, the unhappy King decided to reconcile himself with the great Party which had saved him in the past and which he had so rashly alienated. On September 21st, the day after the royal return from Chatham, a Proclamation was issued promising the exclusion of Catholics from the forthcoming Parliament. Yet even this spoke of the hated proposal to remove the penal laws. For it was not in James' nature to make a bold and shameless Elizabethan withdrawal. Instead he fell back, after the manner of his father, step by step, and always a step too late.[11]

During the last days of September he interviewed the Bishops and

* 'He told me the Dutch were now coming to invade England in good earnest. I presumed to ask if he really believed it. To which the King replied with warmth, "Do I see you, my Lord"?' Clarendon, *Diary*, Sept. 24th, 1688.

† 'We are all here in great hurry, and in hourly expectation of an invasion, upon what grounds nobody yet knows.' W. Shaw to J. Ellis, Oct. 2nd, 1688. *Ellis Correspondence* II, 230.

restored Compton, already in the secret counsels of the invaders, to his see. On October 2nd he informed the Lord Mayor, Aldermen and Sheriffs of London that he would restore the ancient Charter and privileges of the City, and ten days later made good the same promise to every borough in England. On the 5th the Ecclesiastical Commission was dissolved. A week later the Anglican President and Fellows of Magdalen College, Oxford, were reinstated. Pepys' learned friend, Dr Thomas Smith, stood with his fellow exiles at the College gate and afterwards marched with them in procession to the hall, where the Bishop of Winchester in pursuance of the royal orders solemnly struck the names of the upstart papist Fellows out of the buttery book. A shoal of dismissals of Roman Catholics from the Lord Lieutenancies and other key positions followed.

Yet the uneasiness and resentment in the public mind were now too deeply rooted to be removed by such belated measures, which most people were convinced were due to nothing but fear. Good and loyal Dr Smith, even while all the bells of Oxford rang with joy at his restoration, could not help suspecting from 'some men's intolerable insolence', that an ill-use would be made of these astonishing changes. 'Oh rare invasion,' wrote one unregenerate malcontent, 'to occasion so many gracious acts in restoring things to their legal foundation which hath been the work of many years past to unhinge!' So far from sharing the King's dread of an invasion a large section of the populace seemed to want it passionately and prayed for an east wind to bring it to their shores. Half the nation was whistling *Lilliburlero*, the scurrilous anti-papist doggerel which the whig Lord Wharton – Swift's universal villain – had set to one of Purcell's irresistible airs. There must be a vengeance on Irishmen, Catholics and Palace politicians before the English would be content to be still again. And the one safety-valve that might have let off the national steam was denied: the writs for a Parliament were recalled on the grounds of the threatened invasion. In the shaken, veering counsels of the Palace the priests had won again. 'The Virgin Mary', explained the profane Jeffreys, 'is to do all!'[12]

As a matter of fact the devout King was not without hopes also of his Navy. So high were these, that sooner than offend the insular prejudices of his officers and seamen, he expressly refused an offer of French naval assistance. Though to set the battle fleet out to sea just as winter was falling was a feat unknown to the seventeenth century, a general mobilization of all but the largest ships was ordered. On September 24th the senior officer in the Service, Lord Dartmouth, was appointed to the command, with Strickland as his Vice-Admiral and Berry Rear-Admiral. As Dartmouth was a firm Protestant, the measure was calculated not only to keep away the invaders but to appease the invaded. To give the appointment a still more Protestant complexion, Pepys invited Dr Peachell, the deprived Master of Magdalene, Cambridge, to accompany Dartmouth as his Chaplain: 'judging', he wrote, 'all the qualifications (piety, authority and learning) wished for therein meet abundantly in you'. But not even Pepys' hint of a bishopric could persuade Peachell to accept. The good man had had enough of politics.[13]

On September 28th orders were given to the entire fleet to assemble at the Buoy of the Nore. Thither the squadron at sea, under Strickland, now judged too light to encounter the impending attack, was ordered to fall back. Other ships were to proceed to the rendezvous as soon as they could be got ready, from Orfordness, Yarmouth, Blackstakes, Chatham, the Hope, Long Reach, Deptford, Woolwich and Portsmouth. Even the Straits fleet at distant Gibraltar was laid under contribution. Nor were they to wait till they could be fully manned but to sail at the first opportunity before an easterly wind brought out the Dutch: if necessary they were to take soldiers aboard to make up their complements. On October 1st Fighting Instructions were issued to the Admiral.[14]

In their attitude to the invasion, which was then hourly expected,* Pepys and his sovereign showed themselves in advance of the strategical conceptions of their time. With troops posted to the north where the main blow was expected to fall, sailors like Sir William Booth and Navy officials like Sir Phineas Pett talked of the importance of 'putting the workmen of the Yards into military form and discipline'. Theirs was the old fatal delusion that an island could be secured from invasion by purely defensive measures. 'You in yours', Pepys wrote to the Commissioner at Chatham, 'do say that you had his Majesty's warrant from me for putting the shipwrights and other workmen into a military posture, whereas the whole scope and purpose of the King's warrant is to oppose and

* 'There can be nothing but the wind to-day to delay their coming forth beyond to-morrow or Friday.' S. P. to Sir A. Deane, Sept. 26th, 1688. *Pepysian MSS., Adm. Letters* xv, 45.

suppress the proposition you and Sir William Booth had . . . made to the King for putting them into such a posture. So before anything can be done in demanding the supplies you desire of arms, powder, swords, etc, I am forced to desire you will consider the King's warrant again and what of that demand will be necessary to be made for enabling you to put in execution what the King's warrant does indeed desire, which is not the marshalling of the workmen and forming them into the same method and under the same discipline as soldiers are, but only distributing them and quartering them to the several posts (the particulars thereof the King does in a great measure reckon up to you in the said warrant) for the securing those their respective posts in case of any approaches of an enemy.'*[15]

But the bolder sea counsels of August 26th were superseded by a more cautious plan.† A Drake, a Blake, a Nelson, and perhaps, had he lived, a Narbrough might conceivably have dared all and met Orange's threat with a shock of frigates amid the Zeeland shoals while the battle fleet was making ready. Honest George Legge did not feel justified in taking so overwhelming a risk on a dead lee shore in a season of tempests. He preferred to keep his fleet in the Thames till he was able to meet the invader with equal or superior force. Recalling the limitations of seventeenth-century ships, it is hard to blame him. The technique of long cruising, and still more of close blockade, had still to be learnt.

For the moment, therefore, the work of defending England depended mainly on Pepys and his subordinates in York Buildings and the river shipyards. And so long as the wind blew hard from the west and William's ships lay bound in their harbours, it might avail. But what if the wind should change before the work was complete? On that question the fate of England depended for five anxious weeks until it was decided, not by a daring Admiral with his guns blazing amid crowded transports, but by the winds of Heaven. In the formal Fighting Instructions which Pepys by orders of the Council drafted on October 1st, Dartmouth was empowered to 'endeavour by all hostile means to sink, burn, take and otherwise

* S. P. to Sir P. Pett, Oct. 11th, 1688. *Pepysian MSS., Adm. Letters* xv, 139–40.
† Mr Powley in his brilliant monograph on the *English Navy in the Revolution of 1688* seems to overlook the fact that the fatal decision to assemble the fleet at the Buoy of the Nore must almost certainly have been made on the advice of Lord Dartmouth, whose appointment to the command it closely followed.

destroy and disable' the 'armed force of foreigners and strangers', which a second William the Conqueror was preparing to launch against his country. Yet so long as Dartmouth remained in the Thames that was just what he could not do.[16]

The story of that fatal month which resolved the destiny of unborn millions is to be found in the daily correspondence between the English Admiral and the Secretary of the Admiralty. It began on October 3rd when Pepys wrote to Dartmouth to congratulate him on his safe arrival at the Buoy of the Nore and to tell him of the steps he was taking, by moving buoys and lighthouses at Harwich and in the mouth of the River, to guard against a Dutch attack before the fleet was ready. It followed three themes – the transmission of news received from the Admiralty scouts, the measures for sending Dartmouth the ships, men, victuals, stores and guns he required, and his persistent attempts to coax his Lordship a little nearer the enemy. The last were conducted, both on his own and the King's account, with scrupulous deference to Dartmouth's proper freedom of action, his rights as a commander, and his feelings as a nobleman.[17]

The Admiral's constitutional reluctance to attack did not extend to epistolary operations against the Admiralty. As was his duty he engaged in these with considerable spirit and persistence. Always inclined to be despondent, and with much embittering experience behind him, Dartmouth in the isolation of his flagship could never rid his mind of the suspicion that the men on shore were denying him a fair deal. With his friend Pepys in command of the administration it was hard to say this in so many words, but the inevitable delays of a hasty mobilization gave him plenty of matter for complaints. These he forwarded daily to Pepys, who passed them on to those concerned and answered them with forbearance. He admitted the delays in the victualling and apologized for them; that over-harassed department, he explained, had just had to take over the additional task of provisioning the military garrisons, which, 'does occasion no small interruption'. And his Majesty had in a single week haled the Victualling Commissioners three times into his presence to impress on them the urgency of his Lordship's needs.[18]

Dartmouth, anxious and weighed down with the responsibility of his position, was less patient in reply. 'I here enclose you Mr

Steventon (Agent to the Commissioners of the Victualling) his Memorial given me this day,' he wrote on the 13th, 'with my remarks thereon, which, after showing his Majesty, I desire you will transmit to the Victualling Office to prevent any further writing about it, or their saying the business is done, but that it may be really so.' Neither then nor at any time in his life could Dartmouth, in ordinary relationships the most obliging and forbearing of men, resist the temptation of writing cutting letters. On at least one occasion Pepys was driven to complain of the injustice of his doing so, but the Admiral was inexorable. 'Sir,' he replied, 'though I am very well assured you have assiduously performed your part as Secretary, yet other officers have not, as I have often repeated to you, and do once more most earnestly desire that all excuses may be laid aside and everything effectually done for his Majesty's service, the pressing necessities whereof oblige me to give you my opinion that a further delay may be of fatal consequence.'*[19]

Pepys bore it all with patience, born of long service and understanding of Dartmouth's feelings. Yet it was not to be expected that the war at sea could be waged without that other and departmental war that always breaks out on such occasions on the home front. There was a sharp though decorous exchange of hostilities between the Secretary and the Admiral over the number of supernumeraries aboard the flagship. Fifty, Pepys explained, was the number allowed to the Lord High Admiral at sea, whereas an Admiral with the union flag at the maintop was only entitled to thirty. When Dartmouth replied with a broadside of historical arguments, Pepys returned his fire with extracts from his own Regulations. 'What may have been done before the date of the last solemn Establishment in 1677 about the supernumerary allowance for flags I know not, or what has been done since, either abroad without order or by order from home, in the time of my absence from the Navy. And I do firmly believe it will never appear that fifty men were ever allowed to any flag but the standard since the date of that Establishment by any order that passed my hand.' There was no shifting Pepys from his guns.[20]

Guns, indeed, were one of the causes of administrative battle. When Dartmouth complained of lack of men and victuals, Pepys,

* Lord Dartmouth to S. P., Oct. 13th, 1688. *Rawl. MSS. A.* 186, f. 353.

weary from long interviews with Watermen's Hall or the Victualling Commissioners, and confronted on his return to York Buildings with another of Dartmouth's angry letters, was sometimes driven to retaliate by allusions to the deficiencies of the Ordnance Department, of which, inconveniently enough, Dartmouth was Master. 'I persuade myself', he wrote of a complaint of lack of gunners' stores, 'I need not trouble the officers of the Ordnance from hence with any intimations of what you observe relating to the wants some ships are still under . . . as being well assured that it will be abundantly done by a better hand, I mean your own.' 'How it has come to pass', he added a little later, 'I know not . . . but the King has understood from Captain Constable that the *St Albans* had four ports on the quarter-deck which the Establishment has provided no guns for.'[21]

Such exchanges were perhaps inevitable: under a fierce strain of mind and body, even the noblest tempers show the marks of human frailty. More usually the tone of Pepys' correspondence with Dartmouth was that of a brother in arms in a common service: 'I pray God with all my heart to give you the fruit of the pains which I am sure you are taking for it.'[22]

Far different was the spirit of some of the gentlemen commanders when confronted with the routine requirements and restrictions of the Navy Board. 'Right Honourables,' wrote Lord Berkeley in his large, childish hand, 'your letter of the 14th this morning came to my hands, where you tell me you have not power to add to my allowance of junk. This for your Honours' sake I ought to keep to myself, for should sarcastical people know it, I fear it would make a mighty jest. Indeed I did not expect to have been denied so small a request, for surely you do not think I should eat or sell the junk? No, but he will suffer his boatswain to bobble him! I should be sorry your Honours had so mean an opinion of my judgment as to think I would be put upon, or of my affection to his Majesty's service to see him cheated for the obliging of such a fellow as a boatswain or carpenter.'* 'We have received your Lordship's answer of the 17th,' the Navy Board replied to this gentlemanly epistle, 'the style of which we know how to observe, though not to imitate, intending to submit it with all humility to the King to judge of the difference.'†

---

* Lord Berkeley to Navy Board, Sept. 17th, 1688. *Rawl. MSS. A.* 186, f. 225.
† Navy Board to Lord Berkeley, Sept. 19th, 1688. *Rawl. MSS. A.* 186, f. 304.

Though the reply was signed by Berry, Pett, Deane and Hewer, one suspects that the Admiralty Secretary may have had a hand in its drafting.[23]

Few of the gentlemen captains of the fleet came well out of the ordeal of mobilization. Perhaps their hearts were with their elder brothers or cousins who plotted rebellion in their country houses and awaited their 'deliverance' at the hands of Dutch William. Pepys told Dartmouth how it grieved him to the heart to hear how senior officers sauntered away their time when there was nobody at their backs: 'I have this evening beseeched the King to lay his commands upon his sea captains that are still walking in Whitehall to repair to their charges, as some of them, to my astonishment as well as grief, to this day do.' Here lay the root of all his difficulties. 'My Lord,' he replied to another of Dartmouth's complaints, 'I observe what you say concerning the wants, or at least demands for supplies of stores, from your ships of the fleet. But it can be thought no new thing to anyone that has known the fitting forth of fleets so long as your Lordship and myself have done. For I hardly ever remember a ship that could not find something or other to ask within ten days after they went out. Nor do I ever expect to see it otherwise till commanders will think fit to observe their instructions more.' It was for him the old, old story.[24]

Those admirable officials, the Special Commissioners, did their best. But they suffered from overwork and could not be everywhere at once: and Pepys had to warn Dartmouth early in October that he could not spare any more of them for the fleet since there were scarcely enough of them left in London to form a Board. On the 4th he found Deane 'extremely indisposed, so as not to be able to stir out of doors, and poor Mr Hewer little better, through the unintermitted succession of business to be dispatched from morning to night, and nobody at present to look after any part of it but them two'. A week later Deane was in bed: 'considering', wrote his loyal chief, 'what has lain upon his hand and his alone for a great while it is my wonder he has held up so long'. 'I wish heartily your health,' he wrote to him on the 12th, 'and were I at my liberty to stir from this place would not have failed to visit you long before now; and shall, I believe, very soon, possibly at night if the Cabinet does not sit beyond 7 at night, that I may be with you and Mr Hewer before 8; but after that hour don't expect me.'*[25]

The mid-hour of mobilization saw the execution of the royal resolution of the previous spring to restore the old administrative constitution of the Navy. On October 12th the Special Commission was formally dissolved and three days later the rule of the Principal Officers revived. Lord Falkland remained as Treasurer and Sir Richard Haddock was recalled to the Comptrollership. Sir John Tippetts was re-appointed Surveyor, James Sotherne Clerk of the Acts, and Sir Phineas Pett, Sir Richard Beach and Balty St Michel Resident Commissioners at Chatham, Portsmouth and Deptford. Sir John Berry and Sir William Booth, now both flying their flags at sea, became Comptroller of Victualling and of Storekeeping Accounts respectively. Deane and Hewer, the two pivot men of the administration, were retained as temporary Commissioners.[26]

The work of the Special Commission passed almost unnoticed. In that crowded hour its very success obliterated it. Contemporaries and posterity were alike almost oblivious of it. Yet its achievement was to remain a coping stone of the British imperial structure. In two and a half years, six months less than its estimated term, it had rebuilt almost wholly twenty ships, all of the line of battle, and repaired sixty-nine others. It had also built three new 4th rates and thirty-three storehouses, and laid down an eight months' reserve of sea stores for every ship – 'such a treasure of stores', Pepys proudly claimed, 'as England was never before mistress of'. Nor, he might have added, of such a treasure of ships. Against the new naval strategy of the future the Special Commission provided Britain with a strength of fifty-nine capital ships of the first three rates. Henceforward the Grand Fleet was to be a permanent influence in the counsels of Europe and the world.

All this, including the ordinary charge of maintaining the Service, had been done at a cost of £307,000 p.a. or 22s. per man per month. Not a pennyworth of debt was left unpaid. And now during the closing weeks of its existence and at a time when navies were wont by immemorial custom to lay up for the winter, the Special Commission had on a sudden alarm prepared for sea no less than sixty-seven ships of war, including twelve 3rd rates of the line and twenty-eight 4th rates. No wonder Pepys was modestly pleased with his handiwork. 'I cannot', he told the retiring Commissioners, 'but with great satisfaction reflect upon the condition you will be remembered to have left the Navy of England in, when it shall appear that the last command you had to execute from the King was upon a warrant for fitting forth of ships presented him by me with blanks for the numbers to be filled at his pleasure with his own royal hand. God grant that this, which I take to be the first instance to be met with of the kind since England had a Navy, may ever be within the power of your successors to follow you in.'[27]

Pepys by his life-work had taught his country how to equip, regulate and maintain a fleet. But he could not teach that fleet how to fight. That was still to be the lesson of her sea Admirals, grasped for a moment under the inspired tuition of such as Drake, Myngs and Blake, but awaiting the genius of the great captains of a later age to transform into a permanent habit and rule. Good honest gentleman that he was, Dartmouth was not such a teacher. The trident which Pepys had fashioned for him was for other hands to grasp.

Without a numerical superiority Dartmouth had no wish to risk his ships in battle with the Dutch. It seemed to him, as it seemed to another British Admiral under very different circumstances two centuries later, that the political issues were too great to be staked on the uncertain fate of a sea fight unless victory could be assured from the first. He had been entrusted with his country's fleet and it was his duty to keep it safe and intact. There are many who hold that by doing so he performed unconsciously the greatest service he could have done her, for it so survived unimpaired to fight a mightier enemy than the Dutch when the transient Stuart cause it failed to defend had vanished into smoke.

Be that as it may, Dartmouth from the start resisted every attempt to hustle his fleet out to sea, though strenuously protesting his desire to meet the enemy. While Pepys in the first week of October, ignoring all deficiencies that could not be remedied in such an emergency, despatched ship after ship to the Buoy of the Nore, telling the Admiral that it was far better he should have them so than wait for their full manning until the wind changed, that cautious warrior contented himself with dictating letters about the need for additional men and victuals. Had he but these, he explained, he would not stay two hours more at his anchorage. Pepys replied that the administration did not wish to fetter him in any way and left everything to his discretion. A letter of October 5th from the King to the Admiral again stressed the importance of getting his ships to sea while he could: 'I need not mind you to lose no time to get out from among the sands as fast as you can.'[28]

But Dartmouth was not going to be hurried. On the 4th one of his scouts had reported that there were only seven Dutch ships of war riding off the Maas: if the prevailing westerly gales continued he did not doubt to be at sea before them. The gales continued: as Pepys put it, 'the wind (thanks be to God) sits'. Next day Dartmouth, commenting on some intelligence from Holland sent him from the Admiralty, gave it as his opinion that the enemy's fleet would try to engage him while the transports took a different direction to effect a landing.*It never seemed to occur to him that his best course might be to attack the latter. In another letter he expressed his belief that the transports would not come out at all so long as his fleet remained in being. 'I well know our being beaten may prove a fatal consequence', was the recurring motif of his correspondence. And he dwelt sadly on his fears that he would be forced to put to sea in the end 'with few ships and those not in the condition they ought to be' in a stormy, inclement season of the year. It was the good, fearful, gallant gentleman's nightmare.[29]

It is only when Dartmouth's unhappy position is fully realized that his inadequacy as England's Admiral at this juncture can be appreciated. It is perfectly true that judged by purely technical considerations he was right not to venture his fleet on the Dutch coast in mid-October. Seventeenth-century ships were not made to stay at sea in autumnal gales. This was as true of the Dutch fleet as of the English: it was even truer of their crowded transports. Had Dartmouth ventured to sea the English fleet might well have been dashed to pieces on the sands of Holland, though more probably it would have been scattered and driven back piecemeal to its own harbours. It was undermanned and still very much under strength: every day it waited for reinforcements, Pepys' labours made it stronger. But, however grateful posterity has cause to be to Dart-

---

* Mr Powley, relying on a later letter of the 12th, holds – mistakenly, it would seem – that Dartmouth never entertained such a belief. See Powley, 60.

mouth for keeping, all unconsciously, his fleet intact to wage the wars of a new dynasty, it is only fair to remember that that was not why he commanded it. He was there to save his master's kingdom from invasion. He was a Protestant, but he was also a loyal gentleman who had eaten the King's bread. Unlike others, he never intended to betray him while drawing his pay.

Viewed in that light, Dartmouth's position was simple. He had everything to gain by engaging William's transports and their escorts and scarcely anything to lose. For once the invader had landed, his own carefully husbanded ships could do little against them. They might cut off his supplies, but a seventeenth-century army could live on the country, especially on so fat a one as England. And the whole point of William's coming was that the people, excited by anti-Catholic propaganda, might rise in his support. Against that possibility was the awkward fact that the would-be deliverer was coming at the head of a Dutch army and under cover of a Dutch fleet, and that the English had no love for the Dutch. For two generations they had been their rivals and antagonists. William's marriage with Mary of England had done much to quiet that antagonism and the fears of France and Catholicism felt by both peoples still more. Yet once let Dutchmen and Englishmen exchange blows, particularly on their ancient battlefield, the sea, and the fires of racial hatred would blaze up anew. William's hope was to avoid that clash at all costs. Dartmouth had it in his power to force it upon him should he venture to sea, though at the price of jeopardizing his master's ships. But if they were not to be jeopardized in so fatal a crisis of his own and his kingdom's fortunes, for what purpose had they been built?

His Majesty and the Secretary of the Admiralty were charmingly patient towards the loyal Admiral to whom they had entrusted their all. 'Though all that are in the Hope should not be quite ready,' wrote the former on October 8th, 'consider well whether you should lose the opportunity of this westerly wind to get out from amongst the sands or venture to have the Dutch come and find you somewhere near the Buoy of the Oaze Edge amongst the sands. For you must expect they will come out and be looking for you with the first easterly wind.' Dartmouth replied on the 12th that the King could not be more desirous to have him out of the sands than he was himself of leaving them, but that storms, lack of victuals and the non-arrival of the ships from Portsmouth prevented him. 'I hope,' he protested, 'I am not blameable to get what I can together for so great a work as I have to do, with an enemy likely to be so much superior to me. And I judge it much more for your service to unite while we have time than to drop out in parcels with the hazard of being separated, especially knowing myself here in the best place to do my business while these winds continue. And be assured, Sir, I will be on sea upon the first alteration.' The memory of the fatal division of the fleet before the Four Days' battle of 1666 still haunted the English memory. At almost any other time but this Dartmouth would have been right.[30]

In the same letter, however, the Admiral suggested that, as soon as the Portsmouth ships joined him and the wind moderated, he should show himself on the Dutch coast. He added, perhaps a little superfluously, that he would be careful not to 'peak himself' or do anything rash. Unfortunately this was the moment that the King, with true Stuart irresolution, chose to waver a little and to remind his Admiral of the season of the year and of 'the blowing weather' to be expected. At any rate he must leave the decision to him, 'being sure you will do what is best for my service, which you that are on the place are the only judges of, and must govern yourselves according to the enemy's motions and as wind and weather will permit'. And, with ill-timed confidence, he pointed out that he had an army and enjoyed the peculiar protection of the Deity. 'The Scots and Irish troops are marching as fast as they can to join me . . . I make no doubt but that God will protect me and prosper my arms both by land and sea.'[31]

On that very day, October 14th, the wind shifted into the east. It was the anniversary of William the Conqueror's victory at Hastings. All England waited for invasion. But Dartmouth, though he had thirty-five fighting ships and fourteen fireships ready to sail* was now powerless. All he could do was to get his fleet as far as the Oaze Edge and there place himself in the best defensive posture he was able. But Pepys, thinking him on the eve of departure, wrote to him on the 16th to bid him God-speed: 'And now, my Lord, not knowing whether your stay may give me opportunity of writing to you before your leaving the river, I do most fervently beg of God Almighty to

* *Rawl. MSS. A.* 186, f. 352.

protect and guide you in your present undertaking so that you may
return with the success and safety which all good men wish you.'
How often before had the little Secretary sent out English fleets with
like wishes![32]

But an evil and treacherous inertia lay over the English naval
action that fatal October. Pepys and his virtuous subordinates
seemed like men running in a dream: they strove furiously yet saw
all things motionless beside them. The victualling barges sent down
the river in haste loitered for days before reaching the fleet, and the
pressed seamen bound for the same destination flung the escorting
musketeers overboard and swam ashore. And such was the conduct
of the gentlemen captains that even Pepys began to despair.
'Unless', he told Dartmouth on the 17th, 'there be another spirit put
into some of their commanders (I mean as to diligence and
concernment for the Service and not making of it as a by-business,
annexed only as a convenience to their employments elsewhere), I
shall bid goodnight to the expectations of any good to the Service
from them, let you and myself make as much on't as we please . . .
But for ought I see gentlemen are got above being jealous of any
censure, or else they would not appear to the King every day at
Court complaining that their ships are not ready, while nothing is
wanting towards making them ready but their own attendance on
board.'[33]

There was worse than slackness: there was black downright
treachery by men in the King's pay. One could not prove it, but one
sensed it was there. Dartmouth thanked God for the sea room at the
Oaze Edge that enabled him to keep his captains aboard their own
ships and thus incapable of caballing. Which, he added, being both
idle and English, they might very well do, particularly with so many
pamphlets and newsletters about. On October 22nd he warned the
King of signs of dissatisfaction among some of his younger commanders. 'I am glad Priestman is not amongst us, and I think he ought
to be a little watched for he sets up for a leading politician. The
Duke of Grafton' – a bastard of the late King and a Protestant – 'was
down here among them a little after my coming, though he would
not let me know it. My Lord Berkeley I am told is very pert, but I
have taken him in the next ship to me and shall know more of their
tempers in a little time.' Yet the Admiral was still convinced that
most of his commanders were men of honour.[34]

For all the fears and jealousies of the nation there were still many who were, and who felt, as one of them put it, that an invader ought to be opposed, whatever his pretexts. 'I trust', wrote honest Charles Hatton on the 16th when the enemy were expected hourly, 'the nation in general will behave themselves with loyalty to their prince and regard to their country that the Dutch in 1688 will succeed no better than the Spaniards in 1588.' They were not likely to if the English fleet could but meet their transports on the high seas. But Dartmouth and his ships were 'hooked' among the sands at the Oaze Edge and could not move.[35]

Pepys, who had warned Dartmouth from the first of the danger of staying there too long, wrote to him on the 17th of the royal fears that he would be surprised by the Dutch taking advantage of the wind that imprisoned him among the sands. Though there were reports that they had suffered damage and delay by the storms their intentions no longer admitted of doubt. They were bringing, he reported, 'an incredible number of coats and other clothing for the men they expect to raise here and small arms without stint, even to the making it a difficulty to buy a hand gun, pistol or sword in all the country . . . and a vast quantity of lime, to what uses your Lordship is a much better judge than myself'.[36]

Dartmouth also was well equipped. Victuals and men were now coming in fast and the Portsmouth ships had at last joined him. This he admitted in his letter to the King of the same day, 'so that now we begin to look in earnest, and the fleet are all in as good heart as can be desired'. And on October 20th, after nearly a week of suspense, the wind shifted back with gale force into the west. Every Catholic face shone. James was jubilant: it was plain, he told his Admiral, that God Almighty wished him well, 'which will give you an opportunity to get out and hinder the enemy from coming over, and give you an opportunity of waiting on them when they shall come out'.[37]

It was one that Dartmouth would not or could not seize. How far he was prevented from acting by the weather we cannot be certain. On the 20th he waited for a final store ship: on the 21st and 22nd for better weather. Pepys, struggling with tired workmen and recalcitrant captains, worked the clock round to get the last six ships down the river: 'I do assure your Lordship', he told him, 'I do with the same zeal continue to press the dispatch of the rest that are left behind that I would do for my victuals if I were hungry. And did it last night to the King at the Cabinet by observing to him in these very words, that these delays are no more than must be expected while gentlemen are allowed to hold ships at sea *in commendam* with troops and companies ashore, at a time when there is an equal necessity for their attendance upon both.'[38]

One example of this kind of thing stuck long in Pepys' memory. Waiting in the Bedchamber for his royal master to leave the Closet for the evening meeting of the Cabinet, at a time when the whole future of England was hanging in the balance, he saw, to his anger and amazement, the captain of one of the new 3rd rates standing in the room. He resolved to expose him there and then in the royal presence, but was prevented by the King's arriving late. During the Cabinet meeting he sat simmering, and the moment the proceedings closed and before the King could rise, interposed, that though his Majesty had nothing further to add, he had something for which he was sorry. He then related what he had seen. 'Upon which', he told Dartmouth, 'the King with some surprise asked me what had brought him up from his ship. I answered I knew not, nor did he think fit upon his seeing me there to say anything of it to me or so much as to take notice of his being where I might not well have expected him. But I added that I took it (to make it at all supportable) that he had his Majesty's leave for it; though I observed to his Majesty that if leaves of that kind be signified to commanders by any hand than mine while I have the honour of serving him in my post, it would be to no purpose for me to pretend longer to give him the account I ought and he expected from me of his fleet.'

But the King, it seemed, had granted no such leave nor had any idea what had brought the truant captain to town. 'My lord,' Pepys continued, 'I do not think myself at liberty to mention anything said in that place on this occasion by any of my Lords. But I think I may be bold here to say what passed between the King and myself only . . . For (in one word) I will have all the world to know that, as considerable as it takes the profit of my employment to be, and indeed by the King's favour it is, it should not, were it ten times greater, purchase my staying in it one day longer than I can see his Service thrive as well as I. And that I am sure it never can, from the moment that such a violation as this in the discipline and honour of it passes uncensored.'

Very different was the case of Captain Tennant of the *Tiger*, who in his eagerness to be gone had carried off the riggers from Chatham Dockyard much to everyone's inconvenience. 'The truth is, Captain Tennant's zeal in getting his ship into condition to join your Lordship again was so laudable and indeed exemplary for others (if they would please to take notice of it) that it would almost have excused the carrying away a priest from the altar.' There were times when even Pepys could approve a breach of his rules.[39]

Those waiting weeks at the end of October 1688 had something of the instability of a nightmare. The King fluctuated between blind confidence and active terror. On the 22nd the whole Palace was turned upside-down by a hastily-staged Presence at which he treated a great concourse of embarrassed noblemen and officials to the authentic tale of the royal delivery, presented with every circumstance of anatomical and womanly detail, even to the blood-stained linen, by a procession of midwives, nurses and ladies-in-waiting. Good Mrs Pearse, whom Elizabeth had once so unaccountably called wench, played a notable part in these matronly revelations. They became, of course, the talk of the town, though not in the way the King had intended: 'the men', wrote one outraged lady, 'are grown very learned: it is shameful to hear what discourse is common amongst them, even to footmen and lackeys'. Four days later, to everyone's astonishment and most people's joy, Lord Sunderland, whose double-dyed treachery had at last become clear even to his credulous master, was dismissed. Meanwhile the London mob burned a Popish chapel and waylaid such luckless Irish soldiers as were rash enough to stray from their quarters into the streets. Two of them taking a Sabbath stroll were chased into St Michael's, Cornhill, where their frantic cries of 'Mercy! Mercy!' were mistaken by the startled congregation for the first sounds of a massacre. On that sudden alarm, one Protestant leg at least was broken as its frightened owner leapt desperately out of a window.[40]

At the heart of a distressed kingdom Pepys pursued his business, looking neither to left nor right. 'You must not wonder if at so busy a time as it has for divers weeks past been here to me in matters that would not admit to any interruption,' he wrote as late as the 30th to old Sir Phineas Pett, 'that I have no sooner answered your letter of the 22nd . . . upon the unseasonable difference . . . between yourself and Sir William Booth. I must confess divisions of that kind between gentlemen of the same commission must have too ill consequences to the king's service that they should be passed over without censure. It was my opinion so in what has not long before happened between Sir John Berry and Sir William Booth. And it is so in this. Nevertheless in a case like this of yours where one denies flatly what the other asserts, you affirming of his calling of you scoundrel, if not rascal, his saying that he cared not a turd for you, his giving you frequently the lie and challenging of you, while . . . he does not seem to own any particular of this, offering to prove upon oath by some of the standers-by that he did not treat you as you say he did, I find not myself able where to determine the right or the wrong to be.' And he asked him to let him know the names of his witnesses.

In the same letter Pepys condoled with Pett on the ill-success of his election at Rochester, 'concerning which I shall only say that tho' I was sorry for it, and I think you pretty hardly used in it by some that might (for the King's sake at least) have done otherwise than they did, though they would not for yours, yet I am far from wondering at it, since I verily persuade myself the greatest part of the Elections of England would have deceived expectations as much as this did yours for reasons out of you and your friends' powers to have prevented. And therefore must as a Philosopher advise you to let it pass as a bad bargain of which few men in their lifetime escape without meeting of some.'* So true a philosopher had Pepys become, that in the midst of repelling an invasion, he even found time to write to the Bishop of London about the scandalous scarcity of chaplains in the Navy, praying the blessing of his Lordship's recommendation in so essential and pious a work: there were only eight, he pointed out, in a fleet of thirty-eight warships and twelve fireships. But the Bishop was otherwise engaged, his strenuous if perjured piety providing the pivot on which the secret course of rebellion was turning. His thoughts were far away – with the invaders whom he had invited into England.[41]

But England's Admiral believed that the danger had passed. On the 14th he moved at last, sailing from the Nore in the morning and anchoring at noon in the Gunfleet. Its position among the Essex sands made it a perilous base at such a juncture, as James had pointed out to Strickland eight months before. But Dartmouth

* S. P. to Sir P. Pett, Oct. 30th, 1688. *Pepysian MSS., Adm. Letters* XIV, 269–70.

seemed well content to be there, with as fine a winter squadron, he told the King, as England had ever set out. 'Sir, we are now at sea before the Dutch after all their boasting, and I must confess I cannot see much sense in their attempts with the hazard of such a fleet and army at the latter end of October . . . I wonder to hear by so many letters of the frights that are ashore, though I thank God they take no effects upon us here . . . Your statesmen may take a nap and recover, the women sleep in their beds, and the cattle I think need not be drove from the shore.' It was, as it were, an Admiral's lullaby to England.[42]

Across the North Sea command was held by men of a steelier temper. Two days later, in the evening of the 26th, Pepys was kept long from his bed by important news from the King's agent in Holland. A week before the Dutch, breaking every canon of naval warfare, had come out with 52 men-of-war and 500 transports from Helvoetsluys, as James, who knew his son-in-law's resolution, had warned Dartmouth they would do. But the sudden change of wind next day had given the King and his cautious champion-at-sea one last chance. The great gale of the week-end had driven back the laden transports and their escort of frigates in confusion to their moorings. Had it come a day later or had the English fleet, or even an outlying squadron of it, been there instead of lying cooped up in the Thames, their fate might well have been a terrible one. So it came to pass that one of the boldest feats of arms statesmen ever undertook* escaped the destruction which in sober truth it seemed to merit and invite.[43]

In the course of the night that brought the news of the first Dutch attempt and the storm that defeated it, Pepys, writing at 2 a.m. on the 17th, urged on Dartmouth the advisability of appearing at once off the enemy's coast and taking advantage of their present confusion. Yet even in that vital hour, this model Secretary of the Admiralty was careful to assure him that under no circumstances would the King press on him any action contrary to his judgment, 'in regard that you at sea keep better account of the courses of the wind, and more true, than we either do or can do here'.[44]

Good subject and admirable seaman, the Admiral saw his fleet, not as a means for annihilating the enemy but as a sacred trust

---

* D'Albeville reported in his letter of 20/30 Oct. that 'Tromp refused to go'. *Pepysian MSS., Adm. Letters* xv, 252.

committed to his charge which it was his duty at all costs to keep intact. From on board his flagship, the ironically named *Resolution*, he wrote to Pepys on the 28th that he felt that this object was so essential to the nation's safety that, considering the time of year, it would be inadvisable to venture to the Dutch coast while the wind stayed in the west. This opinion he had placed before his commanders at a Council-of-War and received from them, with the one exception of Sir William Jennens ('in terms, I think, not very proper'),* their confirmation. The invader's design struck him as utterly desperate and ill-advised. 'The whole proceeding at this season', he told his sovereign, 'looks like the advice of land men, or at least men of desperate fortunes than men that know how to accomplish what they have undertaken.' For his part he would not struggle too much against wind and weather but leave that to the Dutch. 'Their growing mad shall not provoke me to follow their example.' It was the attitude of the professional – careful, unimaginative and correct, and well suited to every occasion but that desperate hour.[45]

The councils of the invaders were moved by a different spirit. Orange, whose ignorance was bliss, had resolved to try again. Under his banner, half the adventurers of Europe were gathered together. Of these none were more desperate than the English and Scottish exiles: 'there is not in Hell a wickeder crew', the Marquis d'Albeville had written from the Hague. Such were the men who had planned treason with Shaftesbury and all but sent Pepys to the gallows in the roaring days of '79.† Among them was Harbord who

* Burchett's view of Jennens' proposal, which he avers was backed by others, was that it carried 'the greatest weight with it, had there been a real design of obstructing the Prince of Orange in his passage to England, but instead of that matters were so concerted and agreed among the commanders (who had frequently private meetings to consider the circumstances of affairs) that had the Admiral come fairly up with the Dutch, it would not have been within his power to have done them much damage, although I have reason to believe that his Lordship and some of the captains would have exerted themselves to the utmost'. Josiah Burchett, *A Complete History of the most Remarkable Transactions at Sea* (1720), 414.

The author of *George Byng, Lord Torrington's Memoirs*, takes the same view, that 'though the great number of captains were steady in their principles for the King, yet the chiefest and most considerable of them were otherwise inclined and . . . brought over a majority of the council to think it was hazarding the fleet to lie on that dangerous coast at this time of the year'.

† 'All the rebels and traitors of the old and new stamp go with them.' Marquis d'Albeville to the King, Oct. 30th, 1688. *Rawl. MSS. A.* 186, f. 90. Printed in Smith ii, 327.

had bribed the false witnesses against him, and the old republican Wildman who had drunk and plotted with Scott. In their cups they spoke merrily of executing King James and of hanging the pretended Prince of Wales in his swaddling clothes. At their head was the dissolute, foul-tongued Herbert to whose desperate hands the great Liberator had entrusted the command of his fleet. By such rough instruments our liberties were made.[46]

Yet they did William's business, and all unknowing England's prudent Admiral gave them his aid. Some among them like Herbert and Russell had counted on dissatisfaction in the English Navy. But with Pepys to administer it and Dartmouth to command it, it was not in its loyalty that the country's first line of defence was to fail. 'I hear', the Admiral wrote of his enemies, 'they wear English colours and talk of treating with us. But pray, Sir, be assured I will suffer no language to be spoke to them but out of your guns.' In his sober prudence he never gave himself a chance to use them.[47]

The divine favour was now offered to one more resolute. He did not refuse it. The final days of October saw the wind blowing again from the east. The anxious crowds who gazed up at the church vanes from the streets of English cities knew now that God was Protestant after all. On the 30th Dartmouth, unable to delude himself any longer as to the Dutch resolve and ability to sail, weighed anchor for the open sea. He was too late. The wind after its long westerly spell now stayed unwaveringly in the east. For more than three days he fought in vain to get clear of the sands off the mouth of the Thames. And on November 1st the Prince of Orange sailed once more from Helvoetsluys with the wind he had waited and prayed for in his sails. His and England's hour of destiny had come.[48]

Pepys, perhaps, knew it. 'A pinch', he wrote on that fatal day as he waited for news from the fleet, 'wherein the very being, as well as honour of his Crown and Government is at stake.' Both that day and next listeners in the villages east of London fancied that they heard the sound of guns. But no gun was fired. Steering first north-west towards the Yorkshire coast, Orange's straggling Armada suddenly turned south-west towards the Channel while Dartmouth and his men-of-war were still trying to clear the Galloper Sand. On the morning of the 3rd the invaders were sighted by the English frigates off the Downs, and an hour after noon watchers on the Dover cliffs saw them driving westwards before the wind, their decks washed by great seas and so numerous that there was no counting them. By eleven that night the King and Pepys had learnt the worst.[49]

In that bitter hour of defeat no word of reproach to the Admiral sullied Pepys' pen. In the letter that he wrote to him in the early hours of the 4th there was not so much as an expression even of regret. He confined himself to recording the bare news and how he had left the King in council with his generals gallantly preparing orders for the despatch of his army towards Portsmouth, now believed to be the invaders' destination. Only long afterwards, and in the secrecy of his private memoranda, did he commit to paper the sense of his own cruel disappointment at the memory of those wasted weeks – wasted by the friend who had wielded the instrument he had so painfully and lovingly made. 'What a pother was heretofore made', he recorded recalling the silly charge that once had sent him to the Tower, 'about the pretended discovery of our sands, etc, to strangers! While it now appears how little use we were able to make of our supposed only knowledge of them ourselves at so critical a juncture as that was when my Lord Dartmouth could not tell how to get his fleet out of them, though there by his own choice and after all the cautions given him by the King against the very evil he betrayed himself and his unhappy master to by going thither.' But whether Pepys was right or Dartmouth, no man now can say for certain.[50]

All next day and the day after news came to London as the invaders passed down the Channel. On November 4th there were reports that the Dutch had landed at Portsmouth, soon contradicted as their sails were sighted further and further to the west. On the 5th Pepys attended the Council and dictated the usual routine letters from the office. It was not till the evening of the 6th, as the King was sitting to Kneller for a picture which Pepys had commissioned that artist to paint of him, that he learnt by letters from the little town of Dartmouth that the enemy were putting ashore in Torbay.[51]

Throughout these lamentable proceedings the English fleet, mobilized with such pains and hopes and now outwitted and out-manoeuvred, alternately pursued its enemy or lay windbound among the sands. In London no one even knew for certain where it was, though on the morning of the 5th the Admiralty was informed that it had been seen passing Dover on the previous afternoon. Spartan in misfortune, Pepys wrote on the 6th to the Admiral at

Portsmouth, where he hoped to find him, indicating rather than stating the extent of the blow that had befallen the kingdom. 'Though all that know your Lordship, and above all the King, is abundantly assured that no part of your disappointment in relation to the Dutch fleet can be charged upon anything within your power to have prevented, yet the consequences of it in the said fleet's passing without the least interruption to the port they were bound for ... are too visible and of too great moment to escape being lamented and very certain I am by none more than yourself ... Upon which I have nothing in command to say to your Lordship by way of comment, saving that, since it has so unhappily fallen out that the Dutch are in all probability at this hour peaceably putting on shore their whole land force and baggage, so there is nothing left within the power of your Lordship to obtain from them in reference to the landing part, and that consequently their men-of-war will now be at an entire liberty to receive or attack you as they shall think fit.' It was the melancholy and inescapable truth.[52]

Hardly had this letter been despatched but news arrived from the unhappy Admiral, who was now lying becalmed off Beachy Head. Not till daybreak on Sunday the 4th had he managed to get his ships clear from the sands in an E.S.E. gale. But it failed him next day – that memorable 5th of November when William landed in the west. 'Thus', the poor man ended his report to his sovereign, 'I have given your Majesty a true account of all my proceedings, which are so far from the vain hopes I had that I take myself for the most unfortunate man living, tho' I know your Majesty is too just to expect more than wind and weather will permit.' In the meantime his flag-officers and commanders were unanimously opposed to attacking the Dutch fleet if a landing had been effected. The only consolation was that the *Swallow* frigate had captured a fly-boat with 200 men of one of the English regiments serving in Holland whom William had pressed into his service. The common soldiers, Dartmouth reported, rejoiced when they were taken.* They seemed to be little in touch with the mood of their country.[53]

Pepys was the most magnanimous of men. Twice again he reassured Dartmouth that he had nothing with which to reproach

---

* Some of them, according to the practice of the time, were allocated by the Admiralty Secretary to make up the complements of the undermanned ships. *Pepysian MSS., Adm. Letters* xv, 310.

himself and that he had done all that a careful and prudent Admiral could do. The King had commanded him to repeat his sense 'of your incapacity of doing more in that exigence for his service than you did, considering the place in which you were then hooked and the wind that then blew to the benefit of the Holland's fleet and disadvantage of yours'. It was rather a big consideration, particularly as the wind had blown in the opposite direction for so long. But of this Pepys said nothing.

13

The Glorious Revolution

'The English confusion to Popery drink
Lilliburlero bullen a la!'

Lord Wharton, *Lilliburlero*.

Far down in the west country, the narrow lanes and little steep hills
that lie to the east of Torbay were thronged with marching men. On
Tuesday, November 6th, the Dutch Prince's advance guard had
reached Newton Abbot, and in the market place of that quiet town
the Declaration of Liberation was read to a gaping audience of
farmers and graziers. The gentry kept out of the way, the prudent
remaining within doors and the more loyal taking horse for London.
On the 7th the march continued, eleven thousand foot and four
thousand horse, of whom at least three parts were foreigners,
passing Chudleigh and the woods of Catholic Ugbrooke where,
unknown to all but the most faithful retainers of the fallen Cliffords,
the Secret Treaty of Dover – first fatal parent of all that had now
come to pass – lay hidden.*

On the 8th watchers on the walls of Exeter saw the glint of steel
and heard the tramp of horses coming out of the south-west. By
nightfall the western capital was a foreign camp. On Friday the
Prince of Orange rode down its twisted, cobbled streets under
rocking steeples, while a large concourse – for it was Fair time and
the city was full of country folk – gazed at the interminable
procession of gentlemen of fortune and exiled adventurers attended
by feathered and turbaned negroes, of furred and breastplated
horsemen from Sweden, of Brandenburgers and Swiss musketeers,
of Dutch foot and cannon that had been dented in a hundred battles
by Meuse and distant Danube, dragged by teams of innumerable
cart-horses. By a strange irony that no one in England seemed to
note, more than a quarter of them were Catholics. The fame of these

---

* Two and a half centuries later, when the present writer stayed in the house, it
was brought in after dinner, according to family custom, with the coffee and proudly
displayed in its beautiful case by an ancient butler.

alien warriors, their stature magnified a hundredfold by popular rumour and casting gigantic shadows across the winter sky, spread fast through the kingdom; an army of giants was about to expel the debased and stunted papists whom the King had recruited from the bogs of Ireland to enslave his people. A popular song, that recounted in innumerable verses the bawdy exploits of a tailor's wife with her spouse's apprentices, was reset to new and more stirring words by those who made it their business to give wings to rumour:

> Poor Berwick, how will thy dear joys
> Oppose this famed viaggio?
> Thy tallest sparks will be mere toys
> To Brandenburg and Swedish boys,
> Coraggio! coraggio!

Afterwards in the cathedral in the presence of empty stalls – for the Bishop and Dean had fled to London, and the Canons, hearing that the prayer for the infant Prince of Wales was to be omitted, had prudently absented themselves – the Liberator listened to Burnet thanking God in brazen tones for his fortunate voyage. And when that worthy instrument of the Lord's pleasure arose to read the Declaration, the very choir rose and scurried out in alarm. For this, they reflected, was downright rebellion.[1]

Of all this Pepys as yet knew nothing. His place was in London among the Admiralty ledgers at York Buildings and in attendance on his master in closet and Council chamber. During those first days of the invasion he continued to work long into each night. He was above all things an Englishman – the very quintessence of that which we mean by English character – and it is the habitude of Englishmen in the hour of crisis and defeat to do the work that comes to their hands after their wonted manner. 'My lord, it's late, and I have much to do to-night', is the phrase that ends Pepys' letters. He had suffered a crushing blow. He was not beaten, for he refused to accept it.

So he told Dartmouth in letters that followed one another in quick succession that he had moved the King at the Cabinet meeting to take up more merchantmen in the River and fit them out as fireships, that he was despatching more men and victuals, and that he could count on every support whenever he should feel himself able to attack the enemy. When Captain Rooth arrived on horseback – sore in the seat from the unwonted exercise – with papers taken from a captured Dutch fly-boat, it was Pepys' part to get them deciphered and pore over the figures and information they revealed. At two in the morning on Sunday, November 11th, he sat down to transmit the conclusions of his labours to Dartmouth: contrary to the Admiral's belief it appeared that the Dutch fleet guarding the transports at Torbay was no stronger in numbers than the English and weaker in quality.[2]

Pepys was again careful to assure Dartmouth that not the least blame attached to him for his failure to intercept the invaders. He knew well his old friend and chief's sensitive, fretting nature and wished to fire, not depress, it. 'I am yet under some fears', he wrote on the 8th in a private letter – the second he had sent him that day – 'of your taking too much to heart your late misfortune.' For such, he added, he was forced to call it. And he related how, after that evening's Council meeting, he had asked the King for a further assurance and received the comforting answer that, however much foolish landsmen or ill-willed seamen might take the liberty of censuring, nothing could be more plain than the impossibility of his Admiral's serving him better than he had done. 'Therefore pray be fully at ease in this matter, depending upon't that if I knew the least cause for the contrary I would tell you of it. For so upon my faith I would. Remember, too, how much worse you were once used even where you were successful, I mean in the business of Tangier, and, withal, how little you were the worse for it ten days after. Once more, therefore, pray be at peace with yourself.' Pepys never showed himself to better advantage than in this correspondence with his over-anxious and irresolute sea-colleague. In his reply Dartmouth told him that his kindness had eased his heart: 'I can never enough acknowledge your share in my sufferings even from Tangier to the Long Sands Head.'[3]

On Saturday, November 10th, a week after the Dutch fleet had passed down the Channel, Pepys heard the King's artillery rumbling along the Strand at the top of the street as it made its way under his old friend, Sir Henry Shere, towards Piccadilly and the Salisbury road. At that moment it still seemed possible that James might add William's head to Monmouth's. At Exeter the Prince of Orange seemed to be waiting in vain for the gentry to join him. 'As yet', Pepys told Dartmouth, 'we do not find one man of quality that stirs, only a multitude of rabble which signifies but little.' The government hoped to concentrate the army on a line from the Dorset coast to the Bristol Channel and so hem in the invaders in the south-western peninsula, as Essex had been in '44 and Monmouth in '85. The corollary, which had sealed the fate of Monmouth, was a naval attack on the invader's transports. Successfully executed, the double plan must spell the Prince's ruin.[4]

Yet, though the Exchange remained thronged with merchants, and the royal troops marched on every road to the west in hopes that one good blow might end all for the best, there were secret forces at work of which the King and Pepys were unaware. So long as any regiments of the standing army were in their neighbourhood, the rustic magnates of northern and midland England remained discreetly in their country houses. But once the dusty backs of the redcoats had faded into the misty lanes of the south and west, the great lords who had invited William over plucked up their courage. And from Exeter and the printing presses of London, the Prince's Declaration circulated among the people, with its promise – so well attuned to anxious ears – of a free and legally constituted Parliament that would redress all grievances, resolve the legitimacy of the warming-pan Prince of Wales, settle the Succession and establish the lawful Protestant religion beyond challenge. And with the Declaration spread rumours that revived the worst fears of '78 and '41 – of stores of knives, gridirons and cauldrons hidden in papist cellars for massacring and roasting Protestants. Twice that week the Guards were forced to disperse riotous apprentices outside the monastery at Clerkenwell and other meeting-places of the hated Catholics.[5]

Nor could the Government, for all its momentary superiority in military force, feel any certainty that new invaders might not arrive. As he sat in his customary place in St Martin's-in-the-Fields on the morning of Sunday, November 11th, Pepys was called back to the office by a messenger from the Postmaster-General. An express had just been received from Harwich that five thousand troops were waiting in transports at Rotterdam for a wind. Twice that day and in the Cabinet in the evening Pepys asked the King for definite orders. But in the end, as usual, all was left to Dartmouth's discretion.[6]

During the second week of November strenuous efforts were made by the Court and Admiralty to prepare the fleet for further action, the King sending his letters to Dartmouth unsealed and open for Pepys to approve and forward. While the Admiral aboard the *Resolution* in the Downs complained of the divisions of his captains, the want of victuals and stores, the state of his ships after the storms, and his fears that the Dutch forces were greater than had been estimated, Pepys continued to pour out letters to subordinates in the hope that something decisive would come at last of all his labours. To those whom he deemed in need of reproof he was more than usually severe, emphasizing the need for speed and 'good husbandry' and censuring mercilessly such iniquities as those of the Fishermen's Company, who instead of providing the statutory quota of seamen from among its own members used its press warrants to rake up all the unseaworthy scum of the town. No irregularity passed unnoticed by the eagle eye in the long panelled room above the Watergate. 'However I have offended you by my ungovernable way of proceeding,' pleaded Sir William Booth, 'I am sure that nothing can make me want gratitude to put all your commands in execution, even to the last drop of my blood or shilling I have in the world. I cannot help your being angry with me now, but I do give you my word that I will never give you the least occasion as long as I have breath, for never man hath been so much mortified as I have been at your angry way of writing. I know you are Christian enough to forgive me.'* For Christian though he was, the great Secretary was apt to require a tooth for a tooth, and more, when crossed.[7]

To Dartmouth's reasons for delay he returned a courteous but firm iteration of the importance of closing with the Dutch fleet: after all the enemy were presumably in the same plight. On the evening of November 12th the Council reviewed two reports of the number of ships of war with the Prince of Orange, the one from a Deal postmaster who had counted them as they passed through the Straits, the other from a Scottish lieutenant in the Dutch service who had deserted at Torbay. The latter, led before the Council, stated that the total force consisted of forty-four ships of war with twelve fireships, instead of the sixty hitherto supposed, and these but of moderate size, indifferently manned and victualled. He was sent off

---

* Sir W. Booth, on board the *Pendennis* in the Downs, to S. Pepys, Nov. 13th, 1688. *Rawl. MSS. A.* 179, f. 86. See also *Pepysian MSS., Adm. Letters* xv, 159.

at once to the Downs with his report. 'An ill horseman as most of us sailors are', he seems to have travelled but slowly.[8]

But though Pepys wrote cheerfully to the Admiral that on this new information 'his Majesty with the advice of all my Lords this night at the Cabinet' had determined upon his being 'authorized to proceed against this fleet', his own resolution was not matched by his master's, who wrote after the Council by the same mail such a letter as only a Stuart would have penned. 'I think that the Buoy of the Nore ought not to be so much as thought on without you were much overpowered by the enemy . . . You best know your own strength and whether you are in a condition to make use of this easterly wind to attempt anything upon them. At least I think there can be no danger of going to the Spithead, and I should think you are in more safety there when the wind should come westerly than in the Downs. T'would be of some reputation even your going but thither, but of much more if you thought yourself strong enough to look out for them . . . And now that I have said this to you, I must leave all to your judgment who are on the place.' Such sentiments would have been admirable in other circumstances or addressed to another man. With his kingdom at stake and with a bold blow needed to recover it, James could no longer afford them.[9]

For a day or two longer, it continued to seem, as one of the Clerks of the Council put it, 'the quietest invasion that ever was'. William remained in Exeter waiting for allies and causing little harm beyond an interruption of the mails. 'Some of the scurf and meaner part run into them', it was reported, 'as they would to see a show, but generally retreat the next day; most of our Western people having ever since Monmouth's time been much troubled with dreams of gibbets.' The nightly sallies of the London 'prentices against the Catholic chapels in Lime Street, Bucklersbury and Clerkenwell were still dispersed without much difficulty: on the beat of drum and the appearance of a few militiamen, 'the young mutineers' scampered away.[10]

So at least it seemed to the Court, where preparations for the forthcoming fight – another Sedgemoor, it was hoped – went on without any signs of unseemly haste. The King had originally intended to set out for the west on Thursday the 15th, but early in the week it became known that he would not leave till the week-end. His health was not good, and the royal train had to be furnished with a special supply of milch asses. Meanwhile it was confidently announced that 'the army, 27,000 strong, will be able to offer battle by Tuesday next on Salisbury Plains and our Imperial monarch at the head of them'.[11]

But already disquieting rumours were beginning to percolate. At first, for all the brave promises of aid offered Orange when he was still safely on the other side of the water, his only reported accessions of strength were a Devonshire hedge-squire and a few Buckinghamshire butchers and maltsters evading their creditors. But in the course of the second week of invasion, it was whispered in London that such whig grandees as the Earls of Shrewsbury and Macclesfield, Lord Mordaunt and Mr Sidney were on their way to the Prince's camp. Then on the evening of the 14th it was learnt by an express from Cirencester that the dissolute Lord Lovelace with a party of a hundred horse had been stopped by the local militia and only disarmed after serious loss of life.

Far worse followed next day. Shortly after noon, as the King was sitting down to dinner, an express arrived from the west. He read it, rose, left his dinner untasted and went into his Closet, leaving a buzz of conversation behind him. Soon all the Palace knew of the desertion on the previous day of the King's nephew by his first marriage, young Lord Cornbury, one of the chief officers of the Army, heir to the tory house of Hyde and grandson of the great Earl of Clarendon who had stood by the Stuarts in the darkest hour of their adversity. Riding out of the royal camp at Salisbury at the head of three regiments of cavalry, he had attempted to lead them into the enemy's lines, and, on the discovery of his treachery, had himself gone over with his chief officers. The private soldiers would not go with him.[12]

In a single hour the bubble of confidence had been pricked. After that there was no trusting anyone in high place. The most tried loyalist was suspect: no one could be absent two days, a courtier wrote, but underwent censure. Other defections were spoken of, the most important being that of the west-country magnate, Edward Seymour, whose loyalty, apart from his Toryism, had always been of a limited nature, it being dubious whether a man so proud and imperious could feel that emotion consistently towards anyone but himself. The 'turbulent mobile', following the lead of their betters, grew bolder: the Convent at Clerkenwell was uproariously pulled down, and by the end of the week terrified Catholics were moving their goods to the foreign embassies. News from the Continent fanned the rising fires of Protestant alarm: in the Palatinate and on the Rhine the armies of the most Catholic King were marching from strength to strength, the Germans being as much taken by surprise by their old tormentors' winter campaigning as James had been by Orange.* On the 16th France declared war on Holland, and all Europe was in the melting-pot. The Protestant English could not forget that Orange was the foe, and their own King the friend, of the French tyrant.[13]

On Saturday, November 17th, James prepared to leave the capital. Before he started for the front he called his officers together and, giving them the choice of laying down their commissions, begged them not to betray him by deserting his standard in the field as Cornbury had done. Afterwards he asked the Cabinet to witness his last will and testament. Pepys' signature to this document appears immediately below the names of the Lords of the Council – Lord Chancellor Jeffreys, Melfort, Belasye and Arundell of Wardour, Preston, the Secretary of State, and Godolphin – and above those of William Blathwayt, the Secretary-at-War, and William Bridgeman, the Clerk of the Council.† For all the sorrow of the occasion it must have been a proud moment for the son of a tailor who owed nothing to birth and everything to his own efforts.[14]

Before the King set out, the Archbishops of Canterbury and York and a group of high tory peers and bishops sought an audience. James showed no pleasure at seeing them. They begged him to call a speedy Parliament and steal the invader's thunder rather than be forced to it by a general insurrection. He refused, saying that he would hold no Parliament while traitors were in arms in the kingdom. He would answer them with steel of their own metal.[15]

At about two o'clock in the afternoon James left for Windsor, taking his infant son with him. The popular feeling about the Prince was such that he dared not leave him in the capital: he felt it safer to send him to Portsmouth. Pepys accompanied his sovereign on the first stage of his journey as far as Windsor. There that night he

---

* '. . . it being sleeping time with the Germans who did not expect a campaign in the depths of the winter'. *Ellis Correspondence* ii, 289.

† *Stuart Papers at Windsor Castle, MSS.*, vol. i, Nov. 17th, 1688. (Communicated by O. F. Morshead.)

thought it advisable to safeguard his own position against an adverse future by a paper acknowledging the sums owing to him on the count of his earlier services. This he got the King to sign:

We do hereby graciously declare our continued sense of the long and faithful services performed to our late dearest Brother and our self by Mr Pepys our Secretary for the affairs of our Admiralty of England, and that his long want of satisfaction to his just pretensions attested by ourself when Duke of York and confirmed by our said dearest Brother in a statement thereof bearing date the second day of March 1678/9 shall be no impediment to his receiving the same from us; we hereby earnestly recommend him to the Lords Commissioners of the Treasury for their doing him full right on our behalf therein, and in what is further due to him in his account as late Treasurer for Tangier. Given at our Castle of Windsor on this 17th day of November 1688.*

The sum at stake was in the neighbourhood of £28,000. If Pepys be judged as over-worldly for reminding his royal master of this ancient debt at such an hour, it should be remembered that he had refrained from doing so during the four and a half years of his second tenure of the Admiralty Secretaryship, when he could have obtained payment for it at almost any time. But he had felt that the Service he controlled had more need of the money than he. Only now, when the solid earth was quaking under his feet, did he ask that his debt on the community should be recorded. He was never paid.[16]

Next morning, Sunday the 18th, the King set out for Salisbury, sending the Prince of Wales towards Portsmouth. Pepys returned to London. He had much to cause him anxiety, for not only was his master's cause committed to an unknown battlefield in the west, but Dartmouth, spurred on by his exhortations, had at last resolved to attack the enemy.† The fleet, after being becalmed for three days, had sailed from the Downs on the afternoon of Friday the 16th with a north-east wind, good weather and a settled hard sky. For a moment it seemed as though the long tide of ill fortune was about to turn. But on Sunday night, after Pepys got back to London, the clear frosty weather broke, the wind shifting into the south-west and

* Letter communicated to the late Dr J. R. Tanner by the late Lieut.-Colonel Frederick Pepys Cockerell.
† 'This is a melancholy time with all of us; what adds to our pain is that our fleet set sail yesterday, in quest it is thought, of the Dutch fleet. God send us good success!' O. Wynne to J. Ellis, Nov. 17th, 1688. *Ellis Correspondence* ii, 301.

rapidly increasing to gale intensity. So it continued for four days while Pepys, gazing out at grey, blowing sky and river, penned anxious and fruitless letters of enquiry. The tragedy for him – and it is hard to over-estimate the bitterness of it – was that had the wintry gales proper to that season commenced a fortnight earlier when the Prince's transports were at sea they might well have driven the invaders to as terrible an end as that which befell their predecessors in that other and greater '88 of a century before. 'It is strange', Dartmouth had written to the King, 'that such mad proceedings should have such success at this time of the year, but I hope God will bless your Majesty's forces at last.' And now, when it might so have come to pass, the scales of fate were depressed still lower against a failing cause. For the long-expected tempest found the King's fleet at sea and the Dutch safe in an English anchorage.[17]

The week ending the 24th November, the third of the invasion, was, for those in London, a time of waiting. The city remained strangely quiet: the sober and richer sort attending to their business and collecting their debts, while the noisier, 'that gad about all day for coffee and news', contented themselves with whispering. Pepys watched the wind and drafted long letters of administrative detail against all contingencies. On Tuesday the 20th he wrote one of six crowded pages to the missing Admiral, and sent it to Portsmouth thinking it might perhaps catch him there. The Navy Office was busy getting six more fireships to drive the Dutch from their moorings, the *Roebuck* had sailed from Sheerness and the *Mermaid* would soon follow; the *Portland* was lying in Long Reach, 'manned, victualled, and in all respects ready to sail excepting the wanting of her guns'. Concerning these Pepys left her commander, he told Dartmouth, 'to make his own moan to your Lordship as he has not spared to do to me'. 'I do with great longings', he concluded, 'to hear of your Lordship and the fleet after the tempestuous weather we have for some days past had.'[18]

During that week of rumours – that the Dutch fleet had been dispersed by the storm and had been sighted in distress off Land's End, that the Prince of Wales had been shipped to France, that a battle had taken place in the west, that Kirke had been killed by his own men on Salisbury Plain, and that fifty thousand French had landed at Dover – Pepys was made an unwilling party to a comic interlude afforded by the childlike temper of his brother-in-law

Balty. On the evening of the 21st there arrived at the Admiralty a long and passionate letter complaining of how on the previous day the *Phoenix*, long delayed at Deptford by easterly winds, had been prevented by the unaccountable absence of her captain from taking advantage of the sudden change to the south-west. It seems that Balty, who was still enjoying his brief heyday of prosperity as Commissioner at Deptford, had risen at half-past six to pursue his day's duties, and, on enquiring why the *Phoenix* had not sailed with the morning tide, was told by the Clerk of the Cheque that Captain Gifford was in London. 'On which', Balty explained, 'my zeal for his Majesty's service could not but move me into some passion for such a neglect!' and he had expressed himself with some freedom to the master. After which he repaired to London for his customary Tuesday meeting with Sir Anthony Deane and Mr Hewer 'on his Majesty's affairs'. Returning in the evening, he found the wind still in the south-west, and the captain of the *Phoenix* still away. He therefore took it upon himself to order her lieutenant to sail with the morning tide. Then, being very weary, he went to bed.[19]

But scarcely had he begun his slumbers when 'rap, rap, at my door comes the "Globe" boy bringing the enclosed note with express order to deliver it to me presently. The contents when you see I leave you to judge . . . Oh! how soon', this virtuous official commented, 'will all government and rule in the Navy be violated and trampled on if the Commissioners thereof may be thus used by every captain!' And he begged for the administration ('under correction of your piercing judgment') of a gentle reprimand to the erring commander. 'Sir, this comes from one who dares to do his duty and will against all discouragements.' He added that his 'well wishes for a fair wind and eager pressing' had since had the desired effect, for the *Phoenix* had sailed for Long Reach that morning.*

Enclosed was Captain Gifford's note, ill-spelt, ill-written but quite as passionate. After applying 'his piercing judgment' to this affecting correspondence Pepys seems to have administered a provisional rebuke both to the captain and to Balty, notifying the former of the charge made against him and enquiring of the latter whether his old fault of hasty anger might not have led him into expressing himself too freely. He was promptly rewarded by indignant letters from both

* Commissioner St Michel to S. P., Nov. 21st, 1688. *Rawl. MSS. A.* 186, ff. 18–19.

protagonists for whom the war with the invaders had now become a minor matter. From Long Reach Captain Gifford expressed in no uncertain terms his sense of outrage at a landsman's interference, declaring it to be entirely the pilot's fault that the *Phoenix* had not sailed on the 20th and complaining that Balty had insulted him before his crew. As for his own absence, he had never been away from his ship for more than a day since he had taken command, and at the time complained of was merely waiting for the pilot with a runner in attendance to summon him the moment he arrived. His diligence, he thought, merited praise from the Commissioner rather than a complaint.

Balty's letter was worthy of his long mastery of the epistolary art. He protested that though he must ever and with all thankfulness acknowledge that his brother-in-law's regard for him had been expressed with tenderness, his own temper was certainly not so overweening and soft as to make him take offence without cause. What he had done had been due to Captain Gifford's 'ingentile, and I may well say rough, if not rude, return to my zealous discharge of the duty and trust incumbent on me for hastening to sea all the additions of force possible at such a time as this, when the King and kingdom are under the highest dangers (probably) thro' a foreign invasion'. No 'personal disrespect or private pique' had swayed him, nor had he used any 'threatening or unhandsome expressions'. With 'all openheartedness, plainness and sincerity' he had told 'the very truth and nothing but the truth'. It was his conviction that this was but another instance of the attempt certain captains ('especially the Court-like finer sort of 'um') were making to weaken the authority of the Special Commission 'by shooting these little arrows through me (a member) at the whole body'.*

Next day when Balty waited on him, Pepys asked him to answer, in writing and with brevity, certain questions: the date of the Navy Board's order for fitting out the *Phoenix*, the degree of experience of the pilot, and the captain's state of sobriety at the time of writing his note. He knew his Navy. Balty replied that he had enquired of the master of the *Globe* who had been drinking with Gifford: 'he says he seemed to be sober, but I am apt to believe (the time of night considered) he might be somewhat warmed with wine.'† He may

---

* B. St Michel to S. P., Nov. 23rd, 1688. *Rawl. MSS. A.* 186, f. 212.
† *Rawl. MSS. A.* 186, f. 25.

well have been, for it seemed that in the flurry of his departure the captain had impressed two Bailiff's officers, a butcher and a weed-cutter by vocation, and kept them forcibly under hatches – an illegality that brought upon him a warrant from the Lord Chief Justice and one of the Admiralty Secretary's sternest rebukes.* The rest is silence. For the storm in a tea-cup roused by these lesser events was now submerged by a greater.[20]

Throughout the latter part of the week, while the gale continued unabated, tidings kept percolating to London of units of the fleet parted from their consorts and driven for shelter into southern harbours. Then on the morning of Saturday the 24th definite news of Lord Dartmouth arrived from Portsmouth. 'It is with an extraordinary degree of content', Pepys wrote to him at noon that day, 'that I have just now received your Lordship's of yesterday from the Spithead . . . giving me ground of hoping that the loss his Majesty has sustained from the late tempests will prove much more tolerable than we have for many days lain under an apprehension it would have done.' For he was able to add to the Admiral's account of the twenty-two ships which had returned with him to harbour – about half his battered fleet – news of another eleven; seven in the Downs, two in Portland Road, and two off the Isle of Wight. At nightfall he wrote again to inform him that a letter dated the 22nd, and opened by the King at Salisbury, had come in from Captain Churchill of the *Newcastle* at Plymouth. That officer, who had much to say about the condition of his ship, gave a graphic description of the leak which had caused his separation from his consorts. The real reason for his defection was to appear later.[21]

Pepys communicated his news to the Lords of the Council and sent an express to his master at Salisbury. But beyond his relief that his beloved fleet was safe, he had little cause to be pleased. The action on which he had pinned his own hopes and his country's had never taken place.

It was a sorry tale that Dartmouth had had to tell of 'such variety of winds and storms as frustrated all my hopes and intentions for his Majesty's service'. On the 19th, three days after he had sailed from the Downs, he had sighted the Dutch in Torbay. But by that time

---

* 'I am sure a more scandalous instance of it can never arise.' S. P. to Capt. Gifford, Nov. 22nd, 1688. *Pepysian MSS., Adm. Letters* xv, 406.

his own fleet was so divided and depleted that he had been forced to put back to St Helen's. 'There is no resisting a storm in the Channel at this time of the year', he informed the King. 'Their fortune hath been extravagant, for there hath been but three fair days since I came to sea, and they had two of them to land in, while I was becalmed off Beachy. But sure I shall have some luck at last, for I will struggle all I can and endure with patience till I can compass that service you expect from me. My business now shall be to get ready soon as possible, tho' the season of the year is intolerable, sixteen hours night to eight hours day with lee shores in the Channel is harder working than any battle. If it had pleased God to have continued the wind and weather, in all probability I could not have failed.' The fact remained that he had done so.[22]

No battle took place on land either, and the power and dominion of England changed hands without a struggle. On Monday, November 19th, the King had reached Salisbury and next day the Prince of Orange, leaving Seymour to govern the west, had started from Exeter to meet him. Somewhere on Salisbury Plain, it seemed, battle would be joined: men spoke of Stonehenge as the place where the fate of the realm would be decided. The advance guards met in skirmish at Wincanton, a troop of Sarsfield's horse falling back before Mackay's invading Scots. The King at the entreaty of Kirke and Churchill had proposed on the Wednesday to inspect his outposts at Warminster. But on the day before he set out, his health, undermined by early excesses and strained beyond endurance by the events of the past few weeks, failed him, and he was driven to his bed by a violent discharge of blood from the nose. During the next few days he remained at Salisbury in the hands of his doctors.[23]

Information of these events had come to the ears of those in authority in London, but public news remained scanty. Meanwhile rumour was busy: the sight of the King's officers in the Tower – Papists it was believed – planting mortars in the White Tower caused something of a panic in the City on Friday. That night news reached the capital from the north: the arch-rebel Delamere, with many 'old Oliverians', was in arms in Cheshire. Worse followed next day; that the Earl of Danby, raising an alarm that papist soldiers were planning a massacre, had roused the local gentry and militia against the tiny garrison of York, seized the city, and declared for the Prince of Orange. Here was no 'old Oliverian' but an eminent

Cavalier whom less than ten years before the Whigs had threatened with a halter and sent to the Tower for his fidelity. Fired by such an example, alarmed by news of fresh triumphs across the water for the French King and with tales of an impending papist massacre, with no Parliament called and the Prince's Declaration in favour of one circulating everywhere, the country began to rise under the malcontent lords. The rabble came out in the towns and the honest gentry and freeholders, clad in their fathers' rusty armour, in the shires. At Nottingham, where the whig Earl of Devonshire declared for Orange on the 22nd, the local worthies announced themselves as 'assembled together . . . for the defence of our laws, liberties, and properties (according to those free born liberties and privileges descended to us from our ancestors, the undoubted birthright of the subjects of this kingdom of England) . . . being by innumerable grievances made sensible that the very fundamentals of our liberty, religion and properties are about to be rooted out by our late Jesuitical Privy Council . . . and not being willing to deliver over our posterity to such conditions of Popery and slavery'. What precise injury to their liberties as free-born Englishmen they had till now suffered, save a slight abrogation of their right to persecute those of another faith, they did not specify. But they would not, they said, be bugbeared by the 'opprobrious term of rebels'. 'Such a riding and travelling about at such a rate as I never seen in my life,' wrote one onlooker, 'they being resolved to subdue Popery.' They were not disloyal, but merely, as was natural to Englishmen in a crisis, a little confused as to what was happening and intensely determined to do what all their neighbours were doing.[24]

Pepys had no share in their feelings. Though like other men he might be blind to the hidden stream of inevitable evolution of which all this turmoil was a part, he knew too much to be deceived by the propagandist cry that had brought out the honest militia of the East Riding. His heart was with the King who had stood beside him in his work of restoring the Navy. Others of his paid servants, fearing for their estates or places, might make this secret peace with the invader. It never occurred to Pepys to do anything so base.

Many did. On the evening of Saturday the 24th at Salisbury, ill in body and heart and feeling that his whole realm was crumbling behind him, James took the advice of his French generals, Feversham and de Duras, and resolved to fall back at once on

London and the Thames. No sooner had the decision been taken, than the two leading English officers of the army, Lord Churchill and the King's nephew, the Duke of Grafton, who had long been in correspondence with the enemy, set out for William's lines. When on Sunday morning their absence became known, the camp broke up in confusion: not since the last tragic hours of King John's reign had such a wholesale betrayal* been seen in England.

On the same afternoon a courier brought the news to London. All that evening the galleries of Whitehall were crowded with a vast, excited throng. Next morning those going to call the Princess Anne found that she had fled from the Palace in the night with Lord Churchill's wife. The rumour spread through the town that she had been murdered by Papists. But as those who started it knew, she was already on the road to the north to join those in rebellion against her father, while Bishop Compton, who had sat with the inquisitors who tried to implicate Pepys back in '78, rode jackbooted and armed by her side.[25]

In that tragic hour a tried friend of Pepys and one with as loyal a heart as his own defined the nature of the dilemma that confronted every good man in authority who still remained true to his trust. At Hartley Row, amid the cares of commanding the King's artillery on the retreat from Salisbury, Sir Henry Shere found time to write a letter to his old comrade, and chief, Lord Dartmouth. He knew well, he told him, what a heavy burden of distress he must be under. 'You have now a part to act, my Lord, which to my weak discerning is by much the most important of your life; which will appear plainer to you when I tell your Lordship that the King is almost quite deserted. You have heard of those who gave the first example, where my Lord Cornbury was the leader, my Lord Abingdon going in with him etc. Yesterday my Lord Churchill, the Duke of Grafton, and many with them besides two regiments, are gone to the Prince of Orange, and just now, while I am writing this, news is come (and I believe it true) that the Prince of Denmark, the Duke of Ormonde,

---

* Like the rest of the world I have read with admiration Mr Winston Churchill's long and brilliant vindication of his great ancestor. Mr Churchill's pages would, if it were possible, increase one's sense of gratitude to Marlborough for his services to his country, and one's admiration of his generosity, his charm and his genius. But nothing can alter the nature of his relationship to King James. It was the same as Pepys', save that it was more intimate.

my Lord Rochester and many others are likewise amongst the deserters. And every day will produce new accounts to add to the list and heap new calamities upon this poor unfortunate prince's head, who has been cursed with fools to his counsellors and knaves in his bosom, the one to advise him to his destruction, the other to desert him in his distress.

'The King is very ill, I fear, I may say dangerously so, at least in my opinion. He rests this night in the neighbouring village and tomorrow proceeds to London, whither we are moving as fast as our great body can march, and may expect tomorrow to have our quarters beaten up.

'Now my dear Lord, what will you do? I know you are a man of honour and I pray God keep you in that mind. You have therefore an insuperable task given you which nothing but divine inspiration can resolve how you will be able to go through with. While you remain firm in your obedience and faithful to your trust, you are sure to draw the envy, enmity and indignation of all those upon you who shall have forfeited that character, which has a fatal aspect on your fortune and future state, and, while you reflect on your family and circumstances, will not choose but cost you some sad reluctancies. And should you quite depart from your duty and allegiance in the high station wherein you now are, you will then be undone to yourself, for it would give you pangs of remorse that would haunt you to your grave.

'What then, is the temper between these extremes? If you contribute in any wise to the bringing in foreign force, you are undone without redemption. If you fight the Dutch fleet it will be as fatal, and little less if you give up your command so that the fleet should fall into hands that may render it useful to any of these ends which you might have prevented. Is it not possible for your Lordship to shun these rocks by artfully keeping the fleet for some days at sea (for their fermentation cannot last ten days) and by that means put it out of your power to obey or refuse? . . . But I am at my wit's end, and you will forgive me, my good Lord, while you know what an aching heart I have for you, and that out of the force of my love, gratitude and duty, I presume thus to interpose my poor opinion. God in his mercy and wisdom, bless and counsel your Lordship and send us a happy meeting.'[26]

The King also wrote to Dartmouth on the same day, sending his letter by Lord Dover. This Catholic convert – the philandering Harry Jermyn of time past – was appointed to the command of the garrison at Portsmouth. He carried secret verbal instructions about the future of the Prince of Wales. At about four o'clock on Monday afternoon the unhappy monarch reached London to find that his second daughter as well as his first had betrayed him. Broken in spirit, he sat till late at night in council. As the only course now remaining, it was resolved to call the Lords Temporal and Spiritual, whose advice he had so summarily declined ten days before.[27]

When at eleven that night the Cabinet broke up, Pepys, who had been spending the day writing routine letters to the British Consuls in the Mediterranean, set down at the King's command for Dartmouth's benefit the circumstances of the Princess Anne's flight lest there should be any misconception about it in the fleet. He related how that morning Mrs Danvers and Sir Benjamin Bathurst had found her bed cold and her clothes of the previous day, even to her shoes and stockings, left behind, and how the Guard at the Cockpit door had seen a coach with six horses drive off in the night. The evilly disposed were now saying that the Papists had forced her away, whereas – so it seemed to Pepys – nothing could be thought more natural 'than that the ladies should think it time to withdraw as soon as they had received tidings of their husbands having done the same'.[28]

Next day, Tuesday the 27th, the Lords Temporal and Spiritual, or such of them as were in the capital and not with the rebels, met the King in the Dining Room of Whitehall. The Archbishop of Canterbury and James' brothers-in-law, the Earls of Clarendon and Rochester, were among them, with the Secretaries of State in attendance. They advised the King – some of them in language frank to the point of brutality – to call a free Parliament, issue an amnesty and appoint commissioners to open negotiations with the Prince of Orange. In an agony of reluctance the King agreed but asked for a further night to consider the last. The thought of any truck with traitors stuck in his throat.[29]

Perhaps it was the knowledge that a Parliament was certain to meet in the near future that caused Pepys to spare time that day from his official correspondence to write to his friends at Harwich. The proposal about re-opening the naval yard there, he told the Mayor and Corporation, had been approved by the King and would be set in hand so soon as the days began to lengthen. The Commissioners of Customs had agreed to the removal of the Customs House from Ipswich to Harwich, the only remaining impediment being the royal reluctance to injure old and deserving officials at the former place. 'Not but that I shall firmly hope,' Pepys explained, 'cloudy as things at this day look, that Almighty God has it in his gracious purpose to support the King and his Government, and thoroughly to protect the Church of England both in its discipline and doctrine. But that hope not being entirely void of apprehensions that things may possibly end otherwise, I would be very glad, and so would Sir Anthony Deane, to do something while we may to the advantage of a place and society from which we have received so many obligations.' And he asked Captain Langley to let him have an account of any expenses he might have been put to in removing the buoys in the river during the invasion, that he might get him reimbursed while still in a capacity for doing it. 'For as matters stand,' he added, 'I know not how little awhile I may be so.'[30]

Next day James agreed to all the proposals of the Lords Temporal and Spiritual. Pepys passed on the good news at once to Dartmouth, telling him that he had just come from attending the King at his Cabinet where he had been graciously pleased to declare his royal purpose of calling a Parliament as speedily as the requisite time for issuing and returning the writs would admit. 'But what a pity it is', he observed, 'that I could not bring this news without meeting something to abate some of the pleasure which the foregoing tidings must give to all good subjects, Mr Frowde' – the Postmaster – 'stopping me in my way to tell me that my Lord of Bath had seized Plymouth for the Prince.'[31]

Those Tories who wished for nothing more than a restoration of the old Cavalier and Church of England supremacy, were well pleased. The King had agreed to all they had asked. Nothing now remained but to make terms with Orange, render him thanks for his service and set the broken Constitution working again. The tory Nottingham, the trimmer Halifax, who eight years before had saved the legitimate succession by his speech in the Exclusion debate, and the inevitable Godolphin were appointed Commissioners to treat with the Prince. The Catholic Lieutenant of the Tower, Sir Edward Hales, was superseded by a Protestant. A free pardon was offered to all in rebellion. It was hoped that the Parliament which was to meet on January 13th would be as tory as that of 1685.[32]

But there were factors in the situation which the loyalist Tories had almost forgotten. There was Orange himself, who had not come to England purely for the spiritual good of that country and certainly not for that of the Cavalier Party. And there were Orange's friends. When Lord Clarendon, fresh from this eleventh-hour understanding with his royal master, hurried to make his peace at the Prince's camp at Salisbury, he was pained to encounter such old-time revolutionaries as Major Wildman and the preacher, Ferguson, very much at their ease and urgent for tory blood. Others both in London and the country appeared to share their hopes: the whig printing presses were never at rest, and lying rumours, disquieting in the extreme to loyal minds, spread like wildfire. The Tories might pay the piper, if they chose, but it was the Whigs who were calling the tune to which the nation was now dancing. And the tune was *Lilliburlero*. A false proclamation, accepted everywhere as genuine, called in the Prince's name on all Protestants to arrest and disarm the papist supporters of the King. And as those who remembered '78 recalled, a Protestant mob inspired by enthusiastic Whigs made little account of the difference between a Tory and a Papist.[33]

There was another factor which should have caused the jubilant Anglican loyalists some misgivings – the state of the King's mind. Of what was passing in it, Pepys perhaps knew more than any other Protestant about him. At the secret Cabinet after the royal return to London on the evening of the 25th, at which Pepys had been present, the question of sending the infant Prince of Wales out of England had been discussed. James' religious convictions being what they were, this was the essential condition on which the bewildered, defeated man would alone consent to call a Parliament whose first act, he knew, would be to insist on his son's education as a Protestant, if it did not – as the coarse libels now on every coffee-house table suggested – challenge his legitimacy. With the husband of the next heir invading the kingdom in arms, this last contingency indeed seemed almost inevitable. As a result of that mournful discussion Pepys next day prepared a secret warrant to Lord Dartmouth for the King's signature. He did so in his own hand, 'as containing a matter which will not bear being known to more than was at the debate of it till we may be morally sure that no advice of it hence by land could prevent the execution'.* The writing of it must have caused him many an anxious thought. It contained orders to aid Lord Dover in transporting the Prince of Wales to France.[34]

But for a few days the warrant and the royal letter to Dartmouth which accompanied it were not despatched. The rest after his travels may have given the ailing King a last flicker of his old courage. He still delayed committing himself to the fatal course to which Father Petre was pressing him. Instead he sent to Dartmouth on the 29th a brief letter, telling him to preserve the fleet at all costs and asking him to consider where best to dispose of his ships. 'You will have an account from Mr Pepys of what passes here and the ill condition my affairs are in on shore, so that I shall say nothing concerning them.' Pepys in his own letter – a long one – reported that as the King did not anticipate any further opportunity of venturing the fleet that winter, rigid economy and retrenchment must now be the order of the day. This was in reply to a somewhat querulous letter from Dartmouth, asking for instructions. The long sequence of failures was straining tempers: Pepys himself became a little tart. 'You are doing a very good work in getting a strict account of the state of your victuals. Pray be pleased to hasten it. For notwithstanding all my pressing for the providing of more, the Service may meet with disappointment therein if the Commissioners of the Victualling here go by one reckoning and the men eat by another.'[35]

Yet on that very day the King, ill and surrounded as he believed by a murderous populace, surrendered once more to his secret terrors. He sought out the French Ambassador and confided to him that his negotiations with Orange were a mere feint to gain time while he smuggled his wife and child to safety. He would never allow a Parliament to meet which would only force him to do what he was determined not to: to abandon his protection of his Catholic subjects and take arms against Louis. He would sooner entrust his sacred cause and dear ones to his French cousin. Once more he wrote to Dartmouth. ''Tis my son they aim at and 'tis my son I must endeavour to preserve whatsoever becomes of me. Therefore I conjure you to assist Lord Dover in getting him sent away in the yachts, as soon as wind and weather will permit, for the first port

* Nov. 26th, 1688. *Pepysian MSS., Adm. Letters* xv, 435–6.

they can get to in France, and that with as much secrecy as may be.' Next day, the last in November, Pepys transmitted orders to the captains of the *Anne* and *Isabella* yachts to fall down the river to Erith.[36]

At noon on December 1st Pepys wrote to Captain Macdonell of the *Assurance* frigate to fit his ship in readiness for any orders the King might give and to repair in person to town with the utmost diligence.* On that day a warrant was also despatched to Portsmouth ordering Dover and Dartmouth to put their fatal instructions into execution. Two days later, on the 3rd, Pepys ordered the *Isabella* yacht to transport the Comte de Lauzun to France. From what followed we know that the Queen was intended to accompany him.[37]

Meanwhile Dartmouth at Portsmouth was at his wit's end. On every hand he was faced by demands for money. One of his captains complained that he had not two sixpences in the world and begged him to spare an old periwig to keep his bald head from the cold. The officers of the Ordnance, snowed under by simultaneous demands from fleet, army and garrisons, protested that they had not the wherewithal to furnish a single ship; and the dockyard hands, denied by Lord Dover the cash which Pepys had sent down to pay them, were on strike. The unhappy Admiral had therefore received the news of the calling of a Parliament with intense relief and despatched a humble Address, signed by himself and his captains, thanking the King for what he had done and beseeching him to open negotiations with Orange. This document, which reached Whitehall on the 2nd, plunged James into the deepest gloom. Coming from his own fleet, it was a terrible blow to his pride. Even Sir Roger Strickland, he noticed, was among the signatories. 'The poor King is mightily broken', wrote a courtier, 'a great heart can't so easily bend.'[38]

In the course of the same day Dartmouth was confronted with his master's shattering instructions. His dilemma was a terrible one. If he sent the Prince overseas, he would give France a hostage and a perpetual temptation to invade England. He would also render himself guilty of treason. With what he described as the greatest grief of heart imaginable he sat down to reply, imploring James to

* *Pepysian MSS, Adm. Letters* xv, 449.

remember how strict the laws were in this matter. 'Pardon me, therefore, Sir, if on my bended knees I beg of you to apply yourself to other councils, for the doing this looks like nothing less than despair to the degree of not only giving your enemies encouragement but distrust of your friends and people, who I do not despair but will yet stand by you in the defence and right of your lawful successor.' And he reminded the King how prophetically he had foretold his former misfortunes and advised him how to avoid them.[39]

Dartmouth prevailed with Dover to delay any further action until he had received a reply to his letter to the King. He was able to do so the more easily because certain of his captains, who were in secret communication with Orange, took it upon themselves to patrol the mouth of the harbour day and night. As the Commissioner of the Dockyard put it, nobody wanted a second Perkin Warbeck. So far as escape from Portsmouth was concerned the game was up, and the King knew it. Dartmouth's letter reached him on the evening of the 4th, and its contents were already common talk in the capital that night. On the morning of the 5th James replied bidding Dartmouth hold his hand until he had had time to consider the matter: in the evening he added a postscript ordering the infant Prince to be sent back to London by land or, if the roads were not safe, by sea to Margate under an escort. Three days later Pepys sent orders to Captain Fazeby of the *Mary* yacht, then at Portsmouth, to take the Prince of Wales and his retinue aboard and transport them to Greenwich. He need not have given himself the trouble, for Lord Dover, suspecting that the traitor captains were planning to seize his charge, had already slipped away with him at dead of night by coach for London.[40]

Here in the capital, the waves of popular feeling, fanned by the winds of rumour, were dashing with gale force against the King and those who stood by him. The hawkers bawled 'A Hue and Cry after Father Petre' outside his now deserted Whitehall lodgings, houses and cellars were searched by the rabble for papist arms, and the magistrates were powerless. In the streets suspected Jesuits were hunted like dogs. The brave roaring days of '78 and '41 were come again. As Orange's army drew nearer, the prudent, fearing a siege, began to lay in provisions.

In the provinces also the malcontents found ready allies in the basest elements of society. At Newcastle, the roughs of the town, urged on by Lord Lumley, threw the King's statue into the Tyne. Hull, Norwich, Chester, Shrewsbury and Worcester in turn went with the tide, the slender forces of order being submerged almost without a struggle in the fierce popular flood.* At Cambridge priests' robes were burnt in the market place: a learned divine from one of the new Catholic colleges was forced to hide for his life in a 'bog-house' and another made to dance naked in a ditch until he promised to change his religion. At Oxford the dissolute Lord Lovelace, released from Gloucester jail by the mob, rode into the East Gate amid a blaze of orange ribands, the drums playing before him and a crowd of 'rusty ruffians' surging after with drawn swords. Only in the Services did loyalty dare to raise its head; the private soldiers and the humbler sort of officers, who had no temptation to ape the treachery of their superiors, looked on with sullen faces. The desertions from the lower ranks of the Navy and Army were astonishingly few. Dartmouth wrote that now a Parliament had been called the seamen seemed perfectly satisfied and that the Prince of Orange would soon find things alter should he obstruct an honourable settlement.[41]

But Orange, who was as astute a politician as his uncle, Charles, threw away no chances. Advancing slowly towards the capital, he maintained a passive silence and left the fury of his baser allies and the folly of the King to do his business. On Saturday, the 8th, after a judicious delay – for every fresh manifestation of private treachery and popular fanaticism would, as he well knew, shake his father-in-law's weak nerves – he received the Royal Commissioners at Hungerford. At the 'Bear' inn, it was proposed that the invaders should halt pending the meeting of Parliament, that the royal troops should withdraw to a like distance the other side of London, and that all Catholic officers should be dismissed. These terms, so artfully contrived that they were too reasonable for loyal men to disapprove and too repugnant for James to accept, were put into writing on the 9th. 'What if the King were to go away?' Halifax, dining with the Prince at Littlecote, asked Burnet. 'There is nothing so much to be wished', was the reply.[42]

On the same day James, in London, his mind full of secret

---

* 'There was scarce an hour but his Majesty received, like Job, some message of some revolt or misfortune or other.' Sir John Reresby, *Memoirs*, 536.

terrors, had come to a similar resolution. His Irish troops hooted in the streets, his priests in hiding and his child secretly conveyed back to London like a parcel of stolen goods, he took his fears once more to the sly and sympathetic Barillon. Many years before his father had warned him that for a King it was never far from the prison to the grave. He thought of himself as Richard II and of his son-in-law as another Bolingbroke. Many a King of England before him had fled and been restored, he told the Ambassador: he would preserve his rights to assert them on another occasion. There should be another year of Restoration, but not another '49. James in his blindness failed to see that the miracle of '60 had only come about because there had been a '49. He proposed to do what his father with all his mistakes had never done: to turn his back on his realm.[43]

In the storm and darkness of the night of December 9th the Queen and her infant son crossed the Thames in an open boat and, soaked in rain, took coach from Lambeth for Gravesend, where Lord Powis was waiting with a yacht to carry them to France. Next day, as soon as he learnt that they had set sail, the King sent for the Lords and for the Lord Mayor and Sheriffs and informed them of what he had done, promising them that, however dark the complexion of his affairs might look, he would not abandon his post. He wrote to Dartmouth in the same vein, acquainting Pepys with the contents of his letter, which he gave to him to send.[44]

Yet there was still something which the King kept even from his most faithful servants. In his heart, the obstinate man had resolved to abandon neither his prerogative of relieving his co-religionists nor his alliance with Louis. Sooner than receive his Commissioners from Hungerford and the conditions they brought, he would leave his unworthy subjects to their fate. That night in the secrecy of his Closet he burnt the unissued writs for summoning Parliament and sent for the Great Seal. Then he penned a letter to Lord Feversham, ordering him to disband the army, and another to Dartmouth telling him what he was about to do. 'My affairs', he wrote, 'are in so desperate a condition that I have been obliged to send away the Queen and the Prince to secure them at least, whatsoever becomes of me that am resolved to venture all rather than consent to anything in the least prejudicial to the crown or my conscience. And having been basely deserted, . . . I could no longer resolve to expose myself to no purpose to what I might expect from the ambitious Prince of

Orange and the associated rebellious Lords, and therefore have resolved to withdraw till this violent storm is over, which will be in God's good time, and hope that there will still remain in this land seven thousand men that will not bow down the knee to Baal and keep themselves free from associations and such rebellious practices.' It had come right once before when times were as bad, or worse: it might do so once again. He would escape from the reality he had been unable to master into the romance of his youth: exile, the odour and sanctity of martyrdom at the court of foreign princes, and above all hope – hope once again of that wonderful miraculous ending. The fleet could sail for Ireland and take service under Tyrconnel, that is if the captains would obey orders, and if not, 'there is no remedy, and this I may say, never any Prince took more care of his sea and land men as I have done, and been so very ill repaid by them. I have not time to say more, being just a going to take horse.'[45]

Pepys, knowing nothing of all this, had also written to Dartmouth. He instructed him that rigid economy must be enforced and pressing cease, the town and Exchange being full of complaints about the disorders of the press-gang: 'and to say the truth,' he added, 'by all the despatch that I can observe made in the manning of the ships here, even with the help of pressing, it looks to me as if they would not be manned till March.' And after a good deal of uninspired detail about victualling and the salaries of muster-masters, he gave the news. The rabble of Dover had taken the Castle, Dragoons had been worsted in a skirmish by the Prince of Orange's troops, a battalion of the Scots Guards at Maidenhead had gone over *en masse* to the invaders. In London the Roman Catholics were flying for their lives. 'God (who only knows what is best) grant a quick and happy issue to that just indignation of his under which we are at this day fallen!' After which he expressed the two letters to Portsmouth and went to bed.[46]

He was awakened early in the morning by one of the King's French pages with a letter, sealed and addressed to Dartmouth in the royal hand. From him he learnt the shattering news that his master had left the Palace in the night, first commanding him to deliver two letters, one to the soldier, de Duras, and the other to Pepys to forward to Lord Dartmouth. This, without examining its contents, he sent off by express to Portsmouth.[47]

14

The Interregnum

'I told him I was for a Parliament and the Protestant religion as well as they, but I was also for the King.' *Sir J. Reresby*.

The King had gone. It soon appeared that he had taken the Great Seal with him or in some way disposed of it. The Lord Chancellor had also gone. So had the writs for assembling Parliament. And the army, it seemed, was going too, for Lord Feversham, true to his orders, was busy dissolving it unpaid. The kingdom had reverted to the state of nature.

It was this presumably that the King. had intended – a just punishment on a stubborn, treacherous and stiff-necked people. They had denied the divine ordinance of kingly government: they should have a taste of the opposite – of anarchy, the 'war of all against all'. By his own withdrawal, his destruction of the writs, his removal of the Great Seal and his desperate orders to the heads of the armed forces, he had removed every recognized agency by which the business of government could be continued. And he had done it with dramatic and staggering suddenness.

It was an interesting situation, and of a kind to puzzle the ingenuity of the most learned of political philosophers. But the English are not a race of abstract philosophers, and James never displayed a more remarkable incapacity to understand them and their institutions than in this fatal and final act. In logic and law alike the government of the kingdom had ceased. The leaders of the English proceeded to act as though it had not ceased at all.

Within a couple of hours, in the midst of a prodigious uproar and confusion, a provisional government had been set up. The King's brother-in-law, the high tory Lord Rochester, ordered the Captain of the Guard to muster his disbanded troop and declare for the Prince of Orange. The leading officers of the army resolved to do the same. The Lords Temporal and Spiritual, or such of them as were in London, assembled at the Guildhall under the presidency of the Archbishop of Canterbury, and constituted themselves a provisional government. They were mostly loyal Tories – for the great whig lords and their less orthodox tory brethren were elsewhere – but they chose a delegation to invite the Prince of Orange to London, appointed a new Governor of the Tower and drew up a Declaration deploring the non-performance of the royal Proclamation to call a speedy Parliament. What was more they announced their expectation that such a Parliament would quickly be called with the Prince's help.[1]

They sent for the Secretaries of State and they sent for Mr Secretary Pepys of the Admiralty, requiring his immediate attendance. At their command, he wrote to Dartmouth recounting the events of that day and instructing him to refrain from acts of hostility against the Prince's fleet and to dismiss all Catholic officers from his own. He added on his own account that he had little thought when he despatched the King's letter on the previous night that he would so soon have had to send another after it. In the light of what had happened since the bewildered awakening of that terrible morning, he must have had misgivings as to what he had done. For by so faithfully and promptly obeying his master's last orders, there was no saying what responsibilities he might have incurred.[2]

But like everyone else in London Pepys had more urgent and terrible anxieties. Roused from its squalid lairs in the outer liberties by the news that the King was fled and the army disbanded, the mob rose and took possession of the city. All that day the sound of its fury shook the windows of York Buildings. As in the days of the Medway disaster and Godfrey's murder, Pepys was faced with the loss of all he possessed. He was fortunate that his house in Buckingham Street stood in a kind of backwater. Those who lived in the Strand above were less fortunate, for here grimy patriots broke down the doors of all suspected of Popery or zeal for the King – at that moment accounted much the same thing – and burnt and plundered on pretext of seeking arms. The Catholic chapels went down in rubble and flame. Somehow Lord Dartmouth's regiment and the artillery train under Henry Shere managed to save the situation for the time being, fighting their way through the crowded streets to the Tower, 'where there was so great a tumult', as Shere recorded, 'that no one could have believed we could have escaped a man of us'.

In the first hour of night the whole sky was ablaze, as the Mass house in Lincoln's Inn Fields was gutted and its contents piled by the howling rabble on to a bonfire. Then the fury of the populace turned against the foreign embassies, where the vanished papists were rumoured to have taken their goods for safety. Wild House, the stately residence of the Spanish Ambassador adjoining the Fields, was sacked, and an outraged grandee of Spain turned trembling and penniless into the night. The Legations of the Elector Palatine and the Grand Duke of Tuscany in the Haymarket, where the captain of the Trained Bands on guard was shot dead, suffered likewise. Barillon's house in St James' Square was only saved by a strong detachment of the Horse Guards, hastily assembled by the Council and armed with ball. Afterwards the mob marched past the soldiers, holding aloft flickering gilt candlesticks in solemn mockery and plundered popish gewgaws, while thousands of hooligans, waving oranges on swords and staves, yelled joyously for the reign of Saturn so miraculously come again. 'No law, no King', was the cry of the hour: next day the whole city should be looted. 'A world', as one mournful Londoner wrote, 'that is like to be very full of trouble!'

The wintry sun of December 12th rose on a ghastly spectacle. 'The capital in many places presented the aspect of a city taken by storm. The Lords met at Whitehall and exerted themselves to restore tranquillity. The Trained Bands were ordered under arms. A body of cavalry was kept in readiness to disperse tumultuous assemblages.'* The houseless Ronquillo, with every hasty honour that could be paid him, was lodged at Whitehall: 'all sober people are extraordinarily concerned at this horrid violation of the law of nations'. Pepys, shaken and ill, transmitted the orders of the Council of Peers to the ports that all outgoing vessels were to be searched and no one allowed to go down the river without a passport from the Lord Mayor.† Meanwhile the Thames was infested with innumerable boats manned by roughs who searched and plundered every passer-by. To thousands of inoffensive, respectable men and women the state of nature described so often by the political theorists seemed to have arrived: 'no King in Israel nor any face of government left us'.[3]

---

* Macaulay, *History of England* (1885 ed.) III, 302.
† *Pepysian MSS., Adm. Letters* xv, 467.

During the day a circumstance occurred which drew the mob eastwards and gave the authorities time to take breath. A scrivener making his way down a Wapping street saw peering out of an ale-house window the coal-blackened, anguished, but unmistakable face of Lord Chancellor Jeffreys. In a few moments the wretched fugitive was driven from his hiding place and surrounded. Pelted with mud and stones he was dragged by the multitude before the Lord Mayor, who was 'so struck with the terror of the rude populace and the disgrace of a man who had made all people tremble before him' that he fell weeping into a fit from which he never recovered. Later Jeffreys, almost torn to pieces, was smuggled into the Tower behind a forest of pikes formed by two regiments of militia, while the people surged after him yelling and holding out halters. Poor Penn, the Quaker, underwent a somewhat similar experience. As though to add to the horror of that day it became known that Titus Oates in his prison had once more put on his long-discarded Doctor's robes.[4]

Evelyn from the quiet of Sayes Court, Deptford, wrote anxiously to his old friend at York Buildings:

> I left you indisposed and send on purpose to learn how it is with you, and to know if in any sort I may serve you in this prodigious Revolution. You have many friends, but no man living who is more sincerely your servant or that has a greater value for you.
>
> We are here as yet (I thank God) unmolested; but this shaking menaces every corner, and the most philosophic breast cannot but be sensible of the motion. I am assured you need no precepts, nor I example so long as I have yours before me. And I would govern myself by your commands.

Methodically Pepys endorsed the letter: 'Upon the great Convulsion of State upon the King's withdrawing'.[5]

A further convulsion was in store that night. The evening began with an attack on Lord Powis' house in Lincoln's Inn Fields. But by now the authorities were ready. The mob was firmly met and driven off by the military. A period of comparative quiet followed. But those who wished for reasons of their own to destroy an ancient society had further resources. A little before midnight, a dreadful rumour, put about by men dressed as yokels, began to spread in the outer suburbs. Within half an hour the shout went up from every street: 'Rise! Arm! Arm! The Irish are cutting throats!' Thousands of papist soldiers, it was reported, were advancing from Knights-bridge towards the centre of the city, setting fire to the houses and massacring man, woman and child. Amid affrighted crying the drums beat to arms. By one o'clock all the principal streets were barricaded and lined by the Trained Bands, while lighted candles blazed from every window. There was no more sleep that night. Not till dawn did the panic subside and the tired citizens withdraw to their houses.

By this time something like únanimity of feeling had been reached by the governing and well-to-do classes. Whatever their earlier differences of opinion, it was clear that only one thing could now save a distracted kingdom – the speedy arrival of the Prince of Orange. In that dark hour, Whig and Tory alike turned to him. Between their cowardly sovereign and the maddened mob, even the most loyal professors of non-resistance took the one road open. 'I hope, dear,' wrote Lady Dartmouth to her husband, 'that you will be so wise to yourself and family as to do what becomes a reasonable man.'[6]

Dartmouth had already done so. Confronted on the 12th by the news of the King's flight and an invitation from the Prince of Orange, long secreted in the rollers of Lieutenant Byng's breeches and now timely placed upon his dressing-table by his politically-minded captains, the Admiral felt at last that his course was clear. 'Oh God!' he confided to Feversham, 'what could make our master desert his kingdom and his friends?' And in the name of himself and of his captains he wrote to the Prince offering his services to help establish 'the Protestant religion and liberties of England'.[7]

Yet the tragic drama was not quite played out. During the past two days no one had had time to think of the King or speculate about his fate. But during the 13th rumours began to reach the capital that he had been captured by some Kentish fishermen – 'a priest-codding' on the Thames – and brought captive to Faversham as a papist refugee. By the evening it was popularly believed that he had died as a result of the barbarous usage he had received. There well may have been many sad and loyal men who felt that it were best so.

But James was alive. He had survived even the indignity of having hands laid upon his person and his breeches rudely torn down while the scaly rabble searched for his jewels and money. The coronation ring, secreted in his pants, they failed to find. Then someone, suspecting the familiar lantern-jaw under his black periwig, had recognized him. Still denied liberty, he had been taken to a country inn and further insulted. Here, proudly defiant and tremblingly abject by turns, he awaited against his will the verdict of his heretic people.

As soon as the Council of Lords at the Guildhall was made aware of his plight, four of their members set out with a troop of Guards to his assistance. One of them, Pepys' friend the loyal Lord Ailesbury, hastened ahead of his companions and, galloping through a terrible night of wind and rain and a countryside insane with terror, reached Faversham by one o'clock next day. He found his sovereign trembling, unshaved and indignant. By quieting his fears and persuading him to return to his capital, this good, simple man almost changed the course of British history.[8]

To those who were not Tories, the unlooked-for news from Kent was not a little disconcerting. The continued presence of the King put a stop to the plans both of those who wanted to establish another Commonwealth and of those more numerous malcontents who wished to substitute William for James. English public opinion had stood for one royal decapitation but was not likely to stand for another; the halo of martyrdom invested the head of James' father and the echoes of that horrid act still sounded in men's ears. Yet from the provinces news continued to pour in of manifestations of the feeling, now released after long damming, against James' religious policy. Rumours of impending massacre by the disbanded and homeless Irish fanned the flames. At Oxford, the Princess Anne, still accompanied by the militant Bishop of London in blue cloak and breastplate, and escorted by eleven hundred horse, was received at the gate of Christ Church by the Chancellor, Vice-Chancellor and Doctors in their scarlet robes: over all this armed pageantry flew the device: '*Nolumus leges Angliae mutare.*' And it followed that if the people of England were so passionately desirous of preserving their laws unchanged – particularly the more intolerant ones – they could not be inordinately anxious to retain a King who was as obstinately determined to change them.[9]

The Tories, who were less logical, wished to keep both their old laws and their old King, at least for so long as he lived and so was King by Divine Right. James' reluctant re-appearance reminded them of both these inescapable facts. But during the past two days in their dire necessity even the most loyal of them had gone so far in

ignoring his existence and hailing his unhallowed rival and conqueror, that his second coming put them into a quandary. Lord
Dartmouth, for instance, who during the interregnum had offered
the fleet to the Prince of Orange, hardly knew which way to turn
when he heard the news of his old master's return. 'Your Majesty
knows', he wrote in desperation, 'what condition you left the fleet
in, and me in the most unsupportable calamity of my life. What
could I do but send to the Prince of Orange when I found the whole
nation did? . . . But I hope all will end in your Majesty's happy re-
establishment. Mr Pepys will acquaint your Majesty with the state
of the fleet.' On the whole the best course seemed to be to lay the
blame on Pepys. The Admiral carefully endorsed the Secretary's
hurried letter of the 11th that had brought him the King's last fatal
order: 'Received the 14th by the common post. Mr Pepys or whom
this was committed to should be answerable for the delay, for this
letter came not till after the Council of War that sent to the Prince
upon the letter from the Lords at Guildhall.' As Pepys expressly
states that he sent it off by express as soon as he received it on the
dawn of the 11th,* its adventures during the intervening three days
of national anarchy must remain a mystery.[10]

Towards four o'clock on the afternoon of Sunday, December 16th,
the King and his retinue approached London. Fearful of his
reception by the populace, he meant to return as he had departed,
by the quiet southern bank and across the Lambeth ferry. But one of
those sudden waves of popular reactionary feeling – so characteristic
of England in time of stress – had set in in his favour. Entering the
cobbled streets of the Borough, James found himself as in the
autumn of '79 on the crest of an unexpected surge of loyalty. Not
fully understanding it, he was yet touched by the acclamations of the
people; 'though they hated his religion', he observed, 'they did not
despise his person'. He resolved therefore to enter his capital openly.
So it came to pass that he went through the Sabbath streets with a
concourse of loyal lords and gentlemen riding before and a crowd
following with loud huzzas, 'to the great but short content', Pepys
reported, 'of all his subjects'. And in the evening there were bonfires
and ringing of bells. Perhaps there flitted across James' tired,
confused mind a memory of that dazzling day thirty years before

* *Rawl. MSS. A.* 186, f. 222. Printed in Braybrooke IV, 243.

when he had ridden thus through the city beside his returning brother.[11]

Yet for all the spontaneous, spasmodic sentimentality of England, the clock could not be put back. For a moment it looked as though a miracle had happened and that the Elizabethan, Clarendonian ideal – so dear to the tory heart – of a perfect union between the legitimate sovereign and the Anglican Church was about to be consummated again as in '60 and '85.* Pepys, hurrying to the Palace with the Admiralty correspondence to welcome his old master, may perhaps have thought so: one suspects there were tears in his eyes as he went his familiar journey up the river that evening. But next day it became amply apparent even to eyes most blinded by loyalty and affection that the momentary vision was only a mirage. The world of fashion and power was with the rising sun in the west. And the King had learnt nothing: he did not wish to learn. He attended Mass and rated his Cabinet and servants for their dealings with the usurping peers at the Guildhall during his absence. It was even said that the old concourse of papists and Jesuits filled the Bedchamber and ante-rooms as though the prodigious revolution of the past few weeks had never been. The only miracle was – if the rumour were true – how these devout gentlemen had so quickly reappeared from nowhere.[12]

'If the King had then prohibited all papists to refrain from coming near to him,' thought Anthony Wood, 'all had been well.' Even so one doubts it. For Tories the course of inexorable time might be reversed. But there were others who did not mean to lose the advantage that James' flight had given them, and the soldier-politician, cold calculating Orange, least of all. He had taken his full measure now of his father-in-law, and he knew that whatever folly he had committed before, given the same circumstances, he would commit again. Fear could always make James do his business for him. He resolved therefore to give James cause to fear.

When the King's messenger, bearing tidings of his return and his readiness to confer with his son-in-law, reached Windsor, the Prince refused to see him and placed him under arrest. Instead he sent a Dutch official to inform James that he would not enter the capital in person until all the armed forces of the kingdom were placed under his

* '. . . All the clouds (as we thought) were vanishing, and a bright day again appearing.' J. Evelyn to his son, Dec. 18th, 1688. *Diary and Correspondence of John Evelyn* (ed. H. B. Wheatley) iii, 428.

command. It was the old Roundhead ultimatum of '42 in a new form. At a council of the Lords who supported William, held at the Castle on the afternoon of the 17th, it was determined that the King must withdraw from London. Three of their number, Halifax, Shrewsbury and the old rebel Delamere, were instructed to tell him so. The invading troops were ordered to advance immediately on the capital.

That evening they closed in from the west. Before dusk they were in occupation of the villages of Kensington and Chelsea. The King was undressing as the Dutch infantry under Count Solms, with fuses lighted for action, poured into the Mall. Old Lord Craven, who more than half a century before had fought for Gustavus Adolphus, begged his master to let him die at the head of the Coldstream Guard sooner than yield the Palace to the foreigner. James coldly refused and the invaders took possession of Whitehall.

Shortly after midnight the Prince's emissaries arrived from Windsor. They insisted that the King, deep in the sleep of weariness and despair, should be woken. They, who a brief while before had been his subjects, told him that he must leave early in the morning for Ham House. James, who had no other thought now but flight, pleaded to be sent instead to Rochester. A messenger was despatched back to William to obtain his permission. It was granted.

Towards midday on Tuesday, December 18th, the King went down the steps of Whitehall for the last time and entered his barge. It was raining. Evelyn, standing with Sir Charles Cottrell and Sir Stephen Fox at one of the windows of the New Buildings, saw him put out into the river with ten or twelve barges of Dutch soldiers following after to protect him, it was claimed, 'from the insults of the mobile'. But of such insults there was now no sign – only silence.[13]

In the pouring rain the victorious Prince of Orange, with General Schomberg sitting beside him in his carriage, drove down Piccadilly about four o'clock the same afternoon. The bells were rung, bonfires lit in the streets, and a crowd with slightly bedraggled favours cheered for the nation's Liberator, though not as loudly, one onlooker noted, as it had for James two days before.* Perhaps the

* 'It is not to be imagined what a damp there was upon all sorts of men throughout the town.' Clarendon, *Diary*, Dec. 19th, 1688. 'The night was spent in ringing of bells, bonfires and other expressions of joy by the rabble; but thinking men of the City seemed displeased at the King's being forced to withdraw a second time.' Sir J. Reresby, *Memoirs*, 541.

presence of so many Dutch troops in their dingy blue uniforms had a damping effect; perhaps it was the rain. However inevitable and utilitarian, there was something a little humiliating to national pride in this revolution. The English, so jealous of foreigners as a rule, are sometimes strangely meek to some particular species of foreigner momentarily in political fashion. They were now accorded their bellyful. The streets round Westminster swarmed with ill-favoured and ill-accoutred Dutchmen instead of the gallant scarlet and gold of England: there were Holsteiners at Woolwich, Brandenburgers at Paddington, 'lousy' Scots at Lambeth, Birkenfeld's Germans at Kensington and other Teutons further afield at Eltham, Kingston and Richmond. It was better, of course, than French papists and Irish cut-throats. But the presence of all these armed foreigners could not but remind the haughty English that, while it had on the whole been a bloodless revolution, it had been a still more bloodless conquest. 'The like was never or will be in story,' wrote one bewildered patriot, 'a King with a great army driven out of his kingdom by a lesser army without fighting.' 'God damn Father Petre,' grumbled Dixie, the King's old coachman, as he drove sadly through the rain to Rochester, 'damn him! But for him, we had not been here.' It was the measure of poor King James' political ineptitude.[14]

The professional placeholders and all those who were great or would be great now went to acclaim the Prince. Evelyn saw him holding levee in the midst of them at St James', 'very stately, serious and reserved'. He seemed more interested in affairs of State than ceremony. Pepys, sadly doing business, one suspects automatically like a man in a dream – there is a shorthand copy of a note of his of that day in response to a request of one of Charles II's daughters, Lady Sussex, to carry her goods to France – received Orange's orders for transmission to Dartmouth at Spithead. The fleet was to be brought with all speed to the Buoy of the Nore. He himself was ordered to attend the Prince next day.[15]

The master who for more than twenty years had watched over Pepys' service, who had learnt to recognize it for what it was and had made him virtual ruler of the Navy, was now fallen beyond hope of recovery. The instrument of power which Pepys had made it his life's work to create had failed utterly to save the cause on which his own fortunes and his sovereign's had depended. His enemies,

William Harbord, Arthur Herbert and Edward Russell, stood at the Prince of Orange's right hand, high in his favour and gratitude. He could look now for little more in life but oblivion, disgrace and perhaps proscription.

On the morning of Wednesday, December 19th, the day set for his audience of the Prince, the weather changed suddenly to intense cold and frost. Seldom can Pepys have looked out on the river beneath his windows with sadder thoughts. What happened at that audience we do not know. Yet it cannot have been altogether unfavourable, for the Prince desired him to remain for the present at his post and Pepys consented. When he got home he found a letter awaiting him that reminded him that there are things in this world more precious than the favours of fortune and the smiles of the great. It came from William Hewer who had been his confidant for twenty-eight years, who once had been beaten by him for staying out late at night, and who had risen in the world in his service and now was richer than he. Couched in the seemingly cold and formal convention of the day, it was the kind of letter which might conceivably have caused the creator of mankind to be not wholly displeased with his handiwork. After wishing that the evening's audience would prove to Pepys' satisfaction, Hewer went on: 'If not, I know you will cheerfully acquiesce in whatever circumstance God Almighty shall think most proper for you, which I hope may prove more to your satisfaction than you can imagine. You may rest assured that I am wholly yours, and that you shall never want the utmost of my constant, faithful and personal service, the utmost I can do being inconsiderable to what your kindness and favour to me has and does oblige me to. And therefore, as all I have proceeded from you, so all I have and am is and shall be at your service.' 'A letter of great tenderness at a time of difficulty', was Pepys' endorsement.[16]

For the present, however, Pepys remained at his post. He had done nothing to save himself which his own conscience or any man could construe as a betrayal of his master. But he was still that which he had been in the far days before the Stuart monarchy was restored, an Englishman with a sense of his duty to his country. To him as to the great nobleman, Halifax, who through dark and devious ways had done so much to guide the course of that revolution, the earth of England, though inferior perhaps to that of many places abroad, had something of divinity in it: he was one who 'would die rather than see a spire of English grass trampled down by a foreign trespasser'. At that hour she was on the verge of war with a great military power. The fleet he had built and reclaimed and tended, and which had failed, through no fault of his, to serve the King, was still needed to serve England. A newsletter of December 25th has a significant note:

Some few days since Secretary Peepes received a letter from an ingenious gentleman in France, who gives an account that the French are setting out 50 sail of men-of-war in their yards in Brittany, and that great numbers of landsmen were drawing down towards the coasts.

Pepys showed the letter at once to the Prince.[17]

On Friday, December 21st, the new ruler of the country gave an audience to some sixty of the temporal and spiritual peers at St James'. He would not, he declared, seize the Crown or declare himself, as some about him suggested, a conqueror. He had come at their invitation to enable Englishmen to reassert their laws and liberties in a free and legally constituted Parliament: he had no intention of going back on his declared word. He would continue to conduct the military affairs of the nation, but he would leave the settling of the civil government in their hands.[18]

The implied promise simplified Pepys' position. The constitution of the kingdom to whose sovereign he had sworn his allegiance remained as before; meanwhile as the administrative officer responsible for the first defensive Service of the realm, it was his plain duty to assist the chief military administrator now accepted as such by King and nation. For the purposes of his work he was now the Prince's man, just as he had been James' when the latter was Duke of York and Lord High Admiral.

His task was not, of course, easy. The Prince was cold, aloof and difficult of access to all but his Dutch confidants, and advising him in naval affairs were men in whose judgment, and still less in whose goodwill, Pepys would not confide. Both Edward Russell and Arthur Herbert in their earlier days as gentlemen captains had felt the lash of the great Secretary's whip. The first, as Harbord's brother-in-law, had recklessly plotted nine years before to take his life and honour, while the other's name was a byword for indiscipline and corruption. But both men now represented something greater than themselves, and Pepys knew what belonged to his place. The correctness of his official attitude revealed the perfected technique of a lifetime. On the 22nd, in reply to a letter of Edward Russell's enclosing a copy of the Prince's orders for bringing the fleet to the mouth of the river, he expressed himself with immaculate and courteous rectitude:

Sir,
     I acknowledge, with many thanks, the favour of yours this morning; and do no less readily subscribe to you for the form than the matter of the enclosed papers.
     I shall endeavour to kiss your hand some time this day if your indisposition, which I am sorry for, will permit it, in order to the discoursing some particulars against the fleet's coming in. Remaining, with very great respect, your faithful and most humble servant,
                                                                    S. Pepys.

In matters of politics Russell and Herbert might far have outdistanced the dry-as-dust Secretary among his ledgers, but when it came to the niceties of battle by administrative correspondence, he was their master every time. More than any other man he evolved the gentle art of bureaucratic defence and offence. It is not the least of his claims to fame that he was the father of the Civil Service and of a system which, for all the challenge of ignorant mobs and authoritarian tanks and bayonets, still maintains throughout the better part of the world to-day. It adds still more to this long dead and unassuming Englishman's stature that that system is supported in the last resort by the same instrument of sea power which Pepys spent his administrative life in creating.[19]
     The Christmas season of 1688 – *Anno Mirabili* as Evelyn dated it – came in with frozen skies. It brought further political changes. On Saturday, December 22nd, the Lords met in their own House to debate the manner of calling the forthcoming Parliament. The majority, led by Archbishop Sancroft, held that to avoid a constitutional break and too great a strain on good men's loyalty, the writs should be issued in the King's name. It was hoped to get the royal consent to this next day, and a delegation was despatched to Rochester to procure it. But on Sunday news reached London that James, blind to the last, had fled secretly in the night and taken ship for France. What William had hoped for had come to pass; no royal ruler but he was left in England and, by his rival's flight into the

arms of Louis, the nation was committed to war with France and dependence on himself and his Grand Alliance.[20]

To the Tories it was the end of their hard-won, brief and chequered spell of prosperity. That union between anointed King, national Church and people for which they had fought so obstinately was now broken beyond hope of mending. 'Our poor master', wrote Francis Gwynn to Dartmouth, 'is once again gone from Rochester, ... and hath so entirely given up all there that there will be no ceremony, I doubt, used towards him or the child, which is the word he is now called by. He chose as ill a time now as he did before, for tomorrow the Lords are to meet concerning a Parliament, and I wish he had stayed to hear what their method had been.' The King's flight meant that an actual revolution must now be followed by what to an ordinary Englishman was far worse, a legal one. 'What', asked Lord Rochester, 'can the most loyal and dutiful body in the world do without a head?' The Whigs were jubilant, for the very ground on which their adversaries stood had opened under their feet. The 'tantivies' had no choice left them but apostasy to their own principles or proscription. It has frequently been the lot of the tory party in England to be betrayed by its own leaders. In the long run this has not harmed it, for the English are a conservative people. But at the time the betrayal has always been paid for by the exclusion from public life of the noblest among the Tories.[21]

The Prince of Orange followed up his victory quickly. On the day the King departed he ordered the French Ambassador to leave England and summoned all available members of Charles II's last House of Commons, together with the Lord Mayor, Aldermen and leading Common Councillors of London, to meet him on the day after Christmas. He thus publicly severed all means of communication with the fugitive King and ensured the support of a body which was certain to be predominantly whig and therefore opposed to any reconciliation with him. Elected in the final flood-tide of the Popish Terror, Charles' last Parliament had been fanatically exclusionist. On Christmas Eve the Lords met under the presidency of Halifax and accepted the *fait accompli*; the Archbishop refrained from attending. Next day they presented an Address begging the Prince to issue circular letters in his name to the electoral bodies to return members to a national Convention, and in the meantime to assume the provisional government of the country. On Boxing Day the assembled Commoners and city fathers, sitting in St Stephen's Chapel under the chairmanship of the exclusionist, Powle, agreed to a like resolution. A tory motion of Sir Robert Sawyer's, intended to limit the Prince's potential claims by giving him the formal title of Administrator, was easily talked out. 'The poor King not considered or mentioned', Lady Dartmouth reported to her absent husband; 'the door shut upon him as if he had never been.' At the time that monarch, accompanied by his priests, was travelling thankfully from Ambleteuse to the Palace of Saint Germain, where Louis the Magnificent was waiting to receive him.[22]

Pepys spent the festive season in the performance of his administrative duties. On Christmas Eve he sat in 'a solemn conference' with Sir Richard Haddock and the other Victualling Commissioners at the Navy Office, wrestling with the dual problem of how to get provisions down the river to a starving fleet in the teeth of an easterly gale, and how to pay for them with cash payments from the Treasury three weeks in arrears. This was the kind of conundrum with which he had formerly been long familiar: 'we are under the last degree of thoughtfulness', he told Dartmouth in a letter written on Christmas Day, 'what possible way is there to remedy this'. With hostilities against France likely to begin at any moment, he had plenty to occupy him. Warned by the Admiral that Guernsey, if not hastily secured, might become a thorn in the flesh of England, he obtained authority from the Prince on Christmas Day to prepare orders for sending frigates there. At the same time he made provision for protecting the Holland packet boats from French privateers.[23]

Pepys' next letter to Dartmouth was written on Boxing Day. It had an unwonted chill about it. For the Admiral, like all the rest of the great world, had taken the not unnatural step of applying to the fount of honour direct, and instead of corresponding as to the disposition of the fleet through the normal medium of the Admiralty, had despatched his private secretary, Phineas Bowles, to London to wait on the Prince and Edward Russell. But neither received him with any enthusiasm, and the Prince subsequently summoned Pepys and handed him Dartmouth's letter. He instructed him to send for Bowles and obtain from him the account of the fleet, 'in order', as Pepys observed in his letter with a certain frigid satisfaction, 'to my reporting the result thereof to him'.

For Pepys was furious. He felt that Dartmouth had not only been unfriendly to him personally but had insulted his office. Only a few months before Bowles had been petitioning him for employment in a most abject manner:* he naturally regarded him as one of his own creatures. That he should now be used to approach the Prince behind his back struck him as outrageous. He showed his displeasure in characteristic fashion. 'Your Lordship judges very rightly of Mr Pepys not being pleased with my coming up to the Prince without application to him,' wrote the discomfited Bowles, 'and this day he has given me a taste of his displeasure on my desiring to know what orders were gone to your Lordship, telling me that they were sent, and that I, bringing nothing to him, he did not think it material to communicate to me, so that he will have me in the dark in the matter . . . I find him much altered since my being with him the first night, but possibly it's more out of personal dislike to me than to your Lordship's proceedings.' For Pepys had now another cause of anger with Dartmouth. 'He is pleased', Bowles continued, 'to call your commissioning Captain Collins for the *Fubbs* yacht a double irregularity, first on the score of Captain Sanders being (as he says) still living, and then next of her not being under your Lordship's command.' For Pepys, as his frowning picture by Kneller reveals, could present a very stern and unforgiving front to those who had done wrong. Nor, in his just indignation, did he make much account of whom he offended.[24]

He even found time at this troubled season for an inter-departmental duel with his *vis-à-vis* of the Army. It was conducted by both sides with scrupulous official politeness. Writing on December 28th to Mr Blathwayt, the Secretary-at-War, about the embarkation of the reinforcements for the Channel Islands, Pepys had occasion to refer to a serious infringement, doubtless accidental, by the military forces, of one of the most sacred rights of the Navy:

There was another particular wherein, upon application expressly made to me this morning by Sir Richard Haddock in the name of himself and the Board, I was necessitated to move his Highness, namely that notice being brought to the Commissioners of the Navy at Deptford of a regiment of the Prince's Foot ordered to be quartered in the town of Deptford, and the Quarter Master's resorting to the said Commissioner with his desire that he

* *Rawl. MSS. A.* 186, f. 173.

may have liberty to quarter some of the officers of the said regiment in the Officers' houses within the Dock and Store-yards there, the Commissioner according to his duty desired and obtained time this day to communicate the same to the Navy Board, who immediately dispatched one of their number (Sir Richard Haddock) in all their names, pressing me to acquaint his Highness with it as a proposal that in no age appears to have been made before, nor can now be admitted without infinite inconveniences and particularly that of exposing his Majesty's ships to fire (as well them in the wet as dry dock) and his Magazines (most of which are combustible) both on float and in the Store houses, not only to fire but to embezzlement. And that too not wholly from what is to be suspected of the soldiers, but even from the King's Officers and workmen themselves when they shall have such a justification ready as the laying it upon the soldiers to the bereaving the Navy Board of the means they now have of challenging a very strict account from the Store-keepers, Watchmen and others charged with the safe custody of them, from the pretence they will raise from this accident of being rendered incapable of answering for their security.

His Highness, upon my opening this to him, was pleased to seem fully satisfied in the Navy Board's reasoning herein, directing me to notify the same to you for your preparing, and doing what is necessary for the Navy Board's satisfaction in it. I very well know how little necessary it is to press them in anything, but the Commissioners of the Navy telling me that they have but this day allowed them for preventing what the Quarter-Master tells them will otherwise be put in execution tomorrow, I leave it to you to give it what dispatch you see reasonable. I am most respectfully

Your humble servant,
S. Pepys.*

For in this as in other matters Pepys was the Navy's watchdog. In whose name he still regarded himself as being such his reference to the King's ships makes plain.[25]

The old year closed and the new year came in with Pepys still performing the familiar routine, waiting on the Prince at St James' and Whitehall for orders and for warrants to be signed, sending men and ships to the Channel Islands and transporting poor disbanded Irish soldiers for internment in the Isle of Wight, allotting frigates to escort the packet boats from Harwich to Holland, and transmitting instructions to Dartmouth. Every care had to be taken to reduce expense, for the outgoings of the past three months had been enormous and scarcely anything was coming in. Eighteen ships were to be left at Spithead for laying up at Portsmouth, and the rest of the

---

* S. P. to Mr Blathwayt, Dec. 28th, 1688. *Royal Society MSS.*, III, 129.

fleet was to make for the River as soon as the unlucky Admiral could get a wind to bring it. But although Pepys wrote almost daily to hasten matters the weather for the last twelve days of December and the first eight of January remained adverse. The cold was so intense that the very Thames began to be frozen over. At the turn of the year Dartmouth managed to get as far as the Downs, but dared come no further for fear of his ships becoming ice-bound.[26]

The quarrel between Pepys and his old friend and colleague was short-lived. On December 28th, after receiving Pepys' protest, Dartmouth penned a letter of apology explaining that the only reason he had sent Bowles up to London was the absence of letters from the Admiralty and his grief and distraction for his royal master. Situated far from the centre of affairs, he had been utterly in the dark as to what was happening. 'I should be very ungrateful if I were capable of making any unkind return to you,' he added. 'Pray deny me not your private and friendly advice, by which I shall be glad to govern myself; and I hope we may yet be helpful to one another. I am sure all things shall be done on my part as becomes your obliged and affectionate friend.'[27]

Though the explanation was not wholly satisfactory, Pepys accepted it. 'I thank you with all my heart', he replied on January 2nd, 'for your last, under your own hand, of me in the particular you mention somewhat unnatural, especially at a juncture so little needing it from one's friends. But, my Lord, you have done both yourself and me right in the trouble you have given yourself for my satisfaction about it. And I assure you, nothing on't shall longer stick with me, but, on the contrary, a desire of rendering your Lordship all the faithful services that (during the little remainder of my abode here) I shall be able to pay you.' For Pepys, though he still had his duty to do, regarded his career as finished. 'It will be matter of great content to me if I may be able by any means to be of use to your Lordship, though I have given over even the thinking on't for myself.' Dartmouth returned his thanks in a letter of genuine affection. 'It is no small part of friendship, in this age,' he wrote, 'to forgive the mistakes even of a friend, which mine really were and no other. Whatever becomes of me or you, I will always own and covet your friendship.'[28]

During the first week of the new year the naval situation changed rapidly. The arrest of English merchants in France and the seizure of their ships had already created a state of virtual war. At the same time news from Ireland showed that that country was on the verge of rebellion. The focus of national interest passed from the armies that had held the stage during the Revolution to the Navy that had stood by watching. Only a few days before the administration had been working out plans for laying up the fleet, 'the Prince intending', as Pepys told Dartmouth, 'with all speed he conveniently can to retrench the present charge of the Navy'. As so often before in the history of seventeenth-century England, the want of money had been the predominant consideration. Even as late as January 3rd orders were given on the Prince's instructions for discharging forty-nine ships.* But a successful appeal made on New Year's Day to the City of London for a loan brought about an immediate change in the situation.[29]

Its effects were felt as early as January 4th. On that day Pepys received orders, first from Captain Russell by letter and later from the Prince in person, that the ships under Dartmouth, instead of going to their respective ports to lay up, should remain together at the Buoy of the Nore. At the same time two frigates were ordered to cruise off the coasts of Ireland.

Dartmouth was anxious to leave the fleet in the Downs, on account of the continued frost, and come up to London to pay his court to the Prince. But on the 8th the wind shifted, and the frost, which had continued since December 19th, broke. Pepys, who visited St James' that day to lay Dartmouth's petition before the Prince, has left us a description of the scene. 'For so soon as the Prince . . . had read your Lordship's letter to him and heard your other to me, he was pleased presently to observe that your Lordship's advice touching the ships and desires concerning yourself being founded all along upon a supposed continuance of the frost and N.E. wind that blew, he did believe that the whole of those measures were now at an end, the wind being come about the S.E. and the frost broke with a great and continued rain, then just before his eyes as we stood in the garden windows; adding that he thought it would be much better that your Lordship should come about (as was before determined) to see the fleet safe brought in, and the rather (to give it you in your own words) because when you are gone

* *Rawl. MSS.* A. 186, f. 119.

there will be nobody to heed it, Sir John Berry being at Portsmouth.'* In another and more personal letter of the same date Pepys expressed his regret that he could not send the Admiral a reply more acceptable to his wishes. 'The truth is,' he assured him, 'the sudden and extraordinary change of weather all this day did naturally administer to his Highness matter for the answer he was pleased to give. Which he gave with so much earnestness, yet with no disregard towards your Lordship, that I thought it of more moment to you to forbear pressing it further.'

Yet Pepys was well aware that if the frost on the Thames had broken, another had set in that boded ill for Dartmouth and himself and showed little sign of thawing. He gave the Admiral a hint of it in his letter, telling him that he concurred with him in his desire to tighten the laws against neglectful masters and pilots – 'and if it ever comes in my way to do aught towards the remedying of it, I am sure I shall. But it must be done in Parliament, and how many things now before must of preference be given them there for the consideration of any matter so remote as that at this day is, is hard to judge.'†[30]

* S. P. to Lord Dartmouth, Jan. 8th, 1689. *Pepysian MSS., Adm. Letters* xv, 507–9.
† *Pepysian MSS., Adm. Letters* xv, 507–9.

Defeat

'Good God! where is loyalty and Christian charity?'
Lord Clarendon, *Diary*, Dec. 29th, 1688.

If Dartmouth had lost his sense of proportion, Pepys had not. The Convention Parliament had been summoned to Westminster on January 22nd and writs had gone out in the Prince's name to the electoral bodies. These had been accompanied by a flood of whig pamphlets and broadsheets, blackening everything that had been done in King James' reign and all who had been his servants. There were plenty of simple folk who expected the forthcoming assembly to effect some wonderful change for the better in the affairs of men; and there was a more than adequate supply of knaves who, for their own ends, encouraged them in that belief. But Pepys had been through too many arbitrary changes and revolutions to be under any further delusions as to what must happen to honest men in the course of them. He was a moderate, if loyal, Tory, which is only another name for a man who wishes to see the world better but is quite certain that it cannot be made so by violence and injustice. His wise old friend, John Evelyn, who was another, forecast what was likely to take place in a letter to his son. 'By what I collect, the ambitious and covetous will be canvassing for places of honour and rich employment . . . .If none of this happen, and that success do not quite alter the principles of men in power, we are to suspect *Astrea* upon earth again. But, as I have often told you, I look for no mighty improvement of mankind in this declining age and catalysis. A Parliament (legally called) of brave and worthy patriots, not influenced by faction nor terrified by power or corrupted by self-interest, would produce a kind of new creation amongst us. But it will grow old, and dissolve to chaos again, unless the same stupendous Providence (which has put this opportunity into men's hands to make us happy) dispose them to do just and righteous things, and to use their empire with moderation, justice, piety and for the public good. Upon the whole matter, those who seek employment before the grandees are served may suspend their solicitation.' Pepys would doubtless have concurred with Evelyn.[1]

His own constituency provided a case in point. On January 1st he wrote to his friends at Harwich offering himself for election to the Convention. But Pepys as head of the naval administration was a very different person from Pepys in his present precarious situation. Excuses began to pour in, even from his most faithful adherents. The alteration in the size of the Corporation by the resumption of the old Charter had made a strange change; the Town Clerk, Daniel Smith, was offended because Pepys had not written to him sufficiently often; the question of the local Lights – Pepys until recently had been Master of Trinity House – prejudiced interested persons. Hints were dropped that he and Deane ought to visit the town if they were to make headway against the two whig candidates who were being put up against them. Mr Sandford wrote on the 5th to let Pepys know that both the Town Clerk and his old correspondent Mr Langley, the Mayor, were secretly working against him: 'Sir, it wounds us to observe such a parcel of ungrateful men.'

Pepys refrained from vain recrimination and replied courteously to them all.* 'As to myself,' he wrote to Mr Seaman on the 8th, 'if they shall think fit to choose me I shall with all respect accept of the same and own myself obliged to 'um by it. But if they have any other in their eye that they do really conceive of better capacity and interest than I, God forbid I should repine at the choice of him.'†

A week before the poll a few loyal supporters were still hopeful: 'as yet', one of them reported on the 8th, 'I have no reason to suspect but that your Honour will carry it'.‡ Two days later Pepys was warned that, though Deane had now withdrawn in his favour, hoping to leave the representation of the Borough to him and Sir Thomas Middleton – 'a very worthy gentleman agreed upon by all parties' – the electors were showing a preference for John Eldred, the whig candidate. On receipt of this blow on the 12th Pepys did for a moment allow himself a modest expression of vexation: had he

* 'I do agree with you in fearing that Sir Anthony Deane and I are not ingeniously dealt with by everybody. I am sensible too of what you say that the Church of England men have got no advantage (among you at least) by the revival of the old charters.' S. P. to Mr Sandford, Jan. 8th, 1689. *Rawl. MSS. A.* 179, f. 156.

† S. P. to Mr Seaman, Jan. 8th, 1689. *Rawl. MSS. A.* 179, f. 156.

‡ Alderman John Browne to S. P., Jan. 8th, 1689. *Rawl. MSS. A.* 179, f. 153.

foreseen such disappointments at Harwich, he told Simon Sandford, he could easily have provided for himself elsewhere. 'But as I have slipped my time, and so it is become too late to talk of any such thing now, so would it make me appear more solicitious for the thing than I really am ... It happens to be a very busy post tonight with me', he added.*

In a letter of the same date to the Mayor he wrote at greater length:

What it is that has wrought a change, I neither know nor think decent for me to enquire into ... I am very loath to believe what I have on this occasion had suggested to me, that there are not wanting some to whom my professions on behalf of the Church of England are made matter of offence. But if that be so, I am contented on that score to be rejected both from Parliament and everything else all the days of my life rather than be once admitted thereto on any other ...

For your advice about my coming down I have had no answer from the Corporation to my late letter encouraging me thereto. And having never heretofore wanted their invitation (nor is it long since the last Mayor brought both Sir Anthony Deane and me a very kind one) I am loath now to go uninvited ... Nor indeed could I at this day (were my encouragements greater), except the Prince's dispensing with my present attendance here, the fleet being but just now brought by my Lord Dartmouth into the river in order to its being part laid up and part set immediately out again in several squadrons for the security of commerce against the insults apprehended from the French.

But as I have heretofore, so I do again pray you not to let my friends want anything of the respect that would be paid them (by way of entertainment) were I myself there. Which I shall with a most ready thankfulness reimburse you for, either here or at Harwich upon demand, whatsoever be the issue of the Corporation's pleasure towards me. Nor shall it be long before I make them a visit in acknowledgment of their old favours, whether they give me any new ones to thank them for on this occasion or no.†

The tide, he knew, was too strong against him: for, as he was warned, men's minds, honesty and manners had altered of late.[2]

---

* *Rawl. MSS. A.* 179, f. 163. Curiously enough there are no entries in the Admiralty Letter Book from Jan. 11th to 13th inclusive. *Pepysian MSS., Adm. Letters* xv, 525. But in *Rawl. MSS. A.* 186, ff. 122 *et seq.* will be found detailed orders, dated Jan. 12th, for despatching squadrons to the Mediterranean, the Channel and Ireland.

† S. P. to the Mayor of Harwich, Jan. 12th, 1689. *Rawl. MSS. A.* 179, f. 165. For the full correspondence between Pepys and his constituents during the election see *Rawl. MSS. A.* 179, ff. 147–77, 210, 221.

Though his enemies were in the gate and at any moment his unyielding vigilance at his post might be visited by a repetition of the fate he had suffered in '79, Pepys abated nothing of his disciplinary zeal or of his precision. At the end of December he reported to the Prince that he had seen more commanders and officers of the fleet in town – without any leave that he knew of from the Admiral – than he ever remembered, 'and this', as he told Dartmouth, 'at a time when nobody can foresee what occasions may arise for the service of their ships'. A fortnight later, in the midst of mobilization, he wrote to his old acquaintance, Captain Graydon of the *Saudadoes*, that he had heard that he had left his command and come to London, 'without any leave that I know of from his Highness, while his Highness was at the time calling upon me once or twice a day to know whether the ships he had ordered to Harwich were gone or no. I told him further that it was an instance of such a piece of liberty as I had never before met with in near 30 years' service and that I believe would not now be adventured upon by any commander in the fleet from the Admiral downwards but yourself, and that for discipline's sake an account ought to be given of it to a court-martial. And when the Service will admit, it shall be no fault of mine if it be not. And this I have the rather done, and do the more frankly tell it you, because I take you for an ingenious man and one that for that reason (though I could have been glad to have been more successful in it) both have and am known to have at all times heretofore endeavoured to do good offices to the King, and should for the same reason (were I to continue in the Navy) very willingly do towards you with his Highness. But at the same time where such an irregularity as this appears, be it in friend or foe, tending to the immediate subversion of all good order in the Navy, it shall never want its full observation from me as long as I have any place in it.'*[3]

Nor did the Secretary in the hour of his decline fear the frown of the great. When the powerful Lord Berkeley, now in high favour with the triumphant party, asked for leave to abandon his squadron in the Downs and come up to London on grounds of pretended ill-health, Pepys, who well knew that his request would be granted,

---

* S. P. to Capt. Graydon of the *Saudadoes*, Jan. 14th, 1689. *Pepysian MSS., Adm. Letters* xv, 525–6. Graydon came to a bad end in the West Indies fifteen years later.

apprised him of the fact but made his displeasure clear. His letter of application arrived too late, he told him – it was past nine at night – to ask the Prince's pleasure on it that day, but he would not fail to do so on the morrow, 'not doubting, your health being concerned in it, but it will be to your satisfaction. Otherwise I could not have encouraged your Lordship to expect it, his Highness having no longer ago than yesterday refused the same request from my Lord Dartmouth, as being unwilling to dispense with a Flag before it had well discharged itself of the body of the ships it was to bring about to the Nore.' To this expression of his disapproval, Pepys added a more direct rebuke for Berkeley's casual attitude towards a disgraceful accident that had befallen one of the 3rd rates under his command. 'It seems a very deplorable story which your Lordship is pleased to give me of the loss of such a ship as the *Sedgemoor* . . . It is what I hope will not be suffered to pass without full justice done upon it, if the persons upon whom the miscarriage is chargeable are, or can be laid hold on.'* A week later Pepys had occasion again to complain of Berkeley, this time in a letter to the Navy Board:

Gentlemen. I cannot but give it you (hoping that it may not yet be too late) as my opinion that my Lord Berkeley has gone a great deal too fast in his ordering the body of the *Sedgemoor* to be broken up before he has authority from the Lord Admiral . . . as being a matter that even the Lord High Admiral himself would be thought to do an extraordinary thing even in his adventuring to order it to be done without the opinion of the Navy Board for it leading him thereto and the approbation of the Prince confirming the same.†

For though, where such great men were concerned, Pepys might now be quite powerless, he was determined that while he remained at his post no irregularity should pass unrebuked, lest the rule of law he had created should be handed down impaired by an ill precedent to his successors.[4]

Sea changes beyond Pepys' capacity to control were happening fast. On January 10th he transmitted orders to Dartmouth to hand over the fleet on its arrival at the Nore to his second-in-command and report at St James'. Two days later, on Saturday the 12th, he was received in an audience with Admiral Herbert – now restored to

---

* S. P. to Lord Berkeley, Jan. 9th, 1689. *Pepysian MSS., Adm. Letters* xv, 513.
† S. P. to Navy Board, Jan. 15th, 1689. *Pepysian MSS., Adm. Letters* xv, 536.

all and more than all his old authority – at which the Prince announced his decision of continuing 10,000 men in sea pay during the remainder of the winter. Twelve ships were to proceed at once to the Mediterranean under Sir John Berry, another eight to Ireland and six to patrol the Channel, while another eighteen, unassigned, were left to be laid up. On Pepys' representing the growing financial straits of the Navy Board and the Victualling Commissioners, the Prince promised to lay the matter immediately before the Commissioners of the Treasury.* During the following week, until cash was forthcoming, Pepys for the last time faced the task of allaying a mutiny among the unpaid seamen. On the 16th he drafted a proclamation to the fleet, denying 'groundless reports of late industriously spread among the seamen touching the uncertainty of their receiving wages due to them', and promising that all arrears should be paid 'according to the known methods of the Navy'.† At that moment the men of at least one of the ships in the Downs were in open mutiny.[5]

Such poor simple folk were easily frightened, and happily as easily appeased. They received their arrears of pay, and the great men proceeded with their task of liquidating the Revolution they had made. The Convention on which so many hopes rested, and so many fears, was due to meet on the 22nd. A week before Evelyn at a meeting at Lambeth Palace found the Church of England Tories sadly divided: some, including most of the Bishops, were for a Regency, some for making the Princess Mary Queen, and a few for calling back the King on conditions. Such tory considerations took little account of the dominant trends of opinion in the country – of the ambitions and fears of the whig peers and politic tory lords, now committed by their own past to undying enmity towards James, of the catchwords of the gullible multitude, of the attitude of the all-powerful Prince himself. It was said in the coffee-houses that Oates had been received at Court and graciously treated, that James was about to put himself at the head of the Papists in Ireland, that King Louis was preparing an army to invade England and restore the exile to his throne. A rumour that the Convention would recall the

* 'His Highness was pleased to be very sensible of the matter.' S. P. to Navy Victuallers, Jan. 14th, 1689. *Pepysian MSS., Adm. Letters*, xv, 527.

† *Rawl. MSS. A.* 186, ff. 125–6. And see *Pepysian MSS., Adm. Letters* xv, 532, 540, 542–3.

King sent prices tumbling in remote country market places; the pamphleteers and the mobmasters, marshalled once more by such cunning contrivers as Pepys' old persecutor, Wildman, knew their business.[6]

On the 17th Pepys issued an order to the captain of the *Fubbs* yacht to sail at once for Holland with Arthur Herbert on board, and another to Sir John Berry to despatch a squadron to Goree to escort Herbert and the Princess of Orange back to England. It was more than ten years since he transmitted similar orders to carry her from her native land as a young bride. Next day he learnt from Harwich that he had lost his election. A certain Captain Ridley, it appeared, had spread a tale in the town that Pepys was a Papist and went to Mass, and that he had frequently seen him in the King's Chapel. The Dissenters, and even 'a kind of Quaker', though disqualified by law from doing so, insisted on recording their votes, and the Mayor's attempts to stop them were 'over-ruled by noise and tumult'. Thereupon in the most arbitrary way Mr Smith, the Town Clerk, had declared Pepys' opponent chosen. Middleton and Eldred carried the two seats and Pepys was left at the bottom of the poll. 'By which', reported Hippolitus de Luzancy, Vicar of Harwich and himself a former convert from Catholicism, 'you may easily be made sensible how we are overrun with pride, heat and faction, and unjust to ourselves to that prodigious degree as to deprive ourselves of the greatest honour and advantage which we could ever attain to in the choice of so great and so good a man as you are. Had reason had the least place among us, or any love for ourselves, we had certainly carried it for you.' After the declaration of the poll, he told Pepys, whilst the victorious members of the Corporation were chairing Eldred up and down the street, a fellow had raised the cry of 'No Tower men! No men out of the Tower!' But no one joined in, the majority of the freemen, who under the ancient and now restored constitution had no votes, declaring roundly that had they had their rights, they would have chosen Pepys. The seamen were particularly friendly towards him.[7]

Pepys took his defeat well. He wrote next day to the Mayor acknowledging his letter. 'If what the Corporation has done gives them but as much content as it do me, I can assure you neither of us have any cause of being dissatisfied with it; nor shall anything that has passed herein lessen the desires I have ever had and shall always have of doing the Corporation and every member of it all the services and good offices I am able whenever they shall give me any opportunity for it. And this even to Mr Smith himself; though I must needs say he has used me a little hardly if his proceedings in this matter towards me have had no better ground than that which he mentioned to you about my preventing the Corporation's obtaining the reversion of the Harwich Lights; the reversion of all Lights having been granted by King Charles the Second, by a Declaration thereof at the Council Table, to the poor of the Trinity House, and myself being also a member (under oath) of that body long before I had any relation to the Corporation of Harwich.

'True it is I am very sorry for the trouble which you and the rest of my friends have sustained for my sake on this occasion, that being (upon my faith) the only uneasiness that falls to my share in this matter. But as I hope both they and you will in your kindness excuse it, so I pray you and them to depend upon it that I shall always remember and thankfully acknowledge it.

'And for what at my desire you have disbursed in the entertainments of my friends on this occasion, pray do me the favour to lay out as much for me (whatever it is) with them in a glass of wine to the Corporation's health, and your own, and theirs, and the gentlemen's your new burgesses.'* A few days later he paid a modest bill for £8. 5s. 6d., £5. 12s. 6d. of which was for wine, £1. 10s. 6d. for meat and £1. 2s. 6d. for beer, bread, oysters, fire and tobacco. The privilege of representing one's fellow citizens cost less in the seventeenth century than it does to-day. It was twenty-one years since Pepys had first contemplated the idea of putting himself forward as a Parliament man should he 'continue in the Navy', and more than fifteen since he had become one. He was little likely now to continue in the Navy, and his absence from a place where he had suffered so much can hardly have caused him much grief.[8]

Thus it came about that the Convention, when it assembled at Westminster on January 22nd to do its useful but rather dubious business, met without Pepys. He would have been uncomfortable there from the start, for the Commons, elected by the old, close, exclusionist Corporations, at once chose Henry Powle, one of his tormentors of earlier days, to be their Speaker. They then agreed on

---

* S. P. to the Mayor of Harwich, Jan. 19th, 1689. *Rawl. MSS. A.* 179, f. 177.

an address of thanks to the Prince of Orange, appointed a day of Public Thanksgiving for his having been made the instrument of the kingdom's deliverance from Popery and arbitrary government and adjourned till the 28th. Among much other hopeful business lying before them was a petition from Dr Titus Oates, setting forth the sad condition he had long lain under and how unjustly he had been used. The only consolation for an old-fashioned Tory who remembered '79 was that Major Wildman was said to be very ill.[9]

Pepys awaited the issue in quiet. He continued to transact the business of the Admiralty from his house in York Buildings, relinquishing nothing of his former severity and refusing leave left and right. He told his friend, Sir William Booth, that the Prince had informed him that 'there were too many already here . . . at a juncture like this when their absence from their duties could be very ill dispensed with'.* Meanwhile he pursued in such leisure as he had the dignified and learned tastes which with the years had become increasingly dear to him. On the day before the Convention met again to consider the state of the nation and dispose of its ancient throne and constitution, he entertained John Evelyn to dinner at the Admiralty, providing as a virtuoso's diversion an infant prodigy, son to one of his other guests. After dinner Pepys and Evelyn put to this child of less than twelve years old many questions which he answered in a most extraordinary manner, so readily and pertly and covering so wide a range of subjects that they decided that his surprising knowledge could never be explained as a mere freak of memory. 'There was not anything', Evelyn afterwards recorded, 'in Chronology, History, Geography, the several systems of Astronomy, courses of the stars, longitude, latitude, doctrine of the spheres, courses and sources of rivers, creeks, harbours, eminent cities, boundaries and bearing of countries, not only in Europe but in any other part of the earth, which he did not readily resolve and demonstrate his knowledge of, readily drawing out with a pen anything he would describe. He was able not only to repeat the most famous things which are left us in any of the Greek or Roman histories, monarchies, republics, wars, colonies, exploits by sea and land, but all the sacred stories of the Old and New Testament; the succession of all the monarchies, Babylonian, Persian, Greek,

---

* S. P. to Sir W. Booth, Jan. 26th, 1689. *Pepysian MSS., Adm. Letters* xv, 562.

Roman with all the lower Emperors, Popes, Heresiarchs and Councils, what they were called about, what they determined of in the controversy about Easter, the tenets of the Gnostics, Sabellians, Arians, Nestorians, the difference between St Cyprian and Stephen about rebaptization, the Schism. We leaped from that to other things totally different, to Olympic years and Synochronisms; we asked him questions which could not be resolved without considerable meditation and judgment, nay of some particulars of the Civil Laws, of the Digest and Code. He gave a stupendous account of both natural and moral philosophy, and even in metaphysics. Having thus exhausted ourselves rather than this wonderful child, or angel rather, for he was as beautiful and lovely in countenance as in knowledge, we concluded in asking him if in all he had read or heard of, he had ever met with anything which was like this expedition of the Prince of Orange, with so small a force to obtain three great kingdoms without any contest. After a little thought he told us that he knew of nothing which did more resemble it than the coming of Constantine the Great out of Great Britain through France and Italy, so tedious a march, to meet Maxentius, whom he overthrew at Pons Milvius with very little conflict, and at the very gates of Rome, which he entered and was received with triumph, and obtained the Empire, not of three kingdoms only, but of all the then known world. He was perfect in the Latin authors, spake French naturally, and gave us a description of France, Italy, Savoy, Spain, ancient and modernly divided; as also of ancient Greece, Scythia and northern countries and tracts. We left questioning further. He did this without any set or formal repetitions, as one who had learned things without book, but as if he minded other things, going about the room, and toying with a parrot there, and as he was at dinner (*tanquam aliud agens*, as it were) seeming to be full of play, of a lively, sprightly temper, always smiling and exceeding pleasant, without the least levity, rudeness or childishness.' One is grateful to Evelyn for the mention of the parrot – brought back, no doubt, by some sailor – that the Admiralty Secretary kept in his hospitable house. With its many opportunities, it must surely have excelled all other fowls of its kind in the wisdom and distinction of its conversation.

Afterwards the father of this 'sweet child', as Evelyn called him, explained that he never made his son learn anything by heart, not even the rules of grammar. His tutor, a Frenchman, read everything to him aloud, first in French and then in Latin. He was already perfect in arithmetic and newly entered into Greek. And he was as earnest at his play as at his work, he told them, playing regularly with other boys of his age four or five hours a day. A little sadly, after enjoying so much happiness, Evelyn who had lost a child of his own of almost equal promise, cautioned the father not to set his heart too much on this jewel: '*Immodicis brevis est aetas, et rara senectus.*'[10]

Next day, Monday, being the 28th January, the Commons resolved themselves into a committee of the whole House to consider the state of the nation. The general expectation was that the Prince and Princess of Orange would be raised to the throne. But it was first necessary to dispose of its present occupant. The spokesman of those who wished to preserve the old constitution unimpaired was Sir Christopher Musgrave, Pepys' companion on his journey through the North in '82, and son to the great Westmorland squire Sir Philip, than whom, as one of his contemporaries wrote, a worthier Englishman was never found. He asked the assembled lawyers whether any Parliament had a right to depose the King. The whig challenge to the Tories, crystallized after half a century of restatement and struggle, was formulated by one with whom Pepys had crossed swords more than once. 'I have heard', said Sir Robert Howard, 'that the King has his crown by a divine right; but we, the people, have a divine right too.' All government was grounded upon a compact with the people. The King had broken it.

It was left to the tory lawyers, who had defended the seven Bishops against the exercise of arbitrary monarchical power, to point out how much more delicate a structure an ancient government was than the whig argument supposed. The social compact was a fiction: the conception of government, so unnatural to the self-seeking animal, man, had grown gradually out of elemental barbarism and anarchy, and could only be preserved from the ever-threatening and destructive forces of individual selfishness by the acceptance of its essential parts as sacred and unalterable. The ancient Estates of the Realm, of which the Crown was one and the Commons another, could not be undermined without grave injury to the whole community, not only in the present generation but in those to come: secured and limited by the rule of known law, they were for all time and of divine ordinance. Sir Robert Sawyer – Pepys' chamber-fellow or 'chum' of Cambridge days – maintained that the Commons had no right to exercise authority over its fellow Estate, the Crown. Nor could it speak for the people as a whole, since it only represented 'the freeholders and the class possessed of property, by no means the nation; perhaps not the fourth part of the nation'. According to a brother lawyer, Sawyer was a proud, affected and poor-spirited man with his eye ever upon prosperity and success. But he acquitted himself courageously that day. He was followed by Sir Heneage Finch, the ex-Solicitor-General, who warned the House against appealing to the hypothetical state of nature 'for in that case where would be the right of property that everybody possessed?' As for the proposal to dispose of the Crown, however badly King James might have governed, he could not forfeit more than he had possessed – the personal exercise of the regal powers. He could not forfeit what was not his to forfeit, the hereditary Crown itself.

But such speakers were few. And their opponents were in no mood to listen. They had suffered a prolonged political eclipse and many of them persecution: they were now in an overwhelming majority. Few of them were philosophers; they were practical and mostly not over-scrupulous men to whom power had come suddenly. One of them put their policy, if not their case, in a nutshell by a brusque 'We found the throne vacant and are to supply the defect. I say we represent the more valuable part and all those who deserve a share in the Government.' And the brazen-faced, bullying apostate, Sir William Williams, the Welsh lawyer who had taken the chief part in the prosecution of the seven Bishops, now declared roundly, 'We come to supply what the King has taken from us.'

It was moved that James II having endeavoured to subvert the constitution by breaking the original contract between King and people, and by the advice of Jesuits and other wicked persons violated the laws and withdrawn himself from the kingdom, had abdicated the government and that the throne had thereby become vacant. At the instance of Colonel Birch, the bluff old Puritan Boanerges against whom Pepys had so often contended, it was also resolved that experience had shown it to be inconsistent with the safety and welfare of a Protestant kingdom to be governed by a popish Prince.

These resolutions were at once carried to the Lords. Here the Tories were stronger, and Rochester and Nottingham, contending

vigorously for respecting the integrity of the Constitution and the
conscience of all those office-holders in Church and State who had
taken the Oath of Allegiance to King James, only failed by two votes
to carry the day in favour of a Regency. It took another week of
wrangling and the sight and sound of the London rabble in Palace
Yard before the Lords were ready to agree with the Commons that
the throne was vacant. During that time the mobmasters wasted no
opportunity of fanning the popular fear of popery and a papist King.
At Oxford, on the day habitually set apart for mourning the
martyrdom of Charles I, a horrible looking instrument was exhibited at the 'Red Lion' with the device, 'Invented, as they say, by a
Popish Bishop to screw Protestants to death by degrees: something
to put into the mouth that they shall make no noises.'*[11]

Pepys was not an hereditary aristocrat nor a great landed
magnate. He was a man of the people, who had risen from the ranks
in the service of the Crown, administering England for the benefit
not of a class but of the people as a whole. He believed in regal
government and a strong executive because in his own limited
sphere he had had to fight for years against those who sought to turn
national interests to class and sectarian ends: for tarpaulins against
ignorant gentlemen commanders, for honest administration against
graft and corrupt contractors, for rule, industry and integrity in the
management of the public service against the arbitrary will of
privileged and irresponsible individuals. That his royal master had
made tragic mistakes he knew as well as any man. But there is little
virtue in loyalty if it is to be dispensed with at the first sign of any
flaw in the human object of that loyalty. And it is when there is a
weak or a bad king that the principle of hereditary monarchy would
seem to depend most on the loyalty of those who subscribe to it.
Pepys may have been wrong: it is easy to argue that he was. But it
cannot be denied that he behaved like a brave and honest man.
Once before he had staked his all and faced Tower, mob and scaffold
sooner than submit to what he knew to be wrong. Though he had
been no supporter of the King's arbitrary courses, still less of his
folly, he knew him for one who had tried to do his duty after his own
lights and had been shamefully traduced and misrepresented by

---

* 'This to make papists odious.' *Anthony Wood, Life and Times* (ed. Clarke, 1894) III,
297.

those who pretended to public motives which in many cases they were far from feeling. He had eaten his bread and sworn him allegiance.

Looking back over the course of our subsequent history, we believe the Revolution of 1688 to have been a necessary and perhaps inevitable step in the evolution of our country, though it may be argued that, by weakening the authority of the central executive unduly, it exposed the English people to that unchecked greed and exploitation of the poor by the strong which accompanied the industrialization of the next century. Samuel Pepys is not to be blamed because he could not think of the Revolution as anything glorious. The magnates who made it might coin noble phrases about the laws and liberties of their country, but they were mostly men who had broken their oaths and who cut a shabbier figure in the eyes of their own contemporaries than they do in ours. And lurking behind the Revolution were the very men – Harbord, Wildman, Aaron Smith – who a few years before had stooped to the lowest depths of perjury and violence in order to destroy both Pepys and his royal master. He could not see them as patriots, even if we now believe that their machinations served the ultimate good of their country. An ignorant porter from Wapping or a bumpkin dazzled by a lace coat and an orange favour might consider such hellrake lords as Lovelace, Wharton and Macclesfield high-spirited tribunes of the people. They did not seem so to Pepys. To Roger North,* who knew them well, the strangest phenomenon of the Revolution was that the reformers of the age were 'the most vicious, lewd and scandalous of all mankind, and the sober and judicious part were those borne hard upon. . . . And for whoring, drunkenness and professed atheism they had not their fellows. Impetuous, injurious and cruel, and yet the cause of religion and property was in their hands, and supported by them as they had the good or ill luck to persuade the world.'

While the Lords were still debating whether the Crown was vacant, the question was being resolved elsewhere as to whom it

* Roger North has often been traduced by later historians, notably by Macaulay. A collation of his writings with contemporary documents does not support the partisan charge of inaccuracy. His account of Samuel Atkins' cross-examination in 1678, for instance, tested by Atkins' manuscript narrative, is remarkably conscientious. Pepys' friend, Lord Clarendon (*Diary*, Jan. 16th, 1689), thought him one of the only two honest lawyers he had met. A well-edited edition of his writings has long been needed.

should be granted and on what terms. The Tories who had been defeated in their hopes of a Regency fell back on yet another expedient: the vesting of the Crown in James' eldest Protestant child, Mary of Orange, who was at least in the line of legal succession. 'I must confess any government is better than none,' pleaded Nottingham in the Lords, 'but I earnestly desire we may enjoy our ancient constitution.'

William saw to it that this proposal had short shrift: he would not, he let it be known, be his wife's subject. But a hope that he might be raised to the throne alone, with the virtual abandonment of all pretence of legality, was felt to savour too much of republicanism and of another military Commonwealth. On Wednesday, February 6th, the Lords in conference with the Commons agreed that the Crown should be offered jointly to William and Mary and the exercise of its powers be vested in William alone. Meanwhile the chief legal experts of the Commons, under the chairmanship of a young whig lawyer of genius named Somers, drew up the heads of the nation's grievances in a formal Declaration of Rights which was to accompany the offer.

The Revolution was now complete. Early on February 12th the yacht that brought the Princess of Orange from Holland dropped anchor off Greenwich. That afternoon she took possession of her fallen father's palace at Whitehall. Next day – Ash Wednesday – in the Banqueting Hall, whence their common grandfather had stepped on to the scaffold in vindication of the ancient laws and constitution of the kingdom, William and Mary accepted King James' throne from the Convention which had declared it vacant. A vast crowd thronged the wet roadway below the Palace all the way to Charing Cross. It is possible that Pepys, who as a boy of fifteen had seen the axe fall in the very place where now Garter-King-at-Arms proclaimed the new sovereigns, was a mute spectator of yet another momentous scene in the history of his country. It is more probable that he remained in his house by the river, hearing only the distant kettle-drums and trumpets and the sound of the acclaiming multitude as the Heralds' procession passed down the Strand towards Temple Bar. His evening mail, read while the sky above the City reflected the glare of a hundred bonfires, struck a note of gentle irony. For good Mr Langley, the Mayor of Harwich, was seeking the advice of his former representative as to how to behave towards an inn-keeper who had been 'so rude as to call his Highness, the Prince of Orange, son of a Flemish bitch!'* History does not relate whether the offending publican was a Jacobite or only the more extreme kind of Whig.[12]

There was nothing now left for Pepys but to lay down his office and go. The last test of loyalty is a man's readiness to sacrifice what he desires for the sake of what he loves. Pepys was one who all his life, though perhaps in a lesser degree as he grew older, had coveted wealth, place and public repute: he was by nature a worldling. But he had been brought up in a school that sets spiritual values above those of this world, however desirable, and through all the changes of life he had remained true at heart to the ideals of his youth. He did not now fail them, nor they him.

Whether the new King, so silent, serious and reserved to all the changing throng about him, would have retained the services of the great Admiralty Secretary against the wishes of such powerful gentlemen of the sea Service as Edward Russell who had invited him to England and Arthur Herbert who had carried him there, one cannot tell. It is possible, for William, however brought over, had not come to England to be the King of the Whigs or even of renegade Tories. When the new government was announced it was found to contain the names of honourable and moderate men like Nottingham and Godolphin. But Pepys left William no option. He acknowledged him as King, and, after his acceptance of the Crown, wrote of him as such in his official letters. But he had sworn oaths of lifelong fealty to another and he would not forswear them. By the standards of either a Christian or a gentleman it is hard to blame him.†[13]

So Pepys, in Evelyn's classic phrase, laid down his office and would serve no more. He did so with courtesy and without haste. William had accompanied his acceptance of the throne with a Proclamation retaining, until his further pleasure should be known,

* T. Langley to S. P., Feb. 12th, 1689. *Rawl. MSS. A.* 179, f. 216.

† For the evidence that Pepys voluntarily laid down his office see the title-page of a bundle of papers in the Bodleian Library, entitled 'A Copy of the Entries of all the Acts of His Royal Highness the Prince of Orange, prepared by Mr Pepys, relating to the Admiralty and Navy from the time of his coming to Whitehall and entrance upon the government to that of Mr Pepys' voluntary ceasing to act further therein'. *Rawl. MSS. A.* 186, ff. 122 *et seq.* See also the famous passage in Evelyn's *Diary* after Pepys' death.

all Protestant office-holders who occupied their present places on the 1st of December. So long as this general suspension of offices continued Pepys was prepared to carry out his familiar duties; he knew it would not be for long, for the rooms of Whitehall were filled with eager seekers after emoluments and power. He arranged for the transport of the Queen-Dowager's servants and goods to Calais, sent out frigates for the last time to deal with the Dunkirk privateers and procured leave for Admiral Berry to wind up his affairs in London before sailing for the Straits. He also did a few last small kindnesses for some old and deserving subordinates: wrote to Sir Phineas Pett asking him to prevent an injustice to James Pearse, purser of the *Britannia* and son of his old friend, the Surgeon-General,* and forwarded Bagwell's name to the Navy Office as the first of three candidates for a vacancy as second assistant at Chatham. Did he, one wonders, recall for a second that remote passionate day when he had strained the forefinger of his right hand struggling with Bagwell's reluctant, dubious, yielding wife?[14]

A week after his succession William issued a further order for a 'public cessation' of all offices until their beneficiaries were authorized to act by fresh powers. It was the signal for Pepys to withdraw. On February 20th he wrote on points of official detail to the Commanders-in-Chief at Portsmouth and the Medway, to the Navy Office about laying up a ship, to Lord Dartmouth as Master-General of the Ordnance about the disposal of her guns, to the captain of the *Defiance* about receiving a chaplain on board and to three of the yacht commanders to afford closer protection to the Harwich packet boats. He also drafted a letter – it cannot have been a very congenial task – to Captain Gifford of the *Phoenix*, ordering him to sail for the Brill to fetch over Mrs Harbord with her 'company, baggage and servants' and another in French to the Duchesse de Bouillon – left behind in the suddenness of Queen Mary of Modena's departure – informing her that the King, on whom he had just waited, had reluctantly decided that he could not spare the *Fubbs* yacht to carry her to Dieppe.[15]

According to Pepys' own account given in the following July to a Parliamentary Committee, February 20th was the last day on which

---

* S. P. to Sir P. Pett, Feb. 22nd, 1689. *Rawl. MSS. A.* 179, f. 262. The request, one is glad to know, was granted. P. Pett to S. P., March 9th. *Rawl. MSS. A.* 170, f. 79.

he acted as Secretary to the Admiralty.* But his Admiralty Letter Book – in which copies of all his correspondence were entered and which, despite many applications, remained in his hands after his resignation – reveals that he continued to dictate official letters for two more days. On February 22nd he wrote to the Navy Board urging that every ship in the Yards should be got ready against the King's need. On the same day he acknowledged the good wishes of several captains of the fleet, assured them of his goodwill so long as it lay in his power to do them any service and wished them good fortune. Their various queries, he explained, he could not answer owing to the general cessation of offices. He hoped, however, that his Majesty would shortly come to a determination about the affairs of the Admiralty.[16]

To one sea captain, an old acquaintance to whom he had formerly entrusted the training of his own nephew, Pepys wrote more implicitly. Though by virtue of the public cessation, he told Tyrrell of the *Mordaunt*, he could not send him any official order, he was privately of opinion that it was the right of the senior captain alone 'to wear the distinction pendant and perform the duty of Commander-in-Chief. Therefore, unless you take yourself to be an older captain than Captain Shovell (which does not appear in any of the Records here), I cannot but think that it will be well taken by the King and those to whom he shall commit the administration of the Admiralty, that you should forbear . . . as being that I hold best to suit with the good order and discipline of the Navy, and what may prevent several inconveniences which may otherwise happen thereto. Which having said out of my friendship to you and the goodwill which I shall always bear towards the prosperity of the Navy, I leave it with you to make use of as you shall think fit.'† With this graceful farewell, Pepys took his leave of the Service.[17]

During the ten days which elapsed between his retirement and the appointment of his successor, three more letters were entered in Pepys' Admiralty Letter Book. All were addressed to Admiral Herbert. The first, dated the 26th of February, dealt with the administrative records of his office. 'I am very sorry for my not being in the way of waiting on you at your calling here this morning. The

* *Rawl. MSS. A.* 170, ff. 178–82, 186 *et seq.*
† S. P. to Capt. Tyrrell, Feb. 22nd, 1689. *Pepysian MSS., Adm. Letters* xv, 591.

list you desired and now enquired after, has been a good while in readiness for you, and as perfect as by any information I can make it.'* On March 1st Pepys wrote again, enclosing much invaluable information about such matters as the pay of pilots, protections to masters and crews of packet boats, the completion of the musters taken by the Navy Office and the return of the officers of the Sheerness Yard to their dwellings lately occupied by the military. 'The following particulars are what you will give me leave (in addition to those I troubled you with last night) to mention now to you as matters that seem to call for some speedy orders.'† No personal differences marred Pepys' farewell to his office. In the closing act of his career he was too great for petty jealousy or spite.[18]

On March 5th the King formally appointed Herbert head of the new Admiralty Commission, joining with him such old political adversaries of Pepys' as Sir Thomas Lee and William Sacheverell and one 'Orange' Tory, Sir John Lowther. On the same day Pepys, still writing from the comely house in York Buildings which he had made the Admiralty of England, forwarded to Herbert a batch of letters from foreign stations with a brief covering note:

Sir,
The enclosed letters coming to hand since my last, you will excuse the trouble of having them transmitted (for the King's service) to you from
		Your most humble servant
				Samuel Pepys.‡

After that there are no further entries in the Admiralty Letter Book. But one other letter of Pepys' of that day was preserved among the unsorted papers which long after his death found their way into the Bodleian Library with the Rawlinson Manuscripts. It was written to his old friend and fellow civil servant, Richard Cooling, who had helped to put him wise to the opportunities of office on his first entering the King's service nearly thirty years before.§ The good man had just been resworn as a Clerk of the Privy Council:

---

* S. P. to Adm. Herbert, Feb. 26th, 1689. *Pepysian MSS., Adm. Letters* xv, 596.
† Do. March 1st, 1689. *Pepysian MSS., Adm. Letters* xv, 597-8.
‡ S. P. to Adm. Herbert, March 5th, 1689. *Pepysian MSS., Adm. Letters* xv, 598.
§ 'He told me how he had a project for all us secretaries to join together and get money by bringing all business into our hands.' *D.* July 5th, 1660.

It is at the suit of the bearer, Mr Stedwell, rather than from any reason I have to think that at this time of day my intercession can be of any avail to him, that I take upon me to be his solicitor to you; though I am persuaded he won't fare the worse with my friend, Mr Cooling, that he uses my name, or that I tell you he was a servant of my Lord Sandwich's and of both our Royal Masters, and has acquitted himself very well for many years together under my observation in the Navy. If any of these considerations, and one more, namely that he married a very good servant of mine, may stand him in any stead in the matter before you, wherein he is recommended, and that I shall acknowledge very thankfully the favour to him, pray let him have your help.*

To anyone acquainted with all that Pepys had been, and done, there is something very moving in this last gentle and persuasive letter.[19]

On assuming office as First Lord of the Admiralty, Herbert appointed Phineas Bowles as Secretary of the new Admiralty Commission. But the office which Pepys had held remained vacant, for with his passing it ceased to exist. Bowles was a senior clerk, dismissible at pleasure and wholly subordinate to a Board of politicians and sea officers – the hired servant and never the administrative ruler of the Navy. His successors, one of whom, Josiah Burchett, Pepys' former clerk, was already working in the office, were for all practical purposes permanent civil servants. But Pepys had been something more: the administrator-in-chief of the Service and at the same time the equivalent of a modern First Lord of the Admiralty, planning and presenting estimates to Treasury and Parliament and representing the Navy in the eyes of the country. During the last four years he had been responsible to the King only. No other subject but he had held any authority in the Admiralty. His remuneration had been that of a high officer of State and four times greater than that of his successor. In all but name he had been Secretary of State for Marine Affairs, like his great contemporary across the water, Jean Baptiste Colbert, Marquis de Seignelay. Had it not been for the Revolution, as has been recently suggested, Pepys might well have been rewarded by the recognition of such an office. He had begun his official career forty years before in an age when rank and birth counted infinitely more than they do to-day, as a subordinate clerk, ignorant of the first rudiments of his profession.

* S. P. to Mr Cooling, March 5th, 1689. *Rawl. MSS. A.* 189, f. 27.

He had attained to a unique mastery of its every aspect. When he ended his work the tonnage of the Navy was 101,032 tons as compared with 62,594 when he began it. Yet, as the sequel was to show, this had been the least part of his achievement.[20]

Epilogue

The three years which had seen the culmination of Pepys' work for the Navy had ended in revolution, the deposition and usurpation of the Crown he had served, and the nemesis and ruin of his world. The Court of the Stuarts, the political ideals which had prevailed there, and his honoured place in it, had vanished as though they had never been. The men he had hated, who had plotted against his life, who had broken – as he imagined, though wrongly – the work to which he had given his all, now inherited the power and the glory. And, lucky to escape in peace, Pepys withdrew into the shades.

Yet, as so often in England, the twilight proved the pleasantest part of the day. In the Indian summer of his closing decade, in the little paradise he had created overlooking the river above Inigo Jones' Watergate – and from which the new Commissioners of the Admiralty tried in vain to dislodge him – Pepys learnt to sublimate defeat and grow old gracefully. Here, ambition laid aside and passion spent, he enjoyed the, for him, incomparable solace of music, cultivated the society of learned friends and the most famous virtuosos of the age – among them Newton, Wren, Dryden, Kneller, Purcell, the scholars Wallis, Wanley and Bentley, and John Evelyn – and, amassing materials for a history of the Navy he never lived to complete, perfected the exquisite library of three thousand beautifully bound books with its unique collection of manuscripts, which he bequeathed with the twelve presses he had specially designed for them, to his old Cambridge college, Magdalene.

Nor did his fidelity to his royal master, or the Revolution and triumph of his enemies, undo, as he had feared, his life's work for the Navy. His hard-won administrative rules and the battle-fleet he had built and repaired assured for his country, even during his lifetime, that primacy in the world's seas which she was never wholly to lose until she relinquished it in our own day. Despite some initial attempts by his political opponents and persecutors to molest him, by the time of his death in 1703 – the year before the Navy captured the great Mediterranean strategic prize of Gibraltar – Pepys was everywhere recognized and esteemed as the great and beneficent public servant he had been. 'To your praises, Sir,' declared the Orator of the University of Oxford in a Latin Diploma presented to him in the closing years of his life, 'the whole ocean bears witness; you have truly encompassed Britain with wooden walls!'

He left his country three legacies – his work for the Admiralty and Navy, the Pepys Library and, unknown to his contemporaries, on the shelves of the latter the six tell-tale shorthand diaries which he had compiled in the days of his early manhood and marriage, and which, first published nearly a century and a quarter after his death, are today recognized as the greatest of all diaries and one of the world's immortal books.

It was left to his friend and fellow diarist, John Evelyn, to epitomize his life. 'This day,' he wrote in his journal, 'died Mr Sam Pepys, a very worthy, industrious, curious person, none in England exceeding him in knowledge of the Navy, in which he had passed thro' all the most considerable offices, Clerk of the Acts and Secretary of the Admiralty, all of which he performed with great integrity. When James II went out of England he laid down his office and would serve no more, but, withdrawing himself from all public affairs, he lived at Clapham with his partner, Mr Hewer, formerly his clerk, in a very noble and sweet place, where he enjoyed the fruits of his labours in great prosperity. He was universally loved, hospitable, generous, learned in many things, skilled in music, a very great cherisher of learned men of whom he had the conversation.'

Appendix A

Letter from Pepys to the Navy Board to do a kindness at the suit of William Penn.

To SIR JOHN TIPPETTS &C.

25th February 1687.

Gentlemen,

At the desire of Mr Penn, this serves to accompany the bearer, mother (as she alleges) to a shipwright slain in the year 1680 by a great shot from the Moors at Tangier, who lays claim to the provision made in the Navy for the mother of persons slain therein, grounded upon that Establishment by which the relations of seamen of the King's ships slain in the land service of that place are to be provided for in the same manner as if they had been killed aboard. But the execution hereof, and the judging of the reasonableness of the claim being left to your Board, I have only out of respect to our old friend Mr Penn wrote this to conduct the woman to you, whose case you will have all fitting regard to, remaining

Gentlemen,

Yours &c.

S. P.

Pepysian MSS., Adm. Letters XIV, 53.

Appendix B

Letter from Pepys to Captain (afterwards Admiral) Clowdisley Shovell on the eve of mobilization, August 1688.

To CAPTAIN SHOVELL, *Dover* in the Downs.

Admiralty *August* 17, 1688.

Sir,

   In answer to yours of the 16th I am to let you know that his Majesty has very lately altered the measures he had before taken about the fleet's going to the westward, his service now requiring their being kept together (for some time at least) where they now are. So that I don't see how it can consist with his Service at this time any of his officers should be absent from their duty; nor do I think his Majesty would receive any motion for such leave very kindly at this conjuncture. And therefore in hopes that your private affairs may without great injury to you dispense with your not being here for some time, I shall yet forbear to move his Majesty till I know from you whether, notwithstanding what I have here said, you shall continue to desire it. And if you do, I will not fail to do my part whatever the success thereof be, though for the sake of the King's Service I could wish your occasions would not put you at present upon desiring. Which is all at present from

Yours &c.

S. P.

Pepysian MSS., Adm. Letters xiv, 349

Appendix C

Letter from Pepys to Captain Cotton of the Navy Yacht ordering him to proceed to the coast of Holland.

To CAPTAIN COTTON, Navy Yacht.

Windsor. *August* 21 1688

Captain Cotton,

If this finds you in the River of Thames as probably it may (my Lord Dartmouth having just now acquainted the King with his having seen you there or at London on Saturday last), this comes by his Majesty's special command to let you know that (all other occasions being set apart) it is his pleasure that you do immediately apply yourself to take the first advantage of wind and weather after receipt hereof for your proceeding with his vessel under your command to the coast of Holland as far as Goree, there, and from thence this way to visit that coast in order to the making of the Dutch fleet or what ships of war of those Provinces you can discover to be come out and now lying or moving anywhere along the coast; using your utmost care and diligence in making the best observations you can concerning them either to number, force or ought else fit for his Majesty's notice and which you can come near enough to descry without coming so near as to be commanded by them. And this having done you are with the like diligence to repair back into the River of Thames there to give me an account of these his Majesty's commands in order to my informing the King thereof. To whom your speedy and effectual execution of the same is at this time of the utmost importance.

I am &c.
S. P.

Pepysian MSS., Adm. Letters XIV, 366.

Appendix D

Pepys' Instructions to the Office from Windsor during the naval mobilization, 23 August 1688.

Memorandum. Windsor. August 23 (88).

By Mr Marratt.*

Mr Atkins will in this packet receive 5 Commissions, namely

Captain Carter to command the *Advice*
Lt. Foulks to be his Lt.
Lt. Coulis to be Lt. of the *Falcon*
Captain Boatham to command the *Portsmouth*
Captain Cornwall the *Dartmouth* fireship.

Which Commissions of present use and therefore are first dispatched, but shall very suddenly be followed by others for all the rest. To which end a supply of blank Commissions of every sort more than enough for the present occasion ought to be prepared forthwith for me, with a quantity of blank instructions of every sort that are to attend them.

With these Commissions comes one warrant of the King's to Sir Roger Strickland about increasing the complement of men of his squadron, which must by all means be forwarded to him this night.

Next Mr Atkins will find these warrants, one for Ambrose Staniford, his being house-carpenter of Portsmouth yard, with another for the payment of Judge Advocates' travelling charges for the last Court Martial held in the Downs, and another for the sending some provisions to the Adventurers upon the Wreck; all which Mr Atkins will dispose of as they ought to be.

To which I am to add that not being able to attend the Office myself tomorrow morning for the swearing of the Masters of merchant ships for their Passes, I must desire my good neighbour,

---

* The Admiralty messenger.

Captain Brideall, to do me the favour which he has heretofore done me in the like case in my absence and would have him attend for me about it.

I am in the next place to desire that notice may be given to Mr Thornton, the map-maker in the Minories, that he and Mr Browne are not to come to me tomorrow at noon (as I had determined) but in lieu thereof on Saturday in the morning about 8 of the clock, when I doubt not to be in town to meet them there.

Lastly I send a letter to Captain Wren for the hastening to the Downs which I desire may be forwarded this night by the post to Plymouth.

As to myself I am under a necessity of staying here tomorrow upon an occasion of the public Council to be held here in the afternoon, at the rising of which I doubt not to be at liberty (which will be in the evening) to set out for York Buildings; desiring in the meantime that Mr Hewer may be advertised thereof in order to his dining with me on Saturday, it being my fear that I may be under a necessity of returning thither the same day in the evening.

S. P.

Pepysian MSS., Adm. Letters xiv, 362–3.

Appendix E

A letter which Pepys received shortly before his retirement from a foreign correspondent, Mrs Egmont, from the Hague. It is dated 30 January, 1689 and addressed to 'Squire Pips' at York Buildings. It is conceivable, though not, I think, probable that the writer was Deborah Willett, the 'Deb' of the closing months of the Diary whose liaison with Pepys made poor Elizabeth so jealous.

Honoured Sir,

Having had formerly the honour to serve you, hope you will be pleased to be kind to the bearer hereof, which is my husband, in all you can. I am to come to England as soon as possible I can. Meantime I do beseech you to advise and asist my dear husband in what you in your prudence and wisdom and goodness thinks best, having heard his request. My service to yourself and Mr Yures and his mother and aunt and the whole family. Pleas to pardon my boldness assuring you that whatever you do for my husband shall be thankfully taken from

> Your humble servant
> Deborah Egmont.

Mr Dispontain hath his love to you.

Rawl. MSS. A. 179, f. 57.

Appendix of References

Introductory Note

As in the earlier volumes, I have preferred to group my reference notes together for each paragraph rather than scatter the page with digits to the inconvenience of the general reader. A kind of miniature bibliography is thus appended to every paragraph or group of paragraphs. Despite certain obvious drawbacks, the advantage of this method is that the reader who is so inclined can test the extent and value of the evidence as a whole on which each conclusion is based. To obviate as far as possible the difficulty of the student who is thus forced to refer to a whole group of authorities to discover the source of a single reference, I have added at the foot of each page in the text the MS. source of any quotation which has not hitherto been printed.

Abbreviations Used

Manuscript Sources

Pepysian MSS. In the Pepys Library, Magdalene College, Cambridge.
  Adm. Letters. Admiralty Letters.
  Mis. Miscellanies.
  Mornamont. 'My Two Volumes of Mornamont', *Pepysian MSS.* No. 2881–2.
Bodl. Bodleian Library, Oxford.
Rawl. MSS. Rawlinson Manuscripts, Bodleian Library.
B.M. British Museum, London.
P.R.O. Public Record Office, London.
S.P. State Papers, Public Record Office.
Tanner and Wheatley MSS. Manuscript notes collected by the late Mr H. B. Wheatley and the late Dr J. R. Tanner, in the possession of the author.

Printed Sources

Ailesbury. Memoirs of Thomas, Earl of Ailesbury. Roxburghe Club. 1890.
Bramston. The Autobiography of Sir John Bramston. Camden Society. 1845.
Braybrooke IV. Vol. IV of Diary and Correspondence of Samuel Pepys. Ed. Lord Braybrooke. 1898.
Burchett. J. Burchett. A Complete History of the Most Remarkable Transactions at Sea. 1720.
Burnet. Bishop Burnet. History of his own Time. 1833.
Cartwright. Dr Thomas Cartwright, Diary. Camden Society. 1843.
Churchill. Winston Churchill. Marlborough, his Life and Times. 1933.
C.J. Commons' Journals.
Clarendon. The State Letters of Henry Earl of Clarendon. Ed. S. W. Singer. 1828.

Clarke. Life of James II. Ed. J. S. Clarke. 1816.

C.P. MSS. A Descriptive Catalogue of the Naval Manuscripts in the Pepysian Library. Ed. J. R. Tanner. 1903–23.

C.S.P.D. Calendar of State Papers, Domestic series.

D. Diary of Samuel Pepys. Ed. H. B. Wheatley. 1893–6.

Dalrymple. J. Dalrymple, Memoirs of Great Britain and Ireland (4th ed.). 1773.

Davey. S. J. Davey, Catalogue. 1889.

D'Orleans. F. J. D'Orleans, The History of the Revolutions in England (2nd ed.). 1722.

Echard. L. Echard, History of England (3rd ed.). 1720.

E.H.R. English Historical Review.

Ellis. The Ellis Correspondence. Ed. G. J. W. Agar-Ellis, 1829.

Evelyn. J. Evelyn, The Diary of Ed. A. Dobson. 1908.

Feiling. K. Feiling, A History of the Tory Party, 1640–1714. 1924.

Fox. C. J. Fox, A History of the Early Part of the Reign of James the Second. 1808.

Grey. A Grey, Debates of the House of Commons. 1769.

Hatton. Correspondence of the Family of Hatton. Camden Society. 1876.

H.M.C. Historical Manuscripts Commission Reports.

Howarth. Letters and the Second Diary of Samuel Pepys. Ed. R. G. Howarth. 1932.

L.C.C. Survey. London County Council Survey of London. Vol. xviii, The Strand (The Parish of St Martin's-in-the-Fields, Part II). 1937.

Lediard. T. Lediard, The Naval History of England. 1735.

L.J. Lords' Journals.

Luttrell. N. Luttrell, A Brief Historical Relation of State Affairs. 1857.

Macaulay. Lord Macaulay, History of England (Albany ed.). 1898.

Mackintosh. Sir James Mackintosh, History of the Revolution in England. 1834.

Macpherson. Original Papers . . . arranged by James Macpherson. 1775.

Mazure. F. A. J. Mazure, Histoire de la Révolution de 1688 en Angleterre. 1825.

Memoires. Pepys's Memoires of the Royal Navy, 1679–1688. Ed. J. R. Tanner. 1906.

Naval Minutes. Samuel Pepys's Naval Minutes. Ed. J. R. Tanner. 1926.

North. Roger North, Lives of the Norths. 1890 ed.

Parlt. Hist. The Parliamentary History of England. Ed. W. Cobbett. 1806–20.

Petty-Southwell Corr. The Marquis of Lansdowne, The Petty-Southwell Correspondence 1676–1687. 1928.

Powley. E. B. Powley, The English Navy in the Revolution of 1688. 1928.

Prideaux. Letters of Humphrey Prideaux. Ed. E. M. Thompson. Camden Society. 1875.

Ranke. L. von Ranke, A History of England principally in the seventeenth century. 1875.

Reresby. Memoirs of Sir John Reresby. Ed. Andrew Browning. 1936.

Routh. E. M. G. Routh, Tangier, England's Lost Atlantic Outpost. 1912.

Smith. The Life, Journals and Correspondence of Samuel Pepys. Ed. Rev. J. Smith. 1841.

Tangier Papers. The Tangier Papers of Samuel Pepys. Ed. E. Chappell. Navy Records Society. 1935.

Tanner, Corr. Private Correspondence and Miscellaneous Papers of Samuel Pepys, 1679–1703. Ed. J. R. Tanner. 1926.

Torrington. Memoirs relating to the Lord Torrington. Ed. J. K. Laughton. Camden Society. 1889.

Verney Memoirs. Memoirs of the Verney Family. 1925 ed.

Welwood. J. Welwood, Memoirs of the Most Material Transactions in England for the Last Hundred Years (6th ed.). 1718.

Whitear. W. W. Whitear, More Pepysiana. 1927.

Wood. The Life and Times of Anthony Wood. Ed. A. Clark. 1891.

Bibliographical Notes

CHAPTER I. VOYAGE TO TANGIER

[1] *Routh* 365–9 et passim; *Tangier Papers* 1–4, 269; *Roxburghe Ballads* II, 582; *C.T.B.* II, Intr. xvi–xvii; III, Part I, Intr. xx; *Rawl. MSS. D.* 916; H.M.C. *Dartmouth* I, 83–5; III, 39–40.

[2] *C.P. MSS.* I, 223; *Smith* II, 150; *Howarth* 151–2; *Tangier Papers* 5–6, 9–12, 14, 18, 253; *H.M.C. Rep.* VII (*Verney* 481); *H.M.C. Dartmouth* III, 39–40.

[3] *C.P. MSS.* I, 266–95; *P.R.O. Addit. MSS.* 51/407; *Tangier Papers* 269–70.

[4] *Tangier Papers* 7–8, 270; *Rawl. MSS. C.* 859, f. 220v; *Naval Minutes* 248.

[5] *Tangier Papers* 8, 109–11; *Rawl. MSS. C.* 859, f. 93 v.

[6] *Tangier Papers* 8–9, 67–71, 270; *H.M.C. Dartmouth* III, 34; *Rawl. MSS. A.* 196.

[7] *Tangier Papers* 9–12

[8] *Tangier Papers* 12, 106, 109, 113, 117, 119, 122–4.

[9] *Tangier Papers* 9, 12–14, 118, 126–9.

[10] *Tangier Papers* 10, 13–16, 75–83; *Diary of Henry Teonge* (ed. Manwaring) 14 July 1675.

[11] *Tangier Papers* 16–17, 111, 333; *G.P., The Present State of Tangier* (1676); *Rawl. MSS. A.* 190, f. 23; *C.* 384, ff. 28–35.

[12] *Tangier Papers* 17, 72–5, 272, 332–4.

[13] *Tangier Papers* 17, 271–96.

CHAPTER II. AFRICAN ADVENTURE

[1] *G.P., The Present State of Tangier* (1676); *Routh* 292; *Smith* 1, 236–7.

[2] *Tangier Papers* 17–18, 90; *Rawl. MSS. A.* 190, f. 42.

[3] *Rawl. MSS. A.* 196, ff. 1–12; *Tangier Papers* 18; *H.M.C. Dartmouth* III, 34–40.

[4] *Tangier Papers* 18–19; *H.M.C. Dartmouth* III, 34; *Rawl. MSS. A.* 196, ff. 13–17.

[5] *Rawl. MSS. A.* 190, f. 13; 196, ff. 17–19; *Howarth* 162–3; *Tangier Papers* 20.

[6] *Tangier Papers* 20–2, 28.

[7] *Tangier Papers* 21–2.

[8] *Rawl. MSS. A.* 196. ff. 20–4; *Tangier Papers* 23; *H.M.C. Dartmouth* III, 34.

[9] *Tangier Papers* 23–4; *H.M.C. Dartmouth* III, 40.

[10] *Rawl. MSS. A.* 196, ff. 24, 27–9; *Tangier Papers* 24–6.

[11] *Tangier Papers* 26–8; *Rawl. MSS. A.* 196, f. 29; *Sir F. W. Hamilton, The Origin and History of the First or Grenadier Guards* (1874) I, 259–60; *H.M.C. Dartmouth* I, 51, 94; III, 34, 40, 51.

[12] *Tangier Papers* 28–30; *Rawl. MSS. A.* 196, ff. 29–30.

[13] *Rawl. MSS. A.* 196, ff. 29–36; C. 859, ff. 247, 248v, 249v; *Tangier Papers* 30–1, 89–90; *H.M.C. Dartmouth* III, 34.

[14] *Rawl. MSS. A.* 196, ff. 31–7; *Tangier Papers* 31–7; *H.M.C. Dartmouth* I, 95; III, 35–6.

[15] *Tangier Papers* 33, 35–7.

[16] *Howarth* 158–60.

[17] *Tangier Papers* 37–44; *H.M.C. Dartmouth* III, 34–8; *Rawl. MSS. A.* 196 passim.

[18] *Tangier Papers* 38–40, 42–5; *H.M.C. Downshire* I, i, 20–1.

[19] *Howarth* 162–3; *Rawl. MSS. A.* 190, f. 13; *Tangier Papers* 33, 39, 40, 42–4, 47–8.

[20] *Tangier Papers* 37–8, 41, 43–8, 51–5, 93, 149–50; *Routh* 262–3, 361–3, 366–8.

[21] *Tangier Papers* 47, 49, 50.

[22] *Tangier Papers* 93–5.

[23] *Tangier Papers* 95–7.

[24] *Rawl. MSS. C.* 859, ff. 81, 111v–112, 225v, 247–9v, 251v; *Tangier Papers* 90, 102–3.

[25] *Tangier Papers* 49–50, 97–9.

[26] *Rawl. MSS. A.* 190, f. 12; *Howarth* 160–2; *Tangier Papers* 89.

[27] *Tangier Papers* 41, 75–83, 89, 91–2, 141.

[28] *Tangier Papers* 50; *Routh* 261–2; *Col. John Davis, History of the Queen's Regt.* 1, 240.

[29] *Tangier Papers* 51–5, 148, 153, 157, 160–1; *Howarth 160–3; Smith* I, 415–16; *H.M.C. Downshire* I, i, 21–2; *H.M.C. Dartmouth* III 35, 220.

[30] *Tangier Papers* 100–2, 164.

[31] *Tangier Papers* 139, 141–3, 148.

[32] *Tangier Papers* 101; *Rawl. MSS. A.* 859, f. 250.

[33] *Tangier Papers* 53–7.

[34] *Tangier Papers* 56–7, 103.

CHAPTER III. SPANISH HOLIDAY

[1] *Tangier Papers* 251–2; *Rawl. MSS. A.* 859, ff. 164, 167; *H.M.C. Dartmouth* III, 130–1; *Howarth* 163–4.

[2] *Rawl. MSS. A.* 190, ff. 182, 208; *Tangier Papers* 177; *H.M.C. Dartmouth* III, 130–1; *Smith* I, 415–16; *Howarth* 163–4.

[3] *Tangier Papers* 257, 281; *Howarth* 164–5.

[4] *H.M.C. Downshire* I, i, 21–2; *Tangier Papers* 257–63; *Rawl. MSS. A.* 190, ff. 146, 185; *Howarth* 165; *Smith* II, 9–10.

[5] *H.M.C. Dartmouth* I, 105–6.

[6] *Rawl. MSS. A.* 190, ff. 128, 133, 182; *H.M.C. Dartmouth* I, 107–8; *Howarth* 166–7; *Smith* II, 11–13, 31–2; *Tangier Papers* 354–63; *Tanner, Corr.* I, 240–3; *Evelyn* 16 Sept. 1685.

[7] *Tangier Papers* 254–5; *Rawl. MSS. A.* 190, ff. 128, 133, 182.

[8] *Tangier Papers* 255–6.

[9] *Tangier Papers* 168–71, 258; *Rawl. MSS. C.* 859, ff. 117v, 118.

[10] *Tangier Papers* 167–9, 191–3, 196–7.

[11] *Rawl. MSS. A.* 190, ff. 133, 185; *Howarth* 166–7; *Smith* II, 11–13; *H.M.C. Dartmouth* I, 107–8; *Braybrooke* (1898) IV, 232.

[12] *Tangier Papers* 256–7; *Pepysian MSS.* No. 2612 passim.

[13] *Tannner, Corr.* II, 104; *Rawl. MSS. A.* 190, ff. 133, 135, 148, 161; *Smith* II, 1–4.

[14] *Howarth* 163.

[15] *Rawl. MSS. A.* 171, f. 155; *A.* 190, f. 135; *Tangier Papers* 179; *Howarth* 164–6; *Braybrooke* (1898) IV, 232.

[16] *Tangier Papers* 180.

[17] *Tangier Papers* 172–3, 176–84, 196.

[18] *Tangier Papers* 172, 180; *Rawl. MSS. A.* 171, ff. 154–6; *C.* 859, f. 117.

[19] *Tangier Papers* 181–4; *Rawl. MSS. A.* 171, ff. 154–6; *C.P. MSS.* I, 65.

[20] *Tangier Papers* 184–8.

[21] *Tangier Papers* 187–8, 190–1.

[22] *Tangier Papers* 188–90, 196, 207.

[23] *Tangier Papers* 189, 191–2, 196–7, 200, 203.

[24] *Rawl. MSS. A.* 190, ff. 128, 130–1; *Tangier Papers* 194, 207; *Smith* II, 31–2.

[25] *Tangier Papers* 204–5, 207, 288–9; *H.M.C. Dartmouth* III, 47; *Rawl. MSS. A.* 190, ff. 87, 148.

[26] *Tangier Papers* 173, 289.

CHAPTER IV. THE GREAT STORM

[1] *Tangier Papers* 175, 195–6, 213, 289–90.

[2] *Tangier Papers* 290–1; *Routh* 264–6; *Rawl. MSS. A.* 190.

[3] *Tangier Papers* 215–16, 224, 290–1.

[4] *Tangier Papers* 217.

[5] *Tangier Papers* 232, 291–2.

[6] *Tangier Papers* 173, 232, 234, 239, 292–3.

[7] *H.M.C. Dartmouth* I, 111, 122; *Tangier Papers* 231, 234, 293.

[8] *Tangier Papers* 223–8, 240–1, 294–5.

[9] *Tangier Papers* 173–4, 209–10.

[10] *Tangier Papers* 225–6.

[11] *Tangier Papers* 110, 150, 153–4, 166, 206–7, 212–15, 228.

[12] *Tangier Papers* 148, 207–8, 214, 240.

[13] *Tangier Papers* 136, 219–20, 223–4, 229, 233–4, 239, 242–3.

[14] *Tangier Papers* 295.

[15] *Tangier Papers* 215, 220, 233–4, 236, 239.

[16] *Tangier Papers* 221, 229–32, 242.

[17] *Tangier Papers* 145, 152, 207, 215, 220–1, 224, 227, 229, 237–8, 240, 309.

[18] *Tangier Papers* 11, 90, 101, 113, 122, 138, 147, 152, 155, 162, 209–10, 216, 223–5, 318; *Rawl. MSS.C.* 859, f. 112.

[19] *Tangier Papers* 148, 216–18, 219, 221, 244.

[20] *Tangier Papers* 241–2, 248–9, 295.

[21] *Tangier Papers* 243–4, 296; *Evelyn* 28 March, April 1684; *H.M.C. Dartmouth* I, 111.

[22] *Tangier Papers* 243–4, 296; *H.M.C. Dartmouth* III, 47–8.

[23] *Tangier Papers* 296, 311–12; *H.M.C. Dartmouth* I, 112–14.

CHAPTER V. RECALL TO THE ADMIRALTY

[1] *H.M.C. Dartmouth* I, 112–14; *Howarth* 167–9; *Smith* II, 43–4; *Letters from the Bodleian Library* (1813) II, 260.

[2] *Howarth* 169; *Smith* II, 45–6; *H.M.C. Dartmouth* III, 46–9.

[3] *Tangier Papers* 321–4; *Rawl. MSS. C.* 859, ff. 192–3; *A.* 190, f. 105; *Petty-Southwell Corr.* 120–2.

[4] *Evelyn* 30 April 1684; *H.M.C. Fleming* 194; *Tanner, Corr.* II, 23–4.

[5] *Pepysian MSS., Misc.* XI, 224–5; *C.P. MSS.* I, 58; *H.M.C. Dartmouth* III, 48–50; *Luttrell* I, 307.

[6] *H.M.C. Dartmouth* I, 122; *Smith* II, 48 n; *Court Book of the Clothworkers' Company* 15 April 1684; *Luttrell* I, 304–5; *London Gazette* 12/15 May 1684; *Pepysian MSS.* No. 2867, Naval Precedents 169; *Misc.* XI, 225; *Rawl. MSS. A.* 190, ff. 74, 76; *Memoires* 7; *C.P. MSS.* I, 65; *Echard* III, 712; *Reresby* 338; *H.M.C. Rep.* VII (*Graham* 370); *Evelyn* 12 May 1684.

[7] *Rawl. MSS. A.* 177, ff. 125, 127, 134; *A.* 190, ff. 174, 176; *Pepysian MSS.* No. 2867, Naval Precedents 39; *Adm. Letters* XI, 5, 7; *Misc.* XI, 226.

[8] *Memoires* 8–9; *Tangier Papers* 332; *Pepysian MS.* No. 1490, p. 86; *Rawl. MSS. A.* 189, ff. 308 et seq.

[9] *Pepysian MSS., Adm. Letters* X, 1–10.

[10] *Rawl. MSS. A.* 177, f. 134; *Tangier Papers* 329–30.

[11] *Rawl. MSS. A.* 190, ff. 97, 192; *C.* 859, f. 191; *Clothworkers' Company Records*, cit. Mrs Esdaile, 'Pepys, Le Seur and Gibbons', *Times Lit. Suppl.* 7 June 1928; *Pepysian MS., Adm. Letters* X, 5, 7, 261.

[12] *Rawl. MSS. C.* 859, ff. 192–4; *Pepysian MSS., Adm. Letters* X, 28.

[13] *Rawl. MSS. C.* 859, ff. 193–4, *P.R.O. Chancery Proceedings, Mitford* C. 8, 376, No. 69.

[14] *H.M.C. Hodgkin* 177–8; *Davey* Item 2861; *Luttrell* I, 306–13; *H.M.C. Portland* III, 380.

[15] *Luttrell* I, 314; *Evelyn* 2 July, 10 Aug. 1684; *Pepysian MSS., Adm. Letters* X, 8–10, 42, 45, 91, 210.

[16] *Pepysian MSS., Adm. Letters* X, 44; *Tangier Papers* 101–2, 190.

[17] *Tangier Papers* 143, 177, 227, 241; *Pepysian MSS., Adm. Letters* X, 42, 57–8, 61.

[18] *C.P. MSS.* I, 59–60; *Pepysian MSS., Adm. Letters* X, 33, 58, 60, 67, 71.

[19] *H.M.C. Portland* III, 381; *L.C.C. Survey* XVIII, Part II, 65–6, 69–74; *Pepysian MSS., Adm. Letters* X, 60; *Rawl. MSS. A.* 193, f. 233; *London Gazette* 10/14 July 1684; 13/16 Oct. 1684; *Mariner's Mirror* XXIV, No. 2 (D. Bonner-Smith, Samuel Pepys and York Buildings 230).

[20] *Pepysian MSS., Adm. Letters* X, 67, 69–71, 73–4, 90, 95–6, 99, 100.

[21] *Memoires* 9–10.

[22] *Pepysian MSS., Adm. Letters* x, 99–101, 106, 113–16, 142, 198; *F. G. Parsons, History of St Thomas' Hospital.*

[23] *Pepysian MSS., Adm. Letters* x, 89, 113–16, 137, 198, 331, 372, 381, 412, 416; *C.P. MSS.* ɪ, 217–18.

[24] *Pepysian MSS., Adm. Letters* x, 105–8; *H.M.C. Hodgkin* 178; Maggs Catalogue, Autumn 1914, No. 392; *Tangier Papers* 239, 330.

[25] *Rawl. MSS. A.* 177, ff. 142, 150.

[26] *Pepysian MSS., Adm. Letters* x, 114, 144.

[27] *Evelyn* 25 Sept. 1684; *Rawl. MSS. A.* 190 (title-page); *Pepysian MSS., Adm. Letters* x, 130–1; *Pepys Club Occasional Papers* ɪɪ, 64; *L.C.C. Survey of London* xvɪɪɪ (*Strand* 1937), 65–6, 69–74.

[28] *J. R. Tanner, Mr Pepys* 263; *Rawl. MSS. A.* 193, f. 152; *B.M. Sloane MSS.* No. 45, f. 69; *The Periodical* ɪx, No. cxvɪɪ, 349–50.

[29] *Pepysian MSS., Adm. Letters* x, 139, 155, 174–6, 179–80, 189; *P.R.O. Chancery Proceedings, Mitford* C. 8, 376, No. 69.

[30] *Pepysian MSS., Adm. Letters* x, 179–80, 195–6; *Evelyn* 2 Nov. 1684; *Torrington* 6–8.

[31] *Pepysian MSS., Adm. Letters* x, 171, 218–20.

[32] *Pepysian MSS., Adm. Letters* x, 267; *C.P. MSS.* ɪ, 115–16.

[33] *Evelyn* 2 Nov. 1684; *Pepysian MSS., Adm. Letters* x, 210–14, 220; *Tangier Papers* 326; *H.M.C. Dartmouth* ɪ, 121–2; *Rawl. MSS. A.* 464 (title-page).

[34] *Pepysian MSS., Adm. Letters* x, 170, 182, 210, 218–19, 224–5, 227, 229–32, 233–7; *C.P. MSS.* ɪ, 64.

[35] *Pepysian MSS., Adm. Letters* x, 170, 230–2, 233–7, 279–80; *Rawl. MSS. A.* 464 passim; *Pepysian MSS.* Nos. 1490, 1534.

[36] *Clothworkers' Company Records*, cit. *Mrs Esdaile, Times Lit. Suppl.* 7 June 1928; *H.M.C. Rep.* vɪɪɪ (*Ashburnham* 7).

[37] *Pepysian MSS., Adm. Letters* x, 241, 243, 301–2, 314, 316; *Evelyn* ɪ, 25 Jan; 4 Feb 1685; *Pepysian MS.* No. 1490; *Naval Minutes* 236–7.

[38] *A. Bryant, Charles II* 361–70; *Pepysian MSS., Adm. Letters* x, 302–7; *Naval Minutes* 265.

[39] *Pepysian MSS., Adm. Letters* x, 314, 316; *D.* 25 May 1660.

CHAPTER VI. A NEW REIGN

[1] *H.M.C. Fleming* 196; *D'Orleans* 274; *Reresby* 352; *Bramston* 165–6; *Fox* 74–5; *H.M.C. Portland* ɪɪɪ, 383; *Burnet* ɪɪɪ, 7, 13; *Evelyn* 14, 17 Feb.

1685; *Pepysian MSS., Adm. Letters* x, 302–7; *Ranke* iv, 217; *H.M.C. Rutland* ii, 86; *Hatton* ii, 55.

[2] *C.P. MSS.* i, 66; *Pepysian MS.* No. 1490.

[3] *Pepysian MSS., Adm. Letters* x, 299–300, 334, 336, 344; *H.M.C. Rep.* vii, (*Trinity House* 259).

[4] *Naval Minutes* 272–3.

[5] *Bodl. Weston MSS., Thomas Baker's Journal.*

[6] *Rawl. MSS.* A. 189, ff. 251–4.

[7] *H.M.C. Rutland* ii, 88; *Dalrymple* i, 126–7; *Naval Minutes* 157; *Burnet* iii, 21; *Pepysian MSS., Adm. Letters* x, 440–1; *Bodl. Rawl.* 537, *A Description of the Ceremonial Proceedings of the Coronation of their most Illustrious, Serene and Sacred Majesties, King James II and his Royal Consort, Queen Mary* (1685); *Mrs Aphra Behn, Pindarick Poem on the Happy Coronation of his most Sacred Majesty, James II* (1685).

[8] *Bodl. An exact Narrative and Description of the Wonderful and Stupendous Fireworks in honour of their Majesties' Coronation* (1685).

[9] *Evelyn* 5 March 1685; *Luttrell* i, 339; *Fox* xxxvii, lxii; *Howarth* 235– 6.

[10] *Pepysian MSS., Adm. Letters* x, 444.

[11] *H.M.C. Buccleuch (Montagu House)* i, 341; *C.J.* ix, 722; *Sandwich Guildhall MSS., Veer's Books E & F* 248; *D.* i, xlv.

[12] *Evelyn* 7, 10 May 1685; *Luttrell*, 341–3; *Burnett* iii, 37; *Macaulay.*

[13] *Luttrell*, 344; *Reresby* 366–9; *Welwood* 139; *Evelyn* 22 May 1685; *Pepysian MSS., Adm. Letters* x, 272, 446, 454, 457, 485; xi, 6; *Rawl. MSS.* A. 189, f. 186; C.P. MSS. i, iii.

[14] *Pepysian MSS., Adm. Letters* xi, 6–7, 26, 30; *H.M.C. Portland* iii, 384; *C.J.* ix, 719, 727, 738; *Rawl. MSS.* A. 193, ff. 232–40.

[15] *Pepysian MSS., Adm. Letters* xi, 26, 30, 36–7, *Rawl. MSS.* A. 189, f. 286v.

[16] *Pepysian MSS., Adm. Letters* xi, 45–8.

[17] *Pepysian MSS., Adm. Letters* xi, 45–8, 55, 65, 78–9.

[18] *Luttrell* i, 346–8; *C.J.* ix, 738; *Pepysian MSS., Adm. Letters* xi, 61, 69.

[19] *Reresby* 379–80; *Pepysian MSS., Adm. Letters* xi, 78–9, 86–7.

[20] *H.M.C. Rutland* ii, 89; *Hatton*, 57–8; *Rawl. MSS.* A. 189, f. 287; *Pepysian MSS., Adm. Letters* xi, 106, 123; *Maggs Catalogue,* July 1934, Item 598.

[21] *Pepysian MSS., Adm. Letters* xi, 125–6.

[22] *Pepysian MSS., Adm. Letters* xi, 138; *H.M.C. Rutland* ii, 92; *H.M.C. Portland* iii, 385; *Prideaux* 142–3; *Evelyn* 8 July 1685.

[23] *H.M.C. Portland* III, 386; *Pepysian MSS., Adm. Letters* XI, 209–10; *Hatton* II, 60.

[24] *Pepysian MSS., Adm. Letters* XI, 158–9, 174–5.

[25] *Pepysian MSS., Adm. Letters* XI, 174, 183, 203, 207, 213–14; *H.M.C. Hastings* II, 180.

[26] *Ailesbury* I, 111–12; *H.M.C. Rep.* VIII, 259; *J. R. Tanner, Mr Pepys* 264; *E.H.R.* Vol. 44 (Oct. 1929), *J. R. Tanner, Samuel Pepys and the Trinity House* 584–5; *Evelyn* 20 July 1685; *Pepysian MSS., Adm. Letters* XI, 154.

[27] *Rawl. MSS. A.* 193, f. 136; *A.* 289, f. 19.

[28] *Wheatley and Tanner MSS., Council Minutes of Royal Society; Pepysian MSS., Adm. Letters* XI, 214.

[29] *Pepysian MSS., Adm. Letters* XI, 236, 282, 301, 327; *Rawl. MSS. A.* 177, f. 134; *Evelyn* 16 Sept. 1685.

[30] *Evelyn* 17 Sept. 1685; *Pepysian MSS., Adm. Letters* XI, 307, 311, 313, 327.

[31] *Howarth* 169–70; *Evelyn* 2 Oct. 1685.

[32] *Luttrell* I, 357–9; *Hatton* II, 60; *H.M.C. Portland* III, 389; *Evelyn* 3, 5 Nov. 1685; *Mackintosh* 13–33.

[33] *Howarth* 167–71; *Davey* (1889) Item 2857.

[34] *Pepysian MS.* No. 1867, Naval Precedents 116, 225; *C.P. MSS.* I, 208–9; *Rawl. MSS. A.* 464, ff. 112–13.

[35] *Pepysian MSS., Adm. Letters* XI, 301; *Rawl. MSS. A.* 464, ff. 5, 112–13.

CHAPTER VII. THE SPECIAL COMMISSION

[1] *Rawl. MSS. A.* 464, ff. 88–91.

[2] *Pepysian MSS., Adm. Letters* XI, 449–50; *Evelyn* 9, 12 Nov. 1685; *C.J.; Grey* VII, 365–7; *C.J.* IX, 757; *Luttrell* I, 361–3; *Mackintosh* 38–47; *Bramston* 210–16; *Reresby* 394–8; *Ailesbury* I, 126–7; *Welwood* 156.

[3] *Rawl. MSS. A.* 464, ff. 146, 168–99.

[4] *Rawl. MSS. A.* 464, ff. 120–3.

[5] *Pepysian MSS., Adm. Letters* XI, 516; *Rawl. MSS. A.* 189, f. 287; *A.* 464, ff. 168–99.

[6] *Rawl. MSS. A.* 464, ff. 168–99; *Memoires* 13–16; *C.P. MSS.* I, 66–7; *Pepysian MS.* No. 1490, p. 7.

[7] *Pepysian MSS., Misc.* VII, 509; No. 1490, pp. 7, 17.

[8] *Pepysian MSS.* No.1490, pp. 8–9, 15, 18, 75, 81, 123; *Adm. Letters*

xi, 514; *Memoires* 18–23, 26; *C.P. MSS.* i, 69–75; *Rawl. MSS. A.* 189,
f. 308; *A.* 464, ff. 76–85, 92–3.

⁹ *Pepysian MS.* No. 1490, pp. 9–10; *C.P. MSS.* i, 75.

¹⁰ *Pepysian MS.* No. 1490, pp. 103, 155–90, 195; No. 2867, Naval
Precedents 64–81; *C.P. MSS.* i, 66, 72–3; *Memoires* 25–7.

¹¹ *Pepysian MS.* No. 1490, pp. 12–13, 131–4; *C.P. MSS.* i, 75–6, 79;
Rawl. MSS. A. 464, ff. 74–5; *Canon A. C. Deane, Sir Anthony Deane.*

¹² *Pepysian MS.* No. 1490, pp. 10–14, 135–7.

¹³ *Pepysian MS.* No. 1490, pp. 139–42; *Rawl. MSS. A.* 464, ff. 72–3;
C.P. MSS. i, 76; *North* i, 302.

¹⁴ *Pepysian MS.* No. 1490, pp. 14–16.

¹⁵ *Pepysian MS.* No. 1490, pp. 143–52; *Memoires* 28–30; *C.P. MSS.* i,
76–7.

¹⁶ *Pepysian MS.* No. 1490, pp. 16, 153–4.

¹⁷ *Pepysian MS.* No. 1490, pp. 16–18, 21–2, 155–90, 195; No. 2867,
Naval Precedents 64–81, iii; *C.P. MSS.* i, 83–5.

¹⁸ *Pepysian MS.* No. 1490, pp. 21–2; *C.P. MSS.* i, 79–80.

¹⁹ *Pepysian MS.* No. 1490, pp. 22, 34–7; No. 2867, Naval Precedents
109; *C.P. MSS.* i, 79; *Memoires* 24.

²⁰ *Pepysian MS.* No. 1490, pp. 38–44; *Rawl. MSS. A.* 464, ff. 95–101.

²¹ *Pepysian MSS.* No. 1490, pp. 46–54, 353; *Adm. Letters* xii, 50, 59,
67–8; *C.P. MSS.* i, 87–9.

²² *Pepysian MSS.* No. 1490, pp. 21–2, 24–35, 199, 203–5; *Adm.
Letters* xii, 30; *Council Minutes of Royal Society* 17 March 1686; *C.P. MSS.*
i, 86.

²³ *Pepysian MSS.,* No. 1490, pp. 44–6; *Adm. Letters* xii, 46–7.

²⁴ *Pepysian MS.* No. 1490, p. 48; *Rawl. MSS. A.* 171, ff. 82, 137–8.

²⁵ *Pepysian MSS.* No. 1490, pp. 49–50, 57, 257, 261–322; No. 2867,
Naval Precedents 84; *Adm. Letters* xii, 59; *C.P. MSS.* 1, 80–3; *Naval
Minutes* 277–8.

²⁶ *Pepysian MS.* No. 1490, p. 57.

²⁷ *Ellis* 1, 65–6, 73, 82, 93–5.

²⁸ *Rawl. MSS. A.* 464, f. 17; *Pepysian MSS., Adm. Letters* xi, 509, 511,
529.

²⁹ *Pepysian MSS., Adm. Letters* xi, 555.

³⁰ *Pepysian MSS., Adm. Letters* xi, 530.

³¹ *Pepysian MSS., Adm. Letters* xii, 32.

³² *Pepysian MSS., Adm. Letters* xi, 301–3, 517; xii, 434, 438–9;
C.P. MSS. i, 220.

[33] *Pepysian MSS., Adm. Letters* xi, 531–2; *P.R.O. Chancery Proceedings, Mitford* C. 8, 376, No. 69.

[34] *Rawl. MSS. A.* 179, ff. 38–40.

[35] *D.* 29 May 1664.

[36] *Evelyn* 13 Dec. 1685; *Journal Books of the Royal Society*, 1685–6.

CHAPTER VIII. THE GREAT SECRETARY

[1] *Ranke* iv, 280; *D'Orleans* 284–5; *Ellis* i, 7, 20, 55, 60 et seq; *Ailesbury* i, 150, 162–4; *Welwood* 156; *Evelyn* 3 Nov., 4 Dec. 1685; 19, 24, 30 Jan. 1686; *Luttrell* i, 358, 360, 368–71, 376–7; *Mackintosh* 56 et seq.; *Burnet* iii, 75, 79–82; *Bramston* 228 et seq.; *Reresby* 399–400, 416–17; *Ailesbury* i, 103–4, 127–8, 146.

[2] *Pepysian MSS. No.* 1490, pp. 58–60, 66–71; *Adm. Letters* xii, 66; *Rawl. MSS. A.* 177, f. 134; *Memoires* 47–9; *Ellis* i, 119; *C.P. MSS.* i, 86– 7.

[3] *Pepysian MSS.* No. 1490, p. 71; *Adm. Letters* xii, 96–7, 105, 107, 123, 215; *Naval Minutes* 250–1; *Rawl. MSS. A.* 177, f. 134; *A.* 189, f. 8; *Luttrell* i, 384.

[4] *Pepysian MSS., Adm. Letters* xii, 58, 283, 293–6; *Memoires* 38–45, 47–9.

[5] *Memoires* 55–68; *C.P. MSS.* i, 210–12; *Rawl. MSS. A.* 451, f. 32; *Pepysian MS.* No. 2867, Naval Precedents 186, 245.

[6] *Pepysian MSS., Adm. Letters* xii, 248; xiii, 1–2.

[7] *Pepysian MS.* No. 2867, Naval Precedents 156 et seq.; *C.P. MSS.* i, 213–15.

[8] *C.P. MSS.* i, 216; *Pepysian MSS.*, No. 2867, Naval Precedents 639 et seq.; *Adm. Letters* xii, 252–3; *Rawl. MSS. A.* 189, ff. 275–8.

[9] *H.M.C. Rutland* ii, 109–10; *Ellis* i, 127–8, 137, 143; *Pepysian MSS., Adm. Letters* xii, 147, 165, 192, 274–5, 285; *Rawl. MSS. A.* 189, f. 205.

[10] *Rawl. MSS. A.* 171, ff. 26, 98; *Pepysian MSS., Adm. Letters* xii, 85; *Naval Minutes* 250.

[11] *H.M.C. Rep.* vii (*Graham* 379); *Pepysian MSS.*, No. 1490, pp. 58–60; *Adm. Letters* xii, 96–97, 107, 209, 231, 331, 337, 381, 414; *Rawl. MSS. A.* 185, f. 243; *A.* 189, ff. 39–48, 53–9, 60.

[12] *Pepysian MSS., Adm. Letters* xiii, 24, 69, 120–1; *Rawl. MSS. A.* 189, ff. 131, 154; *Howarth* 178–9; *H.M.C. Rep.* vi (*Gordon-Cumming* 687).

[13] *Rawl. MSS. A.* 189, ff. 308–11, 401; *C.P. MSS.* i, 72, 91; *Pepysian MSS.* No. 1490, p. 257; *Naval Minutes* 277–8; *Ellis* i, 195, 197.

[14] *Ranke* IV, 281–302; *Luttrell* I, 376–84; *Ailesbury* I, 125; *Reresby* 420–4; *Burnet* III, 97–100;*Bramston* 225, 234, 238–50; *Evelyn* 25 June, 8 Sept. 1686; *Welwood* 171–5; *H.M.C. Portland* III, 397; *Mackintosh* 56–99; *Ellis* I, 104, 118–19, 122–3, 126–7, 144–50, 172–3.

[15] *H.M.C. Rep.* VII (*Verney* 500); *Pepysian MSS., Adm. Letters* XII, 180–1, 406–7; *Davey* Item 2884; *Ellis* I, 271; *Rawl. MSS. A.* 189, f. 218; *Howarth* 173–4; *Luttrell* I, 383.

[16] *Pepysian MSS., Adm. Letters* XII, 244, 257–8, 351; *Davey* Item 2885.

[17] *Rawl. MSS. A.* 189, ff. 218, 268, 279–80, 329; *Pepysian MSS., Adm. Letters* X, 73–4, 81; XII, 448; *C.P. MSS* I, 220–1; *Howarth* 171–4.

[18] *Pepysian MSS., Adm. Letters* XII, 448; *H.M.C. Rep.* V (*Magdalene College* 484); *Howarth* 176–7; *Rawl. MSS. A.* 189, ff. 145, 294–5, 298, 300–3, 318.

[19] *Howarth* 173; *Rawl. MSS. A.* 189, ff. 233, 331.

[20] *Ranke* IV, 300–11; *Luttrell* I, 383, 391; *Ailesbury* I, 152; *Mackintosh* 130 et seq.; *Reresby* 426, 440–2; *Bramston* 251–4, 259; *Evelyn* 29 Dec. 1686; 17 Jan. 1687.

CHAPTER IX. HIS ORDERS HOLD

[1] *Ellis* I, 83–4, 89, 111.

[2] *Ranke* IV, 309–13; *D'Orleans* 290; *Burnet* III, 102; *Mackintosh* 185; *Bramston* 268–70; *Reresby* 444–5, 447–51; *Pepysian MSS., Adm. Letters* XII, 382, 386–7; *Rawl. MSS. A.* 189, ff. 220, 222, 229, 231, 259; *Smith* II, 51–6.

[3] *Ranke* IV, 334–6; *G. N. Clark, The Later Stuarts* 119; *Burnet* III, 149–55; *Mackintosh* 134–9; *Bramston* 274–7, 301; *Rawl. MSS. A.* 189, f. 318; *Howarth* 176–7.

[4] *Rawl. MSS. A.* 179, f. 6; *A.* 189, f. 145; *Braybrooke* IV (1898 ed.), 239.

[5] *Rawl. MSS. A.* 177, ff. 140–1; *A.* 189, f. 145; *Ranke* IV, 311–12; *Luttrell* I, 396; *Mackintosh* 154; *Burnet* III, 100–1, 274; *Bramston* 270.

[6] *Tanner, Corr.* I, 286; *Pepysian MS.* No. 2141, Letter of 19 March 1682; *Rawl. MSS. A.* 189, ff. 296–7; *C.* 859, f. 151v; *Howarth* 178; *Smith* II, 91–5; *H.M.C. Hodgkin* 180–1; *Mackintosh* 371.

[7] *Cartwright* 54.

[8] *Pepysian MSS., Adm. Letters* XII, 243; *Rawl. MSS. A.* 189, f. 226; *Howarth* 172–7.

[9] *Rawl. MSS. A.* 189, ff. 78, 224–5; *Pepysian MSS., Adm. Letters* XIII, 445.

[10] *Rawl. MSS. A.* 189, ff. 312, 314, 316; *Howarth* 174–5.

[11] *Howarth* 175–6; *Rawl. MSS. A.* 189, ff. 319, 321–2; *Luttrell* I, 396.

[12] *Rawl. MSS. A.* 179, ff. 98, 100; *A.* 189, f. 313; *Howarth* 184, 188, 190–3.

[13] *Pepysian MSS., Adm. Letters* III, 457; *Rawl. MSS. A.* 171, ff. 26–7, 29, 36; *A.* 189, ff. 29, 31; *Smith* II, 75–6, 113–16, 124; *Howarth* 179.

[14] *Rawl. MSS. A.* 179, ff. 30, 113; *A.* 189, ff. 17, 19, 49–52, 85, 135, 198, 318; *Howarth* 176–7, 180, 187; *Smith* II, 74–5, 90–1, 124–5; *Davey* Item 2886.

[15] *Smith* II, 82–4; *Wheatley and Tanner MSS.; Pepysian MS.* No. 1825; *J. R. Tanner, Mr Pepys* 263; *Rawl. MSS. A.* 189, f. 23.

[16] *Rawl. MSS. A.* 171, f. 89; *A.* 189, ff. 261–3.

[17] *Pepysian MSS., Adm. Letters* XIII, 1–2, 237–8; XIV, 12; *Rawl. MSS. A.* 171, f. 116.

[18] *Rawl. MSS. A.* 171, f. 63; *Pepysian MSS., Adm. Letters* XIII, 243; XIV, 2, 10, 27, 53.

[19] *Pepysian MSS., Adm. Letters* XI, 555; XIII, 6, 203.

[20] *Pepysian MSS., Adm. Letters* XIII, 179, 183, 274–9.

[21] *Pepysian MSS., Adm. Letters* XIII, 1, 235, 247.

[22] *Pepysian MSS., Adm. Letters* XIII, 205; *Howarth* 181–5; *Rawl. MSS. A.* 179, ff. 18, 20–1; *A.* 189, ff. 1, 3, 8, 11, 16.

[23] *Pepysian MSS., Adm. Letters* XIII, 2, 8–9, 11, 16, 18, 25, 28–9, 32 et seq.; *Rawl. MSS. A.* 171, f. 161; *A.* 177, ff. 1–76; *A.* 179, f. 226.

[24] *Pepysian MSS. Adm. Letters* XIII, 116–17, 122, 125–7, 128–9, 136–8, 151–2; *Rawl. MSS. A.* 189, ff. 83, 115, 125; *Smith* II, 77–81.

[25] *Pepysian MSS. Adm. Letters* XIII, 175–6, 179, 183, 238, 292, 308–9, 339; *H.M.C. Portland* III, 401; *Naval Minutes* 104; *Luttrell* I, 399, 407, 409.

[26] *Luttrell* I, 397, 407, 413; *Hatton* II, 67–9; *H.M.C. Rep.* VII (*Verney* 482); *Bramston* 282–3; *Rawl. MSS. A.* 189, ff. 370–8; *Pepysian MSS. Adm. Letters* XIII, 175–6, 255–6, 292; XIV, 25–6; *E. F. Ward, Christopher Monck, Duke of Albemarle* (1915) 243–7.

[27] *Bramston* 300; *Rawl. MSS. A.* 189, ff. 15–16; *D.* 1486, f. 15; *Ellis* I, 325; *Smith* II, 58–9, 60–3; *Pepysian MSS., Adm. Letters* XIII, 198–9.

[28] *Pepysian MSS., Adm. Letters* XII, 422–3; XIII, 154; *Misc.* XI, 18, 20; *Ailesbury* I, 107; *C.P. MSS.* I, III, 298–9; *Ellis* I, 197; *Rawl. MSS. A.* 186, ff. 239, 263–4.

CHAPTER X. RECREATIONS OF A VIRTUOSO

[1] *Evelyn* 2 June 1686; 10 March; 10 April; 12 May 1687; *Luttrell* 1, 383, 392–3, 395, 411; *Hatton* II, 69; *Burnet* III, 102–3, 161–7, 184–7, 193–5; *Ellis* I, 226–8, 235–6, 255–6, 260, 272–3, 312–13, 338–9; *Ranke* IV, 310–41; *Macaulay; D'Orleans* 292; *Reresby* 452, 456, 581–2; *Mackintosh* 145–97; *Bramston* 270-2, 280–1, 283–97, 304.

[2] *Luttrell* I, 411; *Bramston* 298; *Mackintosh* 201–2; *Burnet* III, 189–90; *Reresby* 469–70; *Pepysian MSS., Adm. Letters* XIII, 241–2, 253–4, 291, 294; *Ellis* I, 336–7; *Hatton* II, 70–1; *H.M.C. Portland* III, 399–404; *Rawl. MSS. A.* 186, f. 233; *A.* 189, f. 35.

[3] *Rawl. MSS. A.* 186, f. 233; *A.* 189, f. 21; *H.M.C. Portland* III, 400; *Pepysian MSS. Adm. Letters* XIII, 254–5; *A. Wood, Athenae Oxonienses* (1721 ed.) II, 949; *H.M.C. Hodgkin* 181.

[4] *Rawl. MSS. A.*179, f. 8; *A.* 186, f. 233; *Pepysian MSS., Adm. Letters* XIII, 9, 15; No. 2879, Miscellanies XI, 161; *Howarth* 186.

[5] *Rawl. MSS. A.*171, f. 7; *A.* 179, f. 119; *A.* 186, f. 233; *Nichols, Literary Anecdotes* I, 423; III, 613; *Smith* II, 103–4; *Wheatley and Tanner MSS.; Howarth* 189.

[6] *Braybrooke* (1898 ed.) IV, 238; *Rawl. MSS. A.* 171, f. 4.

[7] *H.M.C. Hodgkin* 169; *Rawl. MSS. A.* 171, ff. 137–8; *A.* 177, ff. 126–7, 134; *A.* 189, f. 8; *Smith* II, 215; *Reresby* 401.

[8] *L.C.C. Survey of London* XVIII (*Strand*); *Mariner's Mirror* XXIV, No. 2 (April 1938), *D. Bonner-Smith, Samuel Pepys and York Buildings; Rawl. MSS. A.* 179, f. 78.

[9] *Smith* II, 214–15.

[10] *Smith* II, 110–11; *Rawl. MSS. A.* 179, f. 4; *Hodgkin Autograph Letters* (App. 1914), Lot 239; *Rawl. MSS. A.* 171, f. 17; *A.* 179 f. 4; *A.* 186, ff. 4–5; *A.* 193 (title-page).

[11] *Rawl. MSS. A.* 189, f. 35; *Smith* II, 219; *Davey* Item 2889; *Smith* II, 219/20; *Pepysian MSS., Adm. Letters* XIV, 102–6; *Spectator* No. 187.

[12] *Smith* II, 218–19; *Howarth* 180–1; *Rawl. MSS. A.* 189, ff. 25, 27; *D.* 23 Aug. 1665.

[13] *Smith* II, 219; *Rawl. MSS. A.* 171, ff. 148–53; *A.* 179 ff. 18, 20–1; *A.* 189, f. 35; *Howarth* 184–5.

[14] *Braybrooke* (1825 ed. Reprint) 634; *Rawl. MSS. A.* 189, ff. 327–8.

[15] *Howarth* 178; *Rawl. MSS. A.* 189, ff. 296–7; *Evelyn* 19 April 1687.

[16] *Rawl. MSS. A.* 179, f. 122; *A.* 189, ff. 78, 148; *Smith* II, 216–17, 228–9; *Howarth* 189–90.

[17] *Rawl. MSS. A.* 179, ff. 126–31; *Smith* ii, 132–5; *H.M.C. Hodgkin* 181; *Luttrell* i, 424–5; *Pepys Club Occasional Papers* ii, 71; *D.* 21 July 1664.

[18] *Pepysian MSS., Adm. Letters* xiv, 106; *Rawl. MSS. A.* 177, ff. 238–9; *A.* 179, ff. 26, 28; *A.* 189, ff. 133, 235; *Smith* ii, 58–9, 60–3.

[19] *Rawl. MSS. A.* 177, ff. 235, 238–9; *Ranke* iv, 378–84.

[20] *Ranke* iv, 385; *Macaulay; Burnet; Luttrell* i, 385, 390, 428–9.

[21] *Rawl. MSS. A.* 189, ff. 288–92.

[22] *Rawl. MSS. A.* 170, ff. 171, 215–16; *A.* 171, ff. 34, 110, 114–15; *A.* 186, f. 171; *A.* 189, ff. 308–11; *Pepysian MSS.* No. 1490, pp. 76, 90, 372; *Adm. Letters* xiii, 386–7; *Naval Minutes* 277–8; *Memoires* 85; *Ailesbury* i, 107.

[23] Letter in possession of the Dowager Countess of Gainsborough; *Wheatley and Tanner MSS; Rawl. MSS. A.* 171, f. 76; *Pepysian MSS., Adm. Letters* xiv, 24, 114.

CHAPTER XI. THE GATHERING STORM

[1] *Ranke* iv, 380–4, 401–5; *Rawl. MSS. A.* 186, f. 238; *Mackintosh* 372–3, 399, 402–4; *Luttrell* i, 428–9, 432–3, 434, 436; *Bramston* 305–6.

[2] *Pepysian MSS., Adm. Letters* xiv, 7–8, 44; *Rawl. MSS. A.* 186, ff. 194–5, 243; *Luttrell* i, 426, 429.

[3] *Luttrell* i, 426, 433; *Burnet; Dalrymple; H.M.C. Rep.* v, 378; *Clarendon, Diary* i, 15 January 1688; *Mackintosh* 202–6, 400, 408; *Bramston* 303.

[4] *H.M.C. Portland* iii, 405; *Ranke* iv, 341–5; *Mackintosh* 240–1, 381–90; *Ailesbury* i, 169; *Evelyn* 15, 29 April 1688; *Clarendon, Diary* 6 Feb. 1688; *Luttrell* i, 438–9; *Bramston* 302, 307; *Reresby* 494–5.

[5] *Luttrell* i, 434, 436–8; *Smith* ii, 117–19; *Rawl. MSS. A.* 170, ff. 214–15; *A.* 171, ff. 141–6; *Evelyn* 8 May 1688; *Mackintosh* 422; *Pepysian MSS., Adm. Letters* xiv, 148–9.

[6] *Pepysian MSS., Adm. Letters* xiv, 148–9, 158, 162, 166–7; *Smith* ii, 120–3; *Rawl. MSS. A.* 171, ff. 141–6.

[7] *Rawl. MSS. A.* 186, ff. 245–6; *Mackintosh* 422; *Smith* ii, 120–3; *Ellis* i, 224.

[8] *Pepysian MSS., Adm. Letters* xiv, 145, 156–7, 159; *Smith* ii, 120–3.

[9] *Pepysian MSS.*, No. 2879, Miscellanies xi, 913–25; *Adm. Letters* xiv, 156–7; *Powley* 15–16; *H.M.C. Rep.* v, 378; *Luttrell* i, 438–9; *Clarendon, Diary* 8–9 May 1688.

[10] *Pepysian MSS.* No. 2879, Miscellanies xi, 925–6.

[11] *Rawl. MSS. A.* 179, f. 12; *A.* 186 f. 6; *Pepysian MSS., Adm. Letters* xiv, 15 et passim, 326–7, 337, 344.

[12] *Rawl MSS.* 179, f. 34; *A.* 186, f. 8; *Pepysian MSS., Adm. Letters* xiv, 12, 27, 37, 54, 69, 93, 121, 224.

[13] *Rawl. MSS. A.* 179, ff. 8, 14, 32, 88, 117, 120; *A.* 189, f. 9; *Howarth* 183–4, 186–9; *Smith* ii, 127–8; *Pepysian MSS. , Adm. Letters* xiv, 214.

[14] *Pepysian MSS., Adm. Letters* xiv, 35, 190–1, 277 et seq.

[15] *Ranke; Burnet* iii, 193–5; *Luttrell* i, 429–33; *H.M.C. Portland* iii, 408; *Ailesbury* 162–3; *Bramston* 301–7.

[16] *Pepysian MSS., Adm. Letters* xiv, 79–80; *C.P. MSS.* i, 219; *Rawl. MSS. A.* 171, f. 61; *Smith* ii, 125–7.

[17] *Ranke* iv, 347–51; *Mackintosh* 247–51; *Evelyn* 18, 20 May 1688; *Dalrymple* i, 195; *Clarendon, Diary* 12, 16, 17, 18, 23 May 1688; *T. Lathbury, History of the Non-Jurors* (1845) 5–8; *H.M.C. Portland* iii, 408; *Reresby* 498; *Bramston* 307–8; *Luttrell* i, 438–9, 440; *Verney Memoirs* ii, 456–7; *Burnet* iii, 226–32; *Bevill Higgons, Short View* 333.

[18] *Luttrell* i, 434, 437, 442; *Clarendon, Diary* 18, 20, 28 May; 5, 7, 15 June 1688; *Evelyn* 16 March; 8 May; *Burnet* iii, 228–32; 8 June 1688; *H.M.C. Rep.* vii (*Verney* 501–2); *Hatton* ii, 81; *H.M.C. Portland* iii, 410; *Shakerley MSS. Chester Castle papers; Verney Memoirs* ii, 456; *Dalrymple* i, 197–8; *Mackintosh* 256–63; *Bramston* 309; *Ailesbury* 1, 170.

[19] *W. Cobbett and Howell, State Trials* xii, 349 et seq.; *F. Hargrave, State Trials* (1776) iv, 303–96; *Evelyn* 29 June 1688; *Mackintosh* 263–77; *Ellis* ii, 2–3; *Dalrymple* i, 198–9; *H.M.C. Portland* iii, 413; *Sir H. Ellis, Original Letters,* 2nd Series, iv, 105–6, 109; *Clarendon, Diary* 25, 27–30 June 1688; *Burnet* iii, 233–6.

[20] *Ellis* ii, 5; *Verney Memoirs* ii, 458–9; *Ailesbury* i, 170–1; *Churchill, Marlborough,* i, 270; *Dalrymple* i, 199–200; *Reresby* 501, 503–4; *Burnet* iii, 237, 240–1, 274; *Mackintosh* 408–13, 416–20.

[21] *Pepysian MSS., Adm. Letters* xiv, 220, 222; *Mackintosh* 400–1; *Clarke* ii, 200; *Luttrell* i, 442; *Burnet* iii, 246–57; *D'Orleans* 298; *Evelyn* 10 June 1688; *Dalrymple* i, 201; *Ailesbury* i, 172–4; *Hatton* ii, 81; *Ellis* i, 352, 364; ii, 52, 54–5; *Clarendon, Diary* 15 Jan.; 10, 11 Feb. 1688; *H.M.C. Portland* iii, 311.

[22] *Pepysian MSS., Adm. Letters* xiv, 166–8, 176–7, 200–2, 204–5, 208, 210–11; *Admiralty Papers in P.R.O.* cit. *Powley* 15; *Burnet* iii, 237; *Ailesbury* i, 170–1.

[23] *London Gazette* 28/31 May; 14/18 June 1688; *Hatton* II, 80; *Rawl. MSS. A.* 186, ff. 206; *Dalrymple; Luttrell* I, 443; *H.M.C. Portland* III, 410–11; *Pepysian MSS., Adm. Letters* XIV, 210–12, 218, 220, 228, 232– 3, 240; *E.H.R.* VIII (1893), *J. R. Tanner, Naval Preparations of James II in* 1688 272; *Burchett* 407–8; *Torrington* 18.

[24] *Rawl. MSS. A.* 170, ff. 214–16; *C.P. MSS.* I, 89; *Pepysian MSS.* No. 1490, p. 372; *Verney Memoirs* II, 460; *Ailesbury* I, 107.

[25] *Ranke* IV, 382–404; *Dalrymple; D'Avaux; Prideaux* 147.

[26] *Ranke* 404 et seq.; *Luttrell* I, 441, 445, 450–1; *H.M.C. Portland* III, 411; *Dalrymple* III, App. I, 200–1; *Mackintosh* 422–5,. 457–8; *Burnet* III, 240–1, 260–2, 276–85; *Reresby* 503; *Clarke* II, 176; *Torrington* 18–19, 27; *Ellis* II, 63; *Burchett* 408; *Pepysian MSS., Adm. Letters* XIV, 254, 260–1, 272, 276.

[27] *Luttrell* I, 450–1; *Howarth* 191–2; *Smith* II, 130–2; *Rawl. MSS. A.* 179, f. 70; *Ellis* II, 30, 52, 62, 67; *Pepysian MSS., Adm. Letters* XIV, 278.

[28] *Rawl. MSS. A.* 177, ff. 78, 82–104; *Ellis* II, 98; *Pepysian MSS., Adm. Letters* XIV, 282–3, 288, 290, 294; *Luttrell* I, 453.

[29] *Mackintosh* 427–9; *D'Orleans* 302–3; *Pepysian MSS., Adm. Letters* XIV, 304; *Dalrymple* III, App. 1, 212–15; *Ellis* II, 14, 52, 101; *H.M.C. Rep.* V, 378–9.

[30] *London Gazette* 20 July/2 Aug. 1688; *Torrington* 19; *Luttrell* I, 451; *Rawl. MSS. A.* 186, f. 171; *Francis Edwards, Catalogue* No. 507 (1928), Item 339.

[31] *Luttrell* I, 457; *Rawl. MSS. A.* 179, f. 68; *A.* 186, f. 173; *A.* 189, ff. 100–1.

[32] *Ranke* IV, 384, 403–21; *Dalrymple* III, App. I, 200–4; *Mackintosh* 425, 428–9.

[33] *Prideaux Papers* 147; *Luttrell* I, 420–3, 432–3, 436–7, 439, 455, 457; *Churchill, Marlborough* I, 279–80; *Burnet* III, 19; *Macaulay; Dalrymple* III, App. I, 139–49.

[34] *Pepysian MSS., Adm. Letters* XIV, 296 et seq.; *Rawl. MSS. A.* 179, ff. 42, 179, 253; *Evelyn* 23 Aug. 1688; *Smith* II, 142.

[35] *Rawl. MSS. A.* 186, ff. 57–60, 84, 88; *Pepysian MSS., Adm. Letters* XIV, 345, 386–7; *Luttrell* I, 455; *Burchett* 408; *H.M.C. Hodgkin* 182; *Ellis* II, 128, 130, 139; *Torrington* 19; *Smith* II, 135–7.

CHAPTER XII. INVASION

[1] *Pepysian MSS., Adm. Letters* xiv, 349–52, 334–5, 357–60, 362–3, 366, 376; *Burchett* 408–10; *Torrington* 19–20; *Ellis* i, 125, 148; *E.H.R.* viii, 273–4; *Powley* 18; *Luttrell* i, 455–6; *Rawl. MSS. A.* 179, ff. 92–3; *A.* 186, f. 257.

[2] *Pepysian MSS., Adm. Letters* xiv, 362–76, 409; xv, 1–44, 55; *Rawl. MSS. A.* 179, ff. 92–3; *A.* 186, f. 257; *E.H.R.* viii, 274.

[3] *Hatton* ii, 90.

[4] *Mackintosh* 428–9, 431–2, 436–7; *Dalrymple* iii, App. I, 202–6; *Reresby* 506, 509; *Burchett* 408–11; *Torrington* 20–3; *Powley* 19–20.

[5] *Luttrell* i, 457–8, 460; *H.M.C. Rep.* v, 379; *Powley* 22–3; *Pepysian MSS., Adm. Letters* xiv, 363–70, 371–9, 381–4, 386–7, 389–407, 409–22; xv, 21, 35, 39–41, 49, 79, 90, 93, 100, 119–20, 141, 157, 160, 164–5, 222–3, 228, 241–2, 261, 292, 376; *Ellis* ii, 130–1, 139, 141–2, 147–8, 153–4, 158–9.

[6] *Pepysian MSS., Adm. Letters* xiv, 386, 392; xv, 8–10, 15, 35–8, 40, 42, 46–9, 53–4, 71 et seq.; *Rawl. MSS. A.* 186, f. 311; *Braybrooke* (1825) 645–6; *Ellis* ii, 154, 191.

[7] *Smith* ii, 146–9; *Rawl. MSS. A.* 179, f. 22; *A.* 186, f. 311; *Braybrooke* (1825) 645–6; *Howarth* 193; *H.M.C. Dartmouth* i, 139; *Pepysian MSS., Adm. Letters* xv, 12, 13, 44.

[8] *Ranke; Luttrell* i, 457; *Bramston* 312; *Reresby* 506; *Feiling* 227–8; *Evelyn* 7 Sept. 1688; *Smith* ii, 140–4; *Rawl. MSS. A.* 179, ff. 44, 184, 186; *Braybrooke* (1898) 1v, 243; *Pepysian MSS., Adm. Letters* xv, 30–1; *Ellis* ii, 144, 187.

[9] *Pepysian MSS., Adm. Letters* xiv, 407–9.

[10] *Mackintosh* 442; *Clarke* ii, 177; *Hatton* ii, 91–2; *Luttrell* i, 452, 458, 461; *Rawl. MSS. A.* 186, f. 311; *Braybrooke* (1825) 645–6; *Feiling* 227–8; *Torrington* 23; *Burchett* 411; *Clarendon, Diary* 23–24 Sept. 1688; *Pepysian MSS., Adm. Letters* xv, 1–2, 20, 45, 147–8; *Bramston* 316; *Ellis* ii, 141–2, 162, 203, 218, 230–4; *Evelyn* 18, 30 Sept. 1688.

[11] *Ranke* iv, 422–7; *Feiling* 228–9; *H.M.C. Fleming* 212; *Luttrell* i, 462; *Clarendon, Diary* 22 Sept. 1688; *Reresby* 516; *Ellis* ii, 201–2, 207, 209–10, 231, 235; *Burnet* iii, 316–17.

[12] *Ranke* iv, 425; *Luttrell* i, 464–71; *Mackintosh* 448–9; *H.M.C. Rep.* v, 379; *Clarendon, Diary* 28–30 Sept.; 1–14 Oct. 1688; *Letters from the Bodleian Library* (1813) i, 49–50; *Evelyn* 7 Oct. 1688; *Ellis* ii, 211–12, 219, 224, 227, 245, 247–8; *Burnet* iii, 336; *Bramston* 316–26; *H.M.C.*

Portland III, 418; *H.M.C. Dartmouth* I, 139, 141–43, 167; *Reresby* 522; *H.M.C. Fleming* 213; *Hatton* II, 94–5; *Feiling* 228–9.

[13] *Mackintosh* 441; *Clarke* II, 186; *Burchett* 411–14; *Pepysian MSS., Adm. Letters* xv, 34–6; *Powley* 25; *H.M.C. Dartmouth* 1, 255; *Burnet* III, 285; *Bramston* 319; *H.M.C. Fleming* 212; *H.M.C. Portland* III, 417; *Smith* 11, 149–52.

[14] *Burchett* 410–14; *Pepysian MSS., Adm. Letters* xv, 51–2, 55–9, 63–5, 69–70, 73–4, 81–2, 84–6, 96–7, 102–3; *Torrington* 23–6; *E.H.R.* VIII, 275; *Mackintosh* 453; *Clarke* II, 186–91; *H.M.C. Dartmouth* I, 138, 255; *B.M. Sloane MSS.* 3650, ff. 7–11; *Fighting Instructions* 1536–1826 (ed. J. S. Corbett, 1905) 170–2.

[15] *Pepysian MSS., Adm. Letters* xv, 45, 139–40; *H.M.C. Portland* III, 417; *Hatton* II, 93.

[16] *Rawl. MSS. A.* 186, f. 324; *Smith* II, 153–4; *H.M.C. Dartmouth* I, 141–3; *Hatton* II, 95; *Ellis* II, 241, 250; *Burnet* III, 315; *Burchett* 412; *Lediard* II, 615–16; *B.M. Sloane MSS.* 3650, ff. 7–11; *Fighting Instructions* (ed. J. S. Corbett, 1905) 170–2.

[17] *Pepysian MSS., Adm. Letters* xv, 78–80, 85, 89–92, 94–5, 103–10, 115–21, 123–7, 130–5, 147, 164–71, 180–7, 204–5, 219–23, 241–5, 253–7, 262–6, 283–6; *H.M.C. Dartmouth* I, 139–41 et seq.; *Hatton* II, 93; *Rawl. MSS. A.* 186, f. 332; *Smith* II, 159–62; *E.H.R.* VIII, 267.

[18] *Pepysian MSS., Adm. Letters* xv, 78–80, 82, 89–93, 114, 140–1, 155, 157, 172, 212–13; *H.M.C. Dartmouth* I, 139–43, 149–51; *Rawl. MSS. A.* 186, f. 323; *Smith* II, 155–8.

[19] *Rawl. MSS. A.* 186, f. 353; *Pepysian MSS., Adm. Letters* xv, 89–92.

[20] *H.M.C. Dartmouth* I, 149, 155–7; *Pepysian MSS., Adm. Letters* xv, 130–5.

[21] *Pepysian MSS., Adm. Letters* xv, 21, 49, 78–80, 123–7, 228; *Rawl. MSS. A.* 186, f. 332; *Smith* II, 159–62; *H.M.C. Dartmouth* I, 139–43, 149–55.

[22] *Pepysian MSS., Adm. Letters* xv 127; *H.M.C. Dartmouth* I, 153–5.

[23] *Rawl. MSS. A.* 186, ff. 225–9, 304; *Pepysian MSS., Adm. Letters* xv, 72; *Torrington* 18.

[24] *Pepysian MSS., Adm. Letters* xv, 137, 180–7, 193–5; *Powley* 54–5; *H.M.C. Dartmouth* I, 141–3, 149, 162–7.

[25] *Pepysian MSS., Adm. Letters* xv, 130–3, 145–7; *H.M.C. Dartmouth* I, 141–3, 149, 155–7.

[26] *Pepysian MSS.* No. 1490, pp. 76, 369–81; *Adm. Letters* xv, 90–1,

148–9, 163–4; *C.P. MSS.* I, 89–91, 95–6; *Memoires* 69; *H.M.C. Dartmouth* I, 159.

[27] *Pepysian MSS., Adm. Letters* xv, 148; *C.P. MSS.* I, 90–1; *Ailesbury* I, 107; *Memoires* 69.

[28] *Pepysian MSS., Adm. Letters* xv, 64 et seq.; 211–12; *Rawl. MSS. A.* 186, f. 323; *Smith* II, 155–8, 162–4; *H.M.C. Dartmouth* I, 141–4.

[29] *Rawl. MSS. A.* 186, ff. 323, 332; *Smith* II, 155–62; *H.M.C. Dartmouth* I, 256–8.

[30] *H.M.C. Dartmouth* I, 152, 158, 257–8; *Ailesbury* I, 186; *Powley* 39; *Burnet* 315.

[31] *H.M.C. Dartmouth* I, 158, 257–8.

[32] *Evelyn* 14 Oct. 1688; *Powley* 61–2; *Rawl. MSS. A.* 186, ff. 352, 355; *H.M.C. Dartmouth* I, 162–4; *Pepysian MSS., Adm. Letters* xv, 186–7; *Clarendon, Diary* 16 Oct. 1688..

[33] *Pepysian MSS., Adm. Letters* xv, 99–100, 135–8, 155–6, 159–60, 191, 193–5, 208, 212–16, 228, 261–2; *H.M.C. Dartmouth* I, 159–61, 164–7, 171–4; *H.M.C. Rep.* v, 372.

[34] *Ailesbury* I, 184–5; *H.M.C. Dartmouth* I, 259–61; *Burnet* III, 329; *Torrington; Mackintosh* 475; *Clarke* II, 208.

[35] *Hatton* II, 96; *Ellis* II, 233–5, 241, 246–7, 254; *Shakerley MSS.* Oct. 1688.

[36] *H.M.C. Dartmouth* I, 164–7; *Ellis* II, 253, 256; *Pepysian MSS., Adm. Letters* xv, 196–202.

[37] *H.M.C. Dartmouth* I, 168–70, 259–61; III, 59–60; *Rawl. MSS. A.* 186, f. 364; *Smith* II, 166–70.

[38] *Pepysian MSS., Adm. Letters* xv, 241–5; *Powley* 66; *H.M.C. Dartmouth* I, 168–9, 171–4.

[39] *Pepysian MSS., Adm. Letters* xv, 239–43, 262–7; *H.M.C. Dartmouth* I, 178–80, 267.

[40] *Ellis* II, 240, 257–9, 265, 267–9; *Mackintosh* 449–52; *Clarendon, Diary* 21–23 Oct. 1688; *Reresby* 522–3; *Ailesbury* I, 183; *H.M.C. Dartmouth* I, 167, 169–70; *Pepysian MSS., Adm. Letters* xv, 218, 228; *Burnet* III, 318–23; *H.M.C. Portland* III, 419–20; *Bramston* 327; *Feiling* 230; *Evelyn* 28 Oct. 1688; *H.M.C. Rep.* v, 379; *H.M.C. Fleming* 216.

[41] *H.M.C. Dartmouth* III, 59.

[42] *H.M.C. Dartmouth* I, 158; *Powley* 62–6.

[43] *Pepysian MSS., Adm. Letters* xv, 252–5; *H.M.C. Dartmouth* I, 170, 175; *Mackintosh* 462–4; *Bramston* 327; *Torrington* 28; *H.M.C. Portland* III, 420; *Clarendon, Diary* 27 Oct. 1688; *Burnet* III, 310–13.

[44] *Pepysian MSS., Adm. Letters* xv, 253–5; *H.M.C. Dartmouth* I, 175–8.

[45] *H.M.C. Dartmouth* I, 262; III, 60–1; *Rawl. MSS. A.* 186, f. 368; *Burchett* 414; *Powley* 71–4; *Torrington* 26–8; *Dalrymple* II, App. I, 241.

[46] *Rawl. MSS. A.* 186, f. 90: *Smith* II, 328–9; *Pepysian MSS., Adm. Letters* xv, 266–8; *Burnett* III, 307–8, 324–5.

[47] *H.M.C. Dartmouth* I, 262.

[48] *Ellis* II, 262, 268–9, 273–4; *H.M.C. Dartmouth* I, 183, 262–3; III, 61; *Rawl. MSS. A.* 186, f. 372; *Pepysian MSS., Adm. Letters* xv, 288; *Powley* 78–81; *Dalrymple* III, App. I, 243; *Burnet* III, 325.

[49] *Pepysian MSS., Adm. Letters* xv, 293, 297–8; *H.M.C. Rep.* VII (*Graham* 412); *H.M.C. Dartmouth* I, 181–4; *Powley* 79–81; *Ellis* II, 274; *Bramston* 329; *Torrington* 29; *Clarendon, Diary* 3 Nov. 1688.

[50] *Pepysian MSS., Adm. Letters* xv, 297–8; *Powley* 91–4; *H.M.C. Dartmouth* I, 183–4; *Naval Minutes* 273–4, 292.

[51] *Pepysian MSS., Adm. Letters* xv, 303–9, 311; *H.M.C. Rep.* VII (*Graham* 412–13); *H.M.C. Dartmouth* I, 184–5; *Evelyn* 4, 5 Nov. 1688; *H.M.C. Fleming* 218; *Hatton* II, 98–9; *Burnet* III, 327; *Bramston* 330; *Ellis* II, 280–4; *Clarendon, Diary* 6 Nov. 1688; *J. R. Tanner, Mr Pepys* 267 n.

[52] *H.M.C. Dartmouth* I, 263–5; *Powley* 78–81; *Rawl. MSS. A.* 186, f. 374; *Pepysian MSS., Adm. Letters* xv, 311–12; *Smith* II, 332–5.

[53] *Pepysian MSS., Adm. Letters* xv, 304, 308–9; *Powley* 83–5, 88, 94; *Bramston* 329; *Torrington* 29; *H.M.C. Dartmouth* I, 263–5; III, 61–2; *Rawl. MSS. A.* 186, f. 374.

CHAPTER XIII. THE GLORIOUS REVOLUTION

[1] *Macaulay; Rapin; Ranke* IV, 434, 443–5; *Mackintosh* 431–2, 480–2; *G. N. Clark, The Later Stuarts* 132–3; *H.M.C. Dartmouth* I, 187–90; *Ellis* II, 288–9; *Bramston* I, 333; *Burnet* III, 329–30.

[2] *Pepysian MSS., Adm. Letters* xv, 303–54; *Smith* II, 173–6; *Howarth* 195–6; *H.M.C. Dartmouth* I, 187–94, 265–7; III, 62; *Ellis* II, 289.

[3] *H.M.C. Dartmouth* I, 187–9, 268–9; *Howarth* 197–8; *Smith* II, 176–8.

[4] *H.M.C. Rep.* V, 379; *Bramston* 331; *Ellis* II, 287; *Burnet* III, 330–1, 337–8; *Ranke* IV, 441–3; *Macaulay; H.M.C. Dartmouth* I, 192–4; *Clarke* II, 209; *Macpherson* II, 160; *Mackintosh* 479, 482.

[5] *Ranke* IV, 441–3; *Ellis* II, 291; *Macaulay; Mackintosh* 460, 692–701; *H.M.C. Dartmouth* I, 266–7; *Bramston* 332; *H.M.C. Fleming* 221; *Verney Memoirs* II, 467–8.

[6] *Pepysian MSS., Adm. Letters* xv, 353; *H.M.C. Dartmouth* I, 192–4, 268–9; 111, 260–1; *Howarth* 197–8; *Smith* II, 176–8.

[7] *Pepysian MSS., Adm. Letters* xv, 336–84; *H.M.C. Dartmouth* I, 194–201, 267; *Powley* 99–100; *Ellis* II, 292; *Smith* II, 337–8; *Rawl. MSS. A.* 179, f. 86; *A.* 186, f. 400.

[8] *H.M.C. Dartmouth* I, 194–8; *Smith* II, 337–8; *Ellis* 292; *Pepysian MSS., Adm. Letters* xv, 347, 364, 399–400.

[9] *H.M.C. Dartmouth* I, 194–8; *Powley* 102–4; *Smith* II, 337–8.

[10] *H.M.C. Rep.* VII (*Graham* 416); *Ellis* II, 289–94; *Macaulay.*

[11] *Ellis* II, 289–300, 319–24; *Hatton* II, 99–100.

[12] *Feiling* 232–3; *London Gazette*; *Macaulay: H.M.C. Fleming* 220; *Macpherson* II, 160–1; *Burnet* III, 331–3; *Bramston* 333–4; *Mackintosh* 485–6.

[13] *Ellis* II, 289–94, 319–24; *Burnet; Evelyn* 15, 18 Nov. 1688; *Macaulay; Hatton* II, 102; *G. N. Clark, The Later Stuarts* 134; *Ranke* IV, 444–5; *Verney Memoirs* II, 468.

[14] *Macaulay; Mackintosh* 489–90; *Macpherson* II, 161; *D'Orleans* 311; *Stuart Papers at Windsor Castle, MSS.,* Vol. I, 17 Nov. 1688 (communicated by O. F. Morshead).

[15] *Ranke* IV, 445–6; *Feiling, Tory Party* 232; *Bramston* 334–6; *Ellis* II, 301, 307–8; *Macpherson* II, 161–2.

[16] *H.M.C. Fleming* 220; *H.M.C. Rep.* VII (*Graham* 348); *Ellis* II, 301; *H.M.C. Dartmouth* I, 204; *Tanner and Wheatley MSS.,* letter communicated to the late Dr J. R. Tanner by the late Lt.-Col. Frederick Pepys Cockerell.

[17] *Pepysian MSS., Adm. Letters* xv, 384–5; 387, 399–400; *Powley* 108; *H.M.C. Dartmouth* I, 205–10, 267–8, 270–2; III, 66–8; *Torrington* 29–30; *Ellis* II, 301, 305–13; *Evelyn* 18 Nov. 1688; *Smith* II, 336; *Rawl. MSS. A.* 186, f. 18; *Burnet* III, 329.

[18] *Ellis* II, 305–13; *H.M.C. Rep.* VII (*Graham* 349); *H.M.C. Dartmouth* I, 205–10; *Hatton* II, 106.

[19] *Ellis* II, 309–13, 324–31; *Rawl. MSS. A.* 186, ff. 18–19.

[20] *Rawl. MSS. A.* 186, ff. 18–26; *Pepysian MSS., Adm. Letters* xv, 406–7, 410–11.

[21] *Pepysian MSS., Adm. Letters* xv, 413–16, 421–2; *H.M.C. Dartmouth* I, 211–13; III, 66–8; *Ellis* II, 330–6; *Hatton* II, 111–12; *Rawl. MSS. A.* 186, ff. 106, 108.

[22] *H.M.C. Dartmouth* I, 211–13, 271–2; III, 66–8.

[23] *Ailesbury* I, 188–90; *Ranke* IV, 448; *Macaulay; Sir Patrick Hume,*

Diary 20 Nov. 1688; *Ellis* II, 329; *Burnet* III, 333, 337; *D'Orleans* 311–12; *Macpherson* II, 162; *Churchill, Marlborough* I, 291–4; *Bramston* 336; *Mackintosh* 492–4; *H.M.C. Rep.* VII (*Graham* 417).

[24] *Ranke* IV, 449–50; *H.M.C. Fleming* 220; *Macaulay; H.M.C. Rep.* VII (*Graham* 417, 420); *Ellis* II, 314–19, 324–31; *Feiling* 235; *H.M.C. Leeds* 26; *Reresby* 528–32; *Hatton* II, 111–12.

[25] *Ranke* IV, 448–9; *H.M.C. Rep.* VII (*Graham* 418, 424); *Ellis* II, 331; *Macaulay; Mackintosh* 495–8; *Dalrymple; Burnet; Macpherson* II, 162–3; *Burnet* III, 336; *Churchill, Marlborough* I, 298–303; *Hatton* II, 111–12; *Ailesbury* I, 190–1; *Bramston* 336–7.

[26] *H.M.C. Dartmouth* III, 133–4.

[27] *Dalrymple* III, App. I, 255; *Ellis* II, 336, 340; *Macaulay.*

[28] *Pepysian MSS., Adm. Letters* XV, 427–31; *H.M.C. Dartmouth* I, 214–15; *Smith* II, 179.

[29] *Ranke* IV, 452–3; *Macaulay; H.M.C. Dartmouth* I, 216–17; *Reresby* 535; *G. N.Clark, The Later Stuarts* 135–6; *Burnet* III, 339–40; *Clarendon, Diary* 27, 29 Nov. 1688; *Ailesbury* I, 192–3; *Bramston* 337–8.

[30] *Rawl. MSS. A.* 179, ff. 264–6; *Smith* II, 170–2, 180–1.

[31] *Macaulay; H.M.C. Dartmouth* I, 216; *Ellis* II, 313.

[32] *Ranke* IV, 452–3; *Macaulay.*

[33] *Ranke* IV, 450–4; *Clarendon, Diary* 3, 4 Dec. 1688; *Burnet* III, 336, 339–40; *H.M.C. Rep.* VII (*Graham* 419, 421); *D'Orleans* 313; *Mackintosh* 514.

[34] *Pepysian MSS., Adm. Letters* XV, 435–6; *H.M.C. Dartmouth* I, 214–15, 220; *Macpherson* II, 164–5.

[35] *Ranke* IV, 459; *Pepysian MSS., Adm. Letters* XV, 444–8; *H.M.C. Dartmouth* I, 217–19; III, 68; *Rawl. MSS. A.* 186, f. 214.

[36] *Mazure* III, 218–19; *Macaulay; Mackintosh* 509, 520–3, 526; *H.M.C. Dartmouth* I, 216, 220; *Dalrymple* III, App. I, 256; *Rawl. MSS. A.* 186, f. 218; *Braybrooke* IV, 243; *Pepysian MSS., Adm. Letters* XV, 449–50; *H.M.C. Dartmouth* I, 216, 220.

[37] *Pepysian MSS., Adm. Letters* XV, 449–50; *H.M.C. Dartmouth* I, 216, 220.

[38] *H.M.C. Dartmouth* I, 217, 220–3, 272–4, 275–7; *Powley* 120, 136; *Macaulay; Macpherson* II, 165; *Mackintosh* 517; *Hatton* II, 101; *Nash, History of Worcestershire* I, 501.

[39] *H.M.C. Dartmouth* I, 216, 275–7; *Powley* 134–6; *Dalrymple* III, App. I, 257–60.

[40] *H.M.C. Dartmouth* I, 223–5, 277–8; *Powley* 136–41; *Dalrymple* III,

App. I, 245–7; *Torrington* 33; *H.M.C. Fleming* 225; *Pepysian MSS., Adm. Letters* xv, 457; *Reresby* 536.

[41] *H.M.C. Fleming* 226; *Hatton* II, 120; *Mackintosh* 515; *H.M.C. Dartmouth* I, 227, 277–8; *Macaulay; Clarendon, Diary* 11 Dec. 1688; *Ailesbury* I, 213; *Feiling* 235; *Reresby* 535–6; *Wood* III, 186–7.

[42] *Macaulay; Feiling* 237–9; *Burnet* III, 340–2; *H.M.C. Lindsey* 452; *Ellis* II, 342–4; *Foxcroft, Halifax; Ranke* IV, 455–7; *Clarendon, Diary* 8–9 Dec. 1688.

[43] *Macpherson* II, 165; *Ranke* 459–64; *Burnet* III, 342; *Mazure; Bramston* 341–2; *Ailesbury* I, 194–7.

[44] *Macaulay; Ailesbury* I, 193; *Marquise de Campana de Cavelli, Les Derniers Stuarts à St Germain en Laye* II, 397–413; *J. S. Clarke, Life of James II* 246; *Rapin; Mackintosh* 523–4; *H.M.C. Dartmouth* I, 225–6; *Rawl. MSS. A.* 186, f. 222.

[45] *Ranke* IV, 459–64; *Ailesbury* 194–7; *D'Orleans* 315–16; *Mackintosh* 526–9; *Macaulay; H.M.C. Dartmouth* I, 226; *Reresby* 536–7.

[46] *H.M.C. Dartmouth* I, 226–9; *Pepysian MSS., Adm. Letters* xv, 457–61.

[47] *Rawl. MSS. A.* 186, f. 222; *Braybrooke* IV, 243; *H.M.C. Dartmouth* I, 225–6; *Smith* II, 191–8.

CHAPTER XIV. THE INTERREGNUM

[1] *Ranke* IV, 459–64, 478; *Macaulay; H.M.C. Rep.* VII (*Verney* 502); *G. N. Clark, The Later Stuarts* 136–7; *Feiling* 239; *Reresby* 538–9; *H.M.C. Dartmouth* I, 228–9; *Stuart Papers* I, 77; *London Gazette* 13 Dec. 1688; *Clarke* II, 251; *Ailesbury* I, 197–9; *Mackintosh* 532–4.

[2] *Rawl. MSS. A.* 186, f. 216; *Smith* II, 190; *H.M.C. Dartmouth* I, 228–9; *Pepysian MSS., Adm. Letters* xv, 464–5.

[3] *H.M.C. Dartmouth* I, 229–30, 232–3; *Ellis* II, 346–8, 350–2; *Reresby* 537; *G. N. Clark, The Later Stuarts* 137; *Rapin; H.M.C. Rep.* v, 379; *H.M.C. Portland* III, 420–1; *Hatton* II, 124; *Macaulay; Bramston* 339– 40; *Mackintosh* 529–30; *Feiling* 239; *Howarth* 198; *Rawl. MSS. A.* 179, f. 84; *Verney Memoirs* II, 469–71; *Pepysian MSS., Adm. Letters* xv, 467–8.

[4] *Oldmixon; Macaulay; Bramston* 339; *Burnet* III, 348–9; *Reresby* 537–8; *H.M.C. Dartmouth* I, 232–3; *H.M.C. Portland* III, 421; *Hatton* II, 125–6; *Verney Memoirs* II, 469–70.

[5] *Howarth* 198; *Rawl. MSS. A.* 179, f. 84.

[6] *Ellis* II, 356–7; *Ranke* IV, 479; *Mackintosh* 531–2; *Macaulay; Hatton*

II, 124–6; *Ailesbury* I, 200; *H.M.C. Portland* III, 420–1; *H.M.C. Dartmouth* I, 232–3.

⁷ *H.M.C. Dartmouth* I, 219, 228–9, 231–2, 235, 279; III, 69–70, 135; *Dalrymple* III, App. I, 245; *Powley* 143–7; *Torrington* 30–5.

⁸ *Macaulay; Wood* III, 288–91; *H.M.C. Dartmouth* I, 213–30; *Hatton* II, 123, 125–6; *Reresby* 539; *Mackintosh* 536–41; *H.M.C. Fleming* 228; *Ellis* II, 362–4; *Diary and Correspondence of John Evelyn* (ed. Wheatley, 1906) III, 427; *Macpherson* I, 165–6; *Ailesbury* I, 201–13; *Verney Memoirs* II, 472.

⁹ *H.M.C. Fleming* 229–30; *Shakerley MSS., Chester Castle Letters* Dec. 1888; *Letters from the Bodleian Library* (1812) I, 51–2; *Barillon* 17/27 Dec. 1688; *Wood* III, 291.

¹⁰ *H.M.C. Dartmouth* I, 226, 279–80, 282; *Hatton* II, 126; *Rawl. MSS. A.* 186, f. 222.

¹¹ *Wood* III, 289; *Ellis* II, 262–3, 369; *Mackintosh* 542–3; *Ranke* IV, 465; *Macpherson* I, 166–7; *H.M.C. Dartmouth* I, 236, 238; *Reresby* 540; *London Gazette* 16 Dec. 1688; *D'Orleans* 316–17; *Ailesbury* I, 214–15; *Evelyn* 11 Dec. 1688; *J. S. Clarke, Life of James II* II, 262.

¹² *Diary and Correspondence of John Evelyn* (ed. Wheatley) III, 427–8; *Wood* III, 289; *H.M.C. Dartmouth* I, 240; *Burnet* III, 353; *Dalrymple* III, App. I, 268–9; *Macaulay; Mackintosh* 543–4; *Bramston* 340.

¹³ *Wood* III, 289; *Ailesbury* I, 216–18; *Macaulay; Ranke* IV, 465; *G. N. Clark, The Later Stuarts* 137; *Diary and Correspondence of John Evelyn* (ed. Wheatley) III, 428–9; *Diary* 18 Dec. 1688; *Ellis* II, 372–3; *Burnet* III, 352–8; *Bramston* 340–1; *Tanner, Corr.* I, 24–7; *H.M.C. Dartmouth* I, 236; *Macpherson* I, 167–8; *Reresby* 540; *Clarendon, Diary* 15–18 Dec. 1688; *John Sheffield, Duke of Buckingham, Works* (1753) II, 85; *J. S. Clarke, Life of James II* II, 265; *Mackintosh* 546–51.

¹⁴ *Macaulay; Ellis* II, 369; *Ranke* IV, 482–3; *Reresby* 541; *Clarendon, Diary* 19 Dec. 1686; *Burnet* III, 359; *H.M.C. Dartmouth* I, 236, 238; III, 135; *Ailesbury* I, 218–20.

¹⁵ *Clarendon, Diary* 20 Dec. 1688; *Ellis* II, 373; *Burnet* III, 360–1; *Evelyn* 18 Dec. 1688; *Verney Memoirs* II, 472; *Rawl. MSS. A.* 181, f. 154; *Smith* II, 198–9; *H.M.C. Dartmouth* I, 240.

¹⁶ *Wood* III, 291; *Reresby* 541; *Pepysian MSS., Adm. Letters* XV, 465 et seq.; *Rawl. MSS. A.* 179, ff. 59–60; *Howarth* 198.

¹⁷ *H.M.C. Fleming* 231.

¹⁸ *Macaulay; Ranke* IV, 484; *Clarendon, Diary* 21 Dec. 1688.

¹⁹ *Rawl. MSS. A.* 175, f. 279; *A.* 179, ff. 140–1, 150; *A.* 194, ff.

257–9; *Pepysian MSS., Mornamont* I, 1209, 1223–5; *Tangier Papers* 321–2; *H.M.C. Dartmouth* I, 242; III, 142–3; *Smith* II, 199–200.

[20] *Wood* III; *Clarendon, Diary* 22–23 Dec. 1688; *Ailesbury* I, 222–5; *Macaulay; Clarke* II, 275; *Ranke* IV, 484–5.

[21] *Feiling* 246; *Macaulay; H.M.C. Dartmouth* III, 139–41; *Clarendon, Diary* 24, 29 Dec. 1688.

[22] *Ranke* IV, 466, 487–9; *Feiling* 246; *Clarendon, Diary* 24, 26 Dec. 1688; *Macaulay; H.M.C. Dartmouth* I, 242; III, 140–1; *Bramston* 343–5.

[23] *H.M.C. Dartmouth* I, 239–40; III, 70; *Pepysian MSS., Adm. Letters* xv, 470 et seq.; *Smith* II, 350–1.

[24] *H.M.C. Dartmouth* I, 241, 245, 247; III, 140, 142–2; *Smith* II, 350–1; *Rawl. MSS. A.* 186, f. 173.

[25] *Royal Society MSS., Ne III* 129, 28 Dec. 1688.

[26] *Pepysian MSS., Adm. Letters* xv, 490–500, 504, 507–9, 534; *H.M.C. Dartmouth* I, 242–4; *Powley* 157; *Rawl. MSS. A.* 186, ff. 113–17, 119; *Luttrell* I, 493–4; *Evelyn* 7 Jan. 1689; *Clarendon, Diary* 1, 3 Jan. 1689.

[27] *Smith* II, 200–1.

[28] *H.M.C. Dartmouth* I, 247; *Smith* II, 210–12.

[29] *Pepysian MSS., Adm. Letters* xv, 290, 496–8; *Luttrell* I, 494; *H.M.C. Dartmouth* I, 177–8, 240–1; *Rawl. MSS. A.* 186, f. 119; *H.M.C. Fleming* 232; *Reresby* 545; *Mackintosh* 580–1.

[30] *Rawl. MSS. A.* 170, f. 201; *Smith* II, 211–12; *Pepysian MSS., Adm. Letters* xv, 500–2, 504, 507–9, 518–19; *H.M.C. Dartmouth* I, 249; *Wood* III, 291; *Howarth* 199–200.

CHAPTER XV. DEFEAT

[1] *Wood* III, 297; *Luttrell* I, 494, 497; *Bramston* 345; *Clarendon, Diary* 9, 11 Jan. 1689; *Cambridge Historical Journal* 1937 (*J. H. Plumb, The Elections to the Convention Parliament of* 1689); *Diary and Correspondence of John Evelyn* (ed. Wheatley) III, 429–30.

[2] *Rawl. MSS. A.* 179, ff. 140, 147, 149, 151, 153, 156, 159, 161, 163, 165–7, 173, 225; *Braybrooke* (Chandos Library reprint of 1825 ed.) 647–8.

[3] *H.M.C. Dartmouth* I, 242–4; *Pepysian MSS., Adm. Letters* xv, 525–6, 532, 547–8, 554.

[4] *Pepysian MSS., Adm. Letters* xv, 513–14, 520, 536.

[5] *Pepysian MSS., Adm. Letters* xv, 520, 527, 532; *Rawl. MSS. A.* 186, ff. 121v–6; *Mackintosh* 581–2.

[6] *Evelyn* 15 Jan. 1689; *H.M.C. Portland* III, 421; *H.M.C. Fleming* 232; *Clarendon, Diary* 14, 15, 16, 17 Jan. 1689; *Burnet* III, 373–5; *Mackintosh* 587–90.

[7] *Rawl. MSS. A.* 179, ff. 169, 171, 173, 218, 223, 225; *A.* 186, f. 126v; *Pepysian MSS., Adm. Letters* xv, 542–3; *Howarth* 200; *Braybrooke* IV (1898), 245–6.

[8] *Rawl. MSS. A.* 179, ff. 177, 210, 221; *D.* 4 Dec. 1668.

[9] *Luttrell* I, 497–8; *Grey* IX; *C.J.*; *H.M.C. Portland* III, 422, 424; *Bramston* 346; *Mackintosh* 591.

[10] *Pepysian MSS., Adm. Letters* xv, 562 et seq.; *Evelyn* 27 Jan. 1689.

[11] *Grey* IX; *Ranke* IV, 493–511; *Mackintosh* 599–603; *Macaulay*; *Roger North, Lives of the Norths* (1890) III, 136; *Evelyn* 29 Jan. 1689; *Burnet* III, 375–88; *Reresby* 545–6, 548–9; *C.J.*; *L.J.*; *Clarendon, Diary* 29–31 Jan.; 1–6 Feb. 1689; *Mackintosh* 593–614; *Ailesbury* I, 230–7; *H.M.C. Rep.* XII (*House of Lords*, 1689–90, 15); *H.M.C. Portland* III, 424–5, 427; *Luttrell* I, 497–9; *Feiling* 252–3; *Wood* III, 207.

[12] *Grey* IX; *L.J.*, *C.J.*; *Mackintosh* 620–8; *Macaulay*; *Reresby* 551, 554; *Burnet* III, 390–408; *Foxcroft, Halifax* II, 203–4; *Clarendon, Diary* 6, 12–13 Feb. 1689; *C.S.P.D.* 1689–90: I; *Luttrell* I, 500–2; *H.M.C. Portland* III, 428; *Mackintosh* 615–28; *Wood* III, 298; *Evelyn* 6, 21 Feb. 1689; *Feiling* 246, 253–5; *H.M.C. Rep.* V, 376; *Ranke* IV, 509–11, 516–18; *Rawl. MSS. A.* 179, f. 216.

[13] *Rawl. MSS. A.* 186, ff. 112, 138–40; *Pepysian MSS., Adm. Letters* xv, 586; *Evelyn* 26 May 1703; *Ailesbury* I, 227, 236–7; *Clarendon, Diary* 1 March 1689.

[14] *Evelyn* 26 May 1703; *Luttrell* I, 501–2; *H.M.C. Fleming* 235–6; *Rawl. MSS. A.* 170, f. 79; *A.* 179, f. 262; *A.* 186, ff. 112, 134–5, 138–40; *Pepysian MSS., Adm. Letters* xv, 524–5, 575–98; *D.* 20 Feb. 1665.

[15] *Pepysian MSS., Adm. Letters* xv, 586, 590; *H.M.C. Stuart Papers* I, 35.

[16] *Rawl. MSS. A.* 170, ff. 176, 178–82, 186; *A.* 186, ff. 138–40; *H.M.C. House of Lords*, 1689–90, 185; *Pepysian MSS., Adm. Letters* xv, 589–92.

[17] *Pepysian MSS., Adm. Letters* xv, 589–92.

[18] *Pepysian MSS., Adm. Letters* xv, 596–8.

[19] *Luttrell* I, 504, 507; *Pepysian MSS., Adm. Letters*, 598; *D.* 5 July 1660; *Rawl. MSS. A.* 170, f. 71; *A.* 189, f. 27.

[20] *Mariner's Mirror* XXIII, No. 4 (Oct. 1937); *G. F. James, Josiah Burchett* 477–8; *Torrington* 17; *Wheatley and Tanner MSS.* (from a letter of S. P. to Dr Charles Davenant of 6 Aug. 1697 given to Red Cross Sale by Sir Hercules Reed).

Index